NEW TOPICS IN ENVIRONMENTAL RESEARCH

New Topics in Environmental Research

Daniel Rhodes
Editor

Nova Science Publishers, Inc.
New York

Library of Congress Cataloging-in-Publication Data
Available upon request.

ISBN 1-60021-172-0

Published by Nova Science Publishers, Inc. ✢*New York*

CONTENTS

PREFACE

The environment is considered the surroundings in which an organism operates, including air, water, land, natural resources, flora, fauna, humans and their interrelation. It is this environment which is both so valuable, on the one hand, and so endangered on the other. And it is people which are by and large ruining the environment both for themselves and for all other organisms. This book reviews the latest research in this field which is vital for everyone.

Macroalgae, owing to their sedentary nature, have been widely investigated as effective indicators to assess metal levels (bioavailability) in marine coastal environments. Metals concentrations have been determined by focusing on bioaccumulation that may depend upon species-specific resistance/tolerance, algal development, environmental factors, the metal chemical form and complexation, nutrient and metal ion bioavailability, combination of metals and seasonality. In laboratory studies biphasic metal uptake (fast passive ad/absorption and slow active bioaccumulation) has been described. However complete analyses of adaptive/defence responses at biosynthetic, physiological and ultrastructural levels have been performed only for few macroalgae, where metal-complexes have been also detected by TEM/SEM microscopy combined with X-ray microanalysis. For these reasons and for the lack of toxicity standardised methods, dissimilar experimental approaches render the comparison both between (within) parameters and taxa sensitivities extremely problematic. In addition, debate is still open on the proper dose, the best stress parameters and statistical analysis to be chosen for eco-toxicity tests even for the already assessed protocols for microalgae. In chapter 1 attempts are made also to identify a form (or combination of forms) of a metal that might be bioavailable, thus potentially toxic, the free ion activity model in the interactions metal-organism being criticisable. It is known that many algae absorb and accumulate high concentrations of metals to a similar extent, but still scarce information is available on their ability to recover their physiological processes after the stress. More information on the cell functional recovery might be useful for individuating 'bioaccumulators' suitable for metal bioremoval, since the species capable of a prompt recovery might be reused as 'biofilters' after detoxification in confined ponds. The most 'sensitive', thus unable to recover, might be useful as 'biosensors' for bioassays in water quality monitoring. In the case study the authors report, for the red macroalga *Audouinella saviana* (Meneghini) Woelkerling (Nemaliales) under culture, currently adopted and new parameters for macroalgae were explored and discussed in view of contributing the assessment of a standardised toxicity protocol. After preliminary experiments with different Cd doses and exposure times, thalli were cultured under 5-day exposures to 50-2000 µM Cd range, followed by 5-day recoveries in Cd-free media. Biomass/growth rate, O_2-evolution/consumption, ATP, chl/CAR, soluble/structural protein and biliprotein contents were analysed after 24 hrs and 5 days of both stress and recovery. Within parameters a 'sensitiveness' gradient, *i.e.* chl>ATP>R-PC>O_2-consumption>O_2-evolution, was individuated within 24 hrs. The adaptive responses were induced by 100 μM Cd (EC) and the defence mechanisms activated by LC50>300 μM Cd. In Cd-free medium most functions were at least partially recovered within 5 days. Main considerations may be the following: 1) exploring as many as possible parameters in order to choose the best stress markers, may also furnish information on algal cell physiology/metabolism for a useful comparison with different end-pointed papers; 2) there is a good correspondence between ultrastructural changes and physiological responses; 3) despite the high Cd levels supplied, high Cd-tolerance and detoxification capabilities are shown by *A. saviana* which might be regarded as a bioaccumulator and a potential tool for metal bioremoval.

Metals cannot be chemically degraded; rather they need to be physically removed in cost-intensive and technically complex procedures, highlighting the need for sustainable cost efficient remedial actions. In the last decade, plant-based technologies involving biological processes, including plant uptake, transport, accumulation and sequestration of metals, as well as plant-microbe interactions, are gaining significant interest in this context. Accumulation and exclusion are the two basic widely recognized tolerance strategies plants develop at polluted sites. In addition, arbuscular mycorrhiza (AM) may contribute significantly to plant metal tolerance. Arbuscular mycorrhizal fungi (AMF) (Glomeromycota) are ubiquitous soil microbes considered essential for plant survival and growth in nutrient deficient soils. The significantly reduced AMF diversity frequently found in metal polluted environments is presumably composed of the most stress-adapted strains. Inoculation of host plants with indigenous AMF may play an important role in plant protection from metal toxicity by binding metals and consequently restricting their translocation to the shoots, therefore contributing to successful phytostabilization. In addition, the recently discovered mycorrhizal colonization of hyperaccumulating plants may represent a potentially important biotechnological tool for phytoextraction, another branch of modern phytotechnologies. Chapter 2 highlights current knowledge on the interactions of plants and AMF in metal polluted environments and the potential for their use as a biotechnological tool in contemporary remedial practice.

Fungi play a crucial role in ecosystem processes in all terrestrial biomes. Anthropogenic pollution may decrease fungal performance and therefore affect ecosystem functioning. In spite of a considerable number of case studies and narrative reviews, the general pattern of pollution impact on fungi has not emerged. The goal of our study is to evaluate the magnitude and direction of the effects of aerial pollution on abundance and diversity of soil inhabiting fungi by means of a meta-analysis based on observational studies carried out near point emission sources. Our conclusions are based on 122 publications that reported results of 141 primary studies, conducted during 1969-2003 in impact zones of 62 polluters, including 26 non-ferrous smelters, 5 aluminum smelters and 16 polluters emitting mainly SO_2. Both fungal abundance and diversity decreased with increase in pollution load (effect sizes $r = -0.29$ and -0.59, respectively); diversity effect sizes decreased towards higher latitudes. Polluters with longer impact history showed more adverse effects on fungi. Pollution severity or polluter type did not explain variation in general, but increases in abundance or diversity were related to short pollution history and lower impact level. Polluters emitting mainly SO_2 were less deleterious compared to non-ferrous smelters that emit both SO_2 and heavy metals. Adverse effects of pollution on mycorrhizal abundance were slightly larger than on abundance of saprotrophic fungi. Absence of correlations between the effect sizes and annual emissions of individual pollutants suggests that there is no 'leading' pollutant and that the large fraction of fungal responses is due to indirect effects, e.g. due to pollution induced environmental changes. The meta-analysis did not demonstrate publication bias but revealed shortage of reliable observational data. Chapter 3 concludes that the meta-analysis allowed to find important regularities in fungal response to pollution and also critically evaluate the level of our knowledge, indicating that high quality observational data are still badly needed to explain and hopefully predict impact of environmental pollution on soil inhabiting fungi.

A growing consciousness of the intertwined issues of environment and development and the particular role of energy in the nexus of these issues have been realised at present. As a result of this awareness, voices of concern in support of Environmentally Sound and Sustainable Development (ESSD) are now increasingly heard. The great challenge now is to move from the voicing of concerns to accelerated action and change. The list of environmental issues that are relevant to any discussion of ESSD strategies is long and diverse as reported in chapter 4. Implementing development strategies which include the alleviation of poverty as a central focus must address both the direct and indirect linkages between these environmental issues and poverty.

Chapter 5 includes the data on the concentration of Al, As, Cd, Cu, F, Fe, Mn, N, Ni, Pb, S and Zn in the foliage of forest tree species, fruit tree species and shrubs in Žiarska basin (pollution zones A, B, C) in the year 1995–2003; methodology of sampling and determination of elements. Anthropogenic loading expressed by means of the coefficient of immission loading (K_z) has decreasing trend. Total Kz of all tree species in Žiarska basin represents in 2003 only 4,9 times higher loading and 29.5 times higher loading in 1995. Total loading by F represented for the year 2003 exceeding of F concentration by 8 times what is 14.2% in comparison with 1995. Total loading by S represented for the year 2003 exceeding of S concentration by 1.8 times what is 64.3% in 2003 in comparison with the year 1995. In comparison of the state of pollution of ground layer of the atmosphere with the values from the cleanest locality in Europe (Central Norway) only 5 elements (Br, Cl, I, In, Mn) complied with the norm; 10 elements (Ba, Ca, Cs, Cu, K, Mg, Na, Rb, Se, Zn) represented slight loading (1–3 times) and 6 elements (Co, Fe, Hg, Ni, U, V) moderate loading (3-5 times). 16 elements (Ag, Al, As, Cd, Cr, Hf, La, Mo, Pb, Sb, Sc, Sr, Ta, Tb, Th, Yb) represented higher than 5 times increase. The teeth of roe deer hunted in A pollution zone had the highest concentration of F (550– 4308 mg. kg $^{-1}$). There is statistically significant difference between F concentration from A and B pollution and control locality. F concentration dropped in A pollution zone by 35.7% for last 30 years. On the basis of the analysis of diameter increment of beech in air-polluted area Žiarska basin in the transect in stands Forestry Management Unit Jalná and Forest Management Unit Antol the authors could draw conclusions that emissions from aluminium plant affected more significantly the increment of forest stands only in the year 1990.

In chapter 6 the use of seven modern statistical methods in developing ecotoxicity QSARs was investigated. The statistical methods used were general additive model (GAM), generalized unbiased interaction detection and estimation (GUIDE), least absolute shrinkage and selection operator version 2 (LASSO2), multivariate adaptive regression splines (MARS), neural networks (NN), projection pursuit regression (PPR), and recursive partitioning and regression trees (RPART). Traditional multiple linear regression (MLR) was also employed as a baseline method. A data set that contained the toxicity for 250 phenols acting by various mechanisms of toxic action and seven molecular descriptors was used for model development. Eight QSAR models were developed without regard to toxicity mechanism using the above-mentioned statistical methods. The resultant models were validated using the 10-fold cross validation method. For the data set under consideration, the model based on PPR was found to offer the highest modeling and predicting powers. The ability to identify toxicologically important parameters, transparency, and interpretability of the models based on the modern statistical methods and traditional MLR were discussed.

Within the field of radiological protection it has historically been presumed that measures to ensure the protection of man from the effects of ionising radiation have also served to effect the protection of the environment. Recent times have seen this premise questioned on the basis of its inconsistency with environmental protection standards for other contaminants, the fact that it conflicts with the recommendations of some international advisory bodies and that it is, in some cases, demonstrably not true. Such questions have generated the need for a defensible and transparent system for ensuring the protection of the environment from ionising radiation. The Arctic environment is especially vulnerable to radioactive contamination for a number of reasons including the large number of potential and actual sources of contamination either within the Arctic itself or in locations where discharges may be transported to the Arctic and the specificities of Arctic ecosystems that impose enhanced vulnerabilities on the components of these ecosystems to radioactive contamination. For these reasons, the development of specific strategies and systems to ensure the protection of Arctic ecosystems from radioactive contamination are a matter of some concern. The aim of the EPIC (Environmental Protection from Ionising Contaminants in the Arctic) framework was to develop a methodology for the protection of natural populations of organisms in Arctic ecosystems from radiation via the derivation of dose limits for different Arctic biota. The system was developed by collating information relating to the environmental transfer and fate of selected radionuclides through aquatic and terrestrial ecosystems in the Arctic, identification of reference Arctic biota that can be used to evaluate potential dose rates to biota in different terrestrial, freshwater and marine environments and modelling the uptake of a suite of radionuclides to the selected reference Arctic biota. This work then allowed for the development of a reference set of dose models for Arctic biota and the compilation of data on dose-effects relationships and assessments of potential radiological consequences for reference Arctic biota with the integration of assessments of the environmental impact from radioactive contamination with those for other contaminants. Chapter 7 serves to describe the EPIC framework and its development, the regulatory environment within which the framework was designed to function and presents a case study demonstrating the operation of the framework. Future development and issues of concern are also presented.

In: New Topics in Environmental Research
Editor: Daniel Rhodes, pp. 1-35
ISBN 1-60021-172-0
© 2006 Nova Science Publishers, Inc.

Chapter 1

Marine Algae and Heavy Metal Pollution: Current Status and Future Perspectives

L. Talarico[*]
University of Trieste, Trieste, Italy

Abstract

Macroalgae, owing to their sedentary nature, have been widely investigated as effective indicators to assess metal levels (bioavailability) in marine coastal environments. Metals concentrations have been determined by focussing on bioaccumulation that may depend upon species-specific resistance/tolerance, algal development, environmental factors, the metal chemical form and complexation, nutrient and metal ion bioavailability, combination of metals and seasonality. In laboratory studies biphasic metal uptake (fast passive ad/ab-sorption and slow active bioaccumulation) has been described. However complete analyses of adaptive/defence responses at biosynthetic, physiological and ultrastructural levels have been performed only for few macroalgae, where metal-complexes have been also detected by TEM/SEM microscopy combined with X-ray microanalysis. For these reasons and for the lack of toxicity standardised methods, dissimilar experimental approaches render the comparison both between (within) parameters and taxa sensitivities extremely problematic. In addition, debate is still open on the proper dose, the best stress parameters and statistical analysis to be chosen for eco-toxicity tests even for the already assessed protocols for microalgae. Attempts are made also to identify a form (or combination of forms) of a metal that might be bioavailable, thus potentially toxic, the free ion activity model in the interactions metal-organism being criticisable. It is known that many algae absorb and accumulate high concentrations of metals to a similar extent, but still scarce information is available on their ability to recover their physiological processes after the stress. More information on the cell functional recovery might be useful for individuating 'bioaccumulators' suitable for metal bioremoval, since the species capable of a prompt recovery might be reused as

---

[*] Author for correspondence: e-mail talarico@univ.trieste.it, phone: +39 0405583866, fax: +39 040568855

'biofilters' after detoxification in confined ponds. The most 'sensitive', thus unable to recover, might be useful as 'biosensors' for bioassays in water quality monitoring. In the case study we report, for the red macroalga *Audouinella saviana* (Meneghini) Woelkerling (Nemaliales) under culture, currently adopted and new parameters for macroalgae were explored and discussed in view of contributing the assessment of a standardised toxicity protocol. After preliminary experiments with different Cd doses and exposure times, thalli were cultured under 5-day exposures to 50-2000 μM Cd range, followed by 5-day recoveries in Cd-free media. Biomass/growth rate, O_2-evolution/consumption, ATP, chl/CAR, soluble/structural protein and biliprotein contents were analysed after 24 hrs and 5 days of both stress and recovery. Within parameters a 'sensitiveness' gradient, *i.e.* chl>ATP>R-PC>O_2-consumption>O_2-evolution, was individuated within 24 hrs. The adaptive responses were induced by 100 μM Cd (EC) and the defence mechanisms activated by LC50>300 μM Cd. In Cd-free medium most functions were at least partially recovered within 5 days. Main considerations may be the following: 1) exploring as many as possible parameters in order to choose the best stress markers, may also furnish information on algal cell physiology/metabolism for a useful comparison with different end-pointed papers; 2) there is a good correspondence between ultrastructural changes and physiological responses; 3) despite the high Cd levels supplied, high Cd-tolerance and detoxification capabilities are shown by *A. saviana* which might be regarded as a bioaccumulator and a potential tool for metal bioremoval.

ABBREVIATIONS

APC,	allophycocyanin;
CAR,	total carotenoids;
chl,	total chlorophyll;
EC,	effective dose;
LC50,	dose causing 50% diminution of most parameters;
R-PC,	R-phycocyanin;
R-PE,	R-phycoerythrin;
1r, 5r,	1-5-day recoveries without Cd;
1s, 5s,	1-5 day Cd exposures

INTRODUCTION

Many studies, though with different designs and endpoints, have been focussed on metal bioaccumulation capabilities of micro- and macro- algae.

In the field, macroalgae, owing to their sedentary nature, have been widely investigated as effective indicators to assess metal levels (bioavailability) in marine coastal environments (Cullinane *et al.*, 1987; Barreiro *et al.*, 1993; Leal *et al.*, 1997; Amado Filho *et al.*, 1999; Muse *et al.*, 1999; Kut *et al.*, 2000; Villares *et al.*, 2002; Caliceti *et al.*, 2002; Bruno & Eklund, 2003; Lozano *et al.*, 2003; Topcuoglu *et al.*, 2003). Metals concentrations have been determined by focussing on bioaccumulation that may depend upon species-specific resistance/tolerance (Maeda & Sakaguchi, 1990; Burridge & Bidwell, 2002), algal development (Malea & Haritonidis, 2000; Burridge & Bidwell, 2002), environmental factors, such as light (Hu *et al.*, 1996; Gorbi *et al.*, 2001), temperature, salinity, pH (Peterson *et al.*, 1984; Munda & Hudnik, 1988; Skowronski *et al.*, 1991; Rachlin & Grosso, 1991; Rai *et al.*, 1996; Franklin *et al.*, 2000; Lopez-Suarez *et al.*, 2000; Gupta *et al.*, 2001), the chemical form and complexation (Bruland, 1992; Campbell, 1995; Wong *et al.*, 1997; Gledhill *et al.*, 1999; Lombardi *et al.*, 2002), nutrient (Russell & Hunter, 1992; Lee & Wang, 2001; Wang & Dei, 2001) and metal bioavailability (Meyer, 2002) both in water and in the sediments (Borgmann, 2000; Borgmann & Norwood, 2002; Ligero *et al.*, 2002), combination of metals (Munda & Hudnik, 1986; Rijstenbil *et al.*, 1994; Shehata *et al.* 1999; Vasconcelos & Leal, 2001a; Rijstenbil & Gerringa, 2002) and seasonality (Munda & Hudnik, 1991; Vasconcelos & Leal, 2001b; Caliceti *et al.*, 2002; Villares *et al.*, 2002).

In the laboratory, metal uptake and defence mechanisms have been described as being common for various micro- and macro- algae. The light-dependant metal uptake (Hu *et al.*, 1996; Gorbi *et al.*, 2001), is usually biphasic (Rai *et al.*, 1990; Premuzic *et al.*, 1991; Khoshmanesh *et al.*, 1996; Hu *et al.*, 1996; Zhou *et al.*, 1998; Gupta *et al.*, 2001). Rapid ad/ab-sorption processes take place on the surface and within the cell wall, for the presence of binding sites (*i.e.* charged groups -COOH, =SO_4 in the polysaccharides and glicoproteins) (Mariani *et al.*, 1990; Wehrheim & Wettern, 1994; Amado Filho *et al.*, 1999; Diannelidis & Delivopulos, 1997; Talarico *et al.*, 2001), the capability of chemical binding being strictly related to the degree of sulfuration (Gadd, 1990; Werhheim & Wettern, 1994; Diannelidis & Delivopulos, 1997; Garnham, 1997; Talarico *et al.*, 2001; Perez-Rama *et al.*, 2002; Talarico, 2002). The cell wall represents a strong barrier to the free inward diffusion of metal ions and the modifications of this compartment are the first and main mechanism for reducing metal toxicity. In the red *Audouinella saviana* exposed to increasing Cd concentrations (Talarico, 2002), increases of Golgi bodies, not significantly present in the cytoplasm of untreated cells, the appearance of exocytic vesicles trans-locating new-synthesized material, and the progressive thickening (up to four times the initial) and smoothing of the cell walls were observed on TEM/SEM preparations. Similar cell wall modifications were found also in some brown (Amado Filho *et al.*, 1996; Leonardi & Vasquez, 1999) and green (Andrade *et al.*, 2004) macroalgae. These responses are indicative of enhanced polysaccharide synthesis in order to expose more binding sites for 'blocking' the ions within the cell wall (thickness) and to offer less surface (smoothing) for the 'free' ion inward diffusion. These sites would predominantly belong to sulphated polysaccharides, as suggested by the more abundant presence of X-ray S signals in the cell wall compartment (Talarico *et al.*, 2001; Talarico, 2002).

Metal ions are able to cross cell membranes and several possible mechanisms, such as competition for binding to multivalent ion carriers (Ca^{2+} channels) or binding to thiols (such as cysteine), have been accounted for their 'active' transport (using amino acid transporters) (Pinto *et al.*, 2003). Furthermore, membrane lipid-metal, intracellular ligand-metal, and chelating protein-metal complexes may enter the cell by endocytosis (Silveberg, 1975; Rai *et al.*, 1990; Wong *et al.*, 1997). Electron microscopy, alone or combined with X-ray microanalysis (Silverberg, 1975; Lignell *et al.*, 1982; Pellegrini *et al.*, 1991; Rai *et al.*, 1990; Maranzana *et al.*, 1996; Diannelidis & Delivopoulos, 1997; Talarico *et al.*, 2001; Talarico, 2002), has shown the pathway of Pb, Cd and Cu within the cell. Progressive enrichment of vesicular membrane systems and vacuoles for sequestering the toxicant (Talarico, 2002; Nishikawa *et al.*, 2003) in parallel with the increases of metal concentration and/or exposure time were observed. In particular, in the brown *Lessonia spp.* (Leonardi & Vasquez, 1999) and the green *Enteromorpha flexuosa* (Andrade *et al.*, 2004) Cu have been seen to precipitate primarily at two levels: the periplasmalemmal space and cell wall, the vacuolar system being a third site. In the red *Audouinella saviana* treated with Cd (Talarico, 2002), small-sized metal containing vesicles previously located within the plasmalemma-cell wall interface, were then incorporated into the cell wall itself, occupying progressively larger portions of the cell wall. Within a more and more vacuolated cytoplasm, small electron opaque granule-like particles and larger and larger metal-complexes were seen nearby or surrounding varying-sized vesicles. These complexes, firstly incorporated into small vacuoles, were sequestered finally into a highly enlarged vacuole, as clearly demonstrated by SEM cryopreparations (Talarico *et al.*, 2001; Talarico, 2002). Metal deposits may be in form of various inorganic compounds (Russell & Hunter, 1992) and/or metallorganic complexes (Mushrifah & Peterson, 1991; Campbell, 1995; Wong *et al.*, 1997; Pickering *et al.*, 1999). It has been previously suggested that the resistance/tolerance of different macroalgal species would be related mainly to their more or less efficient sequestration and exclusion inner mechanisms (Maeda & Sakaguchi, 1990). Among these latter it can be included the release of chelating exudates (Sueur *et al.*, 1982), as observed in the brown *Fucus vesiculosus* (Gledhill *et al.*, 1999) and the red *Gracilariopsis longissima* (Brown & Newman, 2003). This organic matter would be primarily polysaccharides particularly enriched in uronic acids (Kaplan *et al.*, 1987), but also other metal-complexing ligands, such as cysteine- and glutathione-like ligands. In fact, Vasconcelos and Leal (2001b) have demonstrated that both quantity and quality of the ligands, exuded by *Porphyra* spp. and *Enteromorpha* spp, were different depending on the metal species. Cd, in particular, stimulated only glutathione-like ligands. In *Audouinella*, TEM/SEM preparations have shown cell walls becoming as thin as in untreated thalli, and with a more tight arrangement of the fibrillar component, as a result of matrix loss after lengthy exposures to high Cd concentrations (Talarico *et al.*, 2001; Talarico, 2002). This may be interpreted as an 'extreme' defence to keep the 'exceeding' ions, or to exclude those already bound (Gledhill *et al.*, 1999) outside the cells. Besides a major capability of releasing chelating compounds, also a higher efficiency for direct ion efflux by primary ATPase pumps (Pinto *et al.*, 2003) might be considered to be a distinct feature of metal-tolerant species.

It is worth to note that, though metals are generally toxic at high concentrations, some of them are micronutrients essential for the activity of many enzymes (Cu, Zn) and essential components of photosystems (Fe), oxygen evolving complexes (Mn) or electron transport chain (Fe, Cu). Therefore the physiological range for essential metals between deficiency and toxicity is extremely narrow and a tightly controlled metal homeostasis network to adjust fluctuations in micronutrient availability is necessary (Clemens, 2006). An exhaustive review on processes and mechanisms controlling the uptake/accumulation of toxic and interactive nutrient metals, at molecular and cellular levels, has been done by Sunda & Huntsman (1998) for phytoplankton. Metal ions are generally taken up into cells by membrane transport proteins designed for acquisition of nutrient metals (Mg, Fe, Mn, Zn, Co, Cu, Mo). However, metals are often taken up by more than one transport system, *e.g.* Mn- and Zn-related systems, so that metal coordination sites are never entirely specific for a single metal. Consequently, biological ligands designed to bind an 'intended' nutrient metal will also bind competing (non-nutritive and toxic) metals with similar ionic radii and coordination geometry. Such competitive binding can occur also for nutrient active sites of intracellular metalloproteins and/or for feedback control sites regulating metal uptake and/or efflux.

Competition for membrane transport and intracellular metabolic binding sites strongly influences the uptake of both nutrient and toxic metals, and resultant physiological effects. For example Cd, Cu and Zn, which are present in polluted environments at concentrations much higher than Mn, have been proven to inhibit uptake of Mn by its cellular transport system in several diatoms and chlorophytes, thus causing deficiency of this micronutrient. Whichever induced deficiencies point to inherent linkages between metal toxicity and metal nutrition (Sunda & Huntsman, 1998). The cell strategy against metal excess for suppressing uncontrolled binding of metal ions to physiologically important functional groups is the expression of high-affinity binding sites. The synthesis of gluthatione-derived metal-binding peptides, the phytochelatins (Cobbett, 2000), represents the major detoxification mechanism (Clemens, 2006) within the cytoplasm. For this reason, excesses of essential and, overall, toxic metals, such as Cd, Pb, Hg are extremely harmful because they play key roles in affecting the precursor glutathione (GSH). Consequently, the reduction of the GSH pool causes increases of the oxydized form (GSSG) which promotes the activities of several antioxidant enzymes (Okamoto et $al.$, 1996; Okamoto & Colepicolo, 1998). An altered oxidative metabolism (for instance, unbalance between synthesis and consumption of GSH) leads to the formation of reactive oxygen species (ROS) (Mates, 2000; Cavas & Yurdakoc, 2005), so that toxicity of metals may be related mainly to their direct involvement in several ROS-generating mechanisms (Pinto et $al.$, 2003) within the inner cell compartments. Although ROS species are normal byproducts of the cell oxidative metabolism, they can be extremely harmful to cells at high concentrations, because they can oxidize proteins, lipids (and nucleic acids), thus causing severe damage to various cell functions and structures, especially chloroplasts and mitochondria. It is well known that metals induce oxidative stress, both by directly increasing the cellular ROS concentrations and by reducing the cellular antioxidant capacity, in microalgae (Okamoto et $al.$, 1996; Okamoto & Colepicolo, 1998; Rijstenbil et $al.$, 1994) as well as in macroalgae (Küpper et $al.$, 2002; Pinto et $al.$, 2003; Cavas & Yurdakoc, 2005), activating also the enzyme phytochelatin-synthase (Tsuji et $al.$, 2003) and other enzymes of the biosynthetic pathway of glutathione (GSH), similarly to higher plants (Clemens, 2006). In fact, responses within cytoplasm occur by chelation of metal ions through this precursor and the neosynthesis of cysteine-rich peptides (Hu et $al.$, 2001; Nagalakshmi & Prasad, 2001; Pinto et $al.$, 2003), $i.$ $e.$ the phytochelatins (PC) of different molecular weight (Gekeler et $al.$, 1988; Ahner et $al.$, 1994; Ahner et $al.$, 1995a; Ahner et $al.$, 1995b; Cobbett, 2000) that coordinate metals using their sulfhydryl groups. Interestingly, increased phytochelatin synthesis would require the formation of a GSH-heavy metal complex, generally Cd, being metal binding to PCs relatively specific for Cd (Pinto et $al.$, 2003). It has been proved that in the Cd-phytochelatin complexes, isolated from maize (Pickering et $al.$, 1999), there is not only Cd-thiolate ligation but also the presence of polynuclear metal clusters that involve bridging thiols as well as bridging sulfides. However, recently Clemens (2006) has drawn the conclusion that metal ions do not play a role as direct activators, but merely as stimulators of PC synthesis in a still unknown fashion. By TEM/SEM microscopy on $Audouinella$ (Talarico et $al.$, 2001; Talarico, 2002), the appearance of ribosomes, not so largely present in cytoplasm of untreated cells, suggested an enhanced ribosome-dependant protein synthesis, whereas the progressive (and parallel) increases of S and Cd X-ray signals, in this compartment, indicated a presumably active phytochelatin (and related cysteine-rich polypeptides) biosynthesis. It is reasonable to speculate that the formation of progressively larger and larger metal-complexes in the diverse cell compartments, may be due to the capacity for Cd to form polynuclear metal clusters (Pickering *et al.*, 1999), besides coordinating thiolate groups.

Among possible other damages reported for metal toxicity are cell membrane alterations (depolarization, lipid peroxidation), various enzymes and biosynthetic pathways inhibition, enhancement of photoinhibition and electron transport chain disruption (Rai *et al.*, 1991; Küpper *et al.*, 2002). Severe threat has been reported especially to chloroplasts and mitochondria, considered to be cell compartments highly susceptible to oxidative injury (Pinto *et al.*, 2003). In the photosynthetic apparatus metal ions may affect reaction centres (RC), with insertion of heavy metal in pheophytin *a* and/or plastocyanin, as well as chlorophyll-protein complexes (CPs) of PSIIs and peripheral LHCII antennae of Chlorophyta, with formation of heavy metal substituted-chlorophylls (hms-chl) (Küpper *et al.*, 2002). Recently also destruction and suppression of D1-protein synthesis (Plekhanov & Chemeris, 2003) have been indicated. Other possible targets, such as Rubisco (Stiborová *et al.*, 1988), oxygen-evolving complex of PSII (Mn-proteins) (Appenroth *et al.*, 2001), D1 protein (Giardi *et al.*, 2001) and cytochrome b-559 (Burda *et al.*, 2003), that have been already identified for higher plants, have been scarcely investigated in algae. For the algae possessing accessory light-harvesting antennae (LHC), *i.e.* phycobilisomes (Talarico, 1996; Talarico *et al.*, 1998; Talarico & Maranzana, 2000), direct damages have yet to be established. In the cyanobacterium *Synechococcus elongatus* (Tumova & Sofrova, 2002) increases of PC/chl and APC/chl ratios, detected on isolated thylakoids, were interpreted as probable rearrangement of these antennae following 1000 μM Cd exposure. In the red *Gracilariopsis longissima* (Brown & Newman, 2003) strong biliprotein decreases, not accompanied by similar chlorophyll reductions, have been attributed either to a major sensitiveness of their 'chemical environment' to perturbation by oxiradicals or to a greater binding affinity to Cu for phycocyanin and phycoerythrin with respect to chlorophyll. In *Audouinella* (Talarico *et al.*, 2001; Talarico, 2002), no appreciable alterations of phycobilisome assembly and/or size, on still well organized lamellae, were apparent till 2000 μM Cd exposure for 15-20 days. It is true that these pigments are rich of cysteine residues (sulfhydryl groups) in their apoprotein environment (Talarico, 1990; Talarico, 1996; Contreras-Martel *et al.*, 2001), however the possible effects of these metals on phycobilisome/phycobiliprotein structure and function are still unclear. Though more or less toxic effects have been reported for algal photosynthetic pigments (Küpper *et al.*, 2002; Tumova & Sofrova, 2002; Brown & Newman, 2003) and thylakoid structure and function (Rai *et al.*, 1990; Rai *et al.*, 1991; Visviki & Rachlin, 1992; De Filippis & Ziegler, 1993; Diannelidis & Delivopoulos, 1997; Leonardi & Vasquez, 1999; Nishikawa *et al.*, 2003; Andrade *et al.*, 2004), it has been suggested that, differently from other metals, Cd (and Ni) interferes with other metabolic processes, for example respiration (Webster & Gadd, 1996), rather than interacting directly with the thylakoid membranes (Pinto *et al.*, 2003). In TEM/SEM preparations of *Audouinella saviana* exposed to Cd, this hypothesis has been confirmed, the smaller metal complexes being only nearby and always outside the chloroplast, which kept its integrity even after lengthy exposures to high Cd doses (Talarico *et al.*, 2001; Talarico, 2002).

Despite this wide literature dealing with mechanisms against the metal challenge and possibly metal-induced damages, it should be emphasized that complete analyses of adaptive/defence responses at biosynthetic, physiological and ultrastructural levels are so far lacking. For this reason and for the lack of toxicity standardised methods for macroalgae

(Eklund & Kautsky, 2003), at present it is difficult to compare the different sensitivity and/or accumulation capacities of species, both in the field and in the laboratory. In fact, this has led to very dissimilar experimental approaches (Muyssen & Janssen, 2001) in terms of certainly toxic doses, generally much higher than naturally occurring levels (Tankere & Statham, 1996), exposure times, temperature, light intensity (and spectral composition)/regime and possibly comparable parameters. Moreover, although toxicity protocols are already assessed for microalgae (Reish & Oshida, 1987; ISO, 1989, 1995; USEPA, 1998), debate is still open on the proper dose (NOEC, LOEC, EC50 or LC50) (Pery et al., 2001), the best stress parameters and statistical analysis to be chosen for eco-toxicity tests (Isnard et al., 2001). Attempts are made also to identify a form (or combination of forms) of a metal that might be bioavailable, the so called 'bioavailable fraction' (Meyer, 2002), thus potentially toxic to the aquatic biota, the 'free ion' activity model in the interactions between metals and aquatic organisms being criticisable (Campbell, 1995). In fact, there are evidences that metals can enter the cells also in form of metal-complexes (Silveberg, 1975; Rai et al., 1990; Wong et al., 1997; Maranzana et al., 1996; Leonardi & Vasquez, 1999; Talarico et al., 2001; Talarico, 2002; Andrade et al., 2004).

In recent years, new devices to be connected directly to PSII (PSII-based biosensors) (Giardi et al., 2001), selected batteries of standardized biotests to verify correspondence between toxicity and chemical-based wastewater indices (Manusadžianas et al., 2003) or selection of microalgal species suitable for being analysed by specialised PAM-fluorometers (Bengston Nash et al., 2005) have been explored in order to assess novel toxicity bioassays. For macroalgae only a limited number of bioassays have been developed. These are based on parameters, such as reproduction and/or growth for the red macroalgae *Champia parvula* (USEPA, 1998; EC, 1999) and *Ceramium* spp. (Bruno & Eklund, 2003) or sporulation for the green *Ulva pertusa* (Han & Choi, 2005). It is currently accepted that single species toxicity testing is one of the principal methods for establishing causal association for the impacts of marine pollutants, whereas biomonitoring studies provide no information on causal association between biota and the pollutant(s) induced stress (Burridge & Bidwell, 2002). However, in developing bioassays with macroalgae several questions arise. Do specific end-points (or single parameters) on single species-testing have ecological relevance without a subsequent *in situ* evaluation of impacts? Do all the taxa have potential for assay development to a similar extent? Within taxa, do parameters, such as reproduction/growth rate or sporulation, have greater sensitivity than, for instance, photosynthetic/respiratory activities or pigment contents? Do the former parameters have the same 'biological weight' as the latter? These considerations may offer substantial scope for screening, species by species, both 'the best' taxa and 'the best' stress markers. Then, logical procedure would be to employ the 'most sensitive' (and significant) parameters and perhaps the 'most sensitive' of the species to be tested ultimately *in situ*, as suggested by Burridge & Bidwell (2002).

It is known that many, but not all the macroalgae, are able to absorb and accumulate high concentrations of metals to a similar extent (Abdel-Shafy & El-Said Farghaly, 1995; Zhou et al., 1998; Yu et al., 1999; Muse et al., 1999; Sawidis et al., 2001; Perez-Rama et al., 2002), but no information is available on their ability to recover their physiological processes after the stress, in absence of the toxicant. In fact, data on macroalgae interpretable as possible recovery are referred only to the renewed uptake capability (Hu et al., 1996). Recovery tests have been conducted on the freshwater microalga *Scenedesmus acutus* with Cr, evaluating either the effects of this metal on sexual reproduction (Corradi et al., 1995) either the metal uptake under different light intensities (Gorbi *et al.*, 2001). More informations on macroalgal cell physiology after the stress might be useful especially for selecting 'bioaccumulators' for metal bioremoval (Barron, 1995; Wren *et al.*, 1995; Garnham, 1997; Cervantes *et al.*, 2001), since the species capable of a prompt recovery might be used several times (recycled) as 'biofilters' after detoxification in confined ponds. The most 'sensitive', thus unable to recover readily, might be useful as 'biosensors' for bioassays in water quality monitoring. Also in this view, there is need of integrated and unified procedures (protocols) among researchers for a useful comparison both between (within) parameters and taxa sensitivities to the metal(s). This approach might help a better understanding of the so far large variety of results and it would facilitate the comparison between (within) algal responses, whichever the goals to be achieved in basic and/or applied research on macroalgae.

THE CASE STUDY

Physiological and biochemical responses of *Audouinella saviana* (Nemaliales-Rhodophyta) cultured under cadmium stress: reviewing an ecotoxicological approach.

Talarico L.(*), Maranzana G. & P. Frisenda, Department of Biology, University of Trieste

The purpose of the case study we present in this chapter was to study the adaptive/defence responses of the red macroalga *Audouinella saviana* (Meneghini) Woelkerling (Nemaliales) under culture in order to evaluate its sensitivity against Cd challenge, and also its ability to detoxify in Cd-free medium. Main goals were: a) to analyse as many as possible parameters for comparison with other papers with different endpoints; b) to ascertain the correspondence between previously seen cell fine structure changes with physiological and biochemical responses; c) to estimate the parameter sensitivities in relation with fixed exposure/recovery times; d) to individuate the EC and LC50 possibly discriminating adaptive from defence responses; e) to ascertain the physiological recovery after the stress, in order to determine weather this macroalga might be regarded as a 'biosensor' or a 'bioaccumulator'. Currently adopted and new parameters for macroalgae were explored and discussed in view of possibly contributing the assessment of a standardised protocol for macroalgae.

MATERIAL AND METHODS

The red alga *Audouinella saviana* (Meneghini) Woelkerling - Nemaliales was cultured under controlled conditions. Thalli consist of uniseriate filaments, moderately to freely and irregularly branched (Figure 1). Erect axes are from 10 to 20 mm long. The cells are cylindrical, 4-8 µm wide and 8-12 µm long, each with a single lobed and peripheral chloroplast containing one pyrenoid (Talarico, 2002).

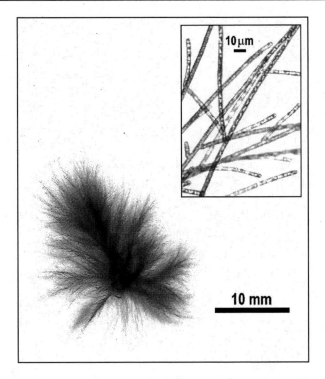

Figure 1. Thallus of the red alga *Audouinella saviana* (Meneghini) Woelkerlig (Nemaliales) with uniseriate filaments (insert).

Maintenance

Thalli were cultured in a modified Erdschreiber medium (Starr & Zeikus, 1993) not containing EDTA chelating trace metals (PIV) and vitamin B_{12}. Thalli were cultured with alga fresh weight (g) : medium volume (L) constant ratio ($FW_{(g)}/V_{(L)} = 1$), at T 23°C, under a diffused light source (Cool White Fluorescent Tubes Philips TLD36W/33) at 6 µmol photons $m^{-2} s^{-1}$ (Flux Radiometer Delta Ohm HD9021) with a L:D = 14:10 photoperiod.

EC, LC50, Exposure/recovery Times

In absence of precise dose-response definitions for macroalgae, EC and LC50 have been considered as the 'dose causing some effect' (either positive either negative) by relating this dose with the magnitude of the effect, and the 'concentration causing the 50% diminution of most physiological and biochemical responses' in the whole thalli, respectively. These doses have been determined with concentrations ranging from 50 µM Cd to 2000 µM Cd after preliminary tests (within 0.001-10 µM Cd range) which did not show clearly toxic effects (Bell, 1995; Maranzana *et al.*, 1996). Following previous analyses of the effects within 1-15 day time intervals, duration of exposure to Cd was fixed in 5 days, then thalli were placed in Cd-free medium and left to recover from 1 to 10 days. Apart from biomass/growth requiring

10 days, the other parameters were tested after 1 and 5 days of both stress (1s, 5s) and recovery (1r, 5r).

Experimental

Cd was added to the medium in form of $Cd(NO_3)_2$ (Talarico, 2002) since, in previous experiments, we ascertained that nitrate enrichment/depletion did not influence the algal responses before 7-14 days, both in cultures with and without Cd (Bell, 1995; Maranzana *et al.*, 1996; Talarico *et al.*, 1997; Maranzana, 1999). The lowest (50 µM) and the highest concentrations (from 1500 µM to 2000 µM Cd) were used only for biomass and protein estimation. The biomass/growth rate estimations were made within intervals of 1, 3, 5, 7, 10 days both in presence and in absence of Cd.

Investigated Parameters

Biomass/Growth Rate
Biomass was estimated as FW (mg) of treated with respect to the untreated thalli (controls) in the same time intervals. The increments/decrements in weight were referred to the DW. Growth rate was calculated as the percentage weight increment in each day (% d^{-1}) according to Haglund *et al.* (1996).

O_2-evolution/consumption and ATP Content
O_2-evolution (at 200 µmol m^{-2} s^{-1} saturating light) and O_2-consumption (in the dark) were estimated by an Hansatech DW1 polarographic Clark Electrode (Delieu & Walker, 1972) and expressed as µmol O_2 min^{-1}g $alga^{-1}$ DW. Total ATP content was determined by the procedure N°366/UV from SIGMA diagnostics for Blood, modified for macroalgae (Maranzana, 1999). Concentrations were expressed as mg g $alga^{-1}$ DW.

Lipo- and Hydro-soluble Pigment Contents
Spectrophotometric analyses (Perkin Elmer 554 UV-VIS Spectrophotometer) were performed on crude 80% (v/v) acetone extracts (Lorenzen, 1967) at $665_{\lambda max}$ nm for chlorophyll (chl) and $475_{\lambda max}$ nm for total carotenoids (CAR), using CAR extinction coefficient of Richards (1952). For biliproteins, crude extracts in 50 mM phosphate buffer pH 6.8 (Talarico, 1990) were analysed at $650_{\lambda max}$ nm, $615_{\lambda max}$ and $565_{\lambda max}$ nm to determine allophycocyanin (APC), R-phycocyanin (R-PC) and R-phycoerythrin (R-PE) amounts, according to MacColl & Guard-Friar (1987). Pigment contents were expressed as µg g $alga^{-1}$ DW.

Total, Soluble/structural Protein Contents
Thalli were homogenized in 0.1M Tris-HCl buffer pH 7.4 with 3 mM β-merchapto-ethanol, cooled for 12 hrs at 4°C, then centrifuged at 3,400 r.p.m. for 5 min. For structural proteins 15% TCA (trichloroacetic acid) and 1N NaOH were added to the residual pellet and centrifugation at 13,000 r.p.m. for 15 min was performed after 24 hrs in the dark at 4°C. All

the samples were analysed according to the Bradford method (1976) and expressed as μg g alga^{-1} DW.

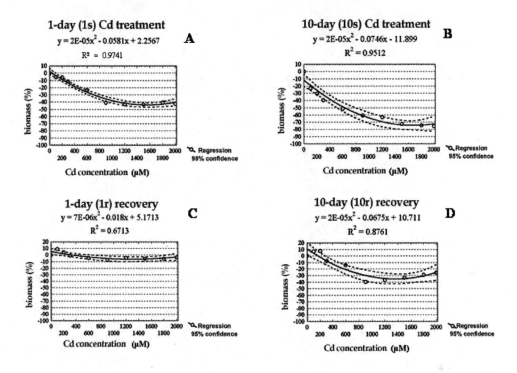

Figure 2. Biomass variations of thalli treated (A and B) with different Cd concentrations (μM) and recovery in absence of the toxicant (C and D). Each value was normalised to the controls (0 line) and expressed as a percentage (%).

RESULTS

Biomass/Growth Rate

Massive biomass decreases (from 40% to 70%) were noticed only within 10 days (Figure 2 A, B) at the highest doses, the 50% loss being localised at 600 μM Cd. During recovery (Figure 2 C, D), at day 10r even algae treated with 2000 μM Cd had recovered more than 50% of the biomass lost at day 10s. Growth rate was always proximate to that of the controls, whichever the Cd concentration (Figure 3 B, C, D), except day 1s showing 40% decrements for doses higher than 900 μM Cd (Figure 3 A).

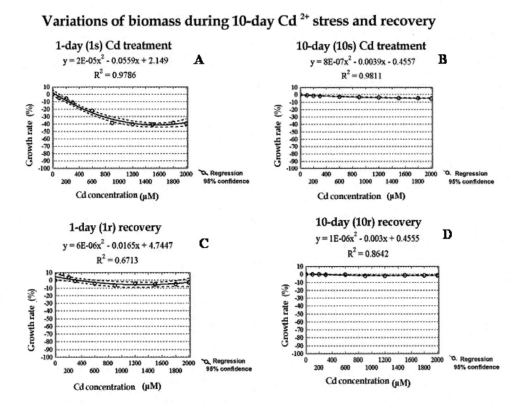

Figure 3. Growth rate variations of thalli treated (A and B) with different Cd concentrations (μM) and recovery in absence of the toxicant (C and D). Values (daily % weight increments) were normalised to the controls (0 line).

O₂-Evolution/consumption and ATP Content

At day 5s, a stimulated photosynthetic activity was detected at the lowest Cd doses. Reductions of about 40% occurred for concentrations around 300 μM Cd (Figure 4 A). The 50% diminution was apparent around 600 μM Cd at day 1s, whereas it was within 300-400 μM Cd at day 5s. The photosynthetic activity, though always much lower than in the controls, was regained moderately (from about 10% to 30%) at day 5r, also at the highest doses (Figure 4 B). All over the stress, O₂-consumption was lowered (Figure 5 A) till reaching the 50% diminution around 400 μM Cd and 600 μM Cd at day 1s and 5s, respectively. In absence of Cd, no evident recovery occurred, the reductions being similar to those of treated thalli (Figure 5 B). The pattern of ATP contents appeared to be similar for both days 1s and 5s, differing only for positive values at 200 μM Cd (1s). In both cases the 50% decrement was reached around 300 μM Cd (Figure 6 A). Also during recovery the 1r and 5r patterns showed similarities, the 5r decrements being less remarkable within 300-600 μM Cd (Figure 6 B). The real recovery with respect to the stressed thalli was around 30%.

Oxygen evolution

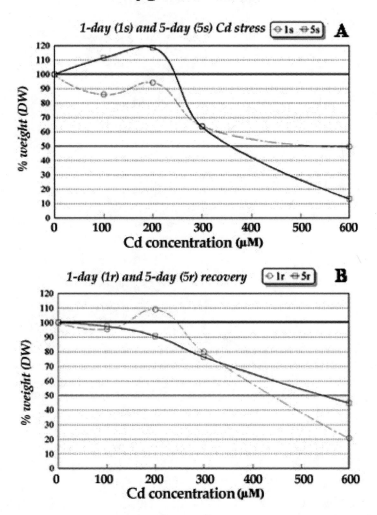

Figure 4. O_2-evolution measurements (μmol O_2 min^{-1} g alga^{-1} DW) at different Cd concentrations (μM) during stress (A) and recovery (B). Values were normalized to the controls (100% thick line) and expressed as a percentage (%). Thin line = 50% decrements (LC50).

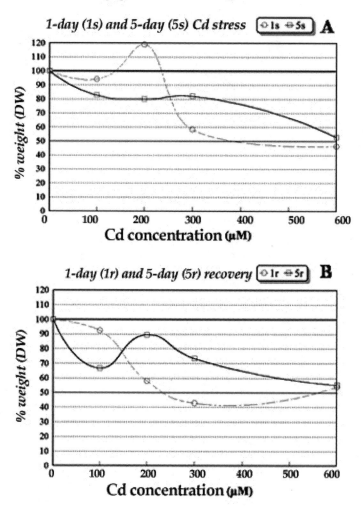

Figure 5. O$_2$-consumption measurements (μmol O$_2$ min^{-1} g alga^{-1} DW) at different Cd concentrations (μM) during stress (A) and recovery (B). Values were normalized to the controls (100% thick line) and expressed as a percentage (%). Thin line = 50% decrements (LC50).

Lipo- and Hydro-soluble Pigment Contents

Apart from APC always proximate to the controls (not presented) and R-PC (which was diminishing), pigments were highly increased within 100-200 μM Cd. Among them, chl was maximally increased to more than 40% since day 1s (Figure 7 A). Pigment reductions were observed for doses > 200 μM Cd, with the most sensitive response for chl (-90% since day 1s). For chl, decrements much higher than 50% were apparent within 200-300 μM Cd, both at days 1s and 5s, whereas for R-PC they were around 50% within 300-400 μM Cd and 400-600 μM Cd at 1s and 5s, respectively (Figure 9 A). Without Cd, chl drastic reductions were fully recovered (from -90% to +30%), with contents largely exceeding those of the controls (Figure 7 B). The hydrosoluble pigments (Figs 9 B and 10 B) also recovered, though to a much lesser extent (10%-20%). In contrast, total CAR increased under all the Cd treatments, reaching values of 40% higher than the controls for 600 µM Cd at day 1s. After Cd deprivation, the stimulating effect was even amplified to 60% more than in the untreated thalli (Figure 8 A, B).

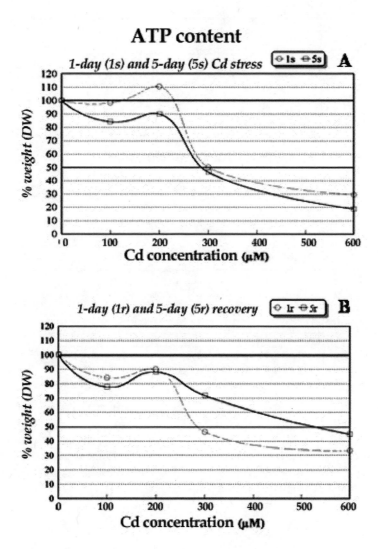

Figure 6. ATP content variations at different Cd concentrations (µM) during stress (A) and recovery (B). Values (mg g alga $^{-1}$ DW) were normalized to the controls (100% thick line) and expressed as a percentage (%). Thin line = 50% decreases (LC50).

Chlorophyll *a* content

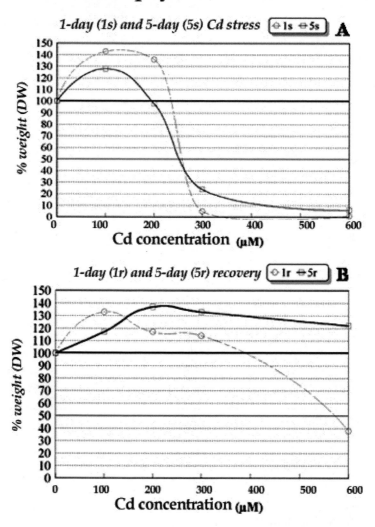

Figure 7. Chl content variations at different Cd concentrations (μM) during stress (A) and recovery (B). Values (μg g alga^{-1} DW) were normalized to the controls (100% thick line) and expressed as a percentage (%). Thin line corresponds to 50% diminutions (LC50).

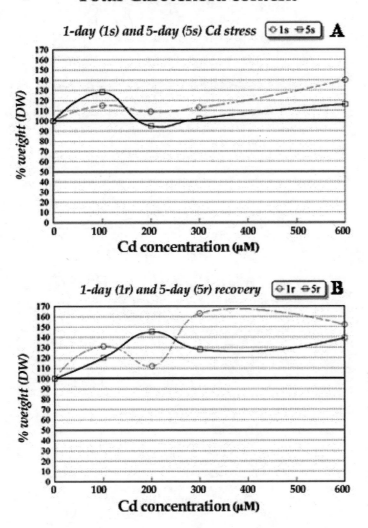

Figure 8. CAR content variations at different Cd concentrations (μM) during stress (A) and recovery (B). Values (μg g alga^{-1} DW) were normalized to the controls (100% thick line) and expressed as a percentage (%). Thin line corresponds to 50% diminutions (LC50).

R-phycocyanin content

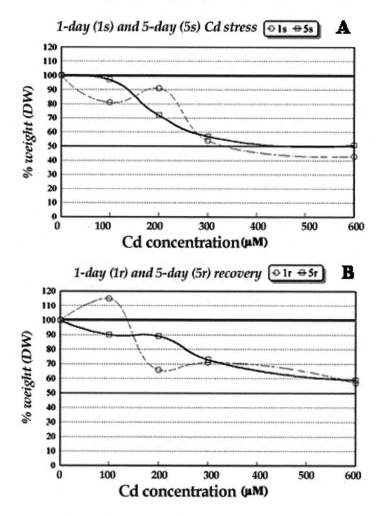

Figure 9. R-PC content variations at different Cd concentrations (µM) during stress (A) and recovery (B). Values (µg g alga^{-1} DW) were normalized to the controls (100% thick line) and expressed as a percentage (%). Thin line corresponds to 50% decrements (LC50).

R-phycoerythrin content

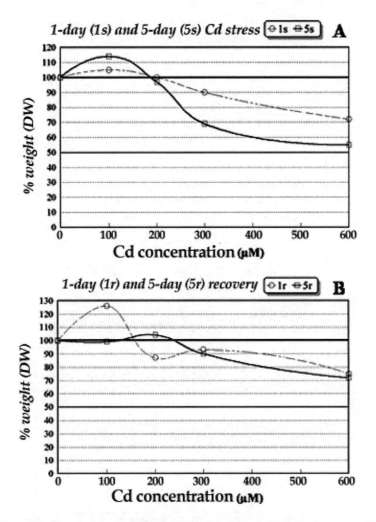

Figure 10. R-PE content variations at different Cd concentrations (μM) during stress (A) and recovery (B). Values (μg g alga^{-1} DW) were normalized to the controls (100% thick line) and expressed as a percentage (%). Thin line corresponds to 50% decreases (LC50).

Soluble/structural Protein Contents

Till 600 μM Cd, total protein contents generally incremented with increasing Cd doses and tended to stabilize around the control values during recovery (not presented data). At 600 μM Cd, the comparison between the structural and the soluble proteins (Figure 11 A) showed that the maximum increases (up to 75%) were due to the structural fraction, the soluble one being enhanced only of 20%. For doses higher than 900 μM Cd, values proximate to the controls were detected for both fractions. During recovery, their contents were always proximate to the controls till 900 μM Cd, with no appreciable variations between the two fractions. Remarkable reductions were seen for higher doses (Figure 11 B).

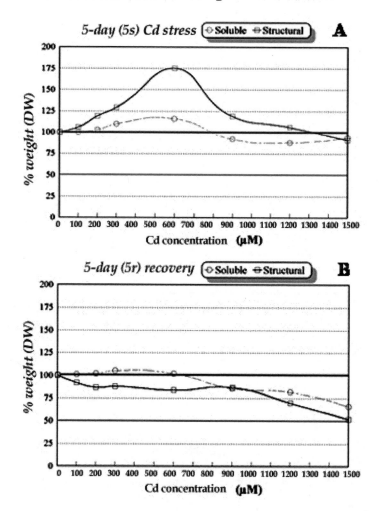

Soluble and structural protein contents

Figure 11. Variations of soluble/structural protein contents (μg g alga^{-1} DW) at different Cd concentrations (μM) during stress (A) and recovery (B). Values were normalized to the controls (100% thick line) and expressed as a percentage (%). Thin line = 50% diminutions (LC50).

EC, LC50 and Parameter Sensitivities

Cd effects are summarised on Table 1. Apart from growth, respiration and R-PC, that were more or less negative as a tendency, parameters, such as chl, CAR, R-PE and proteins, were more or less positively affected within 100-200 μM Cd (presumable EC range). Some of them (ATP and O_2-evolution) showed both positive and negative effects. The certainly toxic effects occurred at different Cd doses, indicating a 'sensitiveness' gradient within parameters which was 'chl>ATP>R-PC>O_2-consumption>O_2-evolution' within 24 hrs (1s). Most parameters showed 50% diminutions within 300-600 μM Cd.

Table 1. Most parameters show positive effects with 100 μM Cd. After 24 hrs, the diverse LC50s (within 300-600 μM Cd) for each parameter individuate a 'sensitiveness' gradient: chl>ATP>R-PC>O_2-consumption>O_2-evolution.

Parameters	EC [Cd] (μM)	Effect (%)	Time (day)	LC50 [Cd] (μM)	Time (day)
Biomass	100 300	-5 -10	1s 1s	600	10s
Growth rate	100 300	-5 -10	1s 1s	None	
O_2-evolution	100 100	-15 +10	1s 5s	600 300-400	1s 5s
O_2-consumption	100 100	-5 -20	1s 5s	400 600	1s 5s
ATP content	200 100	+10 -15	1s 5s	300 300	1s 5s
Chl	100 100	+40 +30	1s 5s	200-300	1s 5s
CAR	100 100	+15 +30	1s 5s	None	
R-PC	100 100	-20 -5	1s 5s	300-400 >400	1s 5s
R-PE	100 100	+5 +15	1s 5s	None	
Total proteins	200	+10	5s	None	
Structural prot.	200	+20	5s	None	
Soluble prot.	200	+5	5s	None	

DISCUSSION

The effects of Cd will be discussed in distinct paragraphs in view of possibly discriminating the adaptive from the defence responses to Cd challenge, by considering also the algal functional recovery. Comparison with other papers will refer necessarily to the stress, since literature possibly interpretable as 'recovery' (Hu *et al.*, 1996) is based on different parameters or referred to a freshwater microalga (Corradi *et al.*, 1995; Gorbi *et al.*, 2001).

Biomass/Growth Rate

The lower concentration range (100-300 μM Cd) seems to have little negative effects. Toxic effects are seen at higher doses (600-2000 μM Cd) which, however, do not seem to block completely the recovery capacities, since the lost biomass was regained (up to 50%) even after a 10-day stress with 2000 μM Cd. Even though with a different metal and much lower doses (maximum around 190 μM Cr), these results may be similar to those observed in the green microalga *Scenedesmus acutus* (Corradi *et al.*, 1995) both at high and low irradiances (Gorbi *et al.*, 2001). When considering the growth rate, only at day 1s toxic effects are seen, and only for concentrations higher than 300 μM Cd. Longer exposures (10s) do not seem to affect particularly growth rate, whichever the Cd concentration and the recovery time. These results indicate that, in long term, the growth rate appears to be less sensitive than biomass (Muyssen & Janssen, 2001) and that Cd, acting on cellular division (cell number) to a lesser extent, influences maximally cellular volume (cell metabolism) (Nishikawa *et al.*, 2003). The biomass increases may be attributed to a newly synthesized material, in agreement with the results on the red macroalga *Gracilariopsis longissima* (Brown & Newman, 2003) for copper. Most of the increased cellular volume would be due to newly formed polysaccharides, as already suggested by previous TEM observations (Talarico, 2002) showing numerous Golgi vesicles trans-locating material for thickening the cell wall, from three to four times. The cell wall widening would result into a higher availability of the cell wall charged groups, as already indicated for different metals in other algae (Mariani *et al.*, 1990; Wehrheim & Wettern, 1994; Amado Filho *et al.*, 1996; Hu *et al.*, 1996; Diannelidis & Delivopulos, 1997). The positive correlation between S and Cd X-ray signals, previously detected (Talarico *et al.*, 2001; Talarico, 2002), would confirm the close relation between the chemical binding capability and the degree of sulfuration already demonstrated for other algae (Gadd, 1990; Wehrheim & Wettern, 1994; Diannelidis & Delivopulos, 1997; Garnham, 1997; Perez-Rama *et al.*, 2002). Cell wall modification would represent the very first adaptive response to low Cd doses, whereas massive doses would activate other intracellular defence responses when cell wall binding sites are saturated (Talarico *et al.*, 2001; Talarico, 2002). The biomass losses at high Cd doses may be due either to the drastically reduced photosynthesis/respiration resulting into less available energy (ATP) for growth, either to the release of organic matter as in the brown *Fucus vesiculosus* (Gledhill *et al.*, 1999) and the red *Gracilariopsis longissima* (Brown & Newman, 2003), both treated with copper. In *Audouinella saviana* such a matter would consist of matrix cell wall polysaccharides, as suggested by the thinner cell wall with abundant and more compact fibrils previously observed by TEM/SEM microscopy (Talarico, 2002). This may be interpreted both as an 'extreme' defence to keep the 'exceeding' metals outside the cells and as an exclusion mechanism to release them into the medium during detoxification. Besides the other defence mechanisms, also the capability of releasing chelating compounds (Diannelidis & Delivopulos, 1997; Gledhill *et al.*, 1999; Brown & Newman, 2003) would correspond to a good tolerance/resistance to the metals (Pinto *et al.*, 2003).

Photosynthesis, Respiration and Energetic Balance (ATP)

The results on photosynthesis and respiration would indicate that 300-400 μM Cd range may discriminate the adaptive from the defence responses, these latter showing more drastic variations of the whole energetic balance (ATP). In short-term, at the lowest doses, it is presumable that the ATP content derives mainly from respiratory process (which was stimulated) rather than from photosynthetic activity (which resulted to be partially inhibited). After prolonged exposure, a major contribution to ATP may derive from the photosynthetic process which was enhanced. With doses higher than 400 μM Cd, especially at day 1s, both the processes are drastically lowered, resulting into a generally low ATP content. Similar reductions of ATP were detected in the green microalga *Chlorella vulgaris* (Rai *et al.*, 1991) and were interpreted as a 'multiple' binding of Zn and Hg with the electron transport systems, the PSII being the primary site of action of these two metals. However, the scarce ATP content may be explained either with a reduced ATP production, either with an increased energetic consumption for active metal transport and sequestration, diverse biosynthetic processes, membrane system 'construction' and cellular restoration processes. Also in the macroalga *Gracilariopsis longissima* (Brown & Newman, 2003) Cu has been seen to induce photosynthesis disruption (PSII damage), but only at high metal levels, whereas respiration was not significantly affected. In *Audouinella*, for quite higher Cd doses, at day 5s the unbalance of the two processes appears to be in favour of respiration which seems to be less affected than photosynthesis. Thus respiration would be the main process sustaining the ATP production in longer time, differently from the red *Antithamnion plumula*, where this activity was proved to be the most affected by copper (Küpper *et al.*, 2002). In *Audouinella*, the defence responses would be based on a modulation of these processes for an energetic balance sufficient for activating protective mechanisms, for sustaining the base metabolism and preserving the cell integrity, as suggested by Brown & Newman (2003). By TEM/SEM microscopy, the integrity of the thylakoid organization and the presence of small metal deposits always outside the chloroplast, observed at the highest doses for long exposures (Talarico, 2002), would confirm the hypothesis that Cd may not interfere directly with the thylakoid structure (Pinto *et al.*, 2003), but preferably with its function, compromising primarily the photosynthetic process at molecular level. The reductions of photosynthesis, in agreement with those detected in other taxa for Cd, Zn, Hg and Cr (Hu *et al.*, 1996; De Filippis & Ziegler, 1993; Gorbi *et al.*, 2001) might derive from presumable damages to different sites of PSII, as already demonstrated in *Anthithamnion* for Cu (Küpper *et al.*, 2002). For Cd a possible interpretation might be also an interaction between Cd and the Mn-proteins of PSII, as suggested for *Chlorella vulgaris* (Rai *et al.*, 1991). In fact, in several diatoms and chlorophytes, it has been demonstrated that high levels of Cd can cause inhibition of Mn uptake by competing for binding either to membrane transport, either to intracellular control sites regulating metal uptake/efflux (Sunda & Huntsman 1998). The consequent deficiency of this micronutrient may result also in the inhibition of growth, as detected in the brown *Fucus vesiculosus* (Munda & Hudnik, 1986), where a Cd-Mn antagonistic action has been hypothesized. Whichever the cause, the appreciable tendency to recover, observed during five days without Cd, would indicate that this metal does not compromise irreversibly the photosynthetic activity. As regards respiration, our results are quite different from those on the green *Ulva lactuca,* where Cd promoted high increases of mithochondrial ATPase activity

(Webster & Gadd, 1996). They are also in contrast with those on the red *Anthithamnion plumula* (Küpper *et al.*, 2002), where respiration resulted to be the most affected at concentrations far lower (around 30 and 270 μM Cu) than those (400 and 600 μM Cd) supplied to *Audouinella*. These differences in the defence responses might be explained with a different bioactive role for these two metals.

Liposoluble Pigments

Differently from the red macroalga *Gracilariopsis longissima* (Brown & Newman, 2003) where chl *a* (and β-carotene) contents were not affected by copper, the lowest Cd doses seem to have some stimulating effect on chlorophyll synthesis, as indicated by the increases observed. This is in agreement with the results on some microalgae for Cd and other metals (Rai *et al.*, 1991; Nagalakshmi & Prasad, 2001; Tumova & Sofrova, 2002). Conversely, doses higher than 300 μM Cd induced drastic reductions, possibly related to Cd competition with the Mg present in the chlorophyll *a* ring, similarly to the red *Anthithamnion plumula* for Cu, where heavy metal substituted-chlorophylls (hms-Chl*a*) within the CPs were detected (Küpper *et al.*, 2002). Nevertheless, in absence of the toxicant, the chlorophyll contents again incremented for the lowest doses since the first day of recovery. After five days without Cd, the contents were also increased, with respect to the controls, for higher doses. These positive values and the wide recovery of chl amounts (up to 120% for day 5r with respect to 5s) would indicate a renewed chlorophyll synthesis, in parallel with a moderate resumption of photosynthetic activity. The positive response of carotenoids, which were increasing both in presence and in absence of cadmium, suggests their involvement in the defence mechanisms, by preventing alterations of the oxidative metabolism (ROS formation) (Mates, 2000; Pinto *et al.*, 2003; Cavas & Yurdakoc, 2005). For microalgae (Okamoto *et al.*, 1996; Okamoto & Colepicolo, 1998), carotenoids together with enzymes, such as superoxide dismutase (SOD), peroxidase and catalase and metal chelators were accounted for the responses against the metal oxidative stress. A presumable defence mechanism might be also the formation of metallorganic complexes (Campbell, 1995), more likely the metal-liposoluble pigment complexes already ascertained for the cyanophyte *Anabaena flos-aquae* under Cd (Mushrifah & Peterson, 1991) and the macrophyte *Cladophora glomerata* under Pb (Wong *et al.*, 1997). During recovery the still large CAR amounts might be explained with their protective action within a still altered cell oxidative metabolism.

Proteins and Hydrosoluble Pigments

Cadmium influences positively the whole protein synthesis, as already suggested by the enhanced presence of ribosomes in TEM preparations (Talarico *et al.*, 2001; Talarico, 2002), both as adaptive and defence responses. If we refer to the structural and the soluble fractions, the first cellular adaptive response involves the structural (highly increased) more than the soluble proteins. Structural proteins would be necessary for building up the thickening cell wall and the highly enriched vesicular membrane systems. During stress within 100-600 μM Cd, the soluble protein fraction is always much higher than that of the controls, also taking into account the possibly strong contribution (up to 60% of the total) of biliproteins (Talarico & Maranzana, 2000). This, together with the highly increased S peak detected within the metal-complexes localised inside the cytoplasm and the final vacuole (Talarico, 2002), would indicate the presence of phytochelatins (Gekeler *et al.*, 1988; Ahner *et al.*, 1994; Ahner *et al.*, 1995a; Ahner *et al.*, 1995b; Cobbett, 2000). Their existence (Rijstenbil & Gerringa, 2002; Tsuji *et al.*, 2003), their chemical structure (Pickering *et al.*, 1999; Hu *et al.*, 2001; Nagalakshmi & Prasad, 2001) and function (Pinto *et al.*, 2003) have been fully elucidated, particularly for microalgae. Interestingly, during recovery, both the soluble and structural fractions were proximate to the control values, possibly indicating some tendency towards both a better balanced oxidative metabolism and a return to the initial cell compartment structures.

Among biliproteins the only stable pigment was APC (not presented data). This pigment, forming the phycobilisome (PBS) core together with the terminal acceptors (PCB-carrying L_{CM} and few diverse APCs), can be considered as a 'membrane pigment' (Talarico, 1996; Talarico & Maranzana, 2000). No variations of APC content and well organized thylakoids with more or less structured PBSs until 1500-2000 μM Cd for 10-15 days (Talarico, 2002) seem to prove no direct damages on this pigment. Conversely, R-PE and R-PC were both affected, though to different extents, by doses higher than 200 μM Cd. Similar biliprotein reductions, detected in *Gracilariopsis longissima* (Brown & Newman, 2003), were interpreted as being due either to a major sensitiveness of their 'chemical environment' to perturbation by oxiradicals or to a high affinity of these biliproteins for Cu. Whichever the cause, the varied pigment composition implies changes in PBS size (Talarico, 1996; Talarico, 2002), thus causing changes of light energy transmission to PSII RCs. Since the photosynthetic performance is not directly related to the biliprotein content, but rather to the presence of more or less structured PBSs (Talarico & Maranzana, 2000), the rearrangement of these antennae may be also accounted for the strong lowering of photosynthetic activity. This is in agreement with the hypothesis formulated for the cyanophyte *Synechococcus elongatus* under Cd stress (Tumova & Sofrova, 2002) despite dissimilar biliprotein variations. Furthermore, being light conditions constant all over the experiments, the drastic and fairly progressive reductions of the 'external' biliproteins (a readily available nitrogen reserve) might be explained also with their consumption due to a higher N-demand when an unbalance occurs. Interestingly, in *Audouinella*, effects on biliprotein contents resembling those described for *Gracilariopsis* (Brown & Newman, 2003) have occurred at doses much higher (100-200 μM Cd) than the highest dose (around 8 μM Cu) supplied to this red macroalga with similar exposure times (5 days versus 7 days). This again suggests a different bioactive role for cadmium and copper, besides a possibly different specific sensitiveness.

EC, LC50, Exposure/recovery Times and Stress Markers

Defined experimental designs for toxicity tests are well assessed only for microalgae (Reish & Oshida, 1987; ISO, 1989; ISO, 1995; USEPA, 1998; Giardi *et al.*, 2001; Manusadžianas *et al.*, 2003; Bengston Nash *et al.*, 2005). Nevertheless, considerable efforts are currently made for choosing the most significant doses for proper and statistically correct analyses (Isnard *et al.*, 2001; Pery *et al.*, 2001). On the other hand, the few assays developed with macroalgae (Bruno & Eklund, 2003; Burridge & Bidwell, 2002; Eklund & Kautsky, 2003; Han & Choi, 2005) are based mostly on reproduction/growth or sporulation, thus parameters other than ours. In absence of precise protocols for macroalgae, the design of our experiments did not allow us to apply any statistical calculations of currently defined doses, lacking the necessary number of replicas and the physiological and biochemical parameters having not the same 'biological weight'. Therefore we have chosen EC as the 'effective concentration' with either positive or negative effects within 24 hrs, and considered the sub-lethal dose (LC50) as the 'effective concentration causing the 50% diminution of most parameters within 24 hrs'. On this basis, from all the results it may be deduced that the EC for *Audouinella saviana* is set around 100 μM Cd, having this dose a major positive influence on algal responses. The first certainly toxic effects were detected within 300-600 μM Cd range, comprehending reasonably the LC50 activating the defence responses. These results indicate that toxic effects for this red macrophyte would occur at Cd doses much higher than those (LC50 = 270 μM Cd) estimated on the 50% mortality of fragments of the agarophyte *Gracilaria tenuistipitata* (Hu *et al.*, 1996), therefore with a quite different approach. This again leads to the need of better defining both the LC50 and the parameters for macroalgae. In fact, different experimental approaches (*i.e.* macroalgal fragments, apical/basal portions *etc.*), derived from protocols assessed for microalgae (Reish & Oshida, 1987; ISO, 1989; ISO, 1995; USEPA, 1998; Giardi *et al.*, 2001; Manusadžianas *et al.*, 2003; Bengston Nash *et al.*, 2005) may be misleading. As regards the exposure time intervals, 24 hours were sufficient for individuating the LC50, discriminating also adaptive from defence responses, but at least 5 days were needed for having a better evaluation of the whole cell functionality. Analogously, a 5-day recovery time was sufficiently indicative for verifying the reversibility of the toxic effects and accumulation processes, with a relatively quick recovery of the cell functionality.

As regards parameters to be possibly chosen as stress markers, considerations may be the following: 1) despite its better sensitiveness in comparison with the growth rate, biomass does not constitute a valid stress parameter because of its long-time requirement; 2) chl represents a valid stress marker for its sensitiveness; 3) the estimation of ATP might be a useful tool for evaluating the energetic balance of photosynthesis and respiration, together with their direct estimation; 4) CAR may be useful, if considered as 'positive' stress markers; 5) among proteins, the structural and the chelating ones might be considered in positive terms (even for doses much higher than 600 μM Cd); 6) for red macroalgae phycocyanin seems to be a valid stress marker for the rapidity and linearity of the response.

If each parameter 'sensitiveness' is put in relation with a fixed exposure (recovery) time, the sensitiveness gradient results to be 'chl>ATP>R-PC>O_2-consumption>O_2-evolution' within 24 hrs.

CONCLUSION

Exploring as many as possible parameters may furnish information on algal cell physiology and metabolism for a useful comparison with other papers with different endpoints. All the results indicate that the first adaptive responses have occurred at 100 μM Cd (EC) and the defence mechanisms were activated by LC50>300 μM Cd.

By summarizing previous ultrastructural observations and physiological and biochemical data, the adaptive responses may be: a) production of matrix polysaccharides to increase cell wall thickness in order to expose more binding sites; b) plasmalemma modifications accompanied by relevant exocytic vesicles involved in translocating new material (*i.e.* matrix polysaccharides); c) stimulation of chl*a* synthesis and photosynthetic activity; d) active ribosome-dependant protein synthesis, with major contribution of the structural fraction, presumably devoted to building up cellular structures capable to block Cd ions.

When Cd ions (Cd-complexes) enter the protoplasm the defence responses may be: a) modulation of photosynthesis/respiration processes with an energetic balance (ATP) sufficient for protective mechanisms, for sustaining base metabolism and preserving cellular integrity, especially the photosynthetic apparatus; b) phycobiliprotein variations, rearrangement of PBSs affecting photosynthetic efficiency and presumable consumption as nitrogen reserve; c) enhanced carotenoid synthesis for an antioxidant action and, possibly, for the formation of metal-liposoluble complexes; d) chelating protein synthesis with formation of metal-complexes within cytoplasm; e) 'construction' of multiple membrane systems, possibly related either to phytochelatin synthesis, either to sequestration of the toxicant into the vacuoles; f) final sequestration into a highly enlarged vacuole; g) metal exclusion by exudate release.

In conclusion, this red alga seems to be a 'high Cd-tolerant' organism, not having thus the potential for bioassays. It behaves as a 'bioaccumulator' rather than a 'biosensor'. In fact, despite Cd levels much higher than those naturally present in seawater (Tankere & Statham, 1996), these doses do not seem sufficiently toxic to compromise irreversibly the alga's growth, physiology and metabolism, since *Audouinella* recoveries its cellular functionality in a relatively short time. Therefore it may represent a potential and renewable (recyclable) tool for metal bioremoval (Barron, 1995; Wren *et al.*, 1995; Garnham, 1997; Cervantes *et al.*, 2001).

GENERAL CONCLUSION

An extensive literature now exists on metals in the aquatic environment and macroalgae have been largely employed as effective indicators to assess metal levels (bioavailability) in marine coastal environments. However, it should be pointed out that our understanding of the biological effects of these metals under natural conditions is very limited, since biomonitoring studies provide no information on causal association between biota and the metal-induced stress, because of the large variability of chemical and physical factors affecting the metal-bioavailability. As a consequence, the levels of metals accumulated by macroalgae may not reflect necessarily the levels of metal pollution. On the other hand metal toxicity, as measured in the laboratory, has led to a pretty good knowledge of the defence mechanisms against the metal(s) challenge, but the responses may be very species-specific because they largely depend on the sensitiveness or tolerance/resistance of the testing alga. Most researchers have performed their experiments with quite different approaches, in terms of stress markers, metal concentrations, effective (EC) or sub-lethal (LC50) doses and exposure times, for the lack of standardized procedures. Furthermore, only few parameters have been used in eco-toxicity tests without considering the possible functional recovery after the stress, and very few analyses of cell fine structure have been conducted. Due to the complexity of aquatic ecosystem and the multifunctional character of toxicity per se, analyzing as many as possible parameters at biosynthetic, physiological and ultrastructural levels may give a more complete information on algal adaptive/defence responses to the toxicant. This would be very useful for individuating the species characteristics (sensitiveness, tolerance/resistance), thus favouring the choice of species suitable for developing bioassays ('biosensors') or for bioremediation (tolerant 'bioaccumulators'). Greater uniformity in assay design, methodology and analysis, with better defined EC/LC50 doses, exposure/recovery times, and accurate choice of the best stress markers, should be the basis for rendering the necessary comparison between and within taxa less problematic, both in the field and in the laboratory research. The development of standardized tests for macroalgae should take into account the different sensitiveness of each species and each parameter, which requires different times, in relation with a well defined exposure time and, possibly, the cell functional recovery. This approach would lead to a better comparison among different species sensitivities and would help to better interpret the outcomes of both monitoring and toxicological studies. First of all, a preliminary screening of the sensitive, the resistant/tolerant species from the field to the lab and vice-versa, would be desirable. In the perspective of a better risk assessment and an adequate management of the coastal ecosystems, unified and integrated approaches between ecotoxicological and ecological research should be encouraged.

REFERENCES

Abdel-Shafy, H. I. & El-Said Farghaly, M. (1995). Accumulation of heavy metals by the benthic algae in the Suez Canal. *Environ. Protect. Engin., 21,* 5-14.

Ahner, B. A., Price, N. M. & Morel, F. M. M. (1994). Phytochelatin production by marine phytoplankton at low free metal ion concentrations: Laboratory studies and field data from Massachusetts Bay. *Proc. Natl. Acad. Sci. USA, 91,* 8433-8436.

Ahner, B. A., Kong, S. & Morel, F. M. M. (1995a). Phytochelatin production in marine algae. 1. An interspecies comparison. *Limnol. Oceanogr., 40 (4),* 649-657.

Ahner, B. A. & Morel, F. M. M. (1995b). Phytochelatin production in marine algae. 2. Induction by various metals. *Limnol. Oceanogr., 40 (4),* 658-665.

Amado Filho, G. M., Karez C. S., Pfeiffer, W. C., Yoneshigue-Valentin, Y. & Farina, M. (1996). Accumulation, effects on growth, and localization of zinc in *Padina gymnospora* (Dictyotales, Phaeophyceae). *Hydrobiologia, 326/327,* 451-456.

Amado Filho, G. M., Andrade, L. R., Karez, C. S., Farina, M. & Pfeiffer, W. C. (1999). Brown algae species as biomonitors of Zn and Cd at Sepetiba Bay, Rio de Janeiro, Brazil. *Mar. Environ. Res., 48,* 213-224.

Andrade, L. R., Farina, M. & Amado Filho, M. (2004). Effects of copper on *Enteromorpha flexuosa* (Chlorophyta) in vitro. *Ecotox. Environ. Saf., 58,* 117-125.

Appenroth, K. J., Stöckel, J., Srivastava, A. & Strasser, R. J. (2001). Multiple effects of chromate on the photosynthetic apparatus of *Spirodela polyrhiza* as probed by OJIP chlorophyll *a* fluorescence measurements. *Environ. Poll., 115,* 49-64.

Barreiro, R., Real, C. & Carballeira, A. (1993). Heavy-Metal Accumulation by *Fucus ceranoides* in Small Estuary in North-West Spain. *Mar. Environ. Res., 36,* 39-61.

Barron, M. G. (1995). Bioaccumulation and Bioconcentration in Aquatic Organisms. In: D. J. Hoffman, B. A. Rattner, G. A. Jr. Burton & J. Jr. Cairns (Eds.) *Handbook of Ecotoxicology* (652-666). Boca Raton, Florida: CRC Press, Lewis Publishers.

Bell, E. M. (1995). A study of the effects of Cadmium on the Photosynthetic Apparatus of the Rhodophyte *Audouinella saviana* in Culture. *Honours Environmental Biology Thesis, ERASMUSSpicUK 1995, University of Trieste, Italy. Supervisor: Talarico, L.,* 1-52.

Bengtson Nash, S. M., Quayle, P. A., Schreiber, U. & Müller, J. F. (2005). The selection of a model microalgal species as biomaterial for a novel aquatic phytotoxicity assay. *Aquat. Toxicol., 72,* 315-326.

Borgmann, U. (2000). Methods for assessing the toxicological significance of metals in aquatic ecosystems: bio-accumulation-toxicity relationships, water concentrations and sediment spiking approaches. *Aquat. Ecosyst. Health Managem., 3,* 277-289.

Borgmann, U. & Norwood, W. P. (2002). Metal bioavailability and toxicity through a sediment core. *Environ. Poll., 116,* 159-168.

Bradford, M. (1976). A rapid and sensitive method for the quantitation of microgram quantities of protein utilizing the principle of protein-dye binding. *Anal. Biochem., 72,* 248-254.

Brown, M. T. & Newmann, J. E. (2003). Physiological responses of *Gracilariopsis longissima* (S. G. Gmelin) Steentoft, L. M. Irvine and Farnham (Rhodophyceae) to sub-lethal copper concentrations. *Aquat. Toxicol., 64,* 201-213.

Bruland, K. W. (1992). Complexation of cadmium by natural organic ligands in the central North Pacific. *Limnol. Oceanogr., 37(5),* 1008-1017.

Bruno, E. & Eklund, B. (2003). Two new growth inhibition test with the filamentous algae *Ceramium strictum* and *C. tenuicorne* (Rhodophyta). *Environ. Poll., 125,* 287-293.

Burda, K., Kruk, J., Schmid, G. H. & Strzalka, K. (2003). Inhibition of oxygen evolution in Photosystem II by Copper (II) ions is associated with oxidation of Cytochrome b-559. *Biochem. J., 371,* 597-601.

Burridge, T. R. & Bidwell, J. (2002). Review of the potential use of brown algal ecotoxicological assay in monitoring effluent discharge and pollution in southern Australia. *Mar. Poll. Bull., 45,* 140-147.

Caliceti, M., Argese, E., Sfriso, A. & Pavoni, B. (2002). Heavy metal contamination in the seaweeds of the Venice lagoon. *Chemosphere, 47,* 443-454.

Campbell, P. J. C. (1995). Interactions between trace metals and aquatic organisms: a critique of the free-ion activity model. In: A. Tessier & D. R. Turner (Eds.), *Metal speciation and bioavailability in aquatic systems* (45-102). Chichester, U.K.: J. Wiley & Sons Publish.

Cavas, L. & Yurdakoc, K. (2005). A comparative study: Assessment of the antioxidant system in the invasive green alga *Caulerpa racemosa* and some macrophytes from the Mediterranean. *J. Experim. Mar. Biol. Ecol., 321 (1),* 35-41.

Cervantes, C., Campos-Garcia, J., Devars, S., Gutierrez-Corona, F., Loza-Tavera, H., Torres-Guzman, J. C. & Moreno-Sanchez, R. (2001). Interaction of chromium with microorganisms and plants. *FEMS Microbiol. Rev., 25,* 335-347.

Clemens, S. (2006). Evolution and function of phytochelatin synthases. *J. Plant Physiol., 163,* 319-332.

Cobbett, C. S. (2000). Phytochelatin biosynthesis and function in heavy metal detoxification. *Plant Biol., 3,* 211-216.

Contreras-Martel, C., Martinez-Oyanedel, J., Bunster, M., Legrand, P., Piras, C., Vernede, X. & Fontecilla-Camps, J. C. (2001). Crystallization and 2,2 Å resolution structure of R-phycoerythrin from *Gracilaria chilensis* : a case of perfect hemihedral twinning. *Acta Cryst., D57,* 52-60.

Corradi, M. A., Gorbi, G. & Bassi, M. (1995). Hexavalent Chromium induced gametogenesis in the freshwater alga *Scenedesmus acutus. Ecotox. Environ. Saf., 30,* 106-110.

Cullinane, J. P., Doyle, T. M. & Whelan, P.M. (1987). Uses of seaweeds as biomonitors of zinc levels in Cork harbour, Ireland. *Hydrobiologia, 151/152,* 285-290.

De Filippis, L. F. & Ziegler, H. (1993). Effect of sub-lethal concentration of Zinc, Cadmium and Mercury on the photosynthetic carbon reduction Cycle of *Euglena. J. Plant Physiol., 142,* 167-172.

Delieu, T. & Walker, D. A. (1972). An improved cathode for measurements of photosynthetic oxygen evolution by isolated chloroplasts. *New Phytol., 71,* 201-225.

Diannelidis, B. E. & Delivopulos, S. G. (1996). The effect of Zinc, Copper and Cadmium on the fine structure of *Ceramium ciliatum* (Rhodophyceae, Ceramiales). *Mar. Environ. Res., 44 (2),* 127-134.

EC (1999). *Guidance Document on Application and Interpretation of Single species-Tests in Environmental Toxicology.* (Environment Canada-Report EPS 1/RM/34, 20 and 25).

Eklund, B. T. & Kautsky, L. (2003). Review on toxicity testing with marine macroalgae and the need for method standardization-exemplified with copper and phenol. *Mar. Poll. Bull., 46,* 171-181.

Franklin, N. M., Stauber, J. L., Markich, S. J. & Lim, R. P. (2000). pH-dependent toxicity of copper and uranium to a tropical freshwater alga (*Chlorella* sp.). *Aquat. Toxicol., 40,* 275-289.

Gadd, G. M. (1990). Biosorption. *Chemistry & Industry, 13,* 421-426.

Garnham, G. W. (1997). The use of algae as Metal Biosorbents. In: J. Wase & C. Forster (Eds.), *Biosorbents for metal ions* (11-37). London, UK: Taylor & Francis Publish.

Gekeler, W., Grill, E., Winnaker, E. L. & Zenk, M. H. (1988). Algae sequester heavy metals via synthesis of phytochelatin complexes. *Arch. Microbiol., 150,* 197-202.

Giardi, M. T., Koblizek, M. & Masojidek, J. (2001). Photosystem II-based biosensors for the detection of pollutants. *Biosensors & Bioelectronics, 16,* 1027-1033.

Gledhill, M., Nimmo, M. & Hill, S. J. (1999). The release of copper-complexing ligands by the brown alga *Fucus vesicolosus* (Phaeophyceae) in response to increasing total copper levels. *J. Phycol., 35,* 501-509.

Gorbi, G., Corradi, M. G., Invidia, M. & Bassi, M. (2001). Light intensity influences chromium bioaccumulation and toxicity in *Scenedesmus acutus* (Chlorophyceae). *Ecotoxicol. Environ. Saf., 48,* 36-42.

Gupta, V. K., Shrivastava, A. K. & Jain, N. (2001). Biosorption of chromium(VI) from aqueous solutions by green algae *Spirogyra* species. *Wat. Res., 35 (17),* 4079-4085.

Haglund, K., Björklund, M., Gunnare, S., Sandberg, A., Olander, U. & Pedersén, M. (1996). New method for toxicity assessment in marine and brackish environments using the macroalga *Gracilaria tenuistipitata* (Gracilariales, Rhodophyta). *Hydrobiologia, 326/327,* 317-325.

Han, T. & Choi, G. W. (2005). A novel marine algal toxicity bioassay based on sporulation in the green macroalga *Ulva pertusa* (Chlorophyta). *Aquat. Toxicol., 75,* 202-212.

Hu, S., Tang, C. H. & Wu, M. (1996). Cadmium accumulation by several seaweeds. *Sci. Tot. Environ., 187,* 65-71.

Hu, S., Lau, K. W. K. & Wu, M. (2001). Cadmium sequestration in *Chlamydomonas reinhardtii. Plant Sci., 161,* 987-996.

Isnard, P., Flammarion, P., Roman, G., Babut, M., Bastien, Ph., Bintein, S., Esserméant, L., Férard, J. F., Gallotti-Schmitt, S., Saouter, E., Saroli, M., Thébaud, H., Tomassone, R. & Vindimian, E. (2001). Statistical analysis of regulatory ecotoxicity tests. *Chemosphere, 45 (4-5),* 659-669.

ISO (1989). Water quality-fresh water algal growth inhibition test with *Scenedesmus subspicatus* and *Selenastrum capricornutum. International Organization of Standardization,* 8692.

ISO (1995). Water quality-marine algal growth inhibition test with *Skeletonema costatum* and *Pheodactylum tricornutum. International Organization of Standardization,* 10253.

Kaplan, D., Christiaen, D. & (Malis) Arad, S. (1987). Chelating properties of extracellular polysaccharides from *Chlorella* spp. *Appl. Environ. Microbiol., 53 (12),* 2953-2956.

Koshmanesh, A., Lawson, F. & Prince, I. G. (1996). Cadmium uptake by unicellular green microalgae. *Chem. Engineer. J., 62,* 81-88.

Küpper, H., Setlìk, I., Spiller, M., Küpper, F. C. & Pràsil, O. (2002). Heavy metal-induced inhibition of photosynthesis: target of *in vivo* heavy metal chlorophyll formation. *J. Phycol., 38,* 429-441.

Kut, D., Topcuoglu, S., Kücükcezzar, R. & Güven, K. C. (2000). Trace metals in marine algae and sediment samples from the Bosphorus. *Water Air Soil Poll., 118,* 27-33.

Leal, M. C. F., Vasconcelos, M. T, Sousa-Pinto, I. & Cabral, J. P. S. (1997). Biomonitoring with Benthic Macroalgae and Direct Assay of Heavy Metals in Seawater of the Oporto Coast (Northwest Portugal). *Mar. Poll. Bull., 34,* 1006-1015.

Lee, W. & Wang, W. (2001). Metal accumulation in the green macroalga *Ulva fasciata*: effects of nitrate, ammonium and phosphate. *Sci. Tot. Environ., 278,* 11-22.

Leonardi, P. I. & Vasquez, J. A. (1999). Effects of copper pollution on the ultrastructure of *Lessonia* spp. *Hydrobiologia, 398/399,* 375-383.

Ligero, R. A., Barrera, M., Cassas-Ruiz, M., Sales, D. & Lopez-Aguayo, F. (2002). Dating of marine sediments and time evolution of heavy metal concentrations in the Bay of Cadiz, Spain. *Environ. Poll., 118,* 97-108.

Lignell, A., Roomans, G. M. & Pedersen, M. (1982). Localization of absorbed Cadmium in *Fucus vesiculosus* L. by X-Ray Microanalysis. *Z. Pflanzenphysiol. Bd., 105 (S),* 103-109.

Lombardi, A. T., Vieira, A. A. H. & Sartori, L. A. (2002). Mucilaginous capsule adsorption and intracellular uptake of copper by *Kirchneriella aperta* (Chlorococcales). *J. Phycol., 38,* 332-337.

López-Suarez, C. E., Castro-Romero, J. M., Gonzalez-Rodriguez, M.V., Gonzalez-Soto, E., Perez-Iglesias, J., Seco-Lago, H. M. & Fernandez-Solis, J. M. (2000). Study of the parameters affecting the binding of metals in solution by *Chlorella vulgaris. Talanta, 50,* 1313-1318.

Lorenzen, C. J. (1967). Determination of chlorophyll and phaeopigments spectrophotometric equation. *Limnol. Oceanogr., 12,* 343-346.

Lozano, G., Hardisson, A., Gutiérez, A. J. & Lafuente, M. A. (2003). Lead and cadmium levels in coastal benthic algae (seaweeds) of Tenerife, Canary Islands. *Environ. Int., 28,* 627-631.

MacColl, R. & Guard-Friar, D. (1987). *Phycobiliproteins.* Boca Raton, Florida: CRC Press Inc., USA.

Maeda, S. & Sakaguchi, T. (1990). Accumulation and detoxification of toxic metal elements by algae. In: I. Akatsuka (Ed.), *Introduction to Applied Phycology* (109-136). The Hague, The Netherlands: SPB Academic Publish.

Malea, P. & Haritonidis, S. (2000). Use of the green *Ulva rigida* C. Agardh as an indicator species to reassess metal pollution in the Thermaikos Gulf, Geece, after 13 years. *J. Appl. Phycol., 12,* 169-176.

Manusadžianas, L., Balkelyte, L., Sadauskas, K., Blinova, I., Pollumaa, L. & Kahru, A. (2003). Ecotoxicological study of Lithuanian and Estonian wastewaters: selection of the biotests, and correspondence between toxicity and chemical-based indices. *Aquat. Toxicol., 63,* 27-41.

Maranzana G. (1999). Effetti di diverse dosi di Cadmio sulle risposte fisiologiche, biochimiche ed ultrastrutturali dell'alga rossa *Audouinella saviana* (Meneghini) Woelkerling in coltura. *Cell Biology Thesis, University of Trieste, Italy,* 1-153.

Maranzana, G., Bell, E., Bozo, S. & Talarico, L. (1996). Response of the red alga *Audouinella saviana* (Meneghini) Woelkerling to Cadmium: preliminary observations. *Giorn. Bot. It., 130 (4-5),* 1078-1081.

Mariani, P., Tolomio, C., Baldan, B. & Braghetta, P. (1990). Cell wall ultrastructure and cation location in some benthic marine algae. *Phycologia, 29,* 253-262.

Mates, J. M. (2000). Effects of antioxidant enzymes in the molecular control of reactive oxygen species toxicology. *Toxicology, 153,* 83-104.

Meyer, J. S. (2002). The utility of terms 'bioavailability' and 'bioavailable fraction' for metals. *Mar. Environ. Res., 53,* 417-423.

Munda, I. M. & Hudnikh, V. (1986). Growth response of *Fucus vesiculosus* to heavy metals, singly and in dual combinations related to accumulation. *Bot. Mar., 29,* 401-412.

Munda, I. M. & Hudnikh, V. (1988). The effects of Zn, Mn, and Co accumulation on growth and chemical composition of *Fucus vesiculosus* L. under different temperature and salinity conditions. *Mar. Ecol., 9,* 213-225.

Munda, I. M. & Hudnikh, V. (1991). Studies on photosynthesis, the associated electron transport system and some physiological variables of *Chlorella vulgaris* under heavy metal stress. *J. Plant Physiol., 137,* 419-424.

Muse, J. O., Stripeikis, J. D., Fernandez, F. M., d'Huicque, L., Tudino, M. B.,. Carducci, C. N. & Troccoli, O. E. (1999). Seaweeds in the assessment of heavy metal pollution in the Gulf San Jorge, Argentina. *Environ. Poll., 104,* 315-322.

Mushrifah, J. & Peterson, P. J. (1991). Uptake and accumulation of cadmium and tin to the insoluble fractions of *Anabaena flos-aquae. Biomed. Letters, 46,* 189-198.

Muyssen, B. T. A. & Janssen, C. R. (2001). Zinc acclimation and its effect on zinc tolerance of *Raphidocelis subcapitata* and *Chlorella vulgaris* in laboratory experiments. *Chemosphere, 45,* 507-514.

Nagalakshmi, N. & Prasad, M. N., V. (2001). Responses of glutathione cycle enzymes and glutathione metabolism to copper stress in *Scenedesmus bijugatus. Plant Sci., 160,* 291-299.

Nishikawa, K., Yamakoshi, Y., Uemura, I. & Tominaga, N. (2003). Ultrastructural changes in *Chlamydomonas acidophila* (Chlorophyta) induced by heavy metals and polyphosphate metabolism. *FEMS Microbiol. Ecol., 44,* 253-259.

Okamoto, O.K., Asano, C. S., Aidar, E. & Colepicolo, P. (1996). Effects of cadmium on growth and superoxide dismutase activity of the marine microalga *Tetraselmis gracilis* (Prasinophyceae). *J. Phycol., 32,* 74-79.

Okamoto, O. K. & Colepicolo, P. (1998). Response of superoxide dismutase to pollutant metal stress in the marine dinoflagellate *Gonyaulax polyedra. Comp. Biochem. Physiol., 119 (1),* 67-73.

Pellegrini, L., Pellegrini, M., Delivopulos, S. & Berail, G. (1991). The effects of cadmium on the fine structure of brown alga *Cystoseira barbata* forma *repens* Zinova et Balugina. *Br. Phycol. J., 26,* 1-8.

Pérez-Rama, M., Abalde, J. A., Herrero, L. C. & Torres, E.V. (2002). Cadmium removal by living cells of the marine microalga *Tetraselmis suecica. Biores. Technol., 84,* 265-270.

Péry, A. R. R., Bedaux, J. J. M., Zonneveld, C. & Kooijman, S. A. L. M. (2001). Analysis of bioassays with time-varying concentrations. *Water Res., 35 (16),* 3825-3832.

Peterson, H. G., Healey, F. P. & Wagemann, R. (1984). Metal toxicity to algae: a highly pH dependent phenomenon. *Can. J. Fish. Aquat. Sci., 41,* 974-979.

Pinto, E., Sigaud-Kutner, T. C. S., Leitao, M. A. S., Okamoto, O. K., Morse, D. & Colepicolo, P. (2003). Heavy metal-induced oxidative stress in algae. *J. Phycol., 39,* 1008-1018.

Pickering, I. J., Prince, R. C., George, G. N., Rauser, W. E., Wickramasinghe, W. A., Watson, A. A., Dameron, C. T., Dance, I. G., Fairlie, D. P. & Salt, D. E. (1999). X-ray absorption spectroscopy of cadmium phytochelatin and model systems. *Biochim. Biophys. Acta, 1492,* 351-364.

Plekhanov, S. E. & Chemeris, Y. K. (2003). Early toxic effects of Zinc, Cobalt, and Cadmium on photosynthetic activity of the green alga *Chlorella pyrenoidosa* Chick S-39. *Biol. Bull., 30 (5),* 506-511.

Premuzic, T. E., Lin, M., Zhu, H. L. & Gremme, A. M. (1991). Selectivity in metal uptake by stationary phase microbial populations. *Arch. Environ. Contam. Toxicol., 20,* 234-241.

Rachlin, J. W. & Grosso, A. (1991). The effects of pH on the growth of *Chlorella vulgaris* and its interaction with cadmium toxicity. *Arch. Environ. Contam. Toxicol., 20,* 505-508.

Rai, L. C., Jensen, T. E. & Rachlin, J. W. (1990). A morphometric and X-ray Energy Dispersive approach to monitoring pH-altered Cadmium toxicity in *Anabaena flos-aquae. Arch. Environ. Contam. Toxicol., 19,* 479-487.

Rai L. C., Sing, A. K. & Mallik, N. (1991). Studies on photosynthesis, the associated electron transport system and some physiological variables of *Chlorella vulgaris* under heavy metal stress. *J. Plant Physiol., 137,* 419-424.

Rai, L. C., Rai, P. K. & Mallik, N. (1996). Regulation of heavy metal toxicity in acid-tolerant *Chlorella*: physiological and biochemical approaches. *Environ. Experim. Bot., 36 (1),* 99-109.

Reish, D. J. & Oshida, P. S. (1987). Manual of methods in aquatic environment research, 10. Short-term static bioassays. *FAO Fish. Tech. Pap., 247,* 1-62.

Richards, F. A. (1952). The estimation and characterisation of plankton population by pigment analysis. I. The absorption spectra of some pigments occurring in diatoms, dinoflagellates and brown algae. *J. Mar. Res., 11,* 147-155.

Rijstenbil, J. W. & Gerringa, L. J. A. (2002). Interactions of algal ligands, metal complexation and availability, and cell responses of the diatom *Ditylum brightwellii* with a gradual increase in copper. *Aquat. Toxicol., 56,* 115-131.

Rijstenbil, J. W., Sandee, A., Van Drie, J. & Wijholds, J. A. (1994). Interaction of toxic trace metals and mechanisms of detoxification in the planktonic diatom *Ditylum brightwellii* and *Thalassiosira pseudonana*. *Microbiol. Rev., 14,* 387-395.

Russell, S. W. & Hunter, K. A. (1992). Influence of phosphorus storage on the uptake of cadmium by the marine alga *Macrocystis pyrifera*. *Limnol. Oceanogr., 37 (7),* 1361-1369.

Sawidis, T., Brown, M. T., Zachariadis, G. & Stratis, I. (2001). Trace metal concentrations in marine macroalgae from different biotopes in the Aegean Sea. *Environ. Int., 27,* 43-47.

Shehata, S. A., Lasheen, M. R., Kobbia, I. A. & Ali, G. H. (1999). Toxic effect of certain metal mixture on some physiological and morphological characteristic of freshwater algae. *Water, Air, Soil Poll., 110,* 119-135.

Silverberg, B. A. (1975). Ultrastructural localization of lead in *Stigeoclonium tenue* (Chlorophyceae, Ulotrichales) as demonstrated by cytochemical and X-ray microanalysis. *Phycologia, 14 (4),* 265-274.

Skovronski, T., Szubinska, S., Pavlik B. & Jakubowski, M. (1991). The influence of pH on Cadmium toxicity to the green alga *Stichococcus bacillaris* and on the Cadmium form present in the culture medium. *Environ. Poll., 74,* 89-100.

Starr, R. C. & Zeikus, J. A. (1993). UTEX-The culture collection of algae at the University of Texas at Austin. *J. Phycol., 29,* 1-106.

Stiborova, M., Ditrichova M. & Brezinova, A. (1988). Mechanism of action of Cu^{2+}, Co^{2+} and Zn^{2+} on Ribulose-1,5-bisphosphate Carboxylase from Barley (*Hordeum vulgare* L.). *Photosynthetica, 22 (2),* 161-167.

Sueur, S., van den Berg, C. M. G. & Riley, J. P. (1982). Measurement of the metal complexing ability of exudates of marine macroalgae. *Limnol. Oceanogr., 27 (3),* 536-543.

Sunda, W. G. & Huntsman, S. A. (1998). Processes regulating cellular metal accumulation and physiological effects: Phytoplankton as model systems. *Sci. Tot. Environ., 219,* 165-181.

Talarico L. (1990). R-phycoerythrin from *Audouinella saviana* (Nemaliales, Rhodophyta). Ultrastructural and biochemical analysis of aggregates and subunits. *Phycologia, 29 (3),* 292-302.

Talarico, L. (1996). Phycobiliproteins and phycobilisomes in red algae: adaptive responses to light. In F. L. Figueroa, F. X. Niell, C. Jimenez & L. Pérez-Llorens (Eds.), *Underwater light and Algal Photobiology* (205-222). Barcelona, Spain: CSIC Press Publish.

Talarico, L. (2002). Fine structure and X-ray microanalysis of a red macrophyte cultured under Cadmium stress. *Environ. Poll., 120 (3),* 813-821.

Talarico, L., Bozo, S. & Maranzana, G. (1997). Preliminary observations on *Audouinella saviana* (Nemaliales, Rhodophyta) cultured at increasing Cd concentrations. *Phycologia, 36 (4)S,* 111.

Talarico, L., Rascio, N., Dalla Vecchia, F. & Maranzana, G. (1998). Some observations on phycobilisomes of *Pterocladiella capillacea* (Gelidiales, Rhodophyta). *Plant Biosystems 132 (2),* 87-96.

Talarico, L. & Maranzana, G. (2000). Light and adaptive responses in red macroalgae: an overview. *J. Photochem. Photobiol. B: Biol., 56,* 1-11.

Talarico, L., Welker, C., Maranzana, G. & Bell, E. (2001). The effects of Cadmium on the fine structure of a red macrophyte under culture. *17ᵗʰ Int. Seaweed Symp., Cape Town, South Africa, Proceed.,* 121.

Tankere, S. P. C. & Statham, P. J. (1996). Distribution of dissolved Cd, Cu, Ni and Zn in the Adriatic Sea. *Mar. Poll. Bull., 32 (8/9),* 623-630.

Topcuoglu, S., Guven, K. C., Balkis, N. & Kirbasoglu, C. (2003). Heavy metal monitoring of marine algae from the Turkish Coast of the Black Sea, 1998-2000. *Chemosphere, 52,* 1683-1688.

Tsuji, N., Hirayanagi, N., Iwabe, O., Namba, T., Tagawa, M., Miyamoto, S., Miyasaka, H., Takagi, M., Hirata, K. & Miyamoto, K. (2003). Regulation of phytochelatin synthesis by zinc and cadmium in marine green alga, *Dunaniella tertiolecta. Phytochemistry, 62,* 453-459.

Tumova, E. & Sofrova, D. (2002). Response of intact cyanobacterial cells and their photosynthetic apparatus to Cd^{2+} ion treatment. *Photosynthetica, 40 (1),* 103-108.

USEPA (1998). Guidance for ecological risk assessment (EPA/630/R-95/002Fa-United States Environmental Protection Agency). *Risk Assessment Forum, Washington DC, USA.*

Vasconcelos, M. T. S. D. & Leal, M. F. C. (2001a). Antagonistic interactions of Pb and Cd on Cu uptake, growth inhibition and chelator release in the marine alga *Emiliana huxleyi. Mar. Chem., 5,* 123-139.

Vasconcelos, M. T. S. D. & Leal, M. F. C. (2001b). Seasonal variability in the kinetics of Cu, Pb, Cd and Hg accumulation by macroalgae. *Mar. Chem., 74,* 65-85.

Villares, R., Puente, X. & Carballeira, A. (2002). Seasonal variation and background levels of heavy metals in two green seaweeds. *Environ. Poll., 119,* 79-90.

Visviki, I. & Rachlin, J. W. (1992). Ultrastructural changes in *Dunaliella minuta* following acute and chronic exposure to copper and cadmium. *Arch. Environ. Contam. Toxicol., 23,* 420-425.

Wang, W. X. & Dei, R. C. H. (2001). Effects of major nutrient additions on metal uptake in phytoplankton. *Environ. Poll., 111,* 233-240.

Webster, E. A. & Gadd, G. M. (1996). Stimulation of respiration in *Ulva lactuca* by high concentrations of cadmium and zinc: evidence for an alternative respiratory pathway. *Environ. Toxicol. Water Qual., 11,* 7-12.

Wehrheim, B. & Wettern, M. (1994). Comparative studies of the heavy metal uptake of whole cells and different types of cell wall from *Chlorella fusca. Biotech. Tech., 8 (4),* 227-232.

Wong, S. L., Nakamoto, L. & Wainwright, J. F. (1997). Detection of toxic organometallic complexes in wastewaters using algal assays. *Arch. Environ. Contam. Toxicol., 32,* 358-366.

Wren, C. D., Harris, S. & Harttrup, N. (1995). Ecotoxicology of Mercury and Cadmium. In D. J. Hoffman, B. A. Rattner, G. A. Jr. Burton & J. Jr. Cairns (Eds.), *Handbook of Ecotoxicology* (392-423). Boca Raton, Florida : CRC Press, Lewis Publish.

Yu, Q., Matheickal, J. T., Yin, P. & Kaewsarn, P. (1999). Heavy metal uptake capacities of common marine macro algal biomass. *Water Res., 33,* 1534-1537.

Zhou, J. L., Huang, P. L. & Lin, R. G. (1998). Sorption and desorption of Cu and Cd by macroalgae and microalgae. *Environ. Poll., 101,* 67-75.

In: New Topics in Environmental Research
Editor: Daniel Rhodes, pp. 37-56

ISBN 1-60021-172-0

Chapter 2

ARBUSCULAR MYCORRHIZA AS A TOLERANCE STRATEGY IN METAL CONTAMINATED SOILS: PROSPECTS IN PHYTOREMEDIATION

Katarina Vogel-Mikuš[*] and Marjana Regvar
University of Ljubljana, Ljubljana, Slovenia

ABSTRACT

Metals cannot be chemically degraded; rather they need to be physically removed in cost-intensive and technically complex procedures, highlighting the need for sustainable cost efficient remedial actions. In the last decade, plant-based technologies involving biological processes, including plant uptake, transport, accumulation and sequestration of metals, as well as plant-microbe interactions, are gaining significant interest in this context.

Accumulation and exclusion are the two basic widely recognized tolerance strategies plants develop at polluted sites. In addition, arbuscular mycorrhiza (AM) may contribute significantly to plant metal tolerance. Arbuscular mycorrhizal fungi (AMF) (Glomeromycota) are ubiquitous soil microbes considered essential for plant survival and growth in nutrient deficient soils. The significantly reduced AMF diversity frequently found in metal polluted environments is presumably composed of the most stress-adapted strains. Inoculation of host plants with indigenous AMF may play an important role in plant protection from metal toxicity by binding metals and consequently restricting their translocation to the shoots, therefore contributing to successful phytostabilization. In addition, the recently discovered mycorrhizal colonization of hyperaccumulating plants may represent a potentially important biotechnological tool for phytoextraction, another branch of modern phytotechnologies.

This chapter highlights current knowledge on the interactions of plants and AMF in metal polluted environments and the potential for their use as a biotechnological tool in contemporary remedial practice.

[*] Corresponding author: Tel: +386 01 4233388, fax: +386 01 2573390; E-mail address: katarina.vogel@bf.uni-lj.si

INTRODUCTION

Acute and diffuse pollution of soil and water by metals and metalloids is a global environmental problem resulting from diverse sources including mining and smelting of metalliferous ores, burning of fossil fuels, municipal wastes, fertilizers, pesticides, sewage sludge amendments and the use of pigments and batteries. All these sources cause accumulation of metals in agricultural soils and pose a threat to food safety and potential health risks due to soil-to-plant transfer of metals (Barceló & Poschenrieder, 2003; Gaur & Adholeya, 2004). Development of environmentally friendly plant-based technologies for the remediation of contaminated soils is therefore of significant interest, but there is a need for better knowledge of the biological processes involved, including plant uptake, transport, accumulation and sequestration of metals and plant-microbe interactions (Barceló & Poschenrieder, 2003; Gaur & Adholeya, 2004; Khan, 2005; Pilon-Smits, 2005; Ernst, 2005).

Exclusion and accumulation are the two basic tolerance strategies that plants develop at metal contaminated sites (Baker, 1981, 1987). In addition, symbiosis with arbuscular mycorrhizal fungi (AMF) may represent another mechanism conferring metal tolerance to plants (Hall, 2002). AMF (Glomeromycota) are one of the most prominent groups of soil micro-organisms (Smith & Read, 1997; Schussler et al., 2001), occurring in almost all habitats and climates, including disturbed soils, and those derived from mine activities (Pawlowska et al., 2000; Pawlowska & Charvat, 2004; Regvar et al., 2006). They expand the interface between plants and the soil environment and contribute to plant growth, particularly in disturbed or metal contaminated sites, by increasing plant access to relatively immobile minerals, such as P (Smith & Read, 1997) and N (Allen, 1991; Read, 1994; Cornelissen et al., 2001) and improve soil texture by binding soil particles into stable aggregates that resist wind and water erosion (Gaur & Adholeya, 2004). AMF are also involved in plant interactions with toxic metals by alleviating metal toxicity to the host by binding metals in the roots thus restricting their translocation to the shoots (Leyval et al., 1997; Leyval & Joner, 2001).

Plant metal tolerance mechanisms with an emphasis on the interactions of plants with AMF and the potential of mycorrhizae for applications in phytoremedial technologies are critically evaluated.

PLANT AND FUNGAL TOLERANCE MECHANISMS IN METAL CONTAMINATED ENVIRONMENTS

Metals in the environment operate as stress factors and may reduce vigor of indigenous organisms or, in the extreme, totally inhibit growth and result in death. The extent to which metals affect organisms is determined by the metal bioavailability, which is influenced by soil total metal concentrations, pH, organic matter content, and cationic exchange capacity (Marschner, 1995, Moreno et al., 1996). Plants and microorganisms, including AMF, can achieve *resistance* to metals by either of two strategies: *avoidance*, when an organism is able to restrict metal uptake and *tolerance,* when the organism survives in the presence of high internal metal concentrations (Baker, 1987, Leyval et al., 1997).

Plant roots are the sites of direct contact with toxic metals, so metal avoidance is attributed to the various mechanisms preventing uptake of metal ions in the roots, thus protecting deeper meristematic root cell layers. Enhanced slough-off of the root cap cells and mucilage secretion is the proposed avoidance mechanism in Cu resistant *Silene armeria* (Llugany et al., 2003), and early cell death of the epidermal cells accompanied by an enhanced secretion of border cells in Al resistant wheat cultivars (Delisle et al., 2001).

Tolerance, on the other hand, is conferred by the possession of specific physiological and biochemical mechanisms employed at the cellular, tissue, organ and/or organismal levels, that collectively enable survival and reproduction of plants in the presence of high concentrations of potentially toxic elements (Baker, 1987; Bert et al., 2000; Hall, 2002). Cellular detoxification mechanisms result from preventing the build–up of excess metal levels in the cytosol by cell-wall binding and/or vacuolar compartmentation (Figure 1). The latter includes active pumping of ions into vacuoles, complexing by organic acids, or by specific metal-binding proteins such as phytochelatins and metallothioneins (Baker, 1987; Hall, 2002; Küpper et al., 1999, 2004). Detoxification mechanisms at the tissue level of the seed start with the seed coats (testa, endosperm) as the first barrier to metal absorption (Figure 1), where the metals are usually found (Seregin & Ivanov, 2001; Mesjasz-Przybylowicz et al., 2001), thus preventing their accumulation in embryonic tissues. In some cases however, metals pass the seed coats and accumulate in the epidermis of cotyledons (Psaras & Manetas, 2001; Vogel-Mikuš et al., 2006), but do not accumulate in the embryonic axis. Germinating plants absorb metals through roots, where they primarily accumulate in the rhizodermis, cortex and root hairs (Figure 1) (Vazquez et al., 1994; Barceló & Poschenrieder, 1999; Seregin & Ivanov, 2001; Liu & Kottke, 2003). The multilayer cortex seems to reduce the toxic effects of metal ions by binding most of them in the cell walls (Barceló & Poschenrieder, 1999; Heumann, 2002) and vacuoles (Heumann, 2002; Liu & Kottke, 2003, 2004). In metal accumulating species however, metals are also accumulated in the endodermis and vascular tissues (e.g. xylem) and are efficiently transported to the above ground tissues (Heumann, 2002). In the leaves, metals are primarily allocated away from photosynthetically active tissues, in epidermal vacuoles and trihomes (Fig 1) (Vazquez et al., 1992; Chardonnens et al., 1999; Seregin & Ivanov, 2001; Ager et al., 2002; Wójcik et al., 2005). On the organ level, two basic detoxification strategies differing in the site of metal detoxification were suggested by Baker (1981). In *metal exclusion*, the detoxification mechanisms employed result in sequestration of the majority of the metal in the roots, restricting metal uptake and transport to the shoots, thus leading to more or less constant low shoot metal levels over a wider range of metal soil concentrations, whereas in *metal accumulation*, the accumulated metals are stored in aerial parts in a detoxified form, with leaves as the main sequestration organ preventing metal uptake in the seeds (Ernst et al., 1992; Ernst, 1996; Li et al., 2005). At the extreme, external detoxification mechanisms such as detachment of the leaves from the plant in the late season represent an additional mechanism for effectively detoxifying the overwintering plant (Baker, 1981).

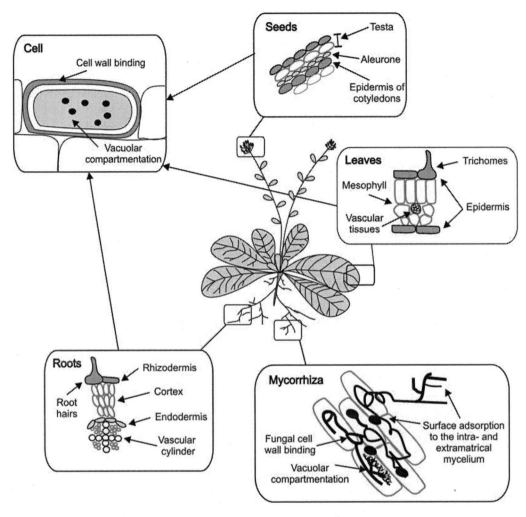

Figure 1. Plant metal tolerance mechanisms at the cellular and tissue level enabling survival and reproduction in metal contaminated environments.

Restricted metal uptake may also result from interactions with mycorrhizal fungi, mainly involving surface adsorption or compartmentation within fungal vacuoles (Figure 1) of tolerant fungal symbionts, as was demonstrated for ectomycorrhizal (Blaudez et al., 2000, Marschner et al., 1998) and arbuscular mycorrhizal fungi (Turnau et al., 1993; Leyval et al., 1997; Joner et al., 2000). Different surface adsorption mechanisms involve ion-exchange, complexation, precipitation and crystallisation of metals on the extra- and intraradical hypal cell wall components (e.g. chitin, cellulose derivatives and melanin) or extracellular slime, which may reduce the intracellular accumulation of metals and their effects on cytoplasmic processes (Turnau et al., 1993; Galli et al., 1994; Denny & Ridge, 1995). Mechanisms within fungal cells however, involve chelation of metal ions by ligands like polyphosphates, metallothioneins and/or compartmentation within vacuoles (Turnau et al., 1993; Kaldorf et al., 1999; Joner et al., 2000; Leyval & Joner, 2001).

Plant tolerance mechanisms on the cellular level therefore in general involve cell wall binding and vacuolar compartmentation, whereas on tissue and organ levels plants tend to protect photosynthetically active tissues and reproductive organs. The metal concentration limits that plants are able to tolerate represent the primary distinction between tolerant, non-tolerant and hyperaccumulating plants, and shoots as the primary storage organs add to the definition of hyperaccumulating plants (Salt & Krämer, 2000). In addition, binding of metals to fungal cell walls and compartmentation in fungal vacuoles of a mycorrhizal root as a whole may add significantly to plant tolerance and may therefore be considered as an important tolerance mechanism at polluted sites.

METAL TOLERANCE OF ARBUSCULAR MYCORRHIZAL PLANTS IN CONTAMINATED SOILS

Soil degradation produces changes in the diversity and abundance of AMF populations (Pawlowska et al., 2000; Regvar et al., 2001). Indigenous AMF ecotypes are the outcome of long-term adaptation to soils with extreme properties (del Val et al., 1999; Weissenhorn et al., 1994), thus resulting in highly metal tolerant strains (Weissenhorn et al., 1993, 1994; Weissenhorn & Leyval, 1995; Hildebrand et al., 1999; Malcova et al., 2003).

The difficulty of demonstrating the possible role(s) of AMF in metal uptake to plants arises from their obligate symbiotic character. Nevertheless, it has been shown that extraradical hyphae can accumulate, translocate and transport [109]Cd from soil to roots using compartmented pot systems in which extraradical hyphae can be separated from plant roots (Joner & Leyval, 1997). Studies addressing this question have shown that the effects of AMF on plant metal accumulation may vary from decreased toward neutral or even increased metal uptake, depending on different plant-AMF combinations, mostly due to both plant and fungal species variations in metal uptake (Leyval et al., 1997; Leyval & Joner, 2001; Malcova et al., 2003). Measurements of the metal-binding capacity of mycorrhizal mycelium showed AMF hyphae have a high metal adsorption capacity (e.g. for Cd), which could represent a barrier for metal translocation to plant tissues (Joner et al., 2000). Similarly, AMF inoculum from metal tolerant *Viola calaminaria* was efficient in sequestering metals in the roots of subterranean clover (Tonin et al., 2001). *Glomus* Br1 isolated from the roots of *V. calaminaria* improved maize growth in polluted soil and reduced root and shoot metal concentrations in comparison to a common *Glomus intraradices* isolate or non-colonized controls (Hildebrandt et al., 1999; Kaldorf et al., 1999). In contrast, higher copper concentrations were found in the shoots of maize plants inoculated with native *G. mosseae* than in non-inoculated plants or plants inoculated with a non-native isolate (Weissenhorn et al., 1995). Nevertheless, the selection of indigenous metal tolerant isolates seems to serve the aim of reducing endogenous concentrations of metals in plants better than non-tolerant ones. In addition, because of the lower sensitivity of fungal hyphae to metals compared to plant roots (Joner & Leyval, 1997), functional symbiosis with metal tolerant AMF strains may confer improved metal tolerance on plants, while maintaining an adequate supply of nutrients like P and N through active hyphal uptake, even when the roots are impaired due to the metal toxicity (Gaur & Adholeya, 2004), thus contributing additionally to a higher survival rate and plant vigor in metal contaminated soils.

Taken together, the tolerance mechanisms that AMF develop at metal contaminated sites may play a crucial role(s) in mediating metal uptake and translocation to plants (Leyval et al., 1997). A range of environmental factors including soil metal concentrations and bioavailability, soil absorption/desorption characteristics, as well as endogenous factors (e.g. the fungal properties and inherent heavy metal uptake capacity of plants), influence the uptake of metals by mycorrhizal plants (Leyval et al., 1997; Pawlowska & Charvat, 2004). The reduced metal uptake, reduced shoot metal translocation, improved mineral nutrition and improved growth rate, which may be achieved after a careful selection of compatible tolerant plant-fungal combinations thus conferring a significant improvement of plant fitness at polluted sites, therefore represents an interesting challenge for any phytoremedial actions.

ARBUSCULAR MYCORRHIZA IN METAL HYPERACCUMULATING PLANTS

Metal hyperaccumulating plants are characterized by exceptionally high concentrations of metals in their above-ground tissues (Reeves & Baker, 2000). Thresholds for plant hyperaccumulation (shoot dry weight) are set at 10 000 mg kg^{-1} for Zn and Mn, 1000 mg kg^{-1} for Ni, Pb, Co, Cu, Se and 100 mg kg^{-1} for Cd (Reeves & Baker, 2000). Metal hyperaccumulating plants are rare, since the majority of metals are usually accumulated in roots (Seregin & Ivanov, 2001). In total 388 metal hyperaccumulating plants belonging to 7 different plant families were recognized by the year 2000, among which 290 hyperaccumulate nickel, 26 cobalt, 24 manganese, 16 zinc and only one hyperaccumulates cadmium (Brooks, 2000). Significant progress has been made in the understanding of the physiological basis of tolerance to, and sequestration of metals in the shoots (Lasat et al., 1998; Küpper et al., 1999; Cosio et al., 2004). However, a considerable uncertainty remains about the mechanisms by which hyperaccumulating plants obtain metals from soil, as well as about the alteration of metal uptake by rhizospheric organisms such as AMF (Vogel-Mikuš et al., 2006).

Many metal hyperaccumulating plants belong to the plant families of Brassicaceae and Caryophyllaceae, that are widely known to possess no or weakly effective associations with AMF (Harley & Harley, 1987; DeMars & Boerner, 1996), and therefore studies of interactions of metal hyperaccumulating plants with AMF have been generally neglected. Recently, mycorrhizal colonization was observed in nickel hyperaccumulating plants belonging to the *Asteraceae* (Turnau & Mesjasz-Przybylowicz, 2003), arsenic hyperaccumulating *Pterydophyta* (Agely et al., 2005; Liu et al, 2005) and Cd and Zn hyperaccumulating *Thlaspi praecox* (Vogel-Mikuš et al., 2005).

A thorough survey of AMF colonization of *Thlaspi* species (Brassicaceae) from metal contaminated soils including *T. caerulescens* hyperaccumulating Zn and Cd, *T. goesingense* hyperaccumulating Ni, *T. calaminare* hyperaccumulating Zn and *T. cepaeifolium* hyperaccumulating Pb indicated poor colonization, with non-discernible arbuscules (Regvar et al., 2003). Meadow *Thlaspi* species from non-polluted sites (*T. praecox, T. caerulescens* and *T. montanum*) on the other hand, showed distinct AMF colonization with the occurrence of hyphae, vesicles and arbuscules. Sequencing of the rDNA PCR- products from *Thlaspi* roots revealed colonization by a common AM fungus *Glomus intraradices*, but none of the sequences obtained was identical to any other *G. intraradices* sequences. These results indicate the existence of slightly different sequences from habitat to habitat, which may point to the existence of a species continuum in the *G. intraradices* clade, and to the existence of

AMF fungal ecotype(s) specifically adapted to heavy metals at such locations (Regvar et al., 2003; Khan, 2005).

Mycorrhizal association of metal tolerant plants with indigenous AMF represents a long term co-evolution between the symbionts, which finally results in a compromise between the costs and benefits provided to the host (Sanders & Fitter, 1992, Whitfield et al., 2004). Higher shoot biomass and higher Ni uptake compared to the non-inoculated plants or plants inoculated with a non-tolerant *Glomus intraradices* (BEG) strain were observed in a greenhouse experiment with Ni hyperaccumulating *Berkheya codii*. The poor arbuscule development observed after inoculation with a non-tolerant AMF strain was attributed to the deleterious effect of Ni on the fungus and/or to possible plant restriction(s) towards a non-beneficial fungus (Turnau & Mesjasz-Przybylowicz, 2003). Similarly, inoculation of the As hyperaccumulator *Pteris vittata* with indigenous AMF from an As-contaminated site resulted in increased frond dry mass and in increased As uptake (Agely et al., 2005). The inoculation of *P. vittata* with *Glomus mosseae* BEG 167, not originating from As- contaminated soils on the other hand, increased frond dry matter and decreased frond As uptake (Liu et al., 2005). Since the production of hyphae is much more economical in terms of organic C than the production of an equivalent length of root, plants may also adjust belowground C allocation and manage with a smaller mycorrhizal root system (Jacobsen et al., 2002). In addition, the mycorrhizal responsiveness of the plant can also be defined in terms of improved nutrition or reproductive capacity (Smith, 2000), which in many cases seems to be more relevant (Koide & Lu, 1992). Similar shoot biomass and reduced root biomass was observed when Cd and Zn hyperaccumulating *Thlaspi praecox* plants inoculated with indigenous metal tolerant AMF were compared to non-inoculated plants. In order to test the efficiency of the symbiosis, mineral nutrient analyses were performed using standard and total reflection X-ray fluorescence (XRF and TXRF). The results confirmed significant transfer of essential nutrients (P, S, Ni and Cu) between metal tolerant *T. praecox* and AMF, thus confirming the significance of the symbiosis (Vogel-Mikuš et al., 2006). The decrease in root biomass of inoculated plants indicates that much of the carbon saved was probably used for the fungal biomass that supplies nutrients to the plant (Smith, 2000). In addition, inoculation of *T. praecox* with indigenous and thus presumably tolerant AMF resulted in decreased Cd and Zn uptake, as well as in changes of Cd, Zn and Pb accumulation strategies, pointing to the alleviation of metal toxicity in Cd, Zn hyperaccumulating *Thlaspi praecox* (Vogel-Mikuš et al., 2006). The above-mentioned results indicate that inoculated hyperaccumulating plants may either accumulate higher metal concentrations or tolerate higher soil metal levels than non-inoculated ones (or both), with obvious consequences for phytoremediation of highly polluted soils.

Because of the lack of establishment of AM symbiosis in *T. praecox* under greenhouse conditions during the vegetative growing period, the functionality of the symbiosis was questioned (Regvar et al., 2003). However, after the induction of flowering by a prolonged vernalization period, distinct mycorrhizal structures were observed in Cd and Zn hyperaccumulating *T. praecox* plants (Vogel-Mikuš et al., 2006). The results are in accordance with the observations of AM development in *Biscutella laevigata* (Brassicaceae), a metallophyte from Polish spoil mounds, where AM colonization was only found during the flowering period (Orlowska et al., 2002). Therefore, in mycorrhizal Brassicaceae plant species the regulation of AM symbiosis development may be connected to changes in hormonal balance during vernalization (Hazebroek & Metzger, 1990) and possibly other physiological/biochemical mechanisms such as changes in glucosinolate profiles during different developmental stages that can also contribute to the regulation of AM development (Rask et al., 2000, Vierheilig et al., 2000). Evidence exists that the level of AM colonization in plants may be regulated in relation to the benefits they receive, but the difficulty in demonstrating this often points to an opposite conclusion (Fitter & Meryweather, 1992). The levels of colonization of *T. praecox* in natural environments, as well as in laboratory experiments, are minute or at best very low (Regvar et al., 2003; Vogel-Mikuš et al., 2005; Vogel-Mikuš et al., 2006). Nevertheless, inoculation of *T. praecox* with AMF significantly increased with increased metal concentrations, additionally pointing to the protective role of AMF against heavy metal toxicity (Vogel-Mikuš et al., 2006). The reasons for mycorrhizal protection in this already tolerant metal hyperaccumulating plant may either have arisen from the need to control metal uptake to the seeds, from possible replacement of high-cost energy demands needed for metal detoxification mechanisms under severe metal pollution conditions, and/or to improve the plant's mineral nutrition (Hagemayer, 1999; Vogel-Mikuš et al., 2006).

Complex biotic and abiotic factors influence plant-AMF interactions that also apply to metal hyperaccumulating plants. In addition, the distinct biochemical and physiological mechanisms involved in the metal tolerance of hyperaccumulating plants inevitably influence the outcome of the interactions between these plants and soil fungi. The benefits plants receive from these interactions may vary from effects on biomass, carbon balance, metal accumulation, mineral nutrition, hormonal balance, reproductive success and other biochemical parameters. Mycorrhizal colonization of rather metal-tolerant plant species may also be seen as the replacement of energy investments in plant metal tolerance mechanisms by symbiosis. As a consequence, the applicability of mycorrhizal hyperaccumulating plants at broader ranges of metal pollution, more efficient phytoextraction because of higher metal concentrations tolerated, or simply improved fitness and survival of these plants for phytostabilisation purposes should be tested in future remedial studies.

ARBUSCULAR MYCORRHIZA AND VEGETATION SUCCESSION AT METAL POLLUTED SITES

The vegetation and flora within an area depend on geological, ecological and seasonal factors resulting from naturally occurring changes in the environment and disturbances in ecosystems induced naturally or by man's activity (Lincoln et al., 1998). Sparse vegetation on bare sand is frequently found throughout post-mining landscapes under specifically unfavorable conditions. With reduced availability of mycorrhizal inoculum, non-mycorrhizal weeds, the dominant early colonizers, are primarily members of the Chenopodiaceae and Brassicaceae (Wiegleb & Felinks, 2001; Allen, 1991). From an ecotechnological viewpoint, succession research may either be viewed as an accompanying element of revegetation experiments to re-establish productive ecosystems, or as an instrument to deliberately direct succession in a desired fashion. Any decision making in contemporary conservation management practice should be based on a solid analysis of the site and related to justified conservation aims. However, there is a lack of knowledge of the course of the succession of the vegetation of post-mining landscapes that are floristically complex and contain several exclusive species with a highly individualistic nature and are thus not easily compared to those of undisturbed areas (Wiegleb & Felinks, 2001).

High soil metal concentrations are reported to reduce AMF spore diversity, spore density and AMF infectivity (Pawlowska et al., 1996; Leyval & Joner, 2001; Regvar et al., 2001). On the basis of spore morphology, several *Glomus* species (e.g. *G. mosseae, G. fasciculatum, G. intraradices, G. aggregatum, G. constrictum*) were frequently identified in metal polluted habitats along with *Scutellospora dipurpurescens, Gigaspora* sp. and *Entrophospora* sp. (Griffioen, 1994; Pawlowska et al., 1996; 2000; Regavar et al., 2001). The low contribution of arbuscular mycorrhizal plant species to the early succession community (Figure 2) was therefore mainly attributed to the low availability of AMF propagules at elevated metal levels (Pawlowska et al., 1996; Leyval et al., 1997). Nevertheless, it was also shown that reduced spore numbers and diversity do not necessarily limit root colonization on polluted sites (Whitfield et al., 2003; Regvar et al. 2006).

Plot	1	2	3	4
Relative plant cover (%)	70	90	100	100
Plant community with dominants	Non-mycorrhizal perennials *Minuartia gerardii* *Sesleria caerulea* *Calamagrostis varia* *Biscutella laevigata* *Thlaspi praecox*	Grassland *Sesleria caerulea* *Calamagrostis epigejos* *Calamagrostis varia* *Minuartia gerardii* *Thlaspi praecox*	Shrubland *Sesleria caerulea* *Erica carnea* *Calamagrostis epigejos* *Thlaspi praecox* *Thymus serphyllum* *Salix caprea*	Early woodland *Sesleria caerulea* *Calamagrostis epigejos* *Calamagrostis varia* *Erica carnea* *Acer psevdoplatanus* *Salix appendiculata*
Mycorrhizal status	Non-mycorrhizal Arbuscular mycorrhizal	Arbuscular mycorrhiza Non-mycorrhizal	Arbuscular mycorrhiza Ericorid mycorrhiza Ectomycorrhiza	Arbuscular-mycorrhiza Ericorid mycorrhiza Ectomycorrhiza
Soil type	Bare rock, erosion	Developing rendzina,	Developing rendzina	Developing rendzina

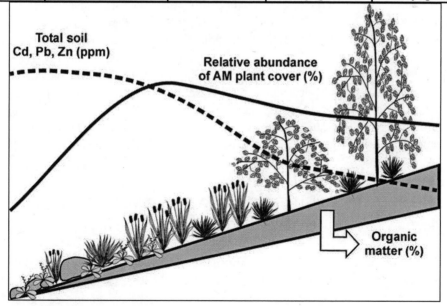

Figure 2. Vegetational and mycorrhizal succession along a metal polluted gradient based on the data of Regvar et al. (2006).

Initial colonizers of heavily disturbed and metal contaminated soils are often metal tolerant plant species, which tend to be non-mycorrhizal or develop low AM colonization levels, with important impacts on the increase of soil organic matter content, and improvement of the soil microclimate. This tends to be conductive to the establishment of plant species favoring higher AM colonization levels and/or favors other mycorrhizal types, particularly ericoid- and ectomycorrhizal (Figure 2). The mycorrhizal succession can therefore be seen as a gradual replacement of non-mycorrhizal with mycorrhizal plant species (Alen 1991; Pawlowska et al., 1996; Leyval & Joner, 1997; Regvar et al., 2006).

The functional significance of plant colonization levels are still a matter of debate, highlighting the lack of understanding of the formation of particular AM structures in plant roots (Fitter & Merryweather 1992; Allen 2001, Regvar et al, 2006). Mycorrhizal rather than non-mycorrhizal grasses (Poaceae) colonize polluted Zn, Cd and Pb mining sites (Leyval & Joner, 1997; Regvar et al., 2006). These grasses (e.g. *Agrostis capillaris*, *Sesleria caerulea*, *Calamagrostis varia*) are able to maintain relatively constant, though moderate (50-80%) levels of mycorrhizal colonization regardless of the levels of pollution (Iestwart et al., 1992; Leyval et al., 1997; Regvar et al., 2006), whereas highly mycorrhizal plant species are mostly found dominating the less polluted sites (Pawlowska et al. 1996, Regvar et al. 2006). These results indicate that lower levels of AM colonization may be beneficial to plants at high metal concentrations and higher AM colonization levels at lower metal concentrations. In addition, intense formation of intraradical spores is frequently found at the most polluted locations. These characteristics of mycorrhizal colonization may therefore be seen as a mycorrhizal strategy at metal polluted sites (Turnau et al., 1996, Regvar et al., 2006).

Increased mycorrhizal activity correlates closely with succession and could be used as a management tool for reclamation of disturbed lands (Allen, 1991; Regvar et al., 2006). The benefits AM confer on the ecosystem level have decisive consequences on the establishment of plant species, soil fertility and quality, floristic richness, competitive ability and community function (Allen, 1991; Francis & Read, 1994; van der Heijden et al., 1998; Barni & Siniscalco, 2000). Increased intraradical spore formation and low levels of mycorrhizal colonization may be seen as a mycorrhizal strategy in polluted environments (Regvar et al., 2006) contributing significantly to plant fitness. The low mycorrhizal colonization levels of the early colonizing AM species may thus represent an important link to bridge initial vegetational stands of early-colonizing successional species with later-stage perennial species. Therefore AM symbiosis should be integrated in future studies of the direction of plant succession and in contemporary facilitation of phytostabilisation schemes.

ARBUSCULAR MYCORRHIZA AND PHYTOREMEDIATION OF METAL POLLUTED SOILS

Remediation of metal contaminated soils is a cost-intensive, technically complex procedure, involving chemical, physical or biological techniques (Khan et al., 2000; Mulligan et al., 2001). The available techniques may be grouped into two categories; *ex situ techniques,* which require removal of contaminated soil for treatment on- or off- site and subsequent disposal and burial at a landfill site, thus merely shifting the contamination problem elsewhere, along with the hazards associated with transportation of contaminated soil and migration of contaminants from the landfill into the adjacent environment. *In situ methods*, on the other hand, remediate without excavation of contaminated soil by diluting the contaminant to safe levels using clean soil, immobilization of inorganic contaminants by complexing, or increasing pH by liming (Khan et al., 2000; Gaur & Adholeya, 2004). In situ soil washing for removing metals from soil is also an alternative to the off-site burial method (Mulligan et al., 2001), but this method is costly and produces a residue rich in heavy metals, which requires further treatment or burial (Gaur & Adholeya, 2004). Unfortunately, in situ physical and chemical methods of remediation of contaminated soils are mainly applicable to relatively small areas and are therefore unsuitable for very large areas such as typical mining sites or industrially/agro-chemically contaminated soils. Furthermore, the above-mentioned techniques render the land useless as a medium for plant growth, since they also remove all biological activities, including useful microbes (e.g. AMF, nitrogen fixing bacteria) (Khan et al., 2000; Khan, 2005). Therefore, environmentally friendly plant-based on-site technologies are gaining significant interest (Barceló & Poschenrieder, 2003; Gaur & Adholeya, 2004; Khan, 2005; Pilon-Smits, 2005; Ernst, 2005).

Current research in the area of contemporary plant-based technologies includes plants and their associated microbes to remediate polluted soils by *phytoremediation*. This improves the biological properties and physical structure of the soil, is environmentally friendly, potentially cheap, visually non-obstructive, and it offers the possibility of bio-recovery of toxic metals (Khan et al., 2000). Phytoremediation covers a range of methods, among which phytostabilisation and phytoextraction are the most suitable for remediating heavily and moderately metal contaminated soils (Barceló & Poschenrieder, 2003; Gaur & Adholeya, 2004; Khan, 2005; Pilon-Smits, 2005; Ernst, 2005). *Phytostabilization* includes immobilization and reduction in the mobility and bioavailability of contaminants by plant roots and their associated microbes. It is the most suitable plant remediation technique for restoring highly poly-metal contaminated sites, such as mine tailings, where phytoextraction would last too long to be economically feasible (Ernst, 2005). Therefore the introduction of plants with metal tolerant mechanisms based on exclusion and the production of an extensive roots system ensures stabilization of metals in the soil and thus hampers the contamination of groundwater and/or the surrounding landscape by wind/or water erosion of mine waste (Barceló & Poschenrieder, 2003; Ernst, 2005). Beside poly-metallic contamination however, mine tailings are also characterized by a very low water holding capacity and poor nutrient (e.g. nitrogen and phosphorus) availability (Ernst, 2005). Because of their improved metal tolerance, nutrient acquisition and water regime, plants colonized with AMF have a selective advantage in colonizing such sites.

The extent to which the natural succession may be altered was recently questioned by several authors (Wilcox, 1998; van der Putten, 2000; Prach & Pyšek 2001; Wiegleb & Felinks, 2001). In the short term, succession on abandoned arable land may be enhanced by sowing seeds of the dominant later-stage perennial grasses (Van der Putten et al., 2000). Plant communities along the metal pollution gradient at a Pb, Cd and Zn polluted area near a lead smelter were compared in order to select the most suitable plant species for the direction of secondary succession, and to test the feasibility of application of the selected species in practice. Based on species richness, species abundance and arbuscular mycorrhizal colonization, *Calamagrostis varia and Sesleria caerulea* were selected as the most suitable candidates, but their seed germination potentials did not allow successful phytoremedial activity. The dominant status of both grass species thus most likely arises predominantly from colonization from a vegetative source during early succession, and thus their seeds had to be collected at more distant locations where pollution effects were already reduced (Regvar et al., 2006) or optionally, commercial seed mixtures could be tested (Regvar et al., 2000).

If indigenous AMF exist in the contaminated soil to be phytoremediated, managing the microbial population in the rhizosphere by using suitable AMF with their associated rhizobial microflora could provide plants with benefits crucial for ecosystem restoration on derelict lands (Khan, 2000). AMF colonization by a mixed inoculum improved the growth of obligate mycotrophic *Andropogon gerardii*, as well as *Festuca arudinacea*, a facultative mycotroph, in a revegetation trial of mine spoils piles, where plants had failed to establish naturally (Hetrick et al., 1994). During soil restoration, the evaluation of mycorrhizal development and other soil microflora could be used as an important indicator of ecosystem efficiency, in order to biomonitor the success of *mycorrhizoremediation* (Haselwandter, 1997; Khan, 2000). However, care should be taken of the environmental factors affecting the levels of mycorrhizal colonization such as soil characteristics, bioavailability of metals, and microclimatic conditions, as well as biotic factors such as the diversity and density of AMF propagules and seasonal variations in AM colonization levels (Allen 1991; Leyval et al., 1997; Pawlowska et al., 2000; Regvar et al., 2006) when using this approach.

Hyperaccumulating plants may become useful for extracting toxic elements from the soil and thus decontaminating and restoring fertility in polluted areas in another branch of modern phytotechnology, termed *phytoextraction*. It includes removal and concentration of contaminants into harvestable plant parts; however it is feasible only for remediation of weakly and moderately contaminated soils (Ensley, 2000; Salt & Krämer; 2000; Ernst, 2005). In recent years, improved knowledge of the mechanisms of uptake, transport and tolerance of high metal concentrations in these plants (Küpper et al., 1999; Lombi et al., 2001; Baker & Whiting, 2002; Küpper et al., 2004) has opened up new avenues for remediation by phytoextraction (Barceló & Poschenrieder, 2003). To be efficient, phytoextraction requires the fulfillment of several basic conditions. An ideal plant species for remediation purposes should grew easily on soils contaminated by metals, possess high soil-to-shoot translocation factors and produce a high biomass quickly. Unfortunately, most metal hyperaccumulating plants grow quite slowly producing low biomass, while plants that produce a high biomass quickly are usually sensitive to high metal concentrations (Blayloch & Huang, 2000; Barceló & Poschenrieder, 2003). The high energy costs of metal tolerance (trade-off hypothesis) are presumably responsible for this phenomenon (Barceló & Poschenrieder, 2003). There are, however, exceptions to this rule (e.g. Ni hyperaccumulating *Berkheya codii*), which indicate that the capacity to accumulate and tolerate high metal concentrations in shoots and to produce high amounts of dry matter are not always mutually exclusive (Turnau & Mesjasz-Przybylowicz, 2003). It has been calculated that it would take 15 years to phytoextract Cd from soil containing 1.450 mmolkg^{-1} Cd by sowing *Thlaspi caerulescens* (ecotype "St. Laurent-le-Miner") with an annual harvest estimated at 5.2 t dry mass ha^{-1}, while the phytoextraction of Zn from the same site (581.4 mmol kg^{-1} soil) would take 650 years (Robinson et al., 1998). However, transformation of high biomass crops to improve their accumulation and tolerance capacity (Pilon-Smits, 2005) represents an intriguing alternative toward the improvement of remedial success by modern green technologies.

The success of phytoextraction also depends on soil metal bioavailability, which may be increased by exuding organic acids (e.g. malic and citric acid) and /or acid phosphatases under P deficiency (Marschner, 1998). The population density and composition of symbiotic and non-infecting micro-organisms in the rhizosphere can enhance root exudation and the concentrations of organic acids, chelators and acid phosphatases released as ectoenzymes from roots, or microorganisms, including AMF (Khan et al., 2000). Many highly productive plant species such as maize or trees can be grown on low to moderately contaminated sites and the addition of appropriate metal-tolerant AMF may enhance their biomass production and thus the extraction process (Ernst, 2005). The potential for phytoextraction can also be enhanced by cultivating metal hyperaccumulating plants and by inoculating metal hyperaccumulating plants with suitable AMF (Turnau & Mesjasz-Przybylowicz, 2003; Khan et al., 2000). In addition, micro-organisms other that AMF should be included in contemporary phytoextraction procedures. Recent studies imply that inoculation of plants used for phytoremediation with rhizobial microbes, co-cropping/intercropping systems or pre-cropping with mycotrophic crops can also enhance phytoextraction of metals from contaminated soils. However, better understanding of the physical, chemical and biological rhizosphere processes and their interactions with hyperaccumulating and non-accumulating plant species is needed in order to efficiently optimize phytoextraction technologies in future field investigation studies (Khan et al., 2000).

Contemporary phytoremediation techniques represent an interesting alternative to both chemical and physical soil remediation methods that are in general cost-intensive, technically complex and frequently render the land devoid of biological activities and thus useless as a medium for plant growth (Khan et al., 2000; Khan et al., 2005). The existence of AMF in metal contaminated soils plays an important role in the successful survival and growth of plants in contaminated soil (Gaur & Adholeya, 2004). However, the complexity of these interactions, combined with the disturbance characteristics (type, extent, distance and gradient), ecological factors controlled by climatic conditions, as well as biotic factors including the composition of local flora, germination establishment probabilities, vitality maintaining factors etc., favors a site-specific phytoremedial approach (Li et al., 2004; Lincoln et al., 1998; Ernst et al., 2005; Pilon-Smiths, 2005). Depending on the conservational aims, either phytostabilisation or phytoextraction may be selected, thus dictating the choice of plants and soil microorganisms, as well as the selection of the most suitable phytotechnology approach. Current results indicate that future contemporary remedial actions will have to work hand-in-hand with basic research studies in order to select the most suitable plant-microbial partners and test the selected model phytotechnologies on the larger scale specifically for each given remedial site.

PROSPECTS FOR FUTURE RESEARCH

The beneficial effects AMF confer on plants have important implications for plant development, fitness and function in metal contaminated soils and should therefore be integrated in future development of contemporary phytoremediation technologies. Plant metal uptake and tolerance depend largely on both plant characteristics and soil factors, including soil micro-organisms, and thus the interactions between plant roots and their symbionts, such as AMF, can play an important role in successful remediation of contaminated soils. Mycorrhizal associations particularly increase the absorptive surface of plants, with their extramatrical mycelium that explores the rhizosphere beyond the root zone, which in turn enhances plant water and nutrient uptake. Due to the high metal-binding capacity of mycorrhizal mycelium, AMF can act further as a barrier preventing metal transfer to plant shoots. The protection and improved mineral nutrition consequently result in greater biomass production, with obvious consequences for successful phytoremediation of polluted sites. Indigenous AMF strains existing naturally in metal polluted soils that are more tolerant than those from unpolluted soils should be used for deliberate direction of the succession in contemporary phytostabilization of highly metal polluted sites. In addition, the potentials of phytoextraction should be further explored by careful selection of the most suitable plant-symbiont partnerships, thus improving plant survival, vigor and the desired accumulation properties of hyperaccumulating plants with the aim of achieving the "magic" limits of commercially successful phytoextraction or even phytomining. Although achieving these rather optimistic goals may lie far ahead, the dawn of modern phytotechologies seem to be promising enough to keep on track and try to preserve the rich biotic legacy we have inherited from our ancestors.

REFERENCES

Agely, A.A., Sylvia, D.M. & Ma, L.Q. (2005). Mycorrhizae increase arsenic uptake by the hyperaccumulator Chinese brake fern (*Pteris vittata* L.). *Journal of Environmental Quality, 34,* 2181-2186.

Ager, F.J., Ynsa, M.D., Domínguez-Solís, J.R., Gotor, C., Respaldiza, M.A. & Romero, L.C. (2002). Cadmium localization and quantification in the plant *Arabidopsis thaliana* using Micro-PIXE. Nuclear Instruments and Methods in Physics Research Section B - *Beam Interactions with Materials and Atoms, 189,* 494-498.

Allen, M.F. (1991). *The Ecology of Mycorrhizae* (1st edition). Cambridge, UK: Cambridge University Press.

Baker, A.J.M. (1981). Accumulators and excluders - strategies in the response of plants to heavy metals. *Journal of Plant Nutrition, 3* (1-4), 643-654.

Baker, A.J.M. (1987). Metal tolerance. *New Phytologist, 106 (Suppl.),* 93-111.

Baker, A.J.M. & Whiting, S.N. (2002). In search of the Holy Grail - a further step in understanding metal hyperaccumulation? *New Phytologist, 155,* 1-4.

Barceló, J. & Poschenrieder, C. (1999). Structural and ultractructural changes in heavy metal exposed plants. In M.V.N. Prasad & J. Hagemayer (Eds.), *Heavy metal Stress in Plants* (1st edition, pp. 183-205). Berlin, Heidelberg, New York, Springer-Verlag.

Barceló, J. & Poschenrieder, C. (2003). Phytoremediation: principles and perspectives. *Contributions to Science, 2,* 333-444.

Barni, E. & Siniscalco, C. (2000). Vegetation dynamics and arbuscular mycorrhiza in old-field successions of the western Italian Alps. *Mycorrhiza, 10,* 63-72.

Bert, V., Macnair, M.R., De Laguerie, P., Saumitou-Laprade, P. & Petit, D. (2000). Zinc tolerance and accumulation in metallicolous populations of *Arabidopsis halleri* (Brassicaceae). *New Phytologist, 146,* 225-233.

Blaylock, M.J. & Huang, J.W. (2000). Phytoextraction of Metals. In I. Raskin & B.D. Ensley, (Eds.), *Phytoremediation of Toxic Metals, Using Plants to Clean up the Environment* (1st edition, pp.53-70). New York, USA: John Wiley & Sons, Inc.

Blaudez, D., Botton B. & Chalot M. (2000). Cadmium uptake and subcellular compartmentation in the ectomycorrhizal fungus Paxillus involutus. *Microbiology UK, 146,* 1109-117.

Brooks, R.R. (2000). General introduction. In R.R. Brooks (Ed.), *Plants That Hyperaccumulate Heavy Metals* (2nd edition pp. 1-14). Cambridge, UK: CAB international.

Chardonnens, A. N., KoBevoets, P. L. M., van Zanten, A., Schat, H. & Verkleij, J. A. C. (1999). Properties of enhanced zinc tolerance in naturally selected zinc-tolerant *Silene vulgaris. Plant Physiology, 120,* 779–785.

Cosio, C., Martinoia, E. & Keller, C. (2004). Hyperaccumulation of cadmium and zinc in *Thlaspi caerulescens* and *Arabidopsis halleri* at the leaf cellular level. *Plant Physiology 134, 1-*10.

Cornelissen, J.H.C., Aerts, R., Cerabolini, B., Werger, M.J.A. & Van der Heijden, M.G.A. (2001). Carbon cycling traits of plant species are linked with mycorrhizal strategy. *Oecologia, 129,* 611-619.

Delisle, G., Champoux, M. & Houde, M. (2001). Characterization of oxidase and cell death in Al- sensitive and tolerant wheat roots. *Plant Cell Physiology, 42,* 324-333.

Del Val, C., Barea, J.M. & Azòn-Aguilar, C. (1999). Assessing the tolerance to heavy metals of arbuscular mycorrhizal fungi from sewage sludge-contaminated soil. Applied Soil Ecology, 11, 261-269.

De Mars, B.G. & Boerner, R.E.J. (1996). Vesicular arbuscular mycorrhizal development in the Brassicaceae in relation to plant life span. *Flora, 191,*179–189.

Denny, H.J. & Ridge, I. (1995). Fungal slime and its role in the mycorrhizal amelioration of zinc toxicity to higher plants. *New Phytologist, 130,* 251-257.

Ensley, B.D. (2000). Rationale for Use of Phytoremediation. In I. Raskin & B.D. Ensley, (Eds.), *Phytoremediation of Toxic Metals, Using Plants to Clean up the Environment* (1st edition, pp. 53-70). New York, USA: John Wiley & Sons, Inc.

Ernst, W.H.O., Verkleij, J.A.C. & Schat, H. (1992). Metal tolerance in plants. *Acta Botanica Neerlandica, 41,* 229-248.

Ernst, W.H.O. (1996). Bioavailability of heavy metals and decontamination of soils by plants. *Applied Geochemistry, 11,* 163-167.

Ernst, W.H.O. (2005). Phytoextraction of mine wastes – options and impossibilities. *Chemie der Erde, 65* S1, 29-42.

Fitter, A.H. & Merryweather, J.W. (1992). Why are some plants more mycorrhizal than others? An ecological enquiry. In D.J. Read, D.H. Lewis, A.H. Fitter, I.J. Alexander (Eds.), *Mycorrhizas in Ecosystems* (1st edition pp. 26-36). Wallington, UK: CAB International,

Francis, R. & Read, D.J. (1994). The contributions of mycorrhizal fungi to the determination of plant community structure. *Plant and Soil, 159,* 11-25.

Galli, U., Schuepp, H. & Brunold, C. (1994). Heavy metal binding by mycorrhizal fungi. *Physiologia Plantarum, 92,* 364–368

Gaur, G. & Adholeya, A. (2004). Prospects of arbuscular mycorrhizal fungi in phytoremediation of heavy metal contaminated soils. *Current Science, 86,* 528-534.

Griffioen, W.A.J. (1994). Characterization of a heavy metal-tolerant endomycorrhizal fungus from the surroundings o a zinc refinery. *Mycorrhiza, 4,* 197-200.

Hagemayer J. (1999). Ecophysiology of plant growth under heavy metal stress. In M.V.N. Prasad & J. Hagemayer (Eds.), *Heavy Metal Stress in Plants* (1st edition, pp. 157-181). Berlin, Heidelberg, Germany: Springer-Verlag.

Hall, J.L. (2002). Cellular mechanisms for heavy metal detoxification and tolerance. *Journal of Experimental Botany, 366,* 1-11.

Haselwandter K. (1997). Soil microorganisms, mycorrhiza and restoration ecology. In: K. Urbanska, N.R. Webb, P.J. Edwards (Eds.), *Restoration Ecology and Sustainable Development* (1st edition, p. 65-80). Cambridge, UK: Cambridge Press.

Harley, J.L. & Harley, E.L. (1987). A check-list of mycorrhiza in the British flora. *New phytologist, supplement to vol. 105,* No. 2, 1-102.

Hazebroek, J.P. & Metzger, J.D. (1990). Thermoinductive regulation of gibberellin metabolism in *Thlaspi arvense* L. I. Metabolism of [^{2}H] kaurenoic acid and [^{14}C] gibberellin A$_{12}$-aldehyde. *Plant Physiology, 94,* 157–165.

Hetrick, B.A.D., Wilson, G.W.T. & Figge, D.A.H. (1994). The influence of mycorrhizal symbiosis and fertilizer amendments on establishment of vegetation in heavy metal mine spoils. *Environmental Pollution, 86,* 171-179.

Heumann, H.G (2002). Ultrastructural localization of zinc in zinc-tolerant *Armeria maritima* ssp. halleri by autometallography. *Journal of plant physiology, 159,* 197-203.

Hildebrandt, U., Kaldorf, M. & Bothe, H. (1999). The zinc violet and its colonization by arbuscular mycorrhizal fungi. *Journal of Plant Physiology, 154,* 709–717.

Ietswaart, J.H., Griffioen, W.A.J. & Ernst, W.H.O. (1992). Seasonality of VAM infection in three populations of *Agrostis capillaris* (Graminae) on soil with or without heavy metal enrichment. *Plant and Soil, 139,* 67-73.

Jacobsen, I., Smith, S.E. & Smith, F.A. (2002). Function and diversity of arbuscular mycorrhizae in carbon and mineral nutrition. In M.G.A. van der Heijden, I.R. Sanders (Eds.), *Mycorrhizal ecology* (1st edition pp. 75-92) Berlin, Heidelberg, New York, Germany: Springer-Verlag.

Joner, E. & Leyval, C. (1997). Uptake of 109Cd by roots and hyphae of a *Glomus mosseae / Trifolium subterraneum* mycorrhiza from soil amended with high ad low concentrations of Cd. *New Phytologist, 135,* 353-360.

Joner, E., Briones, R. & Leyval, C. (2000). Metal-binding capacity of arbuscular mycorrhizal mycelium. *Plant and Soil, 226,* 227-234.

Kaldorf, M., Kuhn, A.J., Schroder W.H., Hildebrandt, U. & Bothe, H. (1999). Selective element deposits in maize colonized by a heavy metal tolerance conferring arbuscular mycorrhizal fungus. *Journal of Plant Physiology, 154,* 718-728.

Khan, A. G., Kuek, C., Chaudhry T.M., Khoo, C.S. & Hayes W.J. (2000). Role of plants, mycorrhizae and phytochelators in heavy metal contaminated land remediation. *Chemosphere, 41,* 197-207.

Khan, A. G. (2005). Role of soil microbes in the rhizosphere of plants growing on trace metal contaminates soils in phytoremediation. *Journal of Trace Elements in Medicine and Biology, 18,* 355-364.

Koide, R. & Lu, X. (1992). Mycorrhizal infection of wild oats, Parental effects on offspring nutrient dynamics, growth and reproduction. In D.J. Read, D.H. Lewis, A.H. Fitter & I.J. Alexander (Eds.). *Mycorrhiza in Ecosystems* (1st edition, pp. 55-58). CAB international.

Küpper, H., Zhao, F.J. & McGrath, S.P. (1999). Cellular compartmentation of zinc in leaves of the hyperaccumulator *Thlaspi caerulescens. Plant Physiology, 119,* 305-311.

Küpper, H., Mijovilovich, A., Klaucke-Mayer, W. & Kroneck, P.H.M. (2004). Tissue and age-dependent differences in the complexation of cadmium and zinc in the cadmium/zinc hyperaccumulator *Thlaspi caerulescens* (Ganges ecotype) revealed by X-ray absorption spectroscopy. *Plant Physiology, 134,* 748-757.

Lasat, M.M., Baker, A.J.M. & Kochian, L.V. (1998). Altered Zn compartmentation in root symplasm and stimulated Zn absorption into the leaf as mechanisms involved in Zn hyperaccumulation in *Thlaspi caerulescens. Plant Physiology, 118,* 875-883.

Leyval, C., Turnau, K., & Haselwandter, K. (1997). Effect of heavy metal pollution on mycorrhizal colonization and function, physiological, ecological and applied aspects. *Mycorrhiza, 7,* 139-153.

Leyval, C. & Joner, E.J. (2001). Bioavailability of heavy metals in the mycorrhizosphere. In R.G. Gobran, W.W. Wenzel & E. Lombi, (Eds.), *Trace Metals in the Rhizosphere* (1st edition pp. 165-185). Florida, USA: CRC Press.

Llugany, M., Lombini, A., Poschenrieder C. & Barceló, J. (2003). Different mechanisms account for enhanced copper resistance in *Silene armeria* from mine spoil and serpentine sites. *Plant and Soil, 251,* 55-63.

Li, J., Loneragan, W.A., Duggin, J.A. & Grant, C.D. (2004). Issues affecting the measurement of disturbance response patterns in herbaceous vegetation – A test of the intermediate disturbance hypothesis. *Plant Ecology, 172,* 11-26.

Li, W., Khan, M.K, Yamaguchi, S. & Kamiya, Y. (2005). Effects of heavy metals on seed germination and early seedling growth of *Arabidopsis thaliana. Plant Growth Regulation, 46,* 45–50.

Lincoln, R., Boxshall, G. & Clark, P. (1998). A dictionary of Ecology, Evolution and Systematics (2nd edition). Cambridge, UK: Cambridge University Press.

Liu, D. & Kottke I. (2003). Subcellular localization of chromium and nickel in root cells of *Allium cepa* by EELS and ESI. *Plant and Soil 19,* 299-311.

Liu, D. & Kottke I. (2004). Subcellular localization of cadmium in the root cells of *Allium cepa* by electron energy loss spectroscopy and cytochemistry. *Journal of Bioscience, 29,* 329-335.

Liu, Y., Zhu, Y.G., Chen, B.D., Christie, P. & Li, X.L. (2005). Influence of the arbuscular mycorrhizal fungus *Glomus mosseae* on uptake of arsenate by the As hyperaccumulator fern *Pteris vittata* L. *Mycorrhiza, 15,* 187-192.

Lombi, E., Zhao, E.J., McGrath, S.P., Young, S.D. & Sacchi, G.A. (2001). Physiological evidence for a high-affinity cadmium transporter highly expressed in a *Thlaspi caerulescens* ecotype. *New Phytologist, 149,* 53-60.

Malcova, R., Vosátka, M. & Gryndler, M. (2003). Effects of inoculation with *Glomus intraradices* in lead uptake by *Zea mays* L. and *Agrostis capillaris* L. *Applied Soil Ecology, 23,* 55-67.

Marschner, H. (1995). *Mineral Nutrition of Higher Plants,* (2nd edition). London, UK: Academic press.

Marschner, H. (1998a). Role of root growth, arbuscular mycorrhizal, and root exudates for the efficiency in nutrient acquisition. *Field crops research, 56,* 203-207.

Marschner, P., Jentschke, G. & Godbold, D.L. (1998b). Cation exchange capacity and lead sorption in ectomycorrhizal fungi. *Plant and Soil, 205,* 93-98.

Mesjazs-Przybylowicz, J., Grodzinska, K., Przybylowicz, W.J., Godzik, B. & Szarek-Lukaszewska, G. (2001). Nuclear microprobe studies of elemental distribution in seeds of

Biscutella laevigata L. from zinc wastes in Olkusz, Poland. Nuclear Instruments and Methods in Physics Research Section B - *Beam Interactions with Materials and Atoms, 181, 634*-639.

Moreno, J.L., Hernandez, C.G. & Pascual, J.A. (1996). Transference of heavy metals from a calcareous soil amended with sewage–sludge compost to barley plants. *Bioresource Technology, 55,* 251–258.

Mulligan, C.N., Yong, R.N. & Gibbs, B.F. (2001). Remediation technologies for metal-contaminated soils and groundwater: an evaluation. *Engineering Geology, 60,* 193-207.

Orlowska, E., Zubek, Sz., Jurkiewitcz, A., Szarek-Lukaszeewska, G. & Turnau, K. (2002). Influence of restoration on arbuscular mycorrhiza of *Biscutella leavigata* L. (Brassicaceae) and *Plantago lanceoolata* (Plantaginaceae) from calamine spoil mounds. *Mycorrhiza, 12,* 1-17.

Pawlowska, T.E., Blaszkowski, J., & Rühling, Å. (1996). The mycorrhizal status of plants colonizing a calamine spoil mound in southern Poland. *Mycorrhiza, 6,* 499-505

Pawlowska, T.E., Chaney, R.L., Chin, M. & Charavat, I. (2000). Effects of metal phytoextraction practices on the indigenous community of arbuscular mycorrhizal fungi at a metal-contaminated landfill. *Applied and Environmental Microbiology, 66* (6), 2526-2530.

Pawlowska, T.E. & Charvat I. (2004). Heavy metal stress and developmental patterns in arbuscular mycorrhizal fungi. *Applied and Environmental Microbiology, 70* (11), 6643-6649.

Pilon-Smits, E. (2005). Phytoremediation. *Annual Review of Plan Biology, 56,* 15-39.

Prach, K. & Pyšek, P. (2001). Using spontaneous succession for restoration of human-disturbed habitats, Experience from Central Europe. *Ecological Engineering, 17,* 55-62.

Psaras, G.K. & Manetas, Y. (2001). Nickel localization in Seeds of the metal hyperaccumulator *Thlaspi pindicum* Hausskn. *Annals of Botany, 88,* 513-516.

Rask, L., Andréasson, E., Ekbom, B., Eriksson, S., Pontoppidan, B. & Meijer, J. 2000. Myrosinase: gene family evolution and herbivore defense in Brassicaceae. *Plant Molecular Biology, 42,* 93-113

Read, D.J. (1994). Plant-microbe mutualism and community structure. In E.D. Schulze & H.A. Mooney, (Eds.), *Biodiversity and Ecosystem Function* (1st edition, pp. 181-209). London-UK: Spriger Verlag,.

Reeves, R.D. & Baker, A.J.M. (2000). Metal accumulating plants. In I. Raskin & B.D. Ensley (Eds.), *Phytoremediation of toxic metals, Using Plants to Clean up the Environment* (1st edition, pp 193-229). New York, USA: John Wiley & Sons Inc.

Regvar, M., Vogel, K., Kugonič, N., Vodnik, D., Jug, M. & Kret, M. (2000). Toward a comprehensive model for revegetation of the heavy metal polluted site in Žerjav. In L. Santoloce, A. Massacci(Eds.), *Intercost workshop on bioremediation, Sorrento 15 to 18 Novembre 2000* (pp. 140-142). Roma, Italy: Istituto di Biochimica ed Ecofisiologia Vegetali.

Regvar. M., Groznik, N., Goljevšček, N. & Gogala, N. (2001). Diversity of arbuscular mycorrhizal fungi at various differentially managed ecosystems in Slovenia. *Acta Biologica Slovenica, 44* (3), 27-34.

Regvar, M., Vogel, K., Irgel, N., Wraber, T., Hildebrandt, U., Wilde, P., & Bothe, H. (2003). Colonization of pennycresses (*Thlaspi* sp.) of the Brassicaceae by arbuscular mycorrhizal fungi. *Journal of Plant Physiology, 160,* 615-626.

Regvar, M., Vogel-Mikuš K., Kugonič, N., Turk, B. & Batič, F. (2006). Vegetational and mycorrhizal successions at a metal polluted site - indications for the direction of phytostabilisation? *Environmental Pollution,* in press.

Robinson, B.H., Leblanc M., Petit, D., Brooks, R.R., Kirkman J.H. & Gregg, P.E.H. (1998). The potential of *Thlaspi caerulescens* for phytoremediation of contaminated soils. *Plant and Soil, 203,* 47-56.

Salt, D.E. & Krämer, U. (2000). Mechanisms of metal hyperaccumulation in plants. In I. Raskin & B.D. Ensley (Eds.), *Phytoremediation of toxic metals: using plants to clean up the environment* (1st edition, pp 193-229). New York, USA: John Wiley & Sons Inc.

Sanders, I.R. & Fitter, A.H. (1992). The ecology and functioning of vesicular-arbuscular mycorrhizas in coexisting grassland species. II. Nutrient uptake and growth of vesicular arbuscular mycorrhizal plants in a semi-natural grassland. *New Phytologist, 120,* 525-533.

Schussler, A., Schwarzott, D. & Walker C. (2001). A new phylum, the Glomeromycota: phylogeny and evolution. *Mycological Research, 105,* 1413-1421.

Seregin, I.V. & Ivanov V.B. (2001). Physiological aspects of cadmium and lead toxic effects on higher plants. Russian Journal of Plant Physiology, 48, 523-544.

Smith, S.E. & Read, D.J. (1997). *Mycorrhizal Symbiosis* (2nd edition). London, UK: Academic Press.

Smith, F.A. (2000). Measuring the influence of mycorrhizas. New Phytologist, 148 (1), 4-6.

Tonin, C., Vandenkoornhuyse, P., Joner, E.J., Straczek, J. & Leyval, C. (2001). Assessment of arbuscular mycorrhizal fungi diversity in the rhizosphere of *Viola calaminaria* and effect of these fungi on heavy metal uptake by clover. *Mycorrhiza, 10,* 161-168.

Turnau, K., Kottke, I. & Oberwinkler, F. (1993). Element localization in mycorrhizal roots of *Pteridium aquilinum* (L.) Kuhn collected from experimental plots with cadmium dust. *New Phytologist, 123,* 313-324

Turnau, K., Miszalski, Z., Trouvelot, A., Bonfante, P. & Gianinazzi, S. (1996). *Oxalis acetosella* as a Monitoring Plant on Highly Polluted Soils. In C. Azcon-Aguilar & J.M. Barea (Eds.), *Mycorrhizas in integrated systems, from genes to plant development. Proceedings of the Fourth European Symposium on Mycorrhizas.* (COST Edition pp 483-486). Brussels, Luxemburg: European Commission.

Turnau, K. & Mesjasz-Przybylowicz, J. (2003). Arbuscular mycorrhizal of *Berkheya codii* and other Ni-hyperaccumulating members of Asteraceae from ultramafic soils in South Africa. *Mycorrhiza, 13,* 185-190.

Van der Heijden, M.G.A., Klironomos, J.N., Ursic, M., Moutoglis, P., Streitwolf-Engel, R., Boller, T., Wiemken, A. & Sanders, I.R. (1998). Mycorrhizal fungal diversity determines plant biodiversity and productivity. *Nature, 396,* 69-72.

Van der Putten, W.H., Mortimer, S.R., Hedlund, K., Van Dijk, C., Brown, W.K., Lepš, J., Rodriguez-Barrueco, C., Roy, J., Diaz Len, T.A., Gormsen, D., Korthals, G.W., Lavorel, S., Santa Regina, I. & Smilauer, P. (2000). Plant species diversity as a driver of early succession in abandoned fields, a multi- site approach. *Oecologia, 124,* 91-99.

Vazquez, M.D., Barceló, J., Poschenreider, C., Mádico, J., Hatton, P., Baker, A.J.M. & Cope, G.H. (1992). Localization of Zinc and Cadmium in *Thlaspi caerulescens* (Brassicaceae), a metallophyte that can hyperaccumulate both metals. *Journal of Plant Physiology, 140,* 350-355.

Vazquez, M.D., Poschenreider, C., Barceló, J., Baker, A.J.M., Hatton, P. & Cope G.H. (1994). Compartmentation of zinc in roots and leaves of the zinc hyperaccumulator *Thlaspi caerulescens* J&C Presl. *Botanica Acta, 107*, 243-250.

Vierheilig H., Bennett R., Kiddle G., Kaldorf, M. & Ludwig-Müller, J. (2000). Differences in glucosinolate patterns and arbuscular mycorrhizal status of glucosinolate- containing plant species. *New Phytologist, 146*, 343-352.

Vogel-Mikuš, K., Drobne, D. & Regvar, M. (2005). Zn, Cd and Pb accumulation and arbuscular mycorrhizal colonization of pennycress *Thlaspi praecox* Wulf. (Brassicaceae) from the vicinity of a lead mine and smelter in Slovenia. *Environmental Pollution, 133*, 233-242.

Vogel-Mikuš, K., Pongrac, P., Kump, P., Nečemer, M. & Regvar, M. (2006). Colonization of a Zn, Cd and Pb hyperaccumulator *Thlaspi praecox* Wulfen with indigenous arbuscular mycorrhizal fungal mixture induces changes in heavy metal and nutrient uptake. *Environmental Pollution, 139*, 362-371.

Vogel-Mikuš, K., Pongrac, P., Kump, P., Nečemer, M. Simčič, J., Pelicon, P., Budnar, M., Povh, B. & Regvar, M. (2006). Localisation and quantification of elements within the seeds of Zn/Cd hyperaccumulator *Thlaspi praecox* by micro-PIXE. *Environmental pollution*, in press.

Weisennhorn, I., Leyval, C. & Berthelin, J. (1993). Cd tolerant arbuscular mycorrhizal (AM) fungi from heavy metal polluted soils. *Plant and Soil, 157*, 247-256.

Weisennhorn, I., Glashoff, A., Leyval, C. & Berthelin J. (1994). Differential tolerance to Cd and Zn of arbuscular mycorrhizal (AM) fungal spores isolated from heavy metal-polluted and unpolluted soils. *Plant and Soil, 167*, 189-196.

Weisennhorn, I. & Leyval, C., (1995). Root colonization of maize by a Cd-sensitive and Cd-tolerant *Glomus mosseae* and cadmium uptake in sand culture. *Plant and Soil 157*, 247-256.

Weisennhorn, I., Leyval, C., Belgy G. & Berthelin, J. (1995). Arbuscular mycorrhizal contribution to heavy metal uptake by maize (*Zea mays*) in pot culture with contaminated soil. *Mycorrhiza, 5*, 245-251.

Whitfield, L., Richards, A.J. & Rimmer, D.L. (2004). Relationships between soil heavy metal concentration and mycorrhizal colonization in *Thymus polytrichus* in northern England. *Mycorrhiza 14*, 55-62.

Wiegleb, G. & Felinks, B. (2001). Primary succession in post-mining landscapes of Lower Lusatia – chance or necessity. *Ecological Engineering, 17*, 199-217.

Wilcox, A. (1998). Early plant succession on former arable land. *Agriculture, Ecosystems and Environment, 69*, 143-157.

Wojcik, M., Vangronsveld, J., Haen, J.D. & Tukiendorf, A. (2005). Cadmium tolerance in *Thlaspi caerulescens* II. Localization of cadmium in *Thlaspi caerulescens*. *Environmental and Experimental Botany 53*, 163-171.

In: New Topics in Environmental Research
Editor: Daniel Rhodes, pp. 57-103
ISBN 1-60021-172-0

Chapter 3

FUNGI AND AIR POLLUTION: IS THERE A GENERAL PATTERN?

*A. L. Ruotsalainen[1, 2] and M. V. Kozlov[2] ***

[1] University of Oulu, Oulu, Finland
[2] University of Turku, Turku, Finland

ABSTRACT

Fungi play a crucial role in ecosystem processes in all terrestrial biomes. Anthropogenic pollution may decrease fungal performance and therefore affect ecosystem functioning. In spite of a considerable number of case studies and narrative reviews, the general pattern of pollution impact on fungi has not emerged. The goal of our study is to evaluate the magnitude and direction of the effects of aerial pollution on abundance and diversity of soil inhabiting fungi by means of a meta-analysis based on observational studies carried out near point emission sources. Our conclusions are based on 122 publications that reported results of 141 primary studies, conducted during 1969-2003 in impact zones of 62 polluters, including 26 non-ferrous smelters, 5 aluminum smelters and 16 polluters emitting mainly SO_2. Both fungal abundance and diversity decreased with increase in pollution load (effect sizes $r = -0.29$ and -0.59, respectively); diversity effect sizes decreased towards higher latitudes. Polluters with longer impact history showed more adverse effects on fungi. Pollution severity or polluter type did not explain variation in general, but increases in abundance or diversity were related to short pollution history and lower impact level. Polluters emitting mainly SO_2 were less deleterious compared to non-ferrous smelters that emit both SO_2 and heavy metals. Adverse effects of pollution on mycorrhizal abundance were slightly larger than on abundance of saprotrophic fungi. Absence of correlations between the effect sizes and annual emissions of individual pollutants suggests that there is no 'leading' pollutant and that the large fraction of fungal responses is due to indirect effects, e.g. due to pollution induced environmental changes. The meta-analysis did not demonstrate publication bias but revealed shortage of reliable

* Corresponding author: Tel +358-2-3335716; Fax +358-2-3336550; E-mail: mikoz@utu.fi

observational data. We conclude that the meta-analysis allowed to find important regularities in fungal response to pollution and also critically evaluate the level of our knowledge, indicating that high quality observational data are still badly needed to explain and hopefully predict impact of environmental pollution on soil inhabiting fungi.

INTRODUCTION

Fungi play a crucial role in ecosystem functioning in all terrestrial biomes. As heterotrophic organisms, fungi are dependent on external carbon sources and interact with their environment as saprotrophs, symbionts or parasites (Dix & Webster 1995; Adams et al. 1997). Soil inhabiting filamentous fungi form a functionally diverse group representing all classes of higher fungi (Paul & Clark 1996). Along with soil bacteria, fungi are key organisms in decomposition processes and nutrient cycling in soil (Dix & Webster 1995; Paul & Clark 1996). Saprotrophic fungi possess a wide range of enzymes that allow them to utilize complex organic molecules, and they only can access carbon via this process (Dix & Webster 1995). Mycorrhizal fungi acquire carbon from their host plants and enhance the nutrient acquisition of their hosts (Smith & Read 1997), forming a considerable link for the photosynthesized carbon to be allocated to soil (Högberg & Högberg 2002). Mycorrhizal symbiosis therefore affects also soil decomposition processes via energy expenditure belowground. Additionally, mycorrhizal relationships have important implications for plant-plant interactions and plant community development (Read 1997; Van der Heijden et al. 1998).

Due to fungal importance for ecosystem processes, the impact of atmospheric pollution on fungi received wide attention during the last decades. In general, when the effect was found, the results indicate that in the severely polluted areas soil microbial processes are decreased, soil fungal biomass and mycorrhizal colonizations are reduced, and fungal community structure is changed relative to control areas (Wainwright 1988; Pennanen et al. 1996; Meharg & Cairney 2000; Erland & Taylor 2002). The sporocarp formation of macrofungi is especially sensitive to heavy metal and nitrogen depositions (Rühling et al. 1984; Bååth 1989; Arnolds 1991). However, the results of observational studies are highly variable, possibly due to differences in pollution levels, polluter types and study methods (Bååth 1989). In particular, 'soft' pollution may be beneficial for soil microfungi (Wainwright 1979; Killham & Wainwright 1984; Wainwright 1988; Lebedeva et al. 1999).

Despite the abundance of original studies and narrative reviews on pollution effects on fungi (Wainwright 1988; Bååth 1989; Tyler et al. 1989; Dighton & Jansen 1991; Fritze 1992; Gadd 1993; Hartley et al. 1997; Leyval et al. 1997; Cairney & Meharg 1999; Meharg & Cairney 2000; Erland & Taylor 2002), conclusions based on precise numerical analyses are still non-existing, and sources of variation in fungal responses to pollution remain unexplored. Different methodological approaches to the problem make the situation even more complex, because the effects reported in relation to regional pollution may well differ from the effects observed near the point emission sources. Point polluters, such as smelters, power plants and other industrial installations, can be considered as models to study air pollution effects on biota (Kozlov & Zvereva 2003), because pollution effects in an isolated impact zone can be more easily related to either distances from the polluter or deposition levels than in large-scale gradients or urban areas, which allows easier interpretation of biological effects (Wainwright 1988; Tyler et al. 1989; Kozlov & Zvereva 2003). Information from pollution gradients can also reveal patterns on the general sustainability of fungal communities, allowing comparison to natural abiotic stress gradients, such as gradients of salinity, temperature or pH (Van Duin et al. 1991; Cairney & Meharg 1999; Erland & Taylor 2002).

Meta-analysis is a technique that allows statistical exploration and combination of results from a number of publications (Gurevitch & Hedges 2001). Meta-analytical approach has been applied in ecology since beginning of the 1990's, and there is a growing body of research compilations based on meta-analysis (Hawkes & Sullivan 2001; Allison & Goldberg 2002; Koricheva 2002; Sheldon & West 2004; Hillebrand 2004; Treseder 2004). The advantage of meta-analysis compared with narrative reviews is it's ability to measure simultaneously the effect direction (positive or negative) and magnitude, and to estimate the statistical significance of the mean effect size (Gurevitch & Hedges 2001).

In order to evaluate the impacts of aerial pollution on the abundance and diversity of the soil inhabiting fungi, we carried out a meta-analysis of the observational data collected near the point emission sources. In addition to the general analysis, i.e. to the identification of the overall effects, we asked whether polluter type, pollution severity and longevity of the impact would affect fungal abundance and diversity. We also checked whether variation in fungal responses could be explained by the geographical position of the polluter (including vegetation zone) and by the differences between fungal functional groups (mycorrhizal vs. saprotrophic fungi).

MATERIALS AND METHODS

Study Organisms

We restricted our meta-analysis to soil and litter inhabiting filamentous fungi; studies on either fungal endophytes in alive plant aboveground tissues or xylotrophic fungi were excluded. The fungal morphology was accounted for because it affects both fungal nutrition and growth, so that fungi growing as filaments differ from unicellular fungi e.g. yeasts (Wood & Wang 1983). However, we are aware only of a couple of studies on soil yeasts along the pollution gradients, thus the last restriction decreased the number of selected publications only slightly.

Suitability Criteria

We limited our meta-analysis to the papers that fit the criteria coined by Kozlov & Zvereva (2003).

1. The study was conducted near a point polluter (like individual factory);
2. The polluter was influencing surrounding habitats primarily via the ambient air;
3. The study involved natural ecosystems, not modified by experimental treatments;

4. The data have been collected from organisms naturally inhabiting the study area;
5. The study involved both impacted and non-impacted ecosystems, allowing their comparison;
6. The study reported biotic effects (i.e. was not restricted to the accumulation of pollutants);
7. The study provided numerical and/or verbal information, allowing calculation of the effect size or at least vote-counting.

We feel it necessary to comment that numerous publications by Evdokimova and co-workers, reporting changes in soil fungal communities near the copper-nickel smelter at Monchegorsk, Russia, were excluded because all these studies were carried out on introduced soil (Evdokimova 1996), a fact which is not clearly mentioned in several publications. We excluded studies related to radionuclides because (a) they rarely are associated with point polluters, and (b) they mostly report accumulation data, whether impact of radionuclides on abundance and diversity of soil microfungi remains unexplored.

Gathering the Data

In March 2005 we searched the following databases (producer of the database given in parentheses): Agricola (CSA), Arctic and Antarctic Regions (NISC), Biological Abstracts (Biosis), Biological Sciences (CSA), Biosis Previews (Biosis), CAB Abstracts (CAB International), Environmental Sciences and Pollution Management (CSA), and Plant Science (CSA). The searches by several key words related to both pollution and fungi yielded 100 hits with promising titles. The key words used were: fungal activity, fungal community, fungal physiology, fungi, hyphal length, macromycetes, micromycetes, mycorrhiza and saprophytes, which were all combined with: emission, pollution, air pollution, heavy metal, power plant, pulp mill, smelter and sulphur dioxide. Also authors' collections and a mycorrhiza reprint collection at the Botanical Museum of the University of Oulu were searched. All identified papers were screened for both their suitability (see the criteria above) and for additional references; some extra references were obtained from the review articles. In total 350+ publications were screened, and 122 of them (Table 1) were accepted for the analysis after removal of publications that repeatedly reported the same data. When one publication reported results from more than one point polluter, these were considered as separate studies (Table 1). We also included two submitted manuscripts by our research team. In spite of the continuous effort, we were unable to obtain some five potentially suitable data sources.

Data Extraction

Fungal parameters were divided into two classes reflecting either abundance or diversity (Table 2). To avoid biases due to the quality of the studies (different numbers of reported parameters) as well as the repeated publication of the same data, the following rules have been used:

Table 1. Basic information[1] about studies included in meta-analysis (sorted alphabetically by location of polluters).

Location	Year of data collection	Number of study sites	Spatial arrangement of study sites	Number of samples	N used in numerical analysis[2]	Objects[3]	Response variables[4]	Reference
Almalyk	1988-1989	3	?	60	5	Mic	A10 (1/1), D1(0/1)	Lebedeva & Lugauskas 1985a
Bratsk	1975-1995	79	?	?	-	Ect	D4 (0/1)	Mikhailova 1997
Bratsk	?	4	?	?	4	Tfb	D3 (1/1)	Petrov 1988. See also Petrov 1992.
Brixlegg	1984	3	Irregular	15	-	Ect	A13 (0/1)	Göbl & Mutsch 1985
Broćéni	1975-1976	4	?	?	4	Mic	A5 (1/3)	Vulfa 1985
Budel	1987-1991	2	1 transect	17	9	Endo	A12 (1/1)	Griffioen et al. 1994
Budel	1987-1988	2	1 transect	80	10	Endo	A12 (1/1)	Ietswaart & Griffioen 1992
Cherepovets	1995, 1997	3	1	60	4	Mic	A5 (0/1), D1 (1/1)	Lebedeva et al. 1999
Cherepovets	1993, 2001	3	1 transect	300	4	Mic	D4 (1/1)	Zachinyaeva & Lebedeva 2003
Chimkent	1976-1978	5	?	35	5	Mic	A5 (1/1)	Babyeva et al. 1980
Chimkent	1978-1980	2	?	90	4	Mic	A5 (1/1), D1 (0/1)	Levin & Babyeva 1985
Chimkent	?	3	?	?	-	Mic	A5 (0/1)	Skvortsova et al. 1982
Dneprodzerzhinsk	1983-1986	4	?	?	4	Mic	A11 (1/1)	Pavlyukova 1986. See also Pavlyukova 1989, Grishko & Pavlyukova 1997.
Dolna Odra	1976-1980	9	1 transect	?	9	Mic	A5 (1/1)	Borowiec et al. 1985
Erzurum	1987	2	1 transect	10	5	Mic	A5 (1/1), D1 (1/1)	Hasenekoglu & Sülun 1990
Głogów	?	6	1 transect	210	4	Ect	A13 (1/1), D1 (0/1), D2 (0/1)	Leski & Rudawska 2003. See also Leski & Rudawska 2002.
Głogów	?	2	1 transect	30-36	11	Ect	A13 (1/1), D2 (0/1)	Rudawska et al. 2002[5]
Głogów	1982-1984	3	1 transect	3	4	Mic	A5 (1/1)	Zwolinski et al. 1987
Gusum	1979-1980	9-10	1 transect	18-20	9	Mic	D4 (1/1)	Nordgren et al. 1985
Gusum	1979-1980	9	1 transect	18	18	HyL, Mic	A1 (1/1), A2 (1/1), A5 (0/1)	Nordgren et al. 1983
Gusum	1971-?	54	Irregular	54	54	Efb, Sfb	A16 (2/2), D1 (3/3), D4 (3/3)	Rühling 1978

Table 1. Basic information[1] about studies included in meta-analysis (sorted alphabetically by location of polluters) (continued).

Location	Year of data collection	Number of study sites	Spatial arrangement of study sites	Number of samples	N used in numerical analysis[2]	Objects[3]	Response variables[4]	Reference
Gusum	1977-1980	10/52	1 transect	variable	52 (only D)	HyL, Mic, Efb	A1 (1/1), A2 (1/1), A5 (1/1), D1 (0/1), D4 (1/1)	Rühling et al. 1984. See also Tyler 1984.
Harjavalta	?	10	1 transect	20	19[6]	HyL	A1 (1/1)	Fritze et al. 1989[7]
Harjavalta	1994	3	1 transect	3	-	PLF	A4 (0/1)	Fritze et al. 1997
Harjavalta	1993-1994	9	1 transect	9	4	Erg	A3 (1/1)	Fritze et al. 1996
Harjavalta	?	12	1 transect	12	12	PLF	A4 (1/1)	Pennanen et al. 1996. See also Fritze et al. 2000.
Henryetta	1972-1973	2	1 transect	8	4	Mic	A5 (1/1)	Pancholy et al. 1975
Jonava	1981-1983	5	1 transect + 1 additional site	50	5	Mic	A10 (1/1)	Lebedeva & Lugauskas 1985a. See also Lebedeva & Lugauskas 1985b; Lebedeva 1986.
Jonava	1981-1983	2	?	?	-	Mic	A1 (0/1), A10 (0/1), D1 (0/1)	Tomilin et al. 1985
Jonava	1981	4	?	?	-	Mic	A11 (0/1)	Vaichis et al. 1991
Kalush	?	3	?	?	-	Mic	A11 (0/1)	Sinitsyna & Stefurak 1986
Kalush	?	3	?	?	-	Mic	A11 (0/1)	Stefurak 1981
Kandalaksha	1994-1995	10	3 transects	10	4	Mic	A1 (0/1), D4 (1/1)	Evdokimova 2001. See also Evdokimova et al. 1997.
Kandalaksha	?	2	1 transect	?	-	Mic	A5 (0/1), D1 (0/1)	Evdokimova et al. 2004
Kedainiai	1981-1983	5	1 transect + 1 additional site	50	5	Mic	A10 (1/1)	Lebedeva & Lugauskas 1985a. See also Lebedeva & Lugauskas 1985b, Lebedeva 1986.
Kedainiai	2000-2002	7	Irregular	21/21	7	Ect, Mic	A5 (1/1), A13 (1/1), D1 (1/1), D5 (0/1)	Stankeviciené & Peciulyté 2004
Keelung	1996-1999	4	1 transect	28-40	4	Mic	A5 (1/1)	Yang & Yang 2001. See also Yang et al. 1999.

Table 1. Basic information[1] about studies included in meta-analysis (sorted alphabetically by location of polluters) (continued).

Location	Year of data collection	Number of study sites	Spatial arrangement of study sites	Number of samples	N used in numerical analysis[2]	Objects[3]	Response variables[4]	Reference
Kirovgrad	?	?	?	?	-	Ect	A13 (0/1)	Veselkin 1995a
Konin	?	2	1 transect	30-36	11	Ect	A13 (1/1), D2 (0/1)	Rudawska et al. 2002
Konin	?	3	1 transect[8]	?	-	Ect	A3 (0/1), D5 (0/1)	Rudawska et al. 2000
Konin	1999	3 (2 used in analysis)	1 transect	(72 used)	18	Ect	A3 (1/1), A13 (1/1), D2 (0/1), D5 (0/1)	Rudawska et al. 2003
Konin	1981	3	1 transect	Not given	4	Mic	A5 (1/1), D1 (1/1), D4 (1/1)	Chwalinski et al. 1987
Kostamuksha	1997	10	2 transects	?	10	Ect	D3 (2/2)	Lositskaya et al. 1999
Kostamuksha	1996-1998	4	Irregular	?	4	Mic	A5 (1/1)	Medvedeva 2000
Kostamuksha	?	4	?	?	-	Mic	A11 (0/1)	Medvedeva et al. 2001
Kostamuksha	1986-1991	3	?	?	4	Mic	A5 (1/1)	Zaguralskaya & Zyalchenko 1994. See also Zaguralskaya 1997.
Koverhar	1989	24	2 transects	24	24	HyL	A1 (1/1)	Fritze 1991
Krasnoturjinsk	1986-1989	?	?	?	-	Mic	A11 (0/2), D1 (0/1)	Babushkina & Luganskii 1990
Krasnouralsk	1987-1988	5	Irregular?	?	4 /5	Endo	A12 (2/2)	Trubina 2002a. See also Trubina 2002b.
Kuopio	1987-1988	17	Irregular	85	4	Ect	A13 (1/1), D2 (1/1), D5 (1/1)	Holopainen et al. 1996. See also Holopainen 1989.
Legnica	?	5	2 transects	40[8]	5	Mic	A5 (1/1)	Zabawski 1983
Loxley	1977	5	1 transect	16	4	Mic	A5 (1/1)	Wainwright 1979[9]
Lubenik	1996	6	1 transect	?	6	Mic	A5 (1/1)	Kautz et al. 2002
Lubenik	1994	6	1 transect	54	6	Mic	A5 (1/1)	Kautz et al. 2001
Lubon	1992-1995	2	1 transect	480	24	Ect	A13 (1/1), D4 (0/1)	Kieliszewska-Rokicka et al. 1997

Table 1. Basic information[1] about studies included in meta-analysis (sorted alphabetically by location of polluters) (continued).

Location	Year of data collection	Number of study sites	Spatial arrangement of study sites	Number of samples	N used in numerical analysis[2]	Objects[3]	Response variables[4]	Reference
Lubon	?	6	1 transect	210	4	Ect	A13 (1/1), D1 (0/1), D2 (0/1)	Leski & Rudawska 2003
Lubon	1992-1994	2	Irregular	48	24 (A), 7 (D)	Ect	A13 (1/1), A13 (1/1), D5 (1/1)	Rudawska et al. 1995. See also Rudawska et al. 2002.
Mednogorsk	1983-1985	4	?	40	4	Mic	A5 (1/1)	Lurie 1986
Mednogorsk	1982-1988	6	?	?	-	Mic	A5 (0/1), D1 (0/1)	Lurie 1983. See also Lurie 1985.
Miasteczko Śląskie	?	2	1 transect	?	-	Ect	A14 (0/2), D4 (0/2)	Kowalski et al. 1989
Miasteczko Śląskie	1978	3	Irregular[8]	18	6 (A), 4 (D)	Ect	A13 (0/1), A14 (1/1)	Kowalski 1987
Miasteczko Śląskie	?	2	1 transect	30	-	Mic	A5 (0/1), D1 (0/1), D4 (0/1)	Kowalski 1996
Miasteczko Śląskie	?	3	1 transect	18	-	Mic	A5 (0/1), D1 (1/3)	Kowalski 1981
Miasteczko Śląskie	?	3[8]	1 transect	?	4	Mic	A5 (1/1), D1 (1/1), D4 (1/1)	Kowalski et al. 1992
Miasteczko Śląskie	1982-1984	3	1 transect	3	4	Mic	A5 (1/1)	Zwolinski et al. 1987
Miasteczko Śląskie	1974	27 (13 used in analysis)	Irregular	Not given	13 (A), 7 (D)	Mic	A5 (1/1), D1 (1/1), D4 (1/1)	Badura et al. 1976
Mississauga	1976	5	Irregular	5	4	Mic	A5 (1/1)	Bisessar 1982
Mogilev	1981	8	?	?	-	Mic	A11 (0/1)	Zimenko et al. 1982
Monchegorsk	1999-2000	?	1 transect	?	-	Efb	D3 (0/1)	Isaeva 2004
Monchegorsk	?	4	1 transect	120	4	Mic	D1 (1/1), D4 (1/1)	Lebedeva 1993a. See also Lebedeva 1993b.
Monchegorsk	?	3[8]	1 transect	?	14	Mic	A7 (1/1)	Nikonov et al. 2001
Monchegorsk	?	3[8]	1 transect	?	12	Mic	A7 (1/1)	Polyanskaya et al. 2001
Monchegorsk	1987-1988	?	?	?	-	Mic	A11 (0/1)	Raguotis 1989
Monchegorsk	1981-1989	?	?	?	-	Ect	A7 (0/1), D5 (0/1)	Yarmishko 1990

Table 1. Basic information[1] about studies included in meta-analysis (sorted alphabetically by location of polluters) (continued).

Location	Year of data collection	Number of study sites	Spatial arrangement of study sites	Number of samples	N used in numerical analysis[2]	Objects[3]	Response variables[4]	Reference
Monchegorsk	1986-1988, 1991	3/3	1 transect	?	4	Mic	A5 (1/1)	Zaguralskaya 1997
Monchegorsk	2003	6	2 transects	96	6	Ect	A14 (1/1), D5 (1/1)	Ruotsalainen et al. 2006b
Monchegorsk	2003	6	2 transects	58	5	Endo	A12 (1/1), A8 (1/1)	Ruotsalainen et al. 2006a
Monchegorsk	1993, 2001	3	1 transect	300	4	Mic	D4 (1/1)	Zachinyaeva & Lebedeva 2003
Nagda	1979	2	1 transect	6	4	Mic	A5(1/1)	Pawar & Dubey 1985
Nazarovo	1983	5	?	?	-	Tfb	D4 (0/1)	Davydova & Volkova 1984
Nazarovo	Before 1990	2	?	?	-	Mic	A7 (0/1), D1 (0/1)	Makarova & Naprasnikova 1990
Nazarovo	?	?	?	?	11	Mic	A5 (1/1)	Naprasnikova & Lut 1980
Nazarovo	?	2	1 transect	15	8	Mic	A5 (1/1)	Nikitina 1991
Nazarovo	1977-1982	3	?	?	-	Mic (HyL)	A1 (0/1)	Nikitina et al. 1988
Nazarovo	Before 1990	5	?	?	-	Mic	A11 (0/1)	Sorokin 1990
Nazarovo	?	5	Irregular	150	30	Mic	A5 (1/1)	Sorokin 1993
Nazarovo	1982-1984	6	?	?	4	Mic	A11 (0/1), D1 (0/1)	Sorokin & Gukasyan 1986
Nazarovo	Before 1989	2	?	?	-	Efb	D1 (0/1)	Volkova 1989
Nazarovo	1982-1984	2	?	?	-	Efb	D1 (0/1)	Volkova & Davydova 1987
Nikel	1991	3	1 transect	30	4	Mic	A5 (2/2), D1 (1/1), D4 (1/1)	Marfenina & Grigoryev 1992
Nikel	2003	6	2 transects	96	6	Ect	A14 (1/1), D5 (1/1)	Ruotsalainen et al. 2006b
Nikopol	1986-1989	4	?	?	-	Mic	A5 (0/1)	Grishko 1989
Nikopol	?	5	?	?	5	Mic	A5 (1/1)	Grishko 1996. See also Grishko 1998.
Nordenham	1998	7	2 transects	7	7	Erg	A3 (1/1)	Chander et al. 2001
Norilsk	1993	8	?	?	4	Mic	A7 (1/1), A10 (1/1), D4 (1/1)	Kirtsideli et al. 1995
Norilsk	1987-1988	?	?	?	-	Mic	A11 (0/1)	Raguotis 1989
Norilsk	1993, 2001	3	1 transect	300	4	Mic	D4 (1/1)	Zachinyaeva & Lebedeva 2003
Novotroitsk	1983-1985	4	?	40	4	Mic	A5 (1/1)	Lurie 1986

Table 1. Basic information[1] about studies included in meta-analysis (sorted alphabetically by location of polluters) (continued).

Location	Year of data collection	Number of study sites	Spatial arrangement of study sites	Number of samples	N used in numerical analysis[2]	Objects[3]	Response variables[4]	Reference
Orsk	1983-1985	3	?	30	9	Mic	A5 (1/1)	Lurie 1986
Palmerton	1972-1973	4	1 transect[8]	24	4	Mic	A5 (1/1), D1 (1/1), D4 (1/1)	Jordan & Lechevalier 1975
Palmerton	1995-1996	5	1 transect	5	4	PLF	A4 (1/1)	Kelly et al. 2003
Perm	Before 1983	2	?	?	-	Mic	A11 (0/1)	Borisova et al. 1983
Perm	1987-1990	10[8]	?	?	-	Efb	A16 (0/1)	Mekhonoshin 1992
Perm	1987-1991	10	?	?	-	Endo, Ect, Tfb	A12 (0/1), A13 (0/1), D3 (0/1)	Selivanov et al. 1992. See also Selivanov et al. 1990.
Perm	1986-1988	6	?	?	4 (A), 6 (D)	Ect, Tfb	A13 (1/1), A15 (1/1), D3 (1/1)	Shkaraba et al. 1991. See also Shkaraba et al. 1989.
Perm	Before 1987	3	Irregular	15	3	Endo	A12 (1/1)	Krjuger & Shkaraba 1987. See also Shkaraba et al. 1991.
Pincher Creek	?	3	Irregular	15	5 (A), 4 (D)	Endo	A9 (1/1), D1 (1/1)	Clapperton & Parkinson 1990
Polevskoi	1986-1989	?	?	?	-	Mic	A11 (0/1), D1 (0/1)	Babushkina & Luganskii 1990
Polevskoi	1989, 1991	4	Irregular	504 (36 used in analysis)	4	Mic	A5 (1/1)	Kovalenko 2004
Polevskoi	1986-1988	5	?	56	5	Mic	D1 (1/1)	Shebalova et al. 1990
Polevskoi	?	?	?	?	-	Ect	D5 (0/1)	Veselkin 2002
Polevskoi	1987-1988	5	Irregular?	?	4/5	Endo	A12 (2/2)	Trubina 2002a. See also Trubina 2002b.
Police	1975-1980	9	1 transect	?	9	Mic	A5 (1/1)	Borowiec et al. 1984
Postorna	1966	6	Irregular	6	6	Mic	A5 (1/1)	Mrkva & Grunda 1969
Revda	?	?	?	?	-	Endo	A12 (0/1)	Mitjushina 2002
Revda	?	4	1 transect	?	4	Ect	A13 (2/2)	Veselkin 1998. See also Veselkin 1995a, Veselkin 1995b, Veselkin 1999.

Table 1. Basic information[1] about studies included in meta-analysis (sorted alphabetically by location of polluters) (continued).

Location	Year of data collection	Number of study sites	Spatial arrangement of study sites	Number of samples	N used in numerical analysis[2]	Objects[3]	Response variables[4]	Reference
Revda	?	3	?	?	4	Ect	D2 (1/1)	Veselkin 1997b. See also Veselkin 1995a, Veselkin 1996, Veselkin 1997a.
Revda	1988-1992	3	1 transect	?	-	Mic,	A11 (0/1), D1 (0/1)	Vorobeichik 1994
Revda	?	3	1 transect	?	4	Efb	D3 (1/1)	Vurdova 2003
Rönnskär	1981	21	2 transects	42	-	HyL	A1 (0/1), A2 (0/1)	Nordgren et al. 1986
Rönnskär	?	39	1 transect	39	39	PLF	A4 (1/1)	Pennanen et al. 1996
Rönnskär	1981-1984	41	1 transect	41	41	Tfb	A16 (1/1), D1 (0/1)	Rühling & Söderström 1990
Shelekhovo	1975-1995	79	?	?	-	Ect	D4 (0/1)	Mikhailova 1997
Sköldvik	1989-1990	20	1 transect	20	20	HyL	A1 (1/1)	Fritze et al. 1992
Sostanj	1998-2001	2	1 transect	13	4	Ect	A13 (1/1), D2 (1/1)	Al Sayegh-Petkovsek 2004
Sostanj	1992-1993	2	1 transect	6-10	5	Ect	A13 (1/1), A14 (1/1), D2 (0/1),	Kraigher et al. 1994. See also Kraigher et al. 1996.
Sostanj	1993	2	1 transect	60	5	Ect	A13 (1/1), D2 (1/1),	Kraigher 1997
Sudbury/Coniston	2001	5	1 transect	?	5	Mic	A5 (3/3)	Anand et al. 2003
Sudbury/Copper Cliff	1976	4	1 transect[8]	156	4	Mic	A5 (1/1)[10]	Freedman & Hutchinson 1980
Tisova	?	3	1 transect	3	4	Mic	A5 (1/1)	Langkramer 1975
Tisova	1971-1973	3	1 transect	3	4	Mic	A5 (1/1)	Langkramer 1974
Tisova	1971-1974, 1978-1979	5	1 transect	5	5	Mic	A5 (1/1)	Lettl & Langkramer 1984. See also Langkramer & Lettl 1982.
Trbovlje	1998-2001	2	1 transect	13	4	Ect	A13 (1/1), D2 (1/1)	Al Sayegh-Petkovsek 2004
Ufa	1996-2000	14	Irregular	?	-	Ect	A13 (0/1), A15 (0/1)	Kulagin et al. 2002
Ufa	?	2	?	?	5	Ect	A13 (0/1), A15 (0/1), D5 (0/1)	Veselkin & Zaitsev 2003. See also Veselkin 2002, Veselkin et al. 2003.
Ufa	?	2	?	?	-	Ect	A13 (0/1)	Zaitsev 2002
Vladikavkaz	1976-1978	9	?	35	7	Mic	A5 (1/1)	Babyeva et al. 1980

Table 1. Basic information[1] about studies included in meta-analysis (sorted alphabetically by location of polluters) (continued).

Location	Year of data collection	Number of study sites	Spatial arrangement of study sites	Number of samples	N used in numerical analysis[2]	Objects[3]	Response variables[4]	Reference
West-Whitecourt	?	3	1 transect	30	5	FRr	A6 (1/1)	Bewley & Parkinson 1985
West-Whitecourt	1982	3	1 transect	15	5	Mic	A5 (1/1)	Bewley & Parkinson 1984
Zerjav	1998	8 (4 used in analysis)	1 transect	?	4	RAF	A8 (1/1), D1 (1/1), D4 (1/1)	Cevnik et al. 2000
Zerjav	2002	8	Irregular	38	10	Endo	A12 (1/1)	Vogel-Mikus et al. 2005

[1] Missing information: ? = unknown, - = non-applicable (for sample size when numerical analysis had not been used).

[2] Note that N = 3 study sites had been converted to N = 4 to allow ES calculation.

[3] Study objects: Ect = ectomycorrhiza, Efb = ectomycorrhizal fruitbodies, Sfb = saprotrophic fruitbodies, Tfb = total fruitbodies (mycorrhizal and saprotrophic species not separated), Mic = microfungi, Endo = endomycorrhizal fungi, RAF = root associated fungi, Erg = ergosterol concentration, HyL = fungal hyphal length, PLF = PLFA concentration, FRr = fungal respiration.

[4] Consult Table 2 for codes of response variables; in parentheses: number of numerical effect sizes / number of verbal conclusions extracted from the study.

[5] Data for root tip number (A13) are the same as in Leski & Rudawska (2003).

[6] Values derived from a figure, only 19 plots were possible to identify.

[7] Includes both experimental treatments and control plots, controls only used in analysis.

[8] Not clearly stated in the article, but presumed on the basis of indirect article information or additional data sources.

[9] Data reported on sulphur-oxidizing microfungi omitted.

[10] Data on filamentous fungi included in the analysis.

Table 2. Classification of fungal parameters (both numerilac and verbal) reported in original studies.

Code[1]	Parameter	Fungal group, for which the parameter was estimated	Number of studies
A1	Total hyphal length	All groups	9
A2	Fluorescein diacetate active hyphal length	All groups; alive only	3
A3	Ergosterol concentration	All groups; alive only	4
A4	Phospholipid fatty acid concentration	All groups; alive only	4
A5	Number of colony forming units	Microfungi	50
A6	Respiration	All groups; alive only	1
A7	Biomass	All groups	5
A8	Colonization by root-associated fungi[2]	Root-associated	2
A9	Arbuscular mycorrhizal spore number	Glomeralean mycorrhizal	1
A10	Number of propagules	Microfungi	5
A11	'Abundance' without additional information	Microfungi	14
A12	Endomycorrhizal root colonization	Glomeralean mycorrhizal, ericoid mycorrhizal	9
A13	Number of mycorrhizal root tips	Ectomycorrhizal	23
A14	Proportion of mycorrhizal root tips	Ectomycorrhizal	5
A15	Thickness of mycorrhizal mantle	Ectomycorrhizal	3
A16	Number of fruitbodies	Ectomycorrhizal and saprotrophic macrofungi	3
D1	Species number	All groups	31
D2	Number of morphotypes	Ectomycorrhizal	11
D3	Number of observations at the generic level	Ectomycorrhizal	6
D4	Shannon–Wiener diversity index based on species data	All groups	21
D5	Shannon–Wiener diversity index based on morphotype data	Ectomycorrhizal	10

[1] Parameter code (starts with A for abundance and with D for species number and diversity estimates).

[2] Includes dark-septate endophytes.

Table 3. Basic information on the polluters.

Location	Country	Polluter type[1]	General type[2]	Established in	Emission data	Annual aerial emission[3], × 10³ kg								Extent (km)[5]	pH impact[6]	Vegetation zone[7]	Severity[8]
						SO₂	F	Cu	Ni	Zn	Pb	NOₓ	others[4]				
Almalyk	Uzbekistan	Cu	Nf	1949	1991	143 000	92	141	?	?	40	1100	-	15	A	DE	H
Bratsk	Russia	Al	Al	1966	1991	11 970	1884	-	-	-	-	3711	H₂S=479	<30	B	CF	L
Brixlegg	Austria	Cu	Nf	1946										<6	A	TF	L
Brocéni	Latvia	Cem	Cem	1938	1991	-	-	-	-	-	-	300	Dust=4613	<10	B	TF	L
Budel	Netherlands	Zn	Nf	1892	1990	904	-	<1	<1	20	<1	37	NH₃=45 Dust=43		A	TF	L
Cherepovets	Russia	Fe	SO₂	1955	1990	47 800	-	-	0.14	-	-	37 300	H₂S=190 NH₃=312 HC=4400	40	A	CF	H
Chimkent	Kazakhstan	Pbzn	Nf	1934	1982	274 000	2800	11	-	260	2800	(111)		<20	A	DE	H
Dneprodzerzhinsk	Ukraine	Chem	Chem	1939	1991	(2350)	-	-	-	-	-	(1100)	NH₃=2074 H₂S=870	<5	B	TG	L
Dolna odra	Poland	Pop	SO₂	1974	1991	66 708	-	-	-	-	-	27 468	Dust=33367	<15	A	TF	L
Erzurum	Turkey	Cem	Cem	1987										<7	B	TG	L
Głogów	Poland	Cu	Nf	1969	1986	57 000	-	?	?	?	?	?	Dust=3000		A	TF	H
Gusum	Sweden	Bra	Nf	(1661), 1970	2002	<1	-	<1	?	<1	<1	?	?	8	A	TF	H
Harjavalta[9]	Finland	Nicu	Nf	1945	1990, 1993	4700	-	50	7	13	6	180	As=11	<8	A	CF	H
Henryetta	USA	Zn	Nf	1916										0.1	A	TF	H
Jonava	Lithuania	Nfer	Fert	1965	1990-1991	1521	-	-	-	-	-	2023	?	<15	B	TF	H
Kalush	Ukraine	Synf	Synf	?	1991	(13 300)	-	-	-	-	-	(4900)	OS=57	25	B	TG	L
Kandalaksha	Russia	Al	Al	1955	1991	3800	1600	-	-	-	-	1400	?	<10	B	CF	L
Kedainiai	Lithuania	Nfer	Fert	1963	1991	2464	-	-	-	-	-	300	?	<15	B	TF	L
Keelung	Taiwan	Pop	SO₂	1985										10	A	TR	L
Kirovgrad	Russia	Cu	Nf	1914	1989/ 1991	107 100	-	318	-	2043	511	18 600	Dust=3259 As=174	15	A	CF	H
Konin[10]	Poland	Al	Al	1966	1969/ 2003, 1980/ 1999	200/60	600/37	-	-	-	-	?	?		B	TF	L

Table 3. Basic information on the polluters (continued).

Location	Country	Polluter type[1]	General type[2]	Established in	Emission data	SO₂	F	Cu	Ni	Zn	Pb	NOₓ	others[4]	Extent (km)[5]	pH impact[6]	Vegetation zone[7]	Severity[8]
									Annual aerial emission[3], × 10³ kg								
Kostamuksha	Russia	Fe	SO_2	1982	1990	62 200	-	-	-	-	-	3400	-	<10	B	CF	L
Koverhar	Finland	Fe	SO_2	1961	1989	1416	-	-	-	-	-	490	Dust=2026	<4	B	CF	L
Krasnoturjinsk	Russia	Al	Al	1943	1991	(121)	3077	-	-	-	-	(4300)		(<30)	B	CF	L
Krasnouralsk	Russia	Cu	Nf	1932	1990	97 400	874	?	?	?	155	1900	As=482	(<80)	A	CF	H
Kuopio	Finland	Pumi	SO_2	1968	1986-1988	11 500	-	-	-	-	-	400	NH_4=16 SP=250	20	B	CF	L
Legnica	Poland	Cu	Nf	1970	1985	21 033	-	73	-	-	56	?			A	TF	H
Loxley	UK	Bri	Bri	?										2.5	B	TF	L
Lubenik	Slovakia	Mag	Mag	1952-58	1996	69	-	?	?	?	?	495	SP=135	8	B	TF	H
Lubon	Poland	Phofe	Fert	1917	1980/1995	2806/115	162/1					850/94		12	B	TF	L
Mednogorsk	Russia	Cu	Nf	1939	1991	94 700	-	?	?	-	?	100	H_2S=1399		A	CF	L
Miasteczko Śląskie	Poland	Zn	Nf	1967	1992	?	-	?	?	23	13	?	?		A	TF	H
Mississauga	Canada	Pb	Nf	1958?										1	A	TF	L
Mogilev	Belarus	Synf	Synf	1968	1991	(6728)	-	-	-	-	-	(1379)	CS_2=3569 H_2S=614 OS=3597	<15	B	TF	L
Monchegorsk	Russia	Nicu	Nf	1939	1991	196 000	-	6500	5000	-	-	6100		80	A	CF	H
Nagda	India	Sulph	Chem	?										2.5	A	TS	L
Nazarovo	Russia	Pop	SO_2	1961	1991	43 900	-	-	-	-	-	8600		15	A	CF	L
Nikel	Russia	Nicu	Nf	1932	1990-1991	189 800	-	92	136	-	-	600	?	<15	A	TU	H
Nikopol	Ukraine	Fe	SO_2	1966	1991	1600	170	-	-	-	-	3600	Mn=2476 t, OS=84	<3	B	TG	L
Nordenham	Germany	Pb	Nf	?										<8.5	A	TF	L
Norilsk	Russia	Nicu	Nf	1943	1991	2 201 700	-	2700	1200	-	(44)	21 600		100	A	TU	H

Table 3. Basic information on the polluters (continued).

Location	Country	Polluter type[1]	General type[2]	Established in	Emission data	Annual aerial emission[3], × 10³ kg								Extent (km)[5]	pH impact[6]	Vegetation zone[7]	Severity[8]
						SO_2	F	Cu	Ni	Zn	Pb	NO_x	others[4]				
Novotroitsk	Russia	Fe	SO_2	1955	1991	(17 540)	-	-	-	-	-	(14 800)	NH_3=352 H_2S=392 HCN=899 OS=677	(<30)	B	CF	L
Orsk	Russia	Ni	Nf	1938	1991	(55)	-	-	642	-	-	(12 700)		(<30)	A	TG	H
Palmerton[11]	USA	Zn	Nf	1898	1960-1975	5563	-	33	?	2555	33	?	Cd=29	40	A	TF	H
Perm	Russia	Synf	Synf	1980	1991	(18 403)	-	-	-	-	-	(15 109)	OS=3974 NH_3=661		B	CF	L
Pincher Creek	Canada	Gas	SO_2	1967	Not given	29 930	-	-	-	-	-	?	-	20	A	TG	L
Polevskoi	Russia	Crio	Crio	1907	1991	6500	149	-	-	-	-	2700	?	7	B	CF	L
Police	Poland	Chem	Chem	1969	2000-2002	4159	14	-	-	-	-	1819	NH_3=3660 Dust=828	<22	B	TF	L
Postorna	Czech	Synf	Synf	1910	?	630	85	-	-	-	-	?	H_2SO_4=188	5	B	TF	L
Revda	Russia	Cu	Nf	1940	1989	134 089	1016	2610	-	1753	564	1800	As=639	25	A	CF	H
Rönnskär	Sweden	Cupbzn	Nf	1928-30	1979	17 400	-	165	?	161	245	?		<55	A	CF	L
Shelekhov	Russia	Al	Al	1962	1991	2 900	2670	-	-	-	-	500		<15	B	CF	L
Sköldvik	Finland	Oil	SO_2	1965	1987	24 000	-	?	?	?	?	4400	OC=4200 Dust=1400	2	B	CF	L
Sostanj[12]	Slovenia	Pop	SO_2	1970?	1990-1992	84 000	-	-	-	-	-	?	SP=1845		A	TF	L
Sudbury/ Coniston	Canada	Nicu	Nf	1913										6	A	TF	H
Sudbury/ Copper Cliff	Canada	Nicu	Nf	1913	1988	658 515	-	?	1019	?	133	?	?	7	A	TF	H
Tisova	Czech	Pop	SO_2	1960	1990-1992	86 000	-	-	-	-	-	?	?	<40	A	TF	L
Trbovlje	Slovenia	Pop	SO_2	1966-68?	1996	23	-	-	-	-	-	1203	SP=503		A	TF	L
Ufa	Russia	Oil	SO_2	1951	1991	(34 823)	-	-	-	-	-	(25 417)	NH_3=674	<10	B	CF	L

Table 3. Basic information on the polluters (continued).

Location	Country	Polluter type[1]	General type[2]	Established in	Emission data	Annual aerial emission[3], × 10³ kg								Extent (km)[5]	pH impact[6]	Vegetation zone[7]	Severity[8]
						SO₂	F	Cu	Ni	Zn	Pb	NOx	others[4]				
Vladikavkaz	Russia	Pbzn	Nf	1898	1991	(111)	-	-	-	135	79	(155)	?	<20	A	TF	H
West-Whitecourt	Canada	Gas	SO₂	1962	1970-76	30 857	-	-	-	-	-	?	-	10	A	TG	L
Zerjav	Slovenia	Pb	Nf	(1746)	1976-1991	2678	-	?	?	?	?	?	Dust=6388		A	TF	L

[1] Polluter type: Al = aluminium smelter, Bra = brass mill, Bri = brick factory, Cem = cement factory, Chem = chemical factory, Crio = criolite factory, Cu = copper smelter, Cupbzn = copper-lead-zinc smelter, Fe = iron smelter, Gas = gas plant, Mag = magnesite plant, Nfer = nitrogen fertilizer factory, Nicu = nickel-copper smelter, Oil = oil refinery, Pb = lead smelter, Pbzn = lead-zink smelter/refinery, Phofe = phosphate fertilizer factory, Pop = power plant, Pumi = pulp mill, Sulph = sulphuric acid factory, Synf = synthetic fibre, Zn = zink smelter/refinery.

[2] General type (used in meta-analysis): Al = aluminium smelter, Bri = brick factory, Cem = cement factory, Chem = chemical factory, Crio = criolite factory, Fert = fertilizer factory, Mag = magnesite plant, Nf = non-ferrous metal smelter, SO₂ = sulphur dioxide emitter, Synf = synthetic fibre factory.

[3] Empty cell = data not available; - = not emitted in substantial amounts. Estimates received indirectly, e.g. by multiplying regional emission by contribution of a certain polluter, are given in brackets.

[4] Other substantial pollutants (>10,000 kg annually). HC = hydrocarbons, OS = organic solvents, OC = organic compounds, SP = solid particles.

[5] Distance from the polluter to the clean control. The sign "<" is used where control was presumably selected far away from the external border of the impact zone. If the study reported an area of the impact zone, in transformation to distance we assumed that the impact zone was circular.

[6] General pH impact of the polluter to the environment (A = acid, B = alkaline).

[7] Vegetation zone: TU = tundra, CF = coniferous forest, TF = temperate forest, TG = temperate grassland, D = desert, TR = tropics, TS = tropical savannas. After De Blij & Muller (1998).

[8] Severity of the pollution impact: H = high: vegetation damage is obvious, at least near the polluter; L = low: detection of biotic effects requires specific investigation.

[9] NOx emission data from year 1990, other emission data from year 1993.

[10] F emission data from years1969/2003 and SO₂ data from years 1980/1999.

[11] SO₂ emission data for the year 1970.

[12] SP emission data for the year 1996.

1. If several soil layers were reported, only the litter and humus layers were considered to maximize the comparability of primary studies (most studies included data from these layers only).
2. If case of repeated sampling the data were averaged before analysis.
3. If the results of the same study were reported in several publications, the conclusions were aggregated, or the less detailed publication was disregarded.
4. If a paper reported several estimates of abundance or diversity, then (i) only one verbal conclusion was extracted (increase, decrease or no effect), but (ii) all effect sizes (ES) were calculated and the ES with the largest absolute value was selected.

Although we generally included one abundance and one diversity parameter per study, in the case of Rühling (1978) and Rühling et al. (1984) we used average sporocarp abundance and diversity in the general analysis and in the analysis for longevity (the studies published in 1978 and 1984 were carried out the same year), but used individual studies and their ES values reported separately for mycorrhizal and saprotrophic fungi to compare pollution effects on fungal functional groups. In the case of Trubina (2002a) two parameters of endomycorrhizal colonization were included, because arbuscular and ericoid mycorrhiza represent different fungal taxa, and in the case of Ruotsalainen et al. (2006a) we included abundance data both on mycorrhizal and dark-septate fungal root colonization. Paper by Stankeviciené & Peciulyté (2004) reported abundance data both on soil microfungi and ectomycorrhiza; both parameters were included in the analysis because the effect sizes for these two groups were opposite. Publications of Bewley and Parkinson (1984) based on plate counts and Bewley and Parkinson (1985) based on respiratory activity were both included although we cannot fully exclude the possibility that these data originate from the same study. We also need to mention that in the case of Al Sayegh-Petkovsek (2004), Rudawska et al. (2002) and Leski & Rudawska (2003), the studies on different polluters were compared to a common, long-distance control site.

While abundance parameters were directly extracted from the primary studies, the diversity estimates were usually constructed from the tabular data. We used Shannon-Wiener index whenever possible; it was calculated by using Species Richness and Diversity software, version 3.02 (Pisces Conservation Ltd, http://www.irchouse.demon.co.uk/).

Information on Polluters

Emission data and the year of polluter establishment (Table 3) were generally not reported in the primary studies, and they were obtained from additional data sources such as other publications, web pages and contacts with authors, regional authorities or company representatives. Emission data for the polluters on the territory of the former USSR are after Berlyand (1992).

We divided polluters (21 classes; Table 3) into acidic and alkaline groups on the basis of their main pH impact on the environment by using criteria and information given by Anttila (1990), Fritze (1992) and J. Derome (pers. comm.). In addition to general analysis of variation among polluter types, we contrasted two largest data sets: SO_2 emitters, like power plants, and non-ferrous metal smelters emitting both SO_2 and heavy metals (Table 3).

Pollution severity classification was somewhat arbitrary: severity was considered high if adverse effects on vegetation, like extensive necroses or forest decline, were obvious near the polluter; otherwise the severity was classified as low. If information on the effects on vegetation was unavailable, we used the emission data and the distance to the unpolluted sites to judge the severity (Table 3).

Pollution severity, polluter type and pH-impact were highly dependent on each other as explanatory factors according to the χ^2-tests (data not shown). Our data did not allow all factors to be systematically explored on other factor levels, which would have been an optimal procedure; however, we explored the pollution severity separately among acid polluters and also among SO_2 emitters and nonferrous smelters.

Longevity of the impact was defined as the difference between the year(s) of data collection and the year of polluter establishment. On the basis of this character, we divided all studies into three classes of approximately equal size; low, moderate, and high longevity correspond to the time intervals of 1-20, 21-50 and 51-318 years, respectively. We classified the Gusum brassworks in Sweden as very old polluter since there had been smelting activity since 1661, although the recently operating brassworks were established in 1970.

To avoid pseudoreplication, we averaged effect sizes (ES) for both abundance and diversity parameters for each polluter prior the analyses of variation related to polluter type, pollution severity, pH-impact, latitude and vegetation zone.

Vote Counting

Since about one third of the selected publications provided only verbal information (see Results), we conducted vote counting (Gurevitch & Hedges 2001) in order to check, whether conclusions of these studies differ from conclusions of studies that included the information suitable for ES calculation. The first analysis was based on the entire data set and the second on the numerical data set. Additionally, we compared (by χ^2 test) distributions of the reported responses in studies that contained numerical information and that provided verbal conclusions only.

Meta-analysis: Effect Size Calculation

Effect sizes were calculated in two ways, either as correlation coefficients (r) or as Hedge's d (Hedges & Olkin 1985). The Pearson correlation between fungal variables and logarithmic distance to the polluter was used when the data from at least three sites were available (a gradient approach). In nine of 11 studies, where distance data were unavailable, we correlated fungal parameters with soil concentrations of the principal pollutant, which were assumedly proportional to the logarithmic distance; and in two other studies we calculated a Spearman rank correlation coefficient. Hedge's d was calculated when the primary study compared two plots, polluted and control (about a half of the studies reporting numerical information). Background calculations, correlations and frequency analyses were carried out by using MS Excel 2000 (Microsoft) and program R, version 2.0.1 (Ihaka & Gentleman 1996).

When the correlation coefficient was based on three sites (15 studies) and d value was calculated for two replicates (one study), the number of observations was changed to four to allow z transformation. These modified data were carefully checked for their impact on the mean effect sizes, and as they did not deviate from the general pattern, they were all kept in the file.

To combine the data sets for d and r, d's were converted into r's by using the following equation: $r^2 = d^2/(d^2 + 4)$. The sign of the effect was kept unchanged, e.g. if d was negative, the r is also negative (Rosenthal 1994). The effect sizes for the Spearman rank correlation coefficients were calculated in the same way as for the Pearson linear correlation coefficients (Glass et al. 1981).

Because r was calculated as a correlation with the distance to polluter, it yielded positive values when the pollution impact was negative, e.g. fungal variables decreased when approaching the polluter. In contrast, Hedge's d in the same situation yielded negative values, because 'treatment' is smaller than 'control'. To combine these two approaches, the sign of correlation coefficients was changed, and further on the negative ES values correspond to the adverse effects of pollution. Effect sizes were then calculated by z-transforming the correlation coefficients and weighing by sample sizes (Rosenberg et al. 2000). ES values obtained either from r or d approach did not differ from each other ($Q_B = 0.01$, df = 1, p = 0.93). After the analysis we back-transformed effect sizes into r to ease their interpretation (Koricheva 2002; Sheldon & West 2004).

Effect sizes were calculated and analyzed by MetaWin version 2.0 software (Rosenberg et al. 2000). We assumed that the studies carried out on different taxonomic groups, variable study methods and approaches do not share a true, common effect size and therefore we applied mixed effect models in the analyses (Gurevitch & Hedges 2001). We first calculated the mean ES and heterogeneity for both abundance and diversity and then we searched for potential sources of variation by using characteristics of the polluters (Table 3: polluter type, pollution impact on the soil pH, pollution severity, and the longevity of the impact), vegetation zone (classification after De Blij & Muller 1998; Table 3) and fungal functional group as explanatory variables. The pollution impact was considered significant when the confidence interval (bias-corrected bootstrap CIs with 999 iterations) of the average ES did not include zero. Bias-corrected confidence intervals are more conservative (Adams et al. 1997), and they also produce more symmetric CIs after back-transformation.

We also checked whether the diversity effect sizes would be confounded by the absolute number of taxa (or morphospecies) identified in the primary study. Since significant pattern was detected (see Results, Figure 4), we carried out some analyses after removal of four studies that were responsible for the detected pattern. This removal greatly improved the results of analyses of pollution longevity, pollution severity and latitudinal trend.

In the analysis of functional groups we contrasted mycorrhizal and saprotrophic fungi in every case when primary studies allowed this comparison. We assumed that all soil microfungi explored by the plate-counting methods were saprotrophic because these methods select for fungi forming spores in soil (Warcup 1955), and reported species lists typically represent saprotrophic fungal taxa (Warcup 1955; Jordan & Lechevalier 1975; Marfenina & Grigoryev 1992; Lebedeva 1993a; Kowalski 1996). In addition, we contrasted (by χ^2 test) the numbers of studies that reported positive vs. negative ES values related to each explanatory factor.

Testing for Publication Bias

The publication biases related to possible paradigm change or selection against non-significant results may be a serious problem in meta-analyses (Light & Pillemer 1984; Møller & Jennions 2001; Kotiaho & Tomkins 2002; Koricheva 2003). First, we checked the bias related to paradigm change by correlating the ES with the year of publication (Jennions & Møller 2002). Second, the publication bias related to the results of primary studies due to publication policy was explored by using the funnel plot technique, i.e. plotting ES vs. sample size (Light & Pillemer 1984; Palmer 1999; Møller & Jennions 2001). In case of no publication bias, the plot shape should be like a funnel because the studies with small sample sizes should include more variation than studies based on larger samples (Light & Pillemer 1984; Møller & Jennions 2001). Correlation between the ES and sample size was also checked for the funnel plot figure. Consequently, we controlled the fail-safe numbers of the meta-analyses to see how robust our results are against the non-published results (Rosenthal 1979). The Rosenthal's fail safe number demonstrates the number of insignificant unpublished studies which are required to turn the significant mean effect size into insignificant. In general, fail-safe number exceeding 5N (where N is the number of studies included in the meta-analysis) is considered as a proof that the analysis is robust against the unpublished results (Rosenthal 1979; Møller & Jennions 2001), although application of any fixed value to judge the results is not straightforward (Becker 1994). In our analysis we considered fail safe number 3N to indicate a relatively robust result.

RESULTS

Data Quality

We analyzed data obtained from 122 publications and two submitted manuscripts, which reported changes in the communities of soil filamentous fungi in surroundings of the point polluters (Table 1). These publications included 141 separate studies, 87 of which reported numeric data sufficient for the effect size calculation (Table 1). After selection and aggregation of results (see above for the criteria) these studies yielded 128 conclusions of abundance and 63 conclusions of diversity (numeric and verbal information pooled). The general effect size analysis was based on 91 values for abundance and 33 values for diversity; sub-analyses were conducted also on lower numbers of ES values.

Field data originated from 21 countries (Table 3, Figure 1), with the largest proportion collected in Russia (43% of studies). The majority of the included studies were published after 1980, and the largest annual numbers of publications were recorded recently (Figure 2a).

Generally, the sampling design was poorly replicated: in 64 studies the plots were situated on a single transect, and 25 studies were based on two study sites only, polluted and unpolluted, i.e. were not replicated (Table 1, Figure 2b). The median number of study sites was four. The number of study sites was not reported in 10 studies (7%), and sample number information was missing from 63 studies (45%). Statistical tools were applied in 38 studies (27%).

Figure 1. Geographical location of the polluters included in the meta-analysis.

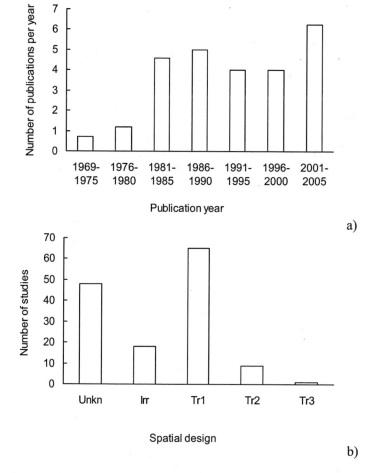

Figure 2. a) Temporal classification of publications in the meta-analysis database (submitted articles by our research team not included). b) Spatial arrangement of the study sites: Unkn = unknown, Irr = Irregular, Tr1 = one transect, Tr2 = two transects, Tr3= three transects.

Data Exploration for Potential Biases

There was no indication of paradigm change during the period when the primary studies were carried out, because both negative and positive results have been published with similar probabilities between 1969 and 2004 (ES vs. the year of publication: $r = -0.05$, N = 91 studies, p = 0.65 for abundance, and $r = -0.08$, N = 33 studies, p = 0.67 for diversity). Sample size neither had effect on ES values (Figure 3). ES values obtained from non-replicated studies (one polluted and one unpolluted plot) did not differ from those obtained from replicated studies ($Q_B = 0.01$, df = 1, p = 0.94). Diversity ES values were found to decrease with increase in the number of groups (taxa or morphospecies) used as the basis of ES estimation (Figure 4).

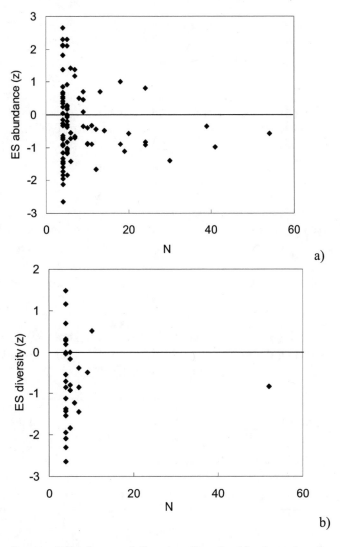

a)

b)

Figure 3. Funnel plot figures of abundance and diversity effect size (z) values plotted against sample sizes on which primary studies were based. $r_s = 0.05$, N = 91 studies, p = 0.61 for abundance, and $r_s = 0.07$, N = 33 studies, p = 0.68 for diversity.

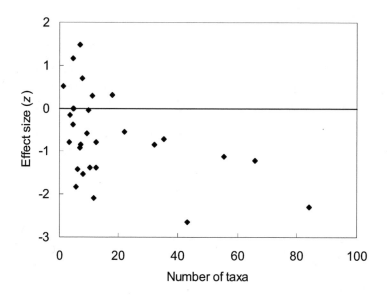

Figure 4. Relationship between the diversity effect size (z) and average number of taxa (or morphospecies) reported in the primary studies ($r = -0.49$, N = 29, p = 0.007).

Vote Counting

Most studies reported negative effects both on abundance and diversity (Table 4); increase in diversity was reported less frequently than increase in biomass. Studies that contained only verbal information did not differ in distribution of the reported responses from studies that also reported numerical values ($\chi^2 = 0.35$, df = 2, p = 0.84). Thus, exclusion of these studies from the further analysis of effect sizes was not expected to bias our conclusions.

Table 4. Vote-counting analysis: numbers of studies that reported decrease, increase or no change for fungal abundance or diversity near the point polluters relative to unpolluted sites.

Studies analysed	Parameter	Numbers of studies reporting different responses			Differences in frequencies of the reported responses	
		Increase	Decrease	No change	χ^2	P
All	Abundance	31	70	27	28.4	<0.0001
	Diversity	6	40	17	27.3	<0.0001
Numerical	Abundance	19	54	18	27.7	<0.0001
	Diversity	2	21	10	16.6	0.0003

Exploration of the Main Effects

We explored the between-class variance heterogeneity to test if the 16 abundance and five diversity parameters (Table 2) could be combined in the meta-analysis. Parameter classes represented by less than two studies were excluded from the heterogeneity analysis that was therefore based on 84 studies on abundance (including classes A1, A3-5, A7, A10, A12-14) and 31 studies on diversity (all classes included) (Table 2). The results did not indicate any statistically significant heterogeneity between the parameter classes (Q_B = 10.22, df = 9, p = 0.33 for abundance and Q_B = 4.88, df = 4, p = 0.30 for diversity), and therefore we decided to use the combined abundance and diversity estimates in the final ES calculation. In addition, heterogeneity among studies was insignificant in all analyses (data not shown).

In the summary analysis we found statistically significant negative effect on fungal abundance (Figure 5), although the robustness of the result against unpublished studies can be questioned (Rosenthals fail safe value 188 vs. 3N = 273). In the case of diversity, the analysis indicated highly negative mean ES, which also had a robust fail safe value (207 vs. 3N = 99).

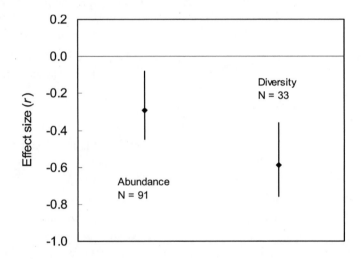

Figure 5. Means and confidence intervals (bias-corrected bootstrap intervals) for abundance and diversity effect sizes (r) in the general meta-analysis. Q_T (abundance) = 105.04, df = 90, p = 0.13, Q_T (diversity) = 33.07, df = 32, p = 0.41. The asymmetrical confidence intervals are due to back-transformation from z to r.

Abundance and diversity may differently respond to the same pollution impact: when both estimates were published in the same study, the ES values did not correlate with each other (r = –0.06, N = 22 studies, p = 0.81). Pollution tended to have more adverse impact on mycorrhizal fungi compared to saprotrophic fungi; however, as the Q_B-values did not indicate statistical difference, we pooled all functional groups in the subsequent analysis (Table 5).

Sources of Variation in Fungal Responses to Pollution

Analysis comparing polluter types included those classes that had minimum two studies (SO_2 emitters, non-ferrous metal smelters, fertilizer, synthetic fibre, chemical and cement factories for abundance and SO_2 emitters, non-ferrous and aluminium smelters and fertilizer factories for diversity). The analysis suggested differences between the polluter types in the case of diversity (abundance $Q_B = 6.89$, df = 5, p = 0.23, diversity $Q_B = 16.29$, df = 3, p < 0.001). Among the compared polluter classes cement factories had a significant negative impact on abundance; diversity significantly decreased near nonferrous and aluminium smelters and fertilizer factories. Polluters emitting both SO_2 and heavy metals (non-ferrous smelters) demonstrated more pronounced impact on diversity then polluters that do not emit heavy metals, while changes in fungal abundance around these two classes of polluters were similar (Table 5). We did not detect statistical difference between acid and alkaline polluters, although the acid polluters tended to have more negative effect on abundance (Table 5).

Pollution severity did not have any statistically significant impact on abundance although the average ES value tended to be more negative among the high impact polluters (Table 5). In the case of diversity the difference between high vs. low impact polluters was more pronounced (Table 5). When effects of pollution severity were compared within two subgroups (among acid polluters and among SO_2 emitters and non-ferrous smelters), there were no differences for changes in abundance in either of the groups ($Q_B = 0.66$, df = 1, p = 0.42, and $Q_B = 0.87$, df = 1, p = 0.35, respectively). In the case of diversity, pollution severity had a statistically significant impact in the latter group ($Q_B = 2.44$, df = 1, p = 0.12, and $Q_B = 5.64$, df =1, p = 0.018, respectively). We did not find any relationship between annual emission of principal pollutants (Table 3) and ES values (correlation analysis, data not shown).

Categorical analysis on pollution longevity indicated that polluters operating during the longest time were most harmful (Table 5). However, correlation analysis failed to detect significant relationship between longevity of impact and ES (abundance: $r = -0.08$, N = 86 studies, p = 0.49; diversity: $r = -0.03$, N = 32 studies, p = 0.86).

Pollution effects on fungal abundance and diversity did not differ significantly between the vegetation zones (abundance: $Q_B = 2.57$, df = 4, p = 0.63; diversity: $Q_B = 2.61$, df = 3, p = 0.46). We did not detect significant latitudinal trend in effects sizes for abundance ($r_s = 0.14$, N = 52 studies, p = 0.30), but in the case of diversity (data set corrected by exclusion of four outliers, see Materials and Methods) adverse effects were stronger in high latitudes, e.g. in Arctic and subarctic regions (Figure 6).

Positive ES values were more often reported in the studies carried out near polluters operating less than 21 yrs than near old polluters ($\chi^2 = 6.5$, df = 2, p = 0.039); near SO_2 emitters compared to non-ferrous smelters ($\chi^2 = 9.3$, df =1, p = 0.002) and near polluters with lower pollution impact compared to high impact polluters ($\chi^2 = 6.9$, df = 1, p = 0.009).

Table 5. Sources of variation in fungal responsers to pollution: summary statistics[1].

Source of variation	Categories	Abundance[2]				Diversity[2]			
		N	r	95% CI	Q_B/P/FS[3]	N	r	95% CI	Q_B/P/FS[3]
Impact longevity (years)	1 - 20	26	− 0.09	− 0.54...0.37	1.93/0.38/236	5	0.16	− 0.36...0.52	7.14/0.03/117
	21 - 50	28	− 0.37	− 0.63...0.03		10	− 0.45	− 0.75...0.05	
	51 - 318	33	− 0.40*	− 0.56...− 0.18		13	− 0.70*	− 0.85...− 0.46	
Pollution severity	High	20	− 0.36	− 0.65...0.10	0.68/0.41/12	8	− 0.61*	− 0.86...− 0.13	0.68/0.41/32
	Low	32	− 0.14	− 0.46...0.15		11	− 0.37	− 0.70...0.06	
Polluter type[4]	SO_2	14	− 0.27	− 0.59...0.18	0.15/0.70/44	6	0.13	− 0.43...0.42	5.88/0.02/7
	NF	24	− 0.37*	− 0.63...− 0.01		8	− 0.62*	− 0.86...− 0.26	
Functional group of fungi	Mycorrhizal	29	− 0.44*	− 0.63...− 0.11	2.84/0.09/43	14	− 0.47*	− 0.72...− 0.06	1.02/0.31/245
	Saprotrophic	48	− 0.08	− 0.36...0.24		18	− 0.66*	− 0.82...− 0.45	
pH	Acid	33	− 0.36*	− 0.58...− 0.08	2.58/0.11/16	12	− 0.44*	− 0.73...− 0.04	1.01/0.31/84
	Alkaline	18	0.05	− 0.41...0.46		10	− 0.70*	− 0.89...− 0.24	

[1]Compareson between functional groups based on the entire data set; other analyses were carried out by using polluter-specific means of ES. Diversity analyses for longevity and severity of pollution were carried out after exclusion of four outliers (see Materials and Methods).

[2]N = sample size; r = mean effect size; 95% CI = confidence interval. Pollution effect is statistically significant (indicated with an asterisk) if 95% CI of the mean effect size does not overlap zero.

[3]Q_B = between class variance heterogeneity; P = probability level (P < 0.05 indicates significant difference between the groups under compareson); FS = fail-safe number (FS > 3N indicates that the result is robust against non-published studies).

[4]SO_2 = polluters emitting mainly sulphur dioxide; NF = non-ferrous metal smelters emitting both SO_2 and heavy metals.

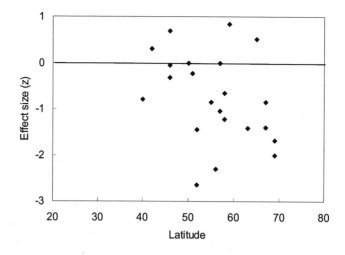

Figure 6. Diversity effect size (*z*) plotted against latitude ($r = -0.49$, N = 19 studies, p = 0.03).

DISCUSSION

Pollution and Soil Fungi: Did the General Pattern Emerge?

Our results suggest that both fungal abundance and diversity decrease with increasing pollution impact with considerably large ES values (–0.29 and –0.59, respectively): we did not find any statistically significant patterns related to pollution severity, pH-impact, vegetation zone or fungal functional groups. The general ES analysis is further supported by the vote-counting, which also suggests significant negative impacts on both abundance and diversity. Our results thus are in line with conclusions published earlier (Wainwright 1988; Pennanen et al. 1996; Meharg & Cairney 2000; Erland & Taylor 2002) and indicate that, in general, pollution impacts on soil fungal communities are negative.

Intriguingly, abundance and diversity ES reported in the same studies did not correlate significantly with each other. This result is difficult to interpret, and as it is based only on a limited data set we suggest that in designing further studies special attention should be paid to the simultaneous exploration of fungal biomass and species richness patterns.

Polluter Type, Longevity and Severity of Impact

Quite predictably, we detected significant variation in fungal responses among the principal types of polluters. In particular, our results suggest that SO_2 emissions alone are less detrimental for fungal diversity than the combined emissions of SO_2 and heavy metals. This could be because SO_2 is not accumulated in soil (Larcher 1995), and there are specialized microbes capable of utilizing reduced sulphur (Killham & Wainwright 1984; Wainwright 1988). In contrast, heavy metals are fungitoxic even at relatively low concentrations, for example copper and zinc are used in fungicides (Trappe et al. 1984), which explains pronounced adverse effects.

Polluters with acid and alkaline impact did not differ in their effects on soil fungi, indicating that toxicity of pollutants is more important than changes in soil pH. For example, aluminium smelters and the magnesite plant, which are classified as alkaline polluters, emit fluorine, SO_2, and nitrogen oxides and therefore cause pronounced toxicity problems in the surrounding ecosystems (Kautz et al. 2001; Evdokimova 2001; Rudawska et al. 2003) like the non-ferrous smelters do (Pennanen et al. 1996; Rigina & Kozlov 2000; Anand et al. 2003).

Several alkaline polluters emitted substantial amount of nitrogen oxide. There is a large literature showing that nitrogen depositions decrease ectomycorrhizal sporocarp production and change the community structure (Ohenoja 1988; Arnolds 1991; Dighton & Jansen 1991; Meharg & Cairney 2000; Erland & Taylor 2002). In contrast, reported effects on arbuscular mycorrhiza, ericoid mycorrhiza and soil saprotrophic fungi have been variable (Heijne et al. 1992; Caporn et al. 1995; Johansson 2000; Egerton-Warburton & Allen 2000; Johansson 2001). Neither abundance nor diversity of soil fungi correlated with N emissions (but this may only indicate that our data are poorly suited to evaluate effects of nitrogen oxides).

Our analysis indicated that polluters with a long history caused larger changes both in fungal abundance and diversity, probably due to both accumulation of pollutants into soil, changes in the field and ground layer vegetation and detrimental changes in ecosystems, leading in particular to deterioration of soil quality (Freedman & Hutchinson 1980; Tyler 1984; Killham & Wainwright 1984; Barkan et al. 1993; Chertov et al. 1993; Anand et al. 2003). This pattern can be interpreted as reflecting the general dose-response relationship, and it contradicts our prior expectation that the effects of newly established polluters could be most detrimental due to lack of genetic adaptations. However, it is difficult to draw conclusions about the effects of adaptation on the diversity parameters based in the present data, because they ignore the changes in taxonomic structure of fungal communities (which is often reported to be altered in polluted areas; see e.g. Bååth 1989; Erland & Taylor 2002).

Surprisingly, we found no major differences in fungal responses to polluters with high and low environmental impacts, although the studies carried out near low impact polluters reported positive results more frequently. Absence of statistical difference can of course be interpreted as the result of improper classification, but it may also be that soil fungi are more sensitive to environmental pollution than higher plants used in severity classification (Tyler 1984; Arnolds 1991). It seems likely that the variation related to composition of pollutants and other environmental factors is so high that the severity effect is difficult to detect.

Out results suggest that mycorrhizal fungi tend to be more sensitive towards pollution impact compared to saprotrophs in terms of abundance, but not in diversity. This difference may result from decreased availability and reduced photosynthetic capacity of host plants at polluted sites (McLaughlin & McConathy 1983), which may constrain carbon acquisition of mycorrhizal fungi. Mycorrhizal fungi have been reported to be sensitive also towards 'soft' nitrogenous and SO_2 pollution (Holopainen et al. 1996; Erland & Taylor 2002; Tarvainen et al. 2003) which may, in contrast, favour saprotrophic fungal taxa (Wainwright 1979; Killham & Wainwright 1984; Wainwright 1988; Tarvainen et al. 2003).

Beneficial Effects of Pollution: Fact or Artefact?

Although our results generally indicate negative impacts of air pollution on fungi, as many as 25 % of studies reported an increase in abundance, and 10 % of studies reported an increase in diversity near the point polluters. We found, quite expectantly, that the 'positive' responses were related to short pollution history, lower pollution levels and polluter type so that SO_2 emissions alone may not be highly harmful. Furthermore, there is nothing unusual in 'positive' effects of pollution: for example, some plants clearly benefit from severe pollution impact due to forest decline which leads to increased light availability (Zvereva & Kozlov 2001; Kozlov 2003), and densities of many herbivorous insects increase near the point polluters due to increase in host quality and depression of natural enemies (Heliövaara & Väisänen 1993; Zvereva & Kozlov 2000; Kozlov 2003). Low levels of heavy metal exposure and nitrogen deposition have also been found to favour some soil fungi, especially saprotrophic ones (Erland & Taylor 2002; Tarvainen et al. 2003; Markkola et al. 2004). We therefore conclude that the 'positive' or neutral effects of pollution on fungal communities do exist, and strongly encourage publication of results that on the basis of preliminary inspection appear strange or unexpected.

Redundancy, Knowledge Gaps and Perspectives

We detected significant correlation between latitude and diversity ES values, which supports the view that Northern ecosystems are most sensitive towards anthropogenic disturbances (Chernov 1985). This result is of especial value because it was obtained despite highly unbalanced sampling design: only three studies from tundra and only two studies from the tropical biome were included in our analysis. However, both increases and decreases in fungal abundance due to pollution impact have been reported from tundra (Raguotis 1989; Marfenina & Grigoryev 1992; Kirtsideli et al. 1995), and we can only conclude that more research in both Arctic and tropical biomes is required before the hypothesis on geographical variation in fungal response to pollution can be rigorously tested.

We detected redundancy in studies conducted near non-ferrous metal smelters and power plants. Although this is probably related to the high relative number of this type of polluters, we suggest that more research efforts should now be directed to other kinds of polluters, especially those having alkaline impact (e.g. aluminium smelters and fertilizer factories).

We also found both functional and taxonomical imbalances within our data set. Studies on soil microfungi and ectomycorrhizal fungi were numerous, but studies on arbuscular and ericoid mycorrhiza - important symbionts of herbaceous and ericaceous plants all over the world (Smith & Read 1997), - as well as studies on dark-septate endophytic fungi (Jumpponen & Trappe 1998), were rather limited.

Designing and Reporting Impact Studies: Methodological Comments

The quality of a number of the primary studies cannot be considered satisfactory. Less than half of the publications allowed numerical treatment, which is partially due to the relatively large proportion of book chapters, conference abstracts and proceedings among the data sources included in our study. However, we were forced to use these publications, since they were the only sources of information on the conducted case studies; thus, data from about a half research projects exploring impact of point polluters on soil fungi have never been published in a comprehensive form. The median number of study sites was four, which reflects the most typical situation where a single gradient was explored. This kind of non-replicated design suggests a very serious confounding effect, where site characteristics actually cannot be distinguished from polluter effects [see Crawley (2002) for confounding effect]. Absence of true replicates agrees with the regular absence of statistical tests, which were made only in about one-third of the primary studies reporting numerical information. In the case of individual studies, interpretation has therefore often been statistically incorrect as based on pseudoreplications, but these data were still valuable for the meta-analysis.

We would like to emphasize the importance of proper design in future field studies along pollution gradients: at least two polluted and two unpolluted plots must be studied, and replicated transects in 2-3 different directions from the emission source would significantly increase reliability of conclusions. In this respect, the study of pine bark bud, *Aradus cinnamomeus* around the Harjavalta smelter in SW Finland can serve as an example: observations were conducted along eight transects starting from the polluter, with 8-9 plots established with regular intervals along each transect (Heliövaara & Väisänen 1986). It was also quite common not to mention pollution source in primary papers; especially this was the case among older studies. Naturally, this kind of information should be most critical and obligatorily required in manuscripts reporting point polluter impacts on biota. Since the estimation of causality and dose-response relationships are of primary importance in pollution ecology, biological data should be interpreted in the light of emission and/or contamination data in all primary publications.

CONCLUSION: WAS THE META-ANALYSIS NECESSARY?

Search for a general pattern is especially important in the field of pollution ecology, where the number of primary studies is high and a need for research synthesis is therefore obvious (Gurevitch & Hedges 2001; Kozlov & Zvereva 2003). Numerous narrative reviews on air pollution impacts on mycorrhiza (Andersen & Rygiewicz 1991; Dighton & Jansen 1991; Leyval et al. 1997; Cairney & Meharg 1999; Erland & Taylor 2002), on fungi in general (Gadd 1993) or on soil microbes (Bååth 1989; Tyler et al. 1989) have pointed out negative impacts both on abundance and diversity, but also strongly emphasized the variability among studies. However, the present meta-analysis based on a holistic approach on different fungal research traditions and methods (which, to the best of our knowledge, is the first attempt to numerically analyze the biotic effects of pollution) revealed a general negative response of soil inhabiting fungi to the impact of diverse point polluters. In particular, our results suggest that mycorrhizal fungi may suffer more from pollution than saprotrophic fungi and that pollution impacts may also appear 'positive', especially when the pollution longevity is short and pollution levels low or moderate. Absence of correlations between the effects sizes and annual emissions of individual pollutants suggests that there is no 'leading pollutant' and that the large fraction of fungal responses is due to indirect effects of pollution, acting via environmental changes. In contrast to our expectations, meta-analysis revealed shortage of reliable observational data, especially concerning fungal diversity; the most critical gaps concern studies from tundra and subtropical / tropical biomes, as well as studies on other mycorrhizal types than ectomycorrhiza. We conclude that the meta-analysis allowed to find important regularities in fungal response to pollution and also critically evaluate the level of our knowledge, indicating that high quality observational data are still badly needed to explain and hopefully predict impact of environmental pollution on soil inhabiting fungi.

ACKNOWLEDGEMENTS

We are grateful to the authors of primary studies, local authorities and representatives of industrial enterprises for responding to numerous requests and providing additional information about experimental design and emission sources. Sami Aikio and Vitaly Zverev are thanked for practical arrangements, Andrei Maisov for help in data extraction, Julia Koricheva for methodological comments, John Derome and Jari Oksanen for useful discussions and Eija Toivonen, Annamari Markkola, Anders Pape Møller and Elena Zvereva for comments on the manuscript. The study was financed by the Academy of Finland (project numbers 201991 and 211734).

REFERENCES

Adams, D. C., Gurevitch, J. & Rosenberg, M. (1997). Resampling tests for meta-analysis of ecological data. *Ecology, 78,* 1277-1283.

Al Sayegh-Petkovsek, S. (2004). Types of ectomycorrhizae and their biodiversity at *Fagus* stands in differently polluted forest research plots. *Zbornik Gozdarstva in Lesarstva, 75,* 5-19. (In Slovenian)

Allison, V. J. & Goldberg, D. E. (2002). Species-level versus community-level patterns of mycorrhizal dependence on phosphorus: an example of the Simpson's paradox. *Functional Ecology, 16,* 346-352.

Anand, M., Ma, K.-M., Okonski, A., Levin, S. & McCreath, D. (2003). Characterising biocomplexity and soil microbial dynamics along a smelter-damaged landscape gradient. *Science of the Total Environment, 311,* 247-259.

Andersen, C. P. & Rygiewicz, P. T. (1991). Stress interactions and mycorrhizal plant response: understanding carbon allocation priorities. *Environmental Pollution, 73,* 217-244.

Anttila, P. (1990). Characteristics of alkaline emissions, atmospheric aerosols and deposition. In P. Kauppi, P. Anttila & K. Kenttämies (Eds.), *Acidification in Finland* (pp. 111-134). Heidelberg, Springer.

Arnolds, E. (1991). Decline of ectomycorrhizal fungi in Europe. *Agriculture, Ecosystems and Environment, 35,* 209-244.

Bååth, E. (1989). Effect of heavy metals in soil on microbial processes and populations. *Water, Air, and Soil Pollution, 47,* 335-379.

Babushkina, L. G. & Luganskii, N. A. (1990). Integrated assessment of the state of forest biogeocoenoses in an industrially polluted area. In D. S. Golod & L. M. Nosova (Eds.), *Problems of dendrology and forest ecology,* 20-23 September 1990, Minsk. Abstracts of presentations, Vol. 2 (pp. 566-568). Minsk, V. F. Kuprevich Institute of Experimental Botany, Byelorussian Academy of Science. (In Russian)

Babyeva, I. P., Levin, S. V. & Reshetova, I. S. (1980). Changes in abundance of microorganisms in soils contaminated by heavy metals. In V. V. Dobrovolsky (Ed.), *Heavy metals in the environment* (pp. 115-120). Moscow, Moscow State University. (In Russian)

Badura, L., Gawlowska, H., Górska, B., Mrozowska, J., Smylla, A. & Zwolinski, J. (1976). The occurrence of bacteria, actinomycetes and microscopic fungi in forest soil contaminated by industrial emission. *Acta Biologica Katowice, 2,* 7-38. (In Polish)

Barkan, V. S., Pankratova, R. P. & Silina, A. V. (1993). Soil contamination by nickel and copper in area polluted by "Severonikel" smelter complex. In M. V. Kozlov, E. Haukioja & V. T. Yarmishko (Eds.), *Aerial pollution in Kola peninsula: Proceedings of the international Workshop,* April 14-16, 1992, St. Petersburg (pp. 119-147). Apatity, Kola Science Centre.

Becker, B. J. (1994). Combining significance levels. In H. Cooper & L.V. Hedges (Eds.), *The Handbook of research synthesis* (pp. 215-230). New York, Russell Sage Foundation.

Berlyand, M. D. (Ed.), (1992). *Annual report on ambient air pollution in cities and industrial centres of Sovjet Union. Emission of pollutants.* St. Petersburg, A. I. Voeikov Main Geophysical Observatory. (In Russian)

Bewley, R. J. F. & Parkinson, D. (1984). Effects of sulphur dioxide pollution on forest soil microorganisms. *Canadian Journal of Microbiology, 30,* 179-185.

Bewley, R. J. F. & Parkinson, D. (1985). Bacterial and fungal activity in sulphur dioxide polluted soils. *Canadian Journal of Microbiology, 31,* 13-15.

Bisessar, S. (1982). Effect of heavy metals on microorganisms in soils near a secondary lead smelter. *Water, Air, and Soil Pollution, 17,* 305-308.

Borisova, G. I., Kasimov, A. K., Kovtun, B. P., Orlyanskaya, N. A., Rau, V. E. & Sorokina, G. A. (1983). Assessment of pollution impact on environment around Perm Factory of Synthetic Deterrents. In P. K. Soldatov & T. K. Khamrakulov (Eds.), *Protection of environment in chemical, petrochemical and fertilizer production industries: Abstracts of All-Union symposium,* 21-23 September 1983 (pp. 78-79). Samarkand, All-Union D. I. Mendeleev Chemical Society. (In Russian)

Borowiec, S., Daca, H., Kwarta, H., Marska, B., Michalcewicz, W. & Wronkowska, H. (1984). Influence of the industrial pollution of "Police" chemical plant on microflora of the cultivated and forest soils. *Zeszyty Naukowe Akademii Rolniczej w Szczecinie, 34,* 37-53. (In Polish)

Borowiec, S., Daca, H., Kwarta, H., Marska, B., Michalcewicz, W. & Wronkowska, H. (1985). The effect of emission from "Dolna odra" power plant on selected microorganisms groups from cultivated and forest soils. *Zeszyty Naukowe Akademii Rolniczej w Szczecinie, 37,* 87-101. (In Polish)

Cairney, J. W. G. & Meharg, A. A. (1999). Influences of anthropogenic pollution on mycorrhizal fungal communities. *Environmental Pollution, 106,* 169-182.

Caporn, S. J. M., Song, W., Read, D. J. & Lee, J. A. (1995). The effect of repeated nitrogen fertilization on mycorrhizal infection in heather [*Calluna vulgaris* (L.) Hull]. *New Phytologist, 129,* 605-609.

Cevnik, M., Jurc, M. & Vodnik, D. (2000). Filamentous fungi associated with the fine roots of *Erica herbacea* L. from the area influenced by the Zerjav lead smelter (Slovenia). *Phyton* (Horn, Austria), *40,* 61-64.

Chander, K., Dyckmans, J., Hoeper, H., Joergensen, R. G. & Raubuch, M. (2001). Long term effects on soil microbial properties of heavy metals from industrial exhaust deposition. *Journal of Plant Nutrition and Soil Science, 164,* 657-663.

Chernov, Y. I. (1985). *The living tundra.* Cambridge, Cambridge University Press.

Chertov, O. G., Nadporozshskaya, M. A., Lapshina, I. N. & Grigorieva, O. A. (1993). Soil degradation in surroundings of "Pechenganikel" smelter complex. In M. V. Kozlov, E. Haukioja & V. T. Yarmishko (Eds.), *Aerial pollution in Kola peninsula: Proceedings of the international Workshop,* April 14-16, 1992, St. Petersburg (pp. 159-162). Apatity, Kola Science Centre.

Chwalinski, K., Kwasna, H. & Sienkiewicz, A. (1987). Mycoflora of forest soils on areas covered by the harmful influence of aluminium works in Konin. *Roczniki Akademii Rolniczej w Poznaniu, 179,* 21-34. (In Polish)

Clapperton, M. J. & Parkinson, D. (1990). The effect of SO_2 on the vesicular-arbuscular mycorrhizae associated with a submontane mixed grass prairie in Alberta, Canada. *Canadian Journal of Botany, 68,* 1646-1650.

Crawley, M. (2002). *Statistical computing. An introduction to data analysis using S-plus.* New York, John Wiley & Sons.

Davydova, N. D. & Volkova, V. G. (1984). Change of soil and vegetation properties under impact of emissions from Nazarovo Power Plant. In V. V. Vorobjev & L. M. Korytnyi (Eds.), *Experimental basis for geographical forecasting of the environmental effect of Kansk-Achinsk Industrial Complex* (pp. 16-34). Irkutsk, Institute of Geography. (In Russian)

De Blij, H. J. & Muller, P. O. (1998). *Physical geography of the global environment.* New York, John Wiley & Sons.

Dighton, J. & Jansen, A. E. (1991). Atmospheric pollution and ectomycorrhizae: More questions than answers? *Environmental Pollution, 73,* 179-204.

Dix, N. J. & Webster, J. (1995). *Fungal ecology.* London, Chapman & Hall.

Egerton-Warburton, L. M. & Allen, E. B. (2000). Shifts in arbuscular mycorrhizal communities along an anthropogenic nitrogen deposition gradient. *Ecological Applications, 10,* 484-496.

Erland, S. & Taylor, A. F. S. (2002). Diversity of ectomycorrhizal fungal communities in relation to the abiotic environment. In M. G. A. Van der Heijden & I. R. Sanders (Eds.), *Mycorrhizal ecology* (pp. 163-200). Berlin, Springer.

Evdokimova, G. A. (1996). Biodiversity of microorganisms in the soils polluted by heavy metals. In F. Bussottui, P. Grossoni, E. Paoletti, R. Raddi & A. Tronconi (Eds.), *Stress factors and air pollution. 17th international meeting for specialists in air pollution effects on forest ecosystems,* 14-19 September, 1996, Florence, Italy (p. 77). Firenze, Centro Stampa 2P.

Evdokimova, G. A. (2001). Fluorine in the soils of the White Sea Basin and bioindication of pollution. *Chemosphere, 42,* 35-43.

Evdokimova, G. A., Beresneva, E. V., Lebedeva, E. V. & Svjatkovskaja, M. V. (2004). The influence of fluorine on the soil fungi of forest podzols in the impact zone of aluminium plant. *Mikologija i Fitopatologija [Mycology and Phytopathology], 38,* 66-70. (In Russian)

Evdokimova, G. A., Mozgova, N. P. & Shtina, E. A. (1997). Soil contamination by fluoride and evaluation of the state of soil microflora in the impact zone of aluminum smelter. *Pochvovedenie [Eurasian Soil Science], 0* (7), 898-905. (In Russian)

Freedman, B. & Hutchinson, T. C. (1980). Effects of smelter pollutants on forest leaf litter decomposition near a nickel-copper smelter at Sudbury, Ontario. *Canadian Journal of Botany, 58,* 1722-1736.

Fritze, H. (1991). Forest soil microbial response to emissions from an iron and steel works. *Soil Biology and Biochemistry, 23,* 151-155.

Fritze, H. (1992). Effects of environmental pollution on forest soil microflora - a review. *Silva Fennica, 26,* 37-48.

Fritze, H., Niini, S., Mikkola, K. & Mäkinen, A. (1989). Soil microbial effects of a Cu-Ni smelter in southwestern Finland. *Biology and Fertility of Soils, 8,* 87-94.

Fritze, H., Kiikkilä, O., Pasanen. J. & Pietikäinen, J. (1992). Soil microbial biomonitoring - the reaction of forest soil microflora to environmental stress along a moderate pollution gradient next to oil refinery. *Plant and Soil, 140,* 175-182.

Fritze, H., Pennanen, T. & Vanhala, P. (1997). Impact of fertilizers on the humus layer microbial community of Scots pine stands growing along a gradient of heavy metal pollution. In H. Insam & A. Rangger (Eds.), *Microbial communities. Functional versus structural aspects* (pp. 69-83). Berlin, Springer.

Fritze, H., Vanhala, P., Pietikäinen, J. & Mälkönen, E. (1996). Vitality fertilization of Scots pine stands growing along a gradient of heavy metal pollution: short-term effects on microbial biomass and respiration rate of the humus layer. *Fresenius Journal of Analytical Chemistry, 354,* 750-755.

Fritze, H., Pennanen, T., Siira-Pietikäinen, A. & Vanhala, P. (2000). Effect of heavy metals on soil microflora. In E. Mälkönen (Ed.), *Forest condition in a changing environment - the Finnish case* (pp. 260-265). Dordrecht, Kluwer Academic Publishers.

Gadd, G. M. (1993). Interactions of fungi with toxic metals. *New Phytologist, 124,* 25-60.

Glass, G. V., McGraw, B. & Smith, M. L. (1981). *Meta-analysis in social research.* Beverly Hills, Saga Publications.

Göbl, F. & Mutsch, F. (1985). Schwermetallbelastung von Wäldern in der Umgebung eines Hüttenwerkes in Brixlegg/Tirol. *Centralblatt für das gesamte Forstwesen, 102,* 28-40.

Griffioen, W. A. J., Ietswaart, J. H. & Ernst, W. H. O. (1994). Mycorrhizal infection of an *Agrostis capillaris* population on a copper contaminated soil. *Plant and Soil, 158,* 83-89.

Grishko, V. N. (1989). *Biological activity of soils under anthropogenic environmental contamination by fluorine. Abstract of PhDn thesis.* Dnepropetrovsk, Dnepropetrovsk State University. (In Russian)

Grishko, V. N. (1996). Effect of fluorine pollution on the structure of a soil microbial cenosis. *Pochvovedenie [Eurasian Soil Science], 0* (12), 1478-1484. (In Russian)

Grishko, V. N. (1998). Microbial cenosis in soils polluted by fluorine-containing acidic industrial emissions. *Mikrobiologija [Microbiology], 67,* 416-421. (In Russian)

Grishko, V. N. & Pavlyukova, N. F. (1997). Effects of gaseous industrial emissions on soil microbocenoses. *Pochvovedenie [Eurasian Soil Science], 0 (2),* 254-260. (In Russian)

Gurevitch, J. & Hedges, L. V. (2001). Meta-analysis. Combining the results of independent experiments. In S. M. Scheiner & J. Gurevitch (Eds.), *Design and analysis of ecological experiments* (pp. 347-369). Oxford, Oxford University Press.

Hartley, J., Cairney, J. W. G. & Meharg, A. A. (1997). Do ectomycorrhizal fungi exhibit adaptive tolerance to potentially toxic metals in the environment? *Plant and Soil, 189,* 303-319.

Hasenekoglu, I. & Sülûn, Y. (1990). A study of microfungi flora of the soils polluted by Askale (Erzurum) cement work. *Turkish Journal of Botany, 15,* 20-27. (In Turkish)

Hawkes, C. V. & Sullivan, J. J. (2001). The impact of herbivory on plants in different resource conditions: a meta-analysis. *Ecology, 82,* 2045-2058.

Hedges, L. V. & Olkin, I. (1985). *Statistical methods for meta-analysis.* New York, Academic Press.

Heijne, B., Hofstra, J. J., Heil, G. W., Van Dam, D. & Bobbink, R. (1992). Effect of the air pollution component ammonium sulphate on the VAM infection rate of three heathland species. *Plant and Soil, 144,* 1-12.

Heliövaara, K. & Väisänen, R. (1986). Industrial air pollution and the pine bark bud, *Aradus cinnamomeus* Panz. (Heteroptera, Aradidae). *Journal of Applied Entomology, 101,* 469-478.

Heliövaara, K. & Väisänen, R. (1993). *Insects and pollution.* Boca Raton, CRC Press.

Hillebrand, H. (2004). On the generality of the latitudinal diversity gradient. *American Naturalist, 163,* 192-211.

Högberg, M. N. & Högberg, P. (2002). Extramatrical ectomycorrhizal mycelium contributes one-third of microbial biomass and produces, together with associated roots, half the dissolved carbon in a forest soil. *New Phytologist, 154,* 791-795.

Holopainen, T. (1989). Ecological and ultrastructural responses of Scots pine mycorrhizas to industrial pollution. *Agriculture, Ecosystems and Environment, 28,* 185-189.

Holopainen, T., Heinonen-Tanski, H. & Halonen, A. (1996). Injuries to Scots pine mycorrhizas and chemical gradients in forest soil in the environment of a pulp mill in Central Finland. *Water, Air, and Soil Pollution, 87,* 111-130.

Ietswaart, J. H. & Griffioen, W. A. J. (1992). Seasonality of VAM infection in three populations of *Agrostis capillaris* (Gramineae) on soil with or without heavy metal enrichment. *Plant and Soil, 139,* 67-73.

Ihaka, R. & Gentleman, R. (1996). R: A language for data analysis and graphics. *Journal of Computational Graphics and Statistics, 5,* 229-314.

Isaeva, L. (2004). Influence of air pollution on species diversity of aphyllophoraceous fungi. In V. Kulikov, V. Razumovskij, O. Chervyakov & O. Kislova (Eds.), *Man and environment in the Barents region at the treshold of the XXI century. International conference proceedings,* August 6-11, 2001, Petrozavodsk – Vodlozero – Varishpelda (pp. 180-182). Petrozavodsk, Karelian Research Centre, Russian Academy of Sciences. (In Russian)

Jennions, M. D. & Møller, A. P. (2002). Relationships fade with time: a meta-analysis of temporal trends in publication in ecology and evolution. *Proceedings of the Royal Society of London, B269,* 43-48.

Johansson, M. (2000). The influence of ammonium nitrate on root growth and ericoid mycorrhizal colonization of *Calluna vulgaris* L. (Hull) from a Danish heathland. *Oecologia, 123,* 418-424.

Johansson, M. (2001). Composition of the saprotrophic fungi in *Calluna* heathland soil and the influence of ammonium nitrate application. *Water, Air, and Soil Pollution: Focus, 1,* 231-239.

Jordan, M. J. & Lechevalier, M. P. (1975). Effects of zinc-smelter emissions of forest soil microflora. *Canadian Journal of Microbiology, 21,* 1855-1865.

Jumpponen, A. & Trappe, J. M. (1998). Dark septate endophytes: a review of facultative biotrophic root colonizing fungi. *New Phytologist, 140,* 295-310.

Kautz, G., Zimmer, M., Zach, P., Kulfan, J. & Topp, W. (2001). Suppression of soil microorganisms by emissions of a magnesite plant in the Slovak Republic. *Water, Air, and Soil Pollution, 125,* 121-132.

Kautz, G., Zimmer, M., Zach, P., Kulfan, J., Topp, W. & Zelinkova, D. (2002). Soil microorganisms suppressed by emissions of a magnesite plant in the Slovak Republic. In B. Mankovska (Ed.), *Long term air pollution effect on forest ecosystems. 20th international meeting for specialists in air pollution effects on forest ecosystems,* 30 August - 1 September, 2002 (p. 143). Zvolen, Forest Research Institute.

Kelly, J. J., Häggblom, M. M. & Tate, R. L. (2003). Effects of heavy metal contamination and remediation on soil microbial communities in the vicinity of a zinc smelter as indicated by analysis of microbial community phospholipid fatty acid profiles. *Biology and Fertility of Soils, 38,* 65-71.

Kieliszewska-Rokicka, B., Rudawska, M. & Leski, T. (1997). Ectomycorrhiza of young and mature Scots pine trees in industrial regions in Poland. *Environmental Pollution, 98A,* 315-324.

Killham, K. & Wainwright, M. (1984). Chemical and microbiological changes in soil following exposure to heavy atmospheric pollution. *Environmental Pollution, 33A,* 121-131.

Kirtsideli, I. J., Vorobjeva, N. I. & Tereshenkova, O. M. (1995). Influence of industrial pollution on the communities of soil micromycetes of forest tundra in Taimyr Peninsula. *Mikologija i Fitopatologija [Mycology and Phytopathology], 29,* 12-19. (In Russian)

Koricheva, J. (2002). Meta-analysis of sources of variation in fitness costs of plant antiherbivore defenses. *Ecology, 83, 176*-190.

Koricheva, J. (2003). Non-significant results in ecology: a burden or a blessing in disguise? *Oikos, 102,* 397-401.

Kotiaho, J. S. & Tomkins, J. L. (2002). Meta-analysis, can it ever fail? *Oikos, 96,* 551-553.

Kovalenko, L. A. (2004). Destabilization of microbial communities in the course of development of adaptation syndrome in soild of forest biogeocenoses of Sverdlovsk region subjected to industrial pollution. In A. N. Semin, I. M. Donnik & M. I. Lukinykh (Eds.), *The food safety - the XXI century: ecological and economic aspects. Collection of scientific papers* (pp. 212-236). Ekaterinburg, Ural State Agricultural Academy. (In Russian)

Kowalski, S. (1981). Communities of soil fungi in the regions polluted by industrial emissions and their influence on the development of *Heterobasidion annosus* [Fr.] Bref. and *Armillariella mellea* [Vahl ex Fr.] P. Karsten. In Anon. (Ed.), *Root and butt rots in Scotch pine stands. European Regional Meeting, IUFRO Working Party, Poznan, Polish Academy of Sciences* (pp.125-137). Poznan, Committee of forest sciences.

Kowalski, S. (1987). Mycotrophy of trees in converted stands remaining under strong pressure of industrial pollution. *Angewandte Botanik, 61,* 65-83.

Kowalski, S. (1996). Biodiversity of soil fungi in converted stands of *Pinus sylvestris* L. as an indicator of environment degradation as the effect of industrial pollution. *Phytopathologia Polonica, 12,* 163-175.

Kowalski, S., Stepniewska, H., Krzan, Z. & Januszek, K. (1992). Communities of rhizosphere fungi as a criterion in evaluating the disease threat to the selected tree species by *Heterobasidion annosum* in converted stands of the upper Silesia industrial district. *Zeszyty Naukowe Akademii Rolniczej im. h. Kollataja w Krakowie, 36,* 137-157. (In Polish)

Kowalski, S., Wojewoda, W., Bartnik, C. & Rupik, A, (1989). Mycorrhizal species composition and infection patterns in forest plantations exposed to different levels of industrial pollution. *Agriculture, Ecosystems and Environment, 28,* 249-255.

Kozlov, M. V. (2003). Density fluctuations of the leafminer *Phyllonorycter strigulatella* (Lepidoptera: Gracillariidae) in the impact zone of a power plant. *Environmental Pollution, 121,* 1-10.

Kozlov, M. V. & Zvereva, E. L. (2003). Impact of industrial polluters on terrestrial ecosystems: a research synthesis. In J. O. Honkanen & P. S. Koponen (Eds.), *Current perspectives in environmental science and technology. 6th Finnish conference of environmental sciences,* 8.-9. May, 2003, Joensuu (pp. 72-75). Joensuu, Finnish Society of Environmental Sciences, University of Joensuu.

Kraigher, H. (1997). Mycobioindication of pollution of two forest sites. *Zbornik Gozdarstva in Lesarstva, 52,* 279-322.

Kraigher, H., Batic, F. & Agerer, R. (1994). Type of ectomycorrhizae on Norway spruce from two differently polluted forest research plots in Slovenia. In R. Cox, K. Percy, K. Jensen & C. Simpson (Eds.), *Air pollution and multiple stresses, 6th International Meeting for specialists in air pollution effects of forest ecosystems* (pp. 365-371). Fredericton, Canadian Forest Services – Atlantic Centre, Natural Resources Canada.

Kraigher, H., Batic, F. & Agerer, R. (1996). Types of ectomycorrhizae and mycobioindication of forest site pollution. *Phyton* (Horn, Austria)*, 36,* 115-120.

Krjuger, L. V. & Shkaraba, E. M. (1987). Mycorrhiza of forest plants in industrially polluted area. *Bulletin of All-Union Institute of Agricultural Biology, 47,* 19-23. (In Russian)

Kulagin, A. Y., Batalov, A. A., Zaitsev, G. A. & Smetanina, E. E. (2002). Adaptive ability of woody plants in industrial environment (with coniferous forests near industrial center of Ufa as an example). In Yu. A. Izrael (Ed.), *Scientific aspects of ecological problems in Russia. Proceedings of All-Russian conference in memory of Acad. A. L. Yanshin,* 13-16 June 2001, Moscow, vol. 1 (pp. 246-251). Moscow, Nauka. (In Russian)

Langkramer, O. (1974). Einfluss der Immissionen auf die Bodenmikroflora in Fichtenbeständen. In Anon. (Ed.), *IX Internationale Tagung über die Luftvereinigung und Forstwirtschaft,* 15-18 October 1974, Mariánské Lázne (pp. 277-281). Zbraslav-Strnady, Ministerium für Forst-and Wasserwirtschaft der CSR Forschungsanstalt für Forstwirtschaft und Jagdwesen.

Langkramer, O. (1975). The influence of immissions on microorganisms and their activities in upper horizons of soils in Norway spruce stands. *Lesnictvi, 48,* 591-612. (In Czech)

Langkramer, O. & Lettl, A. (1982). Influence of industrial atmospheric pollution on soil biotic component of Norway spruce stands. *Zentralblatt für Mikrobiologie, 137,* 180-196.

Larcher, W. (1995). *Physiological plant ecology.* Berlin, Springer.

Lebedeva, E. V. (1986). *Soil micromycetes in surroundings of factories producing nitrate and phosphorous fertilizers. Abstract of PhD thesis.* Vilnus, Botanical Institute, Lithuanian Academy of Sciences. (In Russian)

Lebedeva, E. V. (1993a). Effects of aerial emission on soil microfungi in the Kola peninsula. In M. V. Kozlov, E. Haukioja & V. T. Yarmishko (Eds.), *Aerial pollution in Kola peninsula. Proceedings of the international Workshop*, April 14-16, 1992, St. Petersburg (pp. 272-278). Apatity, Kola Science Centre.

Lebedeva, E. V. (1993b). Soil micromycetes of the nonferrous metallurgy enterprise environs on the Kola Peninsula. *Mikologija i Fitopatologija [Mycology and Phytopathology], 27,* 12-17. (In Russian)

Lebedeva, E. V. & Lugauskas, A. Y. (1985a). Effects of industrial pollution on soil micromycetes. *Mikologija i Fitopatologija [Mycology and Phytopathology], 19,* 16-19. (In Russian)

Lebedeva, E. V. & Lugauskas, A. Y. (1985b). Mycoflora of soils affected by aerial emissions of the fertilizer-producing enterprize. *Proceedings of the Academy of Sciences of the Lithuanian SSR, Ser. B, 4 (92),* 12-20. (In Russian)

Lebedeva, E. V., Nazarenko, A. V. & Vedenyapina, E. G. (1999). Soil micromycetes in the area of "Severstal" metallurgical works (Cherepovets, Russia). *Botanica Lithuanica Suppl., 3,* 107-110.

Leski, T. & Rudawska, M. (2002). Spatial distribution of ectomycorrhizas in Scots pine stand influenced by long term pollution from copper-industrial region in Poland. In B. Mankovska (Ed.), *Long term air pollution effect on forest ecosystems. 20th international meeting for specialists in air pollution effects on forest ecosystems,* 30 August - 1 September, 2002 (p. 157). Zvolen, Forest Research Institute.

Leski, T. & Rudawska, M. (2003). Effect of long-term contrasting anthropogenic emission on ectomycorrhizal community structure of Scots pine stands in Poland. In Anon. (Ed.), *The 4th International Conference on Mycorrhizae (ICOM4),* 10-15 August, 2003, Montreal (p. 714). Montreal.

Lettl, A. & Langkramer, O. (1984). Interrelationships in the soil microbial biocenosis under spruce stand affected by SO_2 immissions. *Ekologia (ČSSR), 3,* 23-34.

Levin, S. V. & Babyeva, I. P. (1985). Impact of heavy metals on the composition and development of yeasts in grey earth. *Pochvovedenie [Eurasian Soil Science], 0* (6), 97-101. (In Russian)

Leyval, C., Turnau, K. & Haselwandter, K. (1997). Effect of heavy metal pollution on mycorrhizal colonization and function: physiological, ecological and applied aspects. *Mycorrhiza, 7,* 139-153.

Light, R. J. & Pillemer, D. B. (1984). *Summing up. The science of reviewing research.* Cambridge, Harvard University Press.

Lositskaya, V. M., Bondartseva, M. A. & Krutov, V. I. (1999). Aphyllophoraceous fungi as indicators of the pine stands status in the Kostomuksha city industrial zone (Karelia). *Mikologija i Fitopatologija [Mycology and Phytopathology], 33,* 331-337. (In Russian)

Lurie, N. Y. (1983). Investigation of population characteristics of micromycetes isolated from soils contaminated by emissions of copper-sulphate factory. In L. G. Dolgova (Ed.), *Ecological aspects of protection and rational exploatation of biological resources: Collection of papers by young scientists* (pp. 76-82). Dnepropetrovsk, Dnepropetrovsk State University. (In Russian)

Lurie, N. Y. (1985). Impact of emissions of metallurgical enterprizes on structure of microbial communities in southern chernozems. *Khimija v Selskom Khozyaistve [Chemistry in Agriculture], 23,* 52-54. (In Russian)

Lurie, N. Y. (1986). *Impact of industrial pollution on structure and function of microbial coenoses in the black earth of Southern Ural. Abstract of PhD thesis.* Moscow, V. V. Dokuchaev Soil Institute. (In Russian)

Makarova, A. P. & Naprasnikova, E. V. (1990). Investigation of the impact of aerosols emitted by power plant on soil microbiota around Kansk-Achinsk industrial complex. In V. A. Krasilov (Ed.), *Ecological problems of wildlife conservation. Abstracts of All-Union conference,* vol. 2 (pp.139-140). Moscow, Academy of Sciences of the USSR. (In Russian)

Marfenina, O. E. & Grigoryev, A. M. (1992). Mycological monitoring of acid precipitation in some coniferous ecosystems at Kola peninsula. In V. Kismul, J. Jerre & E. Lobersli (Eds.), *Effects of air pollutants on terrestrial ecosystems in the border area between Russia and Norway. Proceedings from the first symposium,* 18-20 March, 1992 Svanvik, Norway (pp. 171-176). Oslo, State Pollution Control Authority.

Markkola, A. M., Ahonen-Jonnarth, U., Roitto, M., Strömmer, R. & Hyvärinen, M. (2004). Shift in ectomycorrhizal community composition in Scots pine (*Pinus sylvestris* L.) seedling roots as a response to nickel deposition and removal of lichen cover. *Environmental Pollution, 120,* 797-803.

McLaughlin, S. B. & McConathy, R. K. (1983). Effects of SO_2 and O_3 on allocation of ^{14}C-labeled photosynthate in *Phaseolus vulgaris. Plant Physiology, 73,* 630-635.

Medvedeva, M. V. (2000). Impact of emissions from Kostamuksha ore mining and processing enterprise on biological activity of Karelian forest soils. *Lesnoe Khoziaystvo [Forest Management], 0* (3), 40-42. (In Russian)

Medvedeva, M. V., Bahmet, O. & Yakovlev, A. (2001). Assessment of airborne industrial contamination of soils by microbiological and biochemical methods. In V. Kulikov, V. Razumovskij, O. Chervyakov & O. Kislova (Eds.), *Man and environment in the Barents region at the treshold of the XXI century. International conference proceedings,* August 6-11, 2001, Petrozavodsk – Vodlozero – Varishpelda (pp. 191-193). Petrozavodsk, Karelian Research Centre, Russian Academy of Sciences. (In Russian)

Meharg, A. A. & Cairney, J. W. G. (2000). Co-evolution of mycorrhizal symbionts and their hosts to metal-contaminates environments. *Advances in Ecological Research, 30,* 69-112.

Mekhonoshin, L. E. (1992). Seasonal dynamics of frutification of forest macromycets under impact of pollutants. In V. I. Shubin (Ed.), *Ecology and frutification of macromycets – symbiotrophes of woody plants: Abstracts of presentations* (pp. 39-40). Petrozavodsk, Institute of Forestry. (In Russian)

Mikhailova, T. A. (1997). *Ecological and physiological conditions of forests affected by industrial emissions. Abstract of doctoral thesis.* Irkutsk, Irkutsk State University. (In Russian)

Mitjushina, E. Y. (2002). Study of mycorrhyzas of *Maianthemum bifolium* under industrial impact. In T. K. Golovko (Ed.), *Actual problems of biology and ecology: Abstracts of IX conference of young scientists* (pp. 99-100). Syktyvkar, Institute of Biology of Komi Science Centre. (In Russian)

Møller, A. P. & Jennions, M. D. (2001). Testing and adjusting for publication bias. *Trends on Ecology and Evolution, 16,* 580-586.

Mrkva, R. & Grunda, B. (1969). Einfluss von Immissionen auf die Waldböden und ihre Microflora im Gebiet von Südmähren. *Acta Universitatis Agriculturae Facultas Silviculturae, 38,* 247-269.

Naprasnikova, E. V. & Lut, I. B. (1980). Evaluation of the recent state of microbial communities of basic soils of the Nazarovo depression in the KATEK zone. In A. V. Belov (Ed.), *Integrated geographical researches in the developing regions of Siberia* (pp. 119-126). Irkutsk, Institute of Geography of the Siberia and the Far East. (In Russian)

Nikitina, Z. I. (1991). *Microbiological monitoring of terrestrial ecosystems.* Novosibirsk, Nauka. (In Russian)

Nikitina, Z. I., Naprasnikova, E. V. & Kislotsyna, V. P. (1988). State of microbiota in soils of industrial landscapes. In E. G. Nechaeva & V. A. Snytko (Eds*.), Geography of soils and geochemistry of landscapes in Siberia* (pp. 81-94). Irkutsk, Institute of Geography. (In Russian)

Nikonov, V. V., Lukina, N.V., Polyanskaya, L. M. & Panikova, A. N. (2001). Distribution of microorganisms in the Al-Fe-humus podzols of natural and anthropogenically impacted boreal spruce forests. *Mikrobiologija [Microbiology], 70,* 374-383. (In Russian)

Nordgren, A., Bååth, E. & Söderström, B. (1983). Microfungi and microbial activity along a heavy metal gradient. *Applied and Environmental Microbiology, 45,* 1829-1837.

Nordgren, A., Bååth, E. & Söderström, B. (1985). Soil microfungi in an area polluted by heavy metals. *Canadian Journal of Botany, 63,* 448-455.

Nordgren, A., Kauri, T., Bååth, E. & Söderström, B. (1986). Soil microbial activity, mycelial lengths and physiological groups of bacteria in a heavy metal polluted area. *Environmental Pollution, 41A,* 89-100.

Ohenoja, E. (1988). Effect of forest management procedures on fungal fruit body production in Finland. *Acta Botanica Fennica, 136,* 81-84.

Palmer, A. R. (1999). Detecting publication bias in meta-analysis: a case-study of fluctuating asymmetry and sexual selection. *American Naturalist, 154,* 220-233.

Pancholy, S. K., Rice, E. L. & Turner, J. A. (1975). Soil factors preventing revegetation of a denuded area near an abandoned zinc smelter in Oklahoma. *Journal of Applied Ecology, 12,* 337-342.

Paul, E. A. & Clark, F. E. (1996). *Soil microbiology and biochemistry.* London, Academic Press.

Pavlyukova, N. F. (1986). *Biological activity of soils under contamination with nitrogen-containing chemicals. Abstract of PhD thesis.* Dnepropetrovsk, Dnepropetrovsk State University. (In Russian)

Pavlyukova, N. F. (1989). Interactions between ecosystem components under environmental contamination by nitrogen-containing substances. In A. P. Travleev (Ed.), *Biogeocenological studies of forests in industrial landscapes of Ukrainian steppes* (pp. 126-129). Dnepropetrovsk, Dnepropetrovsk State University. (In Russian)

Pawar, K. & Dubey, P. S. (1985). Changes in soil microflora due to gaseous pollutants from a rayon industry. *Geobios, 12,* 218-220.

Pennanen, T., Fråstegård, Å., Fritze, H. & Bååth, E. (1996). Phospholipid fatty acid composition and heavy metal tolerance of soil microbial communities along two heavy metal-polluted gradients in coniferous forests. *Applied and Environmental Microbiology, 62,* 420-428.

Petrov, A. N. (1988). Ecological structure of the flora of agaric fungi in the area impacted by aerial emissions. In V. A. Mukhin (Ed.), *Investigation of fungi in biocenoses: Abstracts of IV All-Union conference,* Perm, 12-16 September 1988 (p. 140). Sverdlovsk, Institute of Plant and Animal Ecology. (In Russian)

Petrov, A. N. (1992). Symbiotic macromycets in the area impacted by aerial pollution. In V. I. Shubin (Ed.), *Ecology and frutification of macromycets-symbiotrophes of woody plants: Abstracts of presentations* (pp. 47-48). Petrozavodsk, Institute of Forestry. (In Russian)

Polyanskaya, L. M., Nikonov, V. V., Lukina, N. V., Panikova, A. N. & Zvyagintsev, D. G. (2001). Microorganisms of Al-Fe-humus podzols under lichen pine forests affected by aerotechnogenic pollution. *Pochvovedenie [Eurasian Soil Science], 0* (2), 215-226. (In Russian)

Raguotis, A. D. (1989). Impact of industrial emissions on soil microflora in forests of extreme North. In G. M. Kozubov (Ed.), *Ecology of northern forests: Abstracts of presentations of the 1st All-Union meeting,* 2-7 October 1989, vol. 2 (pp. 45-46). Syktyvkar, Institute of Biology, Komi Science Centre. (In Russian)

Read, D. J. (1997). The ties that bind. *Nature, 388,* 517-518.

Rigina, O. & Kozlov, M. V. (2000). The impacts of air pollution impact on the northern taiga forests of the Kola peninsula, Russian Federation. In J. L. Innes & J. Oleksyn (Eds.), *Forest dynamics in heavily polluted regions* (pp. 37-65). Wallingford, CAB International.

Rosenberg, M. S., Adams, D. C. & Gurevitch, J. (2000). *MetaWin: Statistical software for meta-analysis* [2.0]. Sunderland, Massachusetts: Sinauer Associates.

Rosenthal, R. (1979). The "file-drawer problem" and tolerance for null results. *Psychological Bulletin, 86,* 638-641.

Rosenthal, R. (1994). Parametric measures of effect size. In: H. Cooper & L. V. Hedges (Eds.), *The handbook of research synthesis* (pp. 231-244). New York, Russell Saga Foundation.

Rudawska, M., Kielisziewska-Rokicka, B., Leski, T. & Oleksyn, J. (1995). Mycorrhizal status of a Scots pine (*Pinus sylvestris* L.) plantation affected by pollution from a phosphate fertilizer plant. *Water, Air, and Soil Pollution, 85,* 1281-1286.

Rudawska, M., Kielisziewska-Rokicka, B., Staszewski, T., Kubiesa, P. & Szduj, S. (2000). Below-ground mycorrhizal population of Scots pine in three forest stands with different age and impact of air pollutants emitted from the industrial complex in Konin. In D. F. Karnosky (Ed.), *Air pollution, global change and forests in the new millennium. The 19th international meeting for specialists in air pollution effects on forest ecosystems,* 28-31 May 2000, Houghton, Michigan (p. 72). Michigan, Michigan Technological University.

Rudawska, M., Leski, T., Kielisziewska-Rokicka, B. & Staszewski, T. (2002). Effect of long-term contrasting anthropogenic emission on ectomycorrhizal diversity of Scots pine stands in Poland. In B. Mankovska (Ed.), *Long term air pollution effect on forest ecosystem. 20th international meeting for specialists in air pollution effects on forest ecosystems,* 30 August - 1 September, 2002 (p. 164). Zvolen, Forest Research Institute.

Rudawska, M., Kielisziewska-Rokicka, B., Leski, T., Staszewski, T. & Kubiesa, P. (2003). Mycorrhizal community structure of Scots pine trees influenced by emissions from aluminium smelter. In D. F. Karnosky, K. E. Percy, A. H. Chappelka, C. Simpson & J. Pikkarainen (Eds.), *Air pollution, global change and forests in the new millennium* (pp. 329-344). Amsterdam, Elsevier.

Rühling, Å. (1978). Occurrence of higher fungi in an area polluted with copper and zinc. *Staten Naturvårdsverk (SNV) PM, 1028,* 4-32. (In Swedish)

Rühling, Å., Bååth, E., Nordgren, A. & Söderström, B. (1984). Fungi in metal-contaminated soils near the Gusum Brass Mill, Sweden. *Ambio, 13,* 34-36.

Rühling, Å. & Söderström, B. (1990). Changes in fruitbody production of mycorrhizal and litter decomposing macromycetes in heavy metal polluted coniferous forests in North Sweden. *Water, Air, and Soil Pollution, 49,* 75-87.

Ruotsalainen, A. L., Markkola, A. M. & Kozlov, M. V. (2006a). Root fungal colonisation in *Deschampsia flexuosa*: effects of pollution and neighbouring trees. (Submitted manuscript).

Ruotsalainen, A. L., Markkola, A. M. & Kozlov, M. V. (2006b). Mycorrhizal colonisation of mountain birch (*Betula pubescens* subsp. *czerepanovii*) along three environmental gradients: Does life in harsh environment alter plant-fungi relationships? (Submitted manuscript).

Selivanov, I. A., Shkaraba, E. M., Perevedentseva, L. G. & Mekhonoshin, L. E. (1990). Impact of industrial emissions on forest plants interactions with mycorrhizal and pathogenic fungi. In V. A. Krasilov (Ed.), *Ecological problems of nature protection: Abstracts of All-Union conference,* vol. 2 (p. 169). Moscow, USSR State Committee of Nature Protection. (In Russian)

Selivanov, I. A., Shkaraba, E. M., Mekhonoshin, L. E. & Perevedentseva, L. G. (1992). Reaction of mushrooms to environmental contamination. In V. I. Shubin (Ed.), *Ecology and frutification of macromycets – symbiotrophes of woody plants: Abstracts of presentations* (pp. 54-55). Petrozavodsk, Institute of Forestry. (In Russian)

Shebalova, N. M., Kokovkina, T. F. & Babushkina, L. G. (1990). Relationships between accumulation of fluorine-containing substancens in forest soils and litter with species composition of microscopic fungi. *Lesa Urala I Khozyaistvo v Nikh [Forests of Urals and their management], 15,* 163-172. (In Russian)

Sheldon, B. C. & West, S. A. (2004). Maternal dominance, maternal condition and offspring sex ratio in ungulate mammals. *American Naturalist, 163,* 40-54.

Shkaraba, E. M., Krjuger, L. V., Selivanov, I. A., Mekhonoshin, L. E. & Perevedentseva, L. G. (1989). Consortive relationships of forest plants with fungi in the area impacted by emissions of Perm factory of synthetic washing substances. In G. M. Kozubov (Ed.), *Ecology of northern forests: Abstracts of presentations of the 1st All-Union meeting,* 2-7 October 1989, vol. 2 (pp. 94-95). Syktyvkar, Institute of Biology, Komi Science Centre. (In Russian)

Shkaraba, E. M., Perevedentseva, L. G. & Mekhonoshin, L. E. (1991). Consortive relationships of forest plants with fungi in the industrially contaminated area. *Ekologija [Russian Journal of Ecology], 0* (6), 12-17. (In Russian)

Sinitsyna, N. I. & Stefurak, V. P. (1986). Changes in structure of microbial communities and in fermentative activity of soils under impact of aerial pollution. In I. A. Shilov (Ed.), *General problems of biogeocoenology: Abstracts of 2nd All-Union conference,* 11-13 November 1986, Moscow, Vol. 2 (pp. 51-52). Moscow, A. N. Severtsov Institute of Evolutionary Morphology and Ecology of Animals. (In Russian)

Skvortsova, I. N., Stasjuk, N. V. & Gorbatova, V. S. (1982). Structure of microbial community of grey earth under different levels of industrial load. In E. I. Andrejuk & E. V. Balagurova (Eds.), *Structure and functions of microbial communities in soils with different anthropogenic loads: Abstracts of presentations on Republic conference,* 17-21 May 1982, Chernigov (pp. 226-229). Kiev, Naukova Dumka. (In Russian)

Smith, S. E. & Read, D. J. (1997). *Mycorrhizal symbiosis.* London, Academic Press.

Sorokin, N. D. (1990). Microbiological indication of the state of forest ecosystem around Kansko-Achinsk Industrial complex. In G. I. Girs (Ed.), *Diagnostics of the state of vegetation affected by industrial emissions of power plants (recommendations and prognosis)* (pp. 15-21). Krasnoyarsk, V. N. Sukachev Institute of Forest and Timber. (In Russian)

Sorokin, N. D. (1993). Microbiological monitoring of forest ecosystems of Siberia under different anthropogenic impacts. *Uspekhi Sovremennoi Biologii [Advances in Modern Biology], 113,* 131-140. (In Russian)

Sorokin, N. D. & Gukasyan, A. B. (1986). Industrial impact on microbiota of forest ecosystems in Kansk-Achinsk Industrial Complex. In I. A. Shilov (Ed.), *General problems of biogeocoenology: Abstracts of 2nd All-Union vonference,* 11-13 November 1986, Moscow, Vol. 2 (pp. 50-51). Moscow, A. N. Severtsov Institute of Evolutionary Morphology and Ecology of Animals. (In Russian)

Stankeviciené, D. & Peciulyté, D. (2004). Functioning of ectomycorrhizae and soil microfungi in deciduous forests situated along a pollution gradient next to a fertilizer factory. *Polish Journal of Environmental Studies, 13,* 715-721.

Stefurak, V. P. (1981). Impact of industrial pollution on soil microflora. In E. I. Andrejuk (Ed.), *Microbial communities and their sunctioning in soil: Collection of scientific papers* (pp. 158-160). Kiev, Naukova Dumka. (In Russian)

Tarvainen, O., Markkola, A. M. & Strömmer, R. (2003). Diversity of macrofungi and plants in Scots pine forests along an urban pollution gradient. *Basic and Applied Ecology, 4,* 547-556.

Tomilin, B. A., Lebedeva, E. V. & Lugauskas, A. Y. (1985). Fungi as indicators of soil pollution. In T. S. Zakirov & V. N. Li (Eds.), *Proceedings of 7th Congress of All-Union Society of Soil Scientists,* 9-13 September, Tashkent. Part 2 (p. 181). Tashkent, Institute of Soil Science and Agrochemistry, Uzbek Academy of Sciences. (In Russian)

Trappe, J. M., Molina, R. & Castellano, M. (1984). Reactions of mycorrhizal fungi and mycorrhizal formation to pesticides. *Annual Review of Phytopathology, 22,* 331-359.

Treseder, K. K. (2004). A meta-analysis of mycorrhizal responses to nitrogen, phosphorus and atmospheric CO_2 in field studies. *New Phytologist, 164,* 347-355.

Trubina, M. R. (2002a). Fungal symbiosis in plant communities affected by aerial emissions 1. Species characteristics. In Y. M. Alesenkov (Ed.), *Research of forests in Ural. Materials of scientific lectures devoted to the memory of B. P. Kolesnikov* (pp. 65-68). Ekaterinburg, Ural Division RAS. (In Russian)

Trubina, M. R. (2002b). Fungal symbiosis in plant communities affected by aerial emissions 2. Characteristics of plant communities. In Y. M. Alesenkov (Ed.), *Research of forests in Ural. Materials of scientific lectures devoted to the memory of B. P. Kolesnikov* (pp. 68-72). Ekaterinburg, Ural Division RAS. (In Russian)

Tyler, G. (1984). The impact of heavy metal pollution on forests: a case study of Gusum, Sweden. *Ambio, 13,* 18-24.

Tyler, G., Balsberg-Påhlsson, A. M., Bengtsson, G., Bååth, E. & Tranvik, L. (1989). Heavy metal ecology of terrestrial plants, microorganisms and invertebrates. *Water, Air, and Soil Pollution, 47,* 189-215.

Vaichis, M., Armolaitis, K., Barauskas, R., Raguotis, A. D. & Slavenene, L. (1991). Changes in chemical properties and in composition of microflora of forest soils in the impact zone of the factory producing nitrogen fertilizers. In S. V. Zonn (Ed.), *Degradation and rehabilitation of forest soils* (pp. 199-209). Moscow, Nauka. (In Russian)

Van der Heijden, M. G. A., Klironomos, J. N., Ursic, M., Moutoglis, P., Streitwolf-Engel, R., Boller, T., Wiemken, A. & Sanders, I. A. (1998). Mycorrhizal fungal diversity determines plant biodiversity, ecosystem variability and productivity. *Nature, 396,* 69-72.

Van Duin, W. E., Griffioen, W. A. J. & Ietswaart, J. H. (1991). Occurrence and function of mycorrhiza in environmentally stressed soils. In J. Rozema & J. A. C. Verkleij (Eds.), *Ecological responses to environmental stresses* (pp. 114-123). Dordrecht, Kluwer Academic Publishers.

Veselkin, D. V. (1995a). Dynamics of mycorrhiza formation in seedlings of conifers under industrial stress. In E. L. Vorobeichik, S. V. Mukhacheva & I. N. Mikhailova (Eds.), *Mechanisms supporting biodiversity* (pp. 27-28). Ekaterinburg, Institute of Plant and Animal Ecology. (In Russian)

Veselkin, D. V. (1995b). Tolerance of mycorrhizal symbioses of conifers to human impacts. In E. L. Vorobeichik, S. V. Mukhacheva & I. N. Mikhailova (Eds.), *Mechanisms supporting biodiversity* (pp. 28-29). Ekaterinburg, Institute of Plant and Animal Ecology. (In Russian)

Veselkin, D. V. (1996). Mycorrhizal fungi as indicators of industrial disturbance in ecosystems. In E. L. Vorobeichik, S. V. Mukhacheva & I. N. Mikhailova (Eds.), *Problems of basic and applied ecology* (pp. 29-40). Ekaterinburg, Institute of Plant and Animal Ecology. (In Russian)

Veselkin, D. V. (1997a). Diversity of ectomycorrhizas of conifers under pollution impact. In E. L. Vorobeichik & S. V. Mukhacheva (Eds.), *Problems of biodiversity investigation on population and ecosystem levels: Materials of the conference of young ecologists of Ural region,* 1-4 April 1997 (pp.45-51). Ekaterinburg, Institute of Plant and Animal Ecology. (In Russian)

Veselkin, D. V. (1997b). Investigation of mycorrhizal diversity under industrial contamination. *Vertikal: Vestnik of Young Science of Ural, 2,* 59-64. (In Russian)

Veselkin, D. V. (1998). Development of fir on early onthogenetic stages and establishment of mycorrhizas. In I. N. Mikhailova & I. B. Golovachev (Eds.), *Recent problems of population, historical and applied ecology: Materials of the conference of young ecologists* (pp. 12-19). Ekaterinburg, Institute of Plant and Animal Ecology. (In Russian)

Veselkin, D. V. (1999). Response of ectomycorrhiza to industrial impact: the anatomical level. In I. L. Goldberg, I. N. Mikhailova & I. B. Golovachev (Eds.), *Development of ideas by Academician S. S. Schwarz in modern ecology. Proceedings of the conference of young ecologists of the Ural region.* 2-3 April 1999, Ekaterinburg (pp. 11-18). Ekaterinburg, Ekaterinburg Publishers. (In Russian)

Veselkin, D. V. (2002). Diversity of ectomycorrhizas under industrial impact. In: O. Z. Glukhov (Ed.), *Rehabilitation of destroyed natural ecosystems: Materials of the 1st international scientific conference* (pp. 69-73). Donetsk, Donetsk Botanical Garden. (In Russian)

Veselkin, D. V. & Zaitsev, G. A. (2003). Reaction of *Pinus sylvestris* L. ectomycorrhiza under hydrocarbon pollution. In V. G. Sanaev (Ed.) *Eurasian forests - White nights. Materials of the 3rd international conference of young scientists,* 23-29 June 2003 (pp. 232-233). Moscow, Moscow State University of Forestry. (In Russian)

Veselkin, D. V., Zaitsev, G. A., Kulagin, A. Y. & Kuzhleva, N. G. (2003). Reaction of ectomycorrhizas of *Pinus sylvestris* L. on hydrocarbonic contamination. In O. Z. Glukhov (Ed.), *Industrial botany: the state and perspectives of development. Materials of the 4th international conference,* Donetsk, 2003 (pp. 91-93). Donetsk, Donetsk Botanical Garden. (In Russian)

Vogel-Mikus, K., Drobne, D. & Regvar, M. (2005). Zn, Cd and Pb accumulation and arbuscular mycorrhizal colonisation of pennycress *Thlaspi praecox* Wulf. (Brassicaceae) from the vicinity of a lead mine and smelter in Slovenia. *Environmental Pollution, 133,* 233-242.

Volkova, V. G. (1989). Plant resistance under influence of alkaline pollution. *Geografiya i Prirodnye Resursy [Geography and Natural Resources], 0* (3), 34-39. (In Russian)

Volkova, V. G. & Davydova N. D. (1987). *Industrial development and landscape transformation.* Novosibirsk, Nauka. (In Russian)

Vorobeichik, E. L. (1994). Soil microbial community. In E. L. Vorobeichik, O. F. Sadykov & M. G. Farafontov (Eds.) *Ecological standardization of industrial pollution in terrestrial ecosystems (local scale)* (pp. 168-173). Ekaterinburg, Nauka. (In Russian)

Vulfa, L. J. (1985). Impact of calcium-containing dust emissions on soil microbiota. In O. L. Kachalova (Ed.), *Environmental contamination by calcium-containing dust* (pp. 57-60). Riga, Zinatne. (In Russian)

Vurdova, E. V. (2003). Reaction of symbiotrophic fungi to aerial pollution. In I. N. Mikhailova & I. B. Golovachev (Eds.), *Recent problems of population ecology, historical and applied ecology: Materials of the conference of young ecologists* (pp. 234-235). Ekaterinburg, Institute of Plant and Animal Ecology. (In Russian)

Wainwright, M. (1979). Microbial S-oxidation in soils exposed to heavy atmospheric pollution. *Soil Biology and Biochemistry, 11,* 95-98.

Wainwright, M. (1988). Effects of point source atmospheric pollution on fungal communities. *Proceedings of the Royal Society of Edinburgh, 94B,* 97-104.

Warcup, J. H. (1955). On the origin of colonies of fungi developing in soil dilution plates. *Transactions of the British Mycological Society, 38,* 298-301.

Wood, J. M. & Wang, J.-K. (1983). Microbial resistance to heavy metals. *Environmental Science and Technology, 17A,* 582-590.

Yang, C. K. & Yang, S. S. (2001). Microbial ecology of soils surrounding nuclear and thermal power plants in Taiwan. *Environment International, 26,* 315-322.

Yang, S. S., Yang, C. K., Chang, E. H. & Wei, C. B. (1999). The effect of thermal power plant on microbial ecology and environmental quality. *Journal of Microbiology, Immunology and Infection, 32,* 269-277. (In Chinese)

Yarmishko, V. T. (1990). Peculiarities of pine root system development. In B. N. Norin & V. T. Yarmishko (Eds.), *Impact of industrial air pollution on pine forests of the Kola peninsula* (pp. 84-94). Leningrad, V. L. Komarov Botanical Institute. (In Russian)

Zabawski, J. (1983). Seasonal dynamics of microfungi as indicator of soil degradation in the impact zone of the copper smelter. In J. Fabiszewski (Ed.), *Bioindykacja skazen przemyslowych i rolniczych: Materialy pokonferencyjne* (pp. 317-333). Wroclaw, Polish Academy of Science. (In Polish)

Zachinyaeva, A. V. & Lebedeva, E. V. (2003). Micromycetes of polluted soils of the north-west region of Russia and their role in pathogenesis of allergical forms of mycoses. *Mikologija i Fitopatologija [Mycology and Phytopathology], 37,* 69-74. (In Russian)

Zaguralskaya, L. M. (1997). Microbiological monitoring of forest ecosystems in Northern taiga under industrial impact. *Lesovedenie [Forestry], 0* (5), 3-12. (In Russian)

Zaguralskaya, L. M. & Zyalchenko, S. S. (1994). Impact of industrial pollution on soil microbial activity in boreal forests of the Kostomuksha region. *Pochvovedenie [Eurasian Soil Science], 0* (5), 105-110. (In Russian)

Zaitsev, G. A. (2002). Changes in mycorrhyza formation in Sukachev's larch (*Larix sukaczewii* Dyl.) under oil-chemistry contamination from Ufa industrial centre. In T. K. Golovko, S. V. Zagirova & V. G. Zainullin (Eds.) *Actual problems of biology and ecology: Materials of presentations made on 8th conference of young scientists from the Institute of Biology of Komi Science Centre of Ural Branch of the Russian Academy of Sciences* (pp. 295-296). Syktyvkar, Institute of Biology, Komi Science Centre. (In Russian)

Zimenko, T. G., Prokopenko, N. L. & Prokazov, G. F. (1982). Impact of toxic emissions by "Khimvolokno" factory on activity of soil microorganisms. In E. N. Mishustin (Ed.), *Microorganisms as components of biogeocenosis. Materials of All-Union symposium, Alma-Ata, 27-29 September 1982* (pp. 46-47). Alma-Ata, Kazakh State University. (In Russian)

Zvereva, E. L. & Kozlov, M. V. (2000). Pollution suppresses delayed inducible resistance in boreal willow *Salix borealis*. *Ecology Letters, 3,* 85-89.

Zvereva, E. L. & Kozlov, M. V. (2001). Effects of pollution-induced habitat disturbance on the response of willows to simulated herbivory. *Journal of Ecology, 89,* 21-30.

Zwolinski, J., Olszowska, G. & Zwolinska, B. (1987). Soil biological activity as an indicator of industrial pressure on the forest environment (microbiological and biochemical activity). *Acta Agraria et Silvestria, 16,* 25-44.

In: New Topics in Environmental Research
Editor: Daniel Rhodes, pp. 105-112

ISBN 1-60021-172-0
© 2006 Nova Science Publishers, Inc.

Chapter 4

ENERGY, ENVIRONMENT AND POVERTY NEXUS IN DEVELOPING COUNTRIES

Dhulasi Birundha Varadarajan and K. Arockia Raj*

Department of Environmental Economics, School of Economics,
Madurai Kamaraj University, Madurai, India

ABSTRACT

A growing consciousness of the intertwined issues of environment and development and the particular role of energy in the nexus of these issues have been realised at present. As a result of this awareness, voices of concern in support of Environmentally Sound and Sustainable Development (ESSD) are now increasingly heard. The great challenge now is to move from the voicing of concerns to accelerated action and change. The list of environmental issues that are relevant to any discussion of ESSD strategies is long and diverse. Implementing development strategies which include the alleviation of poverty as a central focus must address both the direct and indirect linkages between these environmental issues and poverty.

THE DIMENSIONS OF POVERTY

The concept of poverty refers to an individual's (or family's) lack of access, associated primarily with inadequate income, to basic human needs such as food, shelter, clothing, safe water, sanitation, health care and education.

Operationally, however, poverty standards are typically expressed in single dimensions, the monetary resources that would enable an individual to consume either a fixed bundle of basic goods and services (absolute poverty) or some fraction of the bundle of goods and services that some reference group is able to or actually does, consume (relative poverty).

It has been estimated that, as of 1993, roughly 1.3 billion people in developing countries – 30 percent of their total population – consume less than one dollar per day worth of goods

---

* Correspondence to Dhulasi Birundha Varadarajan: Email: dhulasibirundha@yahoo.com

and services. Statistics on the inability of people in developing countries to satisfy basic human needs corroborate the enormous scale of poverty and highlight its breadth and complexity. For example, an estimated 20 percent of people in developing countries do not have access to health services; 30 percent lack access to safe water and 61 percent lack access to sanitation.

POVERTY AND ENVIRONMENT

The linkages between poverty and the environment are far too complex. An argument is generally made that poor people have a tendency of overusing resources like land, forests and water, thereby degrading them. It was even said one time that poverty is the greatest polluter. There is some evidence to say that the poor are more dependent upon such natural resources. The number of poor being large in several countries, the total environmental damage may look too high. Even then, it is the type of property rights (such as open access, or neglected state properties) that can be a major cause of environmental degradation.

The neglect of the environment in development economics is ironic, because people in poor countries are in great part agrarian and pastoral. Rural people account for about 65 per cent of the population of what the World Bank classifies as low income countries. The proportion of the total labour force in agriculture is a bit in excess of this. The share of agriculture in gross domestic product in these countries is 30 percent. These figures should be contrasted with those from industrial market economies, which are 6 percent and 2 percent, respectively, for the latter two indices (Partha Das Gupta, 1996).

Poor countries are in large measures biomass based subsistence economies, in that the rural poor eke out a living from products obtained directly from their local environment. For example, in its informative study of life in a micro water shed of the Alaknanda river in the Central Himalayas in India, the Indian Centre for Science and Environment reports that, of the total number of hours worked by the villagers sampled, 30 percent was devoted to cultivation, 20 percent to fodder collection, and about 25 percent spread evenly between fuel collection, animal care and grazing. Some 20 percent of time was spent on household chores, of which cooking took up the greatest portion and the remaining 5 percent involved other activities such as marketing.

In Central and West Africa, it has been shown how vital forest products are to the lives of rural people. In many instances, natural resources are of direct value to us as needs for sustaining our lives or as consumption goods (e.g., breathable air, drinkable water and fisheries), in others they are of indirect value, sometimes they are both. The value may be utilitarian (e.g., the resource may be a source of food, or a key stone species in an ecosystem), it may be aesthetic (e.g., a landscape) or it may be intrinsic (e.g., it could be a living animal), indeed, it may be all these things at once. Resource stocks are measured in different ways depending on their character: in mass units (e.g., biomass units for forest, cow-dung and crop residues in number e.g., size of animal herd); in indices of quality e.g., water and air-quality indicators in volume units (e.g., acre-feet for aquifers) and so forth.

Problems of poverty and environmental degradation in developing countries are closely linked (WCED, 1987). The majority of poor people live in rural areas and derive most of their income from soil and forest resources (World Bank, 1990). It has been claimed that poverty may lead to short-planning horizons, which may prevent poor farm households from investing in conservation to protect their natural base. Yet, there have been very few empirical studies of the planning horizon or Rates of Time Preferences (RTPS) among rural poor.

Environmental degradation such as eroding soil, receding forests and vanishing water supplies, is a cause of accentuated poverty among the rural poor in poor countries. There is truth in this. But there is also much accumulated evidence that poverty itself can be a cause of environmental degradation.

This reverse causality arises because some environmental resources (e.g., ponds and rivers) are essential for survival in normal times, while others are a source of supplementary income in times of active economic stress. This mutual influence can offer a pathway along which poverty, environmental degradation and even high fertility feed upon one another in a synergistic manner over time. Indeed, an erosion of the environmental resource base can make certain categories of people destitute even while the economy's GNP increases.

POVERTY ENVIRONMENT AND DEVELOPMENT

Based on the studies after Kuznetz, it can now be said that there is a clear inverse relationship between increase in poverty and economic growth. The relationship between economic development and environmental degradation is quite mixed, between U-shaped, inverted U-shaped, or S-shaped etc. The major issues in the poverty environment and developments are:

An increase in poverty within the community results in increased environmental degradation. Conversely, a reduction in poverty will increase environmental degradation. Other things being equal, an environment inhabited by the poor will be more degraded and become degraded than one inhabited by the rich.

There have been important social changes (policies, external events) that have resulted in concurrent increases in poverty and environmental degradation in a number of developing countries.

Deterioration of the ambient environment hurts the poor more than the rich. But, Jaganathan (1989) looked at rates of deforestation and the level of poverty in West Java and land use and poverty in Nigeria and found little evidence that poverty was a driving force in the deforestation or in the damaging changes in land use.

Policies that change the environment can hurt the poor more than the rich and vice versa. In this regard, Linde Rahr (1998) analyses the effects of income and gender on tree planting. He found that tree planting increases with the increase in female numbers of household members and also increases with the increase in male income.

CPRs AS SOURCE OF LIVELIHOOD

Common property resources also provide the rural poor with partial protection in times of unusual economic stress. For landless people they may be the only non-human assets at their disposal. A number of resources, such as fuel, wood and water for home use, berries and nuts, medicinal herbs, resin and gums are the responsibility of women and children.

The extent of common-property resources as a proportion of total assets in a community varies considerably across ecological zones. In India, they appear to be most prominent in arid regions, mountain regions, and un-irrigated areas. They are least prominent in humid regions and river valleys. The links between under nourishment, destitution and an erosion of the rural common property resource base are close (Das Gupta, 1993, 1996). Jodha (1986) used data from over eighty villages in twelve, districts from six dry tropical states in India to estimate that, among poor families, the proportion of income based directly on the local commons is for the most part in the range 15-25 percent (Jodha, 1995). In his work on the dry lands of India, Jodha (1986) noted a decline in the geographical area covering common property resources ranging from 26 to 63 percent over a twenty-year period. This was in part due to the privatization of land, a good deal of which in his sample had been awarded to the rural non-poor.

The impact of these forms of privatization on the poorest of the poor is confirmed by economic theory. They suggest that privatization of village commons and forest lands, while hallowed at the altar of economic efficiency, can have disastrous distributional consequences, disenfranchising entire classes of people from economic citizenship.

ENERGY POVERTY NEXUS

Energy services are a crucial input to the primary development challenge of providing adequate food, shelter, clothing, water, sanitation medical care, schooling and access to information. Energy therefore is one dimension or determinant of poverty and development, but it is vital.

Energy supports the provision of basic needs such as cooking food, a comfortable living, temperature, high living, the use of appliances, pumping of piped water or sewerage, essential health care, educational aids, communication. Energy also fuels productive activities, including agriculture, commerce, manufacturing, industry and mining. Conversely, a lack of access to energy contributes to economic decline. The energy dimension of poverty – energy poverty – may be defined as the absence of sufficient choice in accessing adequate, affordable, reliable, quality, safe and environmentally benign energy services to support economic and human development.

BIOMASS CONSUMPTION

The reality is that biomass energy is the fuel for the poor. Biomass fuels are used by 3 billion, or half of the Global population, to cook their food everyday. Biomass is contributing as a source of energy in the development and developing world. South Asia, with a population of over 1.2 billion, is largely dependent on biomass energy for meeting the energy needs in member countries. Contribution of such traditional biomass energy in the total energy consumption varies from 33 percent in India to 92 percent in Nepal (Pradeep Chaturvedi, 2000). The WEC projections of biomass energy use are given in Table 1, which shows increasing dependence of biomass energy use.

Table 1. WEC Projection of Bio-Mass Energy use 1998
Role of Bio-mass in Future Global Energy Use (EJ)

Scenario	Year	2025	2050	2100
Shell	1996	85	200-220	-
IPCC	1996	72	280	320
Green Peace	1993	114	181	-
Johnsson et al	1993	145	206	-
WEC	1993	59	94-157	132-215
Dessus et al	1992	135	-	-
Lashof and Tirpak	1991	10	215	-

Scenario	Year	2025	2050	2100
Shell	1996	85	200-220	-
IPCC	1996	72	280	320
Green Peace	1993	114	181	-
Johnsson et al	1993	145	206	-
WEC	1993	59	94-157	132-215
Dessus et al	1992	135	-	-
Lashof and Tirpak	1991	10	215	-

Source: Hall and Screase – WEC's, World Resource Handbook (1998)

FAO's forestry department recently established a Wood Energy Information System (WEIS) which collects the existing data through the implementation of Regional studies (Wood Energy Today for Tomorrow (WETT), 1977). Table 2 explains the wood fuel consumption from 147 countries arranged in line with the FAO classification already used in other documents, such as the state of the world forests. The total production of wood in 1995 reached approx 3900 million cum, out of which 2300 million cum have been used for wood fuels (Table 2). This means that approximately 60 percent of the world's total wood removals from forest and non-forest land have been used for energy purposes. FAO's Regional Wood Energy Development Programme for Asia operating in 16 developing countries in Asia, collected data for their member countries and projected that two-thirds of wood fuels come from non-forest resources (1997).

Table 2. Total Wood Fuel Consumption by Regions 1995

Regions	1000 cum	PJ	Ratio wood Fuel / All Energy	Ratio Wood Fuel / All Wood Uses
Development Countries	1763262	17633	0.15	0.80
Developed Countries	536754	5368	0.02	0.31
World	2300016	23000	0.07	0.59

Source: FAO State, United Nations Energy Year Book 1997, Wood Energy Today for Tomorrow Studies (FAO 1997).

World production of fuel wood for energy use in 1995 is estimated to be about 1.9 billion cum or 1.4 billion tonnes (FAO, 1998). An estimated additional amount equivalent to some

0.3 billion tonnes of wood is recovered and recycled for energy use. The total of 1.7 billion tonnes of fuel wood is equivalent to 550 million tonnes of oil. Compared to 9 giga tonnes of oil equivalent of primary energy supply in 1990, it stands at 6.7 percent. Most of it (76 percent) is used in developing countries. The balance of 24 percent fuel wood used in developed countries represents only 2 percent of their total energy consumption; 44 percent of the total wood fuel consumed in the world is used in Asian countries.

ENERGY CARRIERS

Roughly 2 billion people depend mainly on traditional fuels for cooking. Households use fuel in a variety of activities, including cooking, water heating and lighting. Different energy carriers can be used for each of these activities. These carriers form what is commonly referred to as an energy ladder for that activity. It is well known that people living in poverty tend to rely on a significantly different set of energy carriers than the rich.

Each rung corresponds to the dominant fuel used by a particular income group, and occupy different rungs (Hozier and Dowd, 1987; Reddy and Reddy, 1994). Wood, dung and other biomass fuels represent the lowest rung on the energy ladder for cooking. Charcoal and coal (when available) and kerosene represent higher steps up the ladder to the highest rungs, electricity and LPG.

ENVIRONMENTAL ASPECTS OF BIOMASS CONSUMPTION

The ordering of fuels on the energy ladder also tends to correspond to the efficiency of the associated systems and their cleanliness. For example, the cooking stove efficiencies of firewood, kerosene and gas are roughly 15, 50 and 65 percent respectively.

The emission of wood energy systems normally depend on the type and scale of the system and its operation. Conversion related emissions become lower when the scale of conversion unit increases. The most important emissions that can occur are carbon monoxide Polycylo-Aromatic-Carbon Hydrogens (PACs), Nitrogen Oxide (NO_X) particles. Thermal efficiencies in small scale household wood heaters can be around 50 percent but are much lower in less efficient designs.

It appears that the patterns of energy consumption of people living in poverty tend to increase their misery and aggravate their poverty (Leach, 1992; Das Gupta, 1993) for the following reasons: the use of biomass compromises the health of household members, especially when it is burned indoors without a proper stove to help control the generation of smoke outside. Thus, in addition to its relatively high cost, the use of biomass fuel may also promote higher medical care expenditure and diminish the ability of the poor to work productively.

Traditionally, biomass energy has been associated with environmental degradation and health hazards. Biomass for direct combustion is widely discussed. Production of bio-ethanol for transport vehicles is an emerging application where biomass can substantially avoid carbon emissions. Bio fuel production is regarded as a carbon sink; the total amount of carbon stored per hectare under the bio-energy crop is greater than the level of stored carbon in the vegetation previously on that land.

In India, the National Project on Biogas Development (NPBD, 1981-82) aimed at setting up 12 million biogas plants based on cattle dung, and 2.7 million biogas plants have been set up till March 1998. In the year 1997-98, the improved cooking stove on average saved about 400 kg of fuel wood equivalent per year. Fuel wood based biomass gasifier systems, with capacitities of up to 500 Kw, have been developed indigenously and are manufactured in the country. The biomass based cogeneration programme of 25-30 MW has been attracting the interest of a number of small and medium industries from other countries.

CONCLUSION

To conclude, the challenges of finding more sustainable growth paths and dealing with the nexus of poverty, energy and environment are too great and the intellectual and financial resources available are too scarce for multiple agendas and insensitive or ill-conceived positions.

A consideration of characteristics associated with sustainable development should include: development strategies to provide all people, especially the poor, with livelihoods which are relatively non-polluting, non-resource degrading and less intensive with respect to purchased inputs.

Solving the many problems of the poverty – environment nexus will require many changes, including the empowerment of poor people. Only when poor people have the requisite energy and other natural resources as well as other factors of income and wealth generation, will they be able to and want to act to conserve these resources.

Poor people must have access and control over not just energy and other natural resources, but the other factors of production critical to sustainable development, namely management capacity, to implement this know-how.

Sustainable development means information and management intensive strategies. It is better to educate the rural mass about other matters – namely, the complexities of these intertwined problems of poverty, other natural resource management and the environment, and the challenges in dealing with these problems in societies without well-developed markets, regulatory entities and physical and institutional infrastructure.

Avoid natural resource degradation or depletion except where the economic calculus allowing such depletion explicitly considers the spatial and intertemporal costs and externalities of such depletion. Externalities and use of the common problems are ubiquitous in the developing countries as traditional mechanisms and regulations for common resource management. They often collapse under demographic, commercial and climatic forces.

Thus, if poor people are to have the option of this development path in the midst of many changes, tremendous political, social and financial shifts will be needed. Whether such changes are likely is questionable.

REFERENCES

Jaganathan, V.N. (1989), *Poverty, Public Policies and the Environment*, Environment Working Paper No.24, Washington DC: The World Bank.

Jodha, N.S. (1986), Common Property Resources and the rural poor, *Economic and Political Weekly, 21.*

Jodha, N.S. (1995), Common Property Resources and the Environmental context: Role of biophysical versus social stress, *Economic and Political Weekly, 30,* 3278-3283.

Linde – Rahr (1998), *Rural Deforestation: Gender Effects on Private Investments in Vietnam*, Working paper, Department of Economics: G. Teborg University.

WCED (1987), *Our Common Future*, Oxford University Press, New York.

World Bank (1990), *World Development Report*, The World Bank: Washington DC.

In: New Topics in Environmental Research
Editor: Daniel Rhodes, pp. 113-137

ISBN 1-60021-172-0

Chapter 5

THE IMMISSION LOAD LOWERING WITH THE CHANGE OF THE ALUMINIUM PRODUCTION TECHNOLOGY

Július Oszlányi* and Blanka Maňkovská

Institute of Landscape Ecology, Bratislava, Slovakia

ABSTRACT

Presented report includes the data on the concentration of Al, As, Cd, Cu, F, Fe, Mn, N, Ni, Pb, S and Zn in the foliage of forest tree species, fruit tree species and shrubs in Žiarska basin (pollution zones A, B, C) in the year 1995–2003; methodology of sampling and determination of elements. Anthropogenic loading expressed by means of the coefficient of immission loading (K_z) has decreasing trend. Total Kz of all tree species in Žiarska basin represents in 2003 only 4,9 times higher loading and 29.5 times higher loading in 1995. Total loading by F represented for the year 2003 exceeding of F concentration by 8 times what is 14.2% in comparison with 1995. Total loading by S represented for the year 2003 exceeding of S concentration by 1.8 times what is 64.3% in 2003 in comparison with the year 1995.

In comparison of the state of pollution of ground layer of the atmosphere with the values from the cleanest locality in Europe (Central Norway) only 5 elements (Br, Cl, I, In, Mn) complied with the norm; 10 elements (Ba, Ca, Cs, Cu, K, Mg, Na, Rb, Se, Zn) represented slight loading (1–3 times) and 6 elements (Co, Fe, Hg, Ni, U, V) moderate loading (3-5 times). 16 elements (Ag, Al, As, Cd, Cr, Hf, La, Mo, Pb, Sb, Sc, Sr, Ta, Tb, Th, Yb) represented higher than 5 times increase.

The teeth of roe deer hunted in A pollution zone had the highest concentration of F (550– 4308 mg. kg $^{-1}$). There is statistically significant difference between F

---

* Correspondence to: Július Oszlányi, Director of Institute of Landscape Ecology, Slovak Academy of Sciences, Stefanikova 3, P.O.Box 254, 814 99 Bratislava, Slovak republic. E-mail: julius.oszlanyi@savba.sk. Phone: +421-2- 5249 3882

concentration from A and B pollution and control locality. F concentration dropped in A pollution zone by 35.7% for last 30 years.

On the basis of the analysis of diameter increment of beech in air-polluted area Žiarska basin in the transect in stands Forestry Management Unit Jalná and Forest Management Unit Antol we could draw conclusions that emissions from aluminium plant affected more significantly the increment of forest stands only in the year 1990.

Key words: biomonitoring, air pollution, foliage, mosses, teeth, mapping of F, S, N

INTRODUCTION

Since 1953 problems with the environment pollution in Žiar valley have been connected with the production of aluminium. Aluminium plant is situated on the bank of the river Hron, at the altitude 250 m. Average annual temperature is 8.3°C with extreme temperatures from -30°C in January up to +37.5°C in July. Total precipitation is 706 mm. The region of Žiar valley is closed from several sides, namely in south-west by Pohronský Inovec Mts., in the west and north by Vtáènik Mts. and Kremnické vrchy Mts. and in the east and south-east by Štiavnické vrchy Mts. The area has very unfavourable meteorological conditions regarding the level of the pollution of ground layer of the air by industrial pollutants. About one third of the year is windless, when the valley is aerated badly. In 1967, a new stage of the plant construction continued by the construction of secondary production. A new heating plant was built up in 1986. Annual consumption of raw materials was 600 000 tons (bauxite, coke), 300 000 tons of coal, 150 million m^3 of natural gas, 1300 GWh of electric energy and 14 million m^3 of water. Annual production of Al was 66 000 tons with the production of 315 000 tons of solid and liquid wastes and fallout (fly ashes, Al_2O_3, calcined coke, anthracite) and 17 000 tons of gaseous emission (SO_2, NO_x, F, Cl, Hg). Total production of aluminium reached 2 million tons. Abolishment of a municipality Horné Opatovce, which was situated near to the plant, proves of an injurious effect of this emission. The reconstruction of aluminium plant started in 1986.

A new chapter in the history of the aluminium plant started to be written on 29 February 1996. On that day, the last electrolyser from the old series based on Söderberg technology of aluminium production was shut down. Norwegian company Hydro Aluminium provided a technology for the new production. The implementation of this project contributed to a significant reduction of emission, mainly due to increased efficiency of pollutants' capture. Emission of solid pollutants, fluorine (Fc as HF, Fg as HF, Fs), SO_2, NO_x and CO is being released into the air and measured on emission sources. The mentioned reduction of emission reflected markedly in great reduction of vegetation loading by fluorine (MAŇKOVSKÁ, 1996, 1997, 1998, 2001).

Based on performed works concerning aluminium production it follows that main typical and decisive pollutant is fluorine and from combustion processes sulphur and nitrogen (they are emitted also from other sources) and solid pollutants.

The attention has been paid at the impact of polluted air on forests (Aamlid,Venn, 1993; Abrahamsen, 1980; Ashmore, 1995; Hutchinson et al., 1986; Berg et al., 1995; Karaban et al., 1988; Karaoz, 2003; Nord et al, 2001; Percy et al., 1999; Ruoho et al., 2001; Saare et al.,

2001; Senhou et al., 2002; Stefan, 1995; Stefan et al., 1997; Sutinen ET AL., 1995); forest land (Hovdmand et al., 1997); surface of foliage (PERCY et al., 1995); crown condition and pollution (Solberg et al., 2002); biomonitoring and statistical analyse (Steinnes, 2000; Suzuki et al., 1994; Tokareva, Schepaschenko, 2000; Torseth et al., 2001; Tuovinen et al., 1990).

Following works deal with fluorine emissions (published in the years 1998–2003 by Kluwer Publishing House): Adriano, Doner, 1982; Arnesen, 1997; Arnesen et al, 1995; Arnesen, Krogstad, 1998; Barrow, Ellis, 1986; Neal et al., 1990; Betrand, 1998; Blagojevic Et Al., 2002; Bower, Hatcher, 1967; Braen, Weinstein, 1985; Brewer, 1966; Camargo, Tarazona, 1991; Cameron Et Al., 1986; Care, 1995; Eerden, Van-Der, 1991; Fung et al., 1999; Helrich, 1990 ; Horner, Bell, 1995; Horntvedt, Oyen, 1994; Horntvedt, 1995; Jianyun Ruan, Ming H. Wong, 2000; Muramoto et al., 1991; Phuc, Dam, 1998; Sinha, 1997; Vandersmissen et al., 1993; Weinstein, 1977; Wenzel, Blum, 1992; Wulff, Karenlampi, 1993; Yumada, Hattori, 1977.

With the pollution arising from thermal power plants (published during the years 1998-2003 in Kluwer Publishing House) the following works were dealing: Bellaloui et al., 1999; Brännlund, et al., 1998; Koptsik, Koptsik, Aamlid, 2001; Madhoolika et al., 2000; Meriläinen et al., 2001; Phukan, Bhattacharyya, 2003; Pradhan, Barik, 1999; Rifaat Abdel Wahaab, 2002; Samakovlis, 2003; Wayland et al., 1998).

Emissions of SO_2 cause a noticeable damage to forest stands (Hayami, Ichikawa, 2001; Lindberg, 1992). Many authors deal with accumulation of sulphur in foliage (Ayodele, Ahmed, 2001; Ayrasi et al., 1997; Dogan Kantarci, 2003; Gytarsky et al., 1997); metabolism of sulphur in plants (CRAM et al., 1997; Koivisto et al., 1992; Lofgren et al., 2001; Maňkovská, 1997; Manninen et al., 1977; Maslov, 1978; Raitio, 1992; Rennenberg, 1994).

Emissions of NO_x belong in addition to SO_2 to important injurious agents. Many works dealt with nitrogen, its circulation and influence on growth (Fenn et al., 1999; Flûckner, Braun, 1999; Lovett, 1992; Lovett, et al., 2004; Nellemann, Thomsen, 2001; SIKSTRÖM, 2001). In case of cumulating nitrogen and sulphur in the foliage of forest tree species the ratio of S/N changes and nutrition can be damaged (Bengt et al., 2000; Crescimanno et al., 2000; Ericsson et al., 1993; Kaupenjohan et al., 1989; Tveite et al., 1994; Zöttl, Hüttl, 1986). Simultaneously in addition to the excess of sulphur and nitrogen in the foliage of forest tree species there affect also other injurious agents such as microelements in excess and heavy metals (Haugland et al., 2002; Hlawiczka et al., 2003; Lomander, Johansson, 2001; NYBERG et al., 2001a; Nyberg et al., 2001b).

Some long-term studies about an interaction between leaf surface on trees and atmospheric pollution were carried out (Sharma, 1993; Altieri et al., 1994; SANZ et al., 1995). Effects of atmospheric pollution and epicuticular waxes and stomata were reported through the observations on electron scansion microscope and in some studies was reported the role of SO_2 and other pollutants on morphological leaf wax structure (Gunthard, Goerg, 1991; Krause, Cannon, 1991; Trimbacher, Weiss, 1999, 2004). Alterations in the barrier between tree and atmosphere, the wax cuticle, can have important physiological effects and can therefore be used as a tool to indicate the tree response to abiotic factors. The erosion of epicuticular wax structure and stomatal damage in conifer needles are very widespread phenomena: they are considered important factors in the syndrome of forest decline (Turunen, Huttunen, 1990). SCP - SO_2 and NO_x emissions and organic and solid depositions in Ružomberok forest area was studied and described previously by Maňkovská (1996).

Method of bryomonitoring is based on mapping of heavy metals in the air by means of mosses analyses. There is utilized that characteristic of mosses that they concentrate very effectively heavy metals and other trace elements from the air and precipitation, whereas the concentration of heavy metals in mosses correlates very closely with their concentration in the atmosphere. The methodology is being used intensively for last 20 years in Scandinavian countries and it was adopted by 30 European countries for routine monitoring of metals deposition with very good spatial resolution (Rűhling, Steinnes, 1998). In the framework of the programme "Monitoring of metal atmospheric deposition in the Slovak Republic using mosses analyses" we monitored atmospheric deposition of heavy metals in the years 1991–1997. We carried out mosses sampling on permanent monitoring plots in the grid 16x16 km. On the basis of measurements we constructed element maps, which were presented in the year 1998 in the publication NORD (Rűhling, Steinnes, 1998) and in „Geochemical atlas of Slovak Republic" (Maňkovská, 1996) as well as other publications. In comparison with other European states we can see a significant loading of Slovakia by heavy metals (Maňkovská, 1997). At present the method of biomonitors is being used in many European countries. Two mosses species, which are to forest communities, are being monitored the most frequently In case of each element there was a good linear relation between the concentration of given element in mosses and in precipitation. There is valid equation [concentration in moss] mg.kg^{-1} = [4x atmospheric deposition] mg.m^{-2}.year^{-1} (Rűhling, Steinnes, 1998).

Whole this technique is based on the fact the concentration of heavy metals in mosses correlates very well with atmospheric concentration. It was proven that it is possible to do calibration between the concentration of given element in mosses and the concentration of the same element in the atmosphere (Berg, Steinnes, 1997; BERG et al., 1995).

Primary aim of paper, which is connected with the studies worked out in the years 1995-2002 was solving the effect of polluted air on forest vegetation in Žiarska valley in the year 2003. It was namely evaluation of total concentration of sulphur, nitrogen and fluorine (as the most important air pollutants in broader surroundings) from vegetative organs; air loading in Žiar valley by bioindication by means of mosses on permanent monitoring plots; fauna loading – by means of roe deer and health condition of beech and its diameter increment on 8 plots (SSE transect Opatovce to Počúvadlo) – 1964–2002.

METHODS AND RESULTS

Load of Mosses

The results of analyzing the concentrations of 45 elements (Ag, Al, As, Au, Ba, Br, Ca, Cd, Ce, Cl, Co, Cr, Cs, Cu, Fe, Hf, Hg, I, In, K, La, Mg, Mn, Mo, N, Na, Ni, Pb, Rb, S, Sb, Sc, Se, Sm, Sr, Ta, Tb, Th, Ti, U, V, W, Yb, Zn, Zr) in mosses (mg. m^{-2}.year^{-1}) are given in Table 1. We present separately loading for Žiar nad Hronom and control one - the least polluted central part of Norway.

Table 2 presents exceedance of elements concentrations in comparison with Norway. For Au, Ce, N, S, Sm and Zr data from Norway were not available. As we can see in Table 2, contamination factor for almost all elements is higher than one, it means the concentration of these elements in Slovakia is higher (sometimes 10 up to 100 times higher) than in Norway.

Only the concentration of such elements as bromine and iodine is slightly lower in Slovakia as Norway is a seaside country.

Table 1: Elements concentrations in mosses (mg. m^{-2}.year^{-1})

Element	Žiar	Norway	Element	Žiar	Norway	Element	Žiar	Norway
Ag	0.042	0.005	Hf	0.093	0.002	Sb	0.23	0.01
Al	783	88	Hg	0.040	0.013	Sc	0.120	0.015
As	0.18	0.03	I	0.46	0.50	Se	0.095	0.093
Au	0.0004	-	In	0.02	0.05	Sm	0.060	-
Ba	9.8	4.8	K	1523	750	Sr	17.8	2.9
Br	1.00	1.25	La	0.41	0.07	Ta	0.014	0.001
Ca	1118	780	Mg	428	386	Tb	0.012	0.001
Cd	0.22	0.02	Mn	37	83	Th	0,088	0.010
Ce	0.64	-	Mo	0.27	0.03	Ti	8.5	0.0
Cl	46	50	N	5350	-	U	0.020	0.004
Co	0.175	0.043	Na	80	50	V	1.50	0.34
Cr	1.08	0.17	Ni	0.85	0.28	W	0.063	0.000
Cs	0.08	0.03	Pb	8.0	0.7	Yb	0.045	0.003
Cu	2.1	1.1	Rb	3.00	2.48	Zn	11.3	7.4
Fe	390	91	S	553	-			

Table 2: Exceedance of elements concentrations in comparison with Norway

Element	Žiar	Norway	Element	Žiar	Norway	Element	Žiar	Norway
Ag	7.95	1.00	Hf	61.67	1.00	Sb	16.43	1.00
Al	8.94	1.00	Hg	3.10	1.00	Sc	8.00	1.00
As	5.19	1.00	I	0.92	1.00	Se	1.03	1.00
Ba	2.03	1.00	In	0.37	1.00	Sr	6.17	1.00
Br	0.80	1.00	K	2.03	1.00	Ta	11.20	1.00
Ca	1.43	1.00	La	5.86	1.00	Tb	9.20	1.00
Cd	9.67	1.00	Mg	1.11	1.00	Th	8.75	1.00
Cl	0.93	1.00	Mn	0.44	1.00	U	4.71	1.00
Co	4.12	1.00	Mo	9.81	1.00	V	4.41	1.00
Cr	6.23	1.00	Na	1.61	1.00	Yb	13.85	1.00
Cs	2.46	1.00	Ni	3.09	1.00	Zn	1.53	1.00
Cu	1.95	1.00	Pb	11.89	1.00	K_F	6.60	1.00
Fe	4.27	1.00	Rb	1.21	1.00			

Exceedance of the concentration of elements in mosses in comparison with Norway we expressed by the coefficient of loading by air pollutants K_F and classified it into 4 classes; class 1 – elements are in normal (favourable, standard) concentrations and coefficient does not exceed the value 1; class 2 – light loading (coefficient of loading ranges from 1 to 3); class 3 – moderate loading (coefficient ranges from 3 to 5); class 4 – heavy loading (coefficient is higher than 5) (Table 3).

Table 3: Exceedance of elements concentrations in mosses

Locality	Normal <= 1	Light loading < 1–3>	Moderate loading < 3–5>	Heavy loading > 5
Žiar nad Hronom	Br, Cl, I, In, Mn	Ba, Ca, Cs, Cu, K, Mg, Na, Rb, Se, Zn	Co, Fe, Hg, Ni, U, V	Ag, Al, As, Cd, Cr, Hf, La, Mo, Pb, Sb, Sc, Sr, Ta, Tb, Th, Yb

Contamination of Free Living Roe Deer by Fluorine

Data on the concentration of fluorine in roe deer teeth from three localities in the years 2000-2003 in the vicinity of aluminium plant and control locality Podlavice are given in Table 4. Statistical assessments are presented in Table 5 (Pair comparison of levels pairs) and Table 6 (Comparison of two choices for different dispersions). We found the highest values of fluorine in the locality Lehôtka pod Brehy. The concentration of F ranged from 550 to 4308 mg. kg^{-1}. There is a statistically significant difference between the concentration of F in roe deer teeth from the localities Lehôtka pod Brehy, Lutila, Bartošova Lehôtka and control locality Podlavice. The concentration of F in roe deer teeth ranged from 245 to 410 mg. kg^{-1} in the locality Lutila; in the locality Bartošova Lehôtka from 78 to 264 mg. kg^{-1}; in Trubín it was only 451 mg. kg^{-1}; and in control locality Podlavice it ranged from 178 to 736 mg. kg^{-1}. There is not statistically significant difference between F concentration in roe de er teeth from the localities Lutila, Bartošova Lehôtka and control one Podlavice. Table 7 presents fluorine concentration in roe deer teeth for the years 2000–2003 and 1970 in the vicinity of aluminium plant and control locality. Concentration of F in roe deer teeth in the years 2000–2003 was lower by 35.7% compared to year 1970.

The teeth of roe deer hunted in Lehôtka pod Brehy (A zone of endangerment) had the highest concentration of F (550–4308 mg. kg^{-1}). There is statistically significant difference between F concentration from the mentioned locality and localities Lutila and Bartošova Lehôtka (B zone of loading) and control locality Podlavice. F concentration dropped in A zone of endangerment by *35.7%* for the recent 30 years.

Table 4: Fluorine concentration in roe deer teeth from four localities in the years 2000-2003 in the vicinity of aluminium plant and from control area

Locality	Lutila	Bartošova Lehôtka	Lehôtka pod Brehy	Podlavice	Trubín
X	334	181	2475	420	451
SD	110	95	1796	194	-
Min	245	78	550	178	-
Max	410	264	4308	736	-
Median	367	201	2504	450	-
N	5	3	6	9	1

SD – standard deviation; x – arithmetical mean; med – median; min – minimum; max – maximum;

Table 5: Pair comparison of level pairs – Scheffe method

Compared pair	Difference	Significance	Probability
Lutila – Bartošova Lehôtka	152.8	Insignificant	0.9933
Lutila – Lehôtka pod Brehy	-2141	Significant	0.0012
Lutila – Podlavice	-85.95	Insignificant	0.9974
Bartošova Lehôtka – Lehôtka pod Brehy	-2294	Significant	0.0028
Bart.Lehôtka – Podlavice	-238.8	Insignificant	0.9695
Lehôtka p.Brehy – Podlavice	2055	Significant	0.0006

Table 6: Comparison of two choices for different dispersions

Compared pair	t- test	Critical value	Probability
Lutila – Bartošova Lehôtka	2.321	2.776	0.081[*]
Lutila – Lehôtka pod Brehy	3.923	2.571	0.011[N]
Lutila – Podlavice	1.105	2.228	0.995[*]
Bartošova Lehôtka – Lehôtka pod Brehy	4.192	2.571	0.0086[N]
Bartošova Lehôtka – Podlavice	2.724	2.306	0.0261[*]

[*] Averages are identical; [N] Averages are different

Table 7: Fluorine concentration in roe deer teeth from the year 2000 and 1970 in the vicinity of aluminium plant and in control areas

Endangerment zone	A	B	Control	N
1970	3847		310	15
2002	2475	966	420	21

Note: A (Lehôtka pod Brehy); B (Lutila, Bart.Lehôtka, Trubín); C (Podlavice)

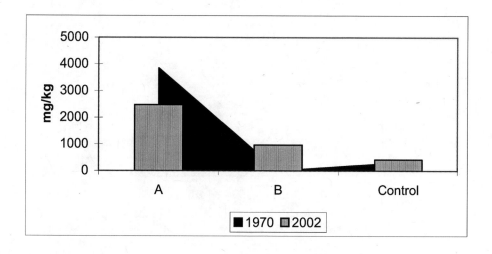

Figure 1: Fluorine concentration in roe deer teeth from the year 2000 and 1970 in the vicinity of aluminium plant and in control areas

Concentration of Elements in Tree Species Foliage in Žiar Valley

Sampling of foliage was conducted in 2003 on the same plots as in 1970–2001 (pollution zone A, B, and C - Figure 1) within the distance of 20 km from the plant. The results of chemical analysis of F, S, N concentration (for the zones A, B, C) are given separately for broadleaved, coniferous and fruit trees for the year 2001 and together with limit values they are presented in the Table 8 with the data for the years 1970–2001. We observed exceeding the limit values for fluorine in all groups of tree species, and for sulphur in broadleaved, fruit trees and shrubs. An interesting fact is exceeding of limit values of nitrogen in broadleaved trees, fruit trees and shrubs. The course of fluorine and sulphur concentrations in 4 groups of tree species for the years 1995–2003 is illustrated in Figure 2. In all tree species groups reduction of fluorine concentration is evident. The course of sulphur concentration in 4 groups of tree species for the years 1995–2003 is illustrated in Figure 3. Sulphur concentration in all studied tree species has slightly decreasing trend, whilst sulphur emission comes also from other emission sources. The course of nitrogen concentration in 4 groups of tree species for the years 1995–2003 is illustrated in Figure 4, whilst in addition to coniferous tree species a slight increase was recorded for other tree species.

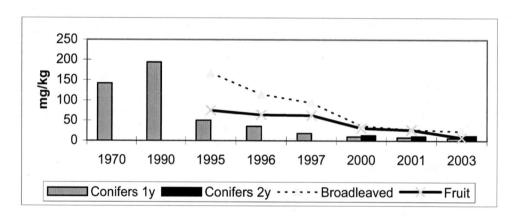

Figure 2: Concentration of F in coniferous and in broadleaved tree species in the years 1970–2003

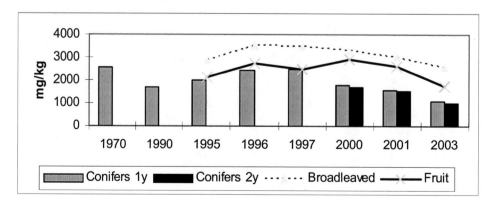

Figure 3: Concentration of S in coniferous and in broadleaved tree species in the years 1970–2003

Table 8. Average concentration of F, S and N in the foliage of 4 groups of tree species in Žiar valley (in mg.kg⁻¹) in the years 1970–2003 in three pollution zones (A, B, C)

Tree species	Coniferous tree species 1 year old	Coniferous tree species 2 years old	Broadleaved tree species	Fruit tree species	Limits* from-to
Element	x(SD)	x(SD)	x(SD)	x(SD)	
F					
1970	*142(97)*	-	-	-	<2.0
1990	*194(67)*	-	-	-	
1995	*50.1(89.5)*	-	*167(410)*	*75.2(51.1)*	
1996	*35.4(50.4)*	-	*115(184)*	*64(58.5)*	
1997	*18.2(12.8)*	-	*94(175)*	*62.7(27.2)*	
2000	*10.0(18.1)*	*13.3(18.4)*	*36.7(61.0)*	*31.1(8.6)*	
2001	*8.0(10.4)*	*10.9(19.9)*	*27.2(52.3)*	*26.4(12.8)*	
2003	*6.6(15.5)*	*12.2(21.6)*	*23.2(56.6)*	*7.7(4.2)*	
N					
1995	16825(3818)	-	*30093(5775)*	24275(5909)	12000–17000
1996	14279(4270)	-	*24612(6396)*	18369(6582)	
1997	15247(3926)	-	*25367(5109)*	19726(5241)	
2000	14338(2005)	14152(2756)	*25117(5454)*	20100(2986)	
2001	14023(3096)	13588(3001)	*26354(4604)*	21440(3968)	
2003	13335(2548)	12485(2156)	*28216(7088)*	24963(5031)	
S					
1970	*2548(605)*	-	-	-	1000–1800
1990	1703(351)	-	-	-	
1995	*1999(468)*	-	*2886(1234)*	*2115(600)*	
1996	*2415(851)*	-	*3503(1618)*	*2735(1172)*	
1997	*2493(566)*	-	*3458(1315)*	*2478(747)*	
2000	1762(214)	1689(265)	*3296(1281)*	*2928(518)*	
2001	1583(358)	1506(379)	*2990 (606)*	*2612(408)*	
2003	1091(308)	1003(229)	*2570(1109)*	1758(481)	

*Innes (1995); Maňkovská (1996); values in italic are exceeded limit values

x – arithmetical mean; SD – standard deviation

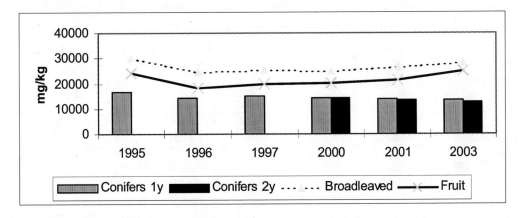

Figure 4: Concentration of N in coniferous, broadleaved tree species and in shrubs in the years 1970–2003

Table 9 presents total concentrations of F, S, N in the foliage of all studied tree species for 3 zones of endangerment (A, B, C) in 2003. Dispersion analysis (ANOVA) is given in Table 10. Comparison of the pairs of concentrations levels for F, S and N for the years 1995–2003 is presented in Table 10. We found statistically significant difference between the concentrations of fluorine in the years 1995/2000, 1995/2001 and 1995/2003.

Statistically significant difference in nitrogen concentrations appeared between the years 1995/2003, 1995/2000, 1996/2000 and 1995/2003. Statistically significant difference in sulphur concentrations appeared between the years 1995/2003, 1996/2000, 1996/2001, 1996/2003 and 2000/2003. T-test for the comparison of concentrations of F, S and N for respective years is given in Table 12. Comparison of the concentrations of F, N and S was statistically significant in respective years and zones of loading.

Table 9: Total concentrations of F, S, N in the foliage of all studied tree species groups for 3 zones of loading (A, B, C) in 2003 (in mg. kg-1)

	F^{95}	F^{96}	F^{00}	F^{01}	F^{03}	N^{95}	N^{96}	N^{00}	N^{01}	N^{03}	S^{95}	S^{96}	S^{00}	S^{01}	S^{03}
X	115	89	25	19	16	25883	19851	19797	20823	21226	2818	3167	2547	2359	1841
SD	277	144	45	39	42	7445	7201	6722	7320	9252	1466	1541	1184	875	1082
Med	22	34	9	6	4	26150	20050	19200	21050	20050	2380	2865	2050	2440	1540
Min	0.01	5.22	2.5	0.6	0.01	10000	7600	10600	8900	8000	1100	940	1347	750	790
Max	2190	868	351	254	303	43800	37490	37500	38500	40300	9450	7320	6849	4500	6330
N	106	76	91	84	90	106	76	91	84	90	106	76	91	84	90

^{95} – 1995; ^{96} – 1996; ^{00} – 2000; ^{01} – 2001; ^{03} – 2003; SD – standard deviation; x – arithmetical mean; med – median; min – minimum; max – maximum;

Table 10: Dispersion analysis (ANOVA), test of significance of factor total effect

Element	Conclusion	Theoretical	Calculated	Probability
F	Significant	2.392	8.705	0.001
N	Significant	2.392	10.901	0.001
S	Significant	2.392	13.429	0.001

Table 11: Comparison of the pairs of the levels of concentrations of F, S and N for the years 1995–2003 (Scheffe methods)

Element Years	F		N		S	
	Difference	Probability	Difference	Probability	Difference	Probability
1995 – 1996	26.09	0.857^N	6032	0.001^*	-349	0.491^N
1995 – 2000	90.03	0.002^*	6086	0.001^*	271	0.686^N
1995 – 2001	95.71	0.001^*	5060	0.001^*	458	0.184^N
1995 – 2003	98.66	0.001^*	4658	0.001^*	977	0.001^*
1996 – 2000	63.95	0.117^N	55	0.999^N	620	0.041^*
1996 – 2001	69.62	0.077^N	-971	0.958^N	808	0.003^*
1996 – 2003	72.57	0.051^N	-1374	0.856^N	1326	0.000^*
2000 – 2001	5.67	1.000^N	-1026	0.940^N	188	0.913^N
2000 - 2003	8.63	0.997^N	-1429	0.812^N	706	0.007^*
2001 - 2003	2.95	0.999^N	-403	0.998^N	518	0.119^N

* – statistically significant difference at the level 0,005; ^{N} – statistically insignificant difference

Table 12: Comparison of the concentrations of F, S and N for respective years of the period 1995–2003

Element	F		N		S	
Years	t- calculated	t- theoretical	t- calculated	t- theoretical	t- calculated	t- theoretical
1995	4.268	1.983[*]	35.794	1.983[*]	19.784	1.983[*]
1996	5.386	1.992[*]	24.034	1.992[*]	17.913	1.992[*]
2000	5.239	1.987[*]	28.095	1.987[*]	20.529	1.987[*]
2001	4.543	1.989[*]	26.072	1.989[*]	24.725	1.989[*]
2003	3.673	1.987[*]	21.763	1.987[*]	16.140	1.987[*]

[*] – statistically significant difference 0.005; [N] – statistically insignificant difference

Table 13 presents the results of correlation between the concentrations of N, S and F in the foliage of tree species according to respective years in the period 1995–2003. The balance of individual elements in plant organisms is a basis for normal growth. Similar chemical characteristics/properties, which follow from about the same ion radicals, probably cause that interactions between respective elements occur inside of plant organism. There exits synergic as well as antagonistic interrelations between individual elements, which are being disturbed by polluted air. MARKERT (1993) as the first explained mutual correlations of P, N, S, K, Ca and Mg for 54 higher and lower plant species. In 2001 and 2003 (Table 13) we found between element pair N/S positive correlation with r higher or equal ± 0.7 in the foliage of all studied tree species in Žiar valley. Mutual correlation with r higher or equal ± 0.5 existed already for N/S in the year 2000 (0.545). Correlation of N/S lower than 0.5 appeared in the year 1995 and 1996. We did not find correlation between N/F and S/F.

Table 13: Correlation between N, S and F for respective years

Elem.	N^{96}	N^{00}	N^{01}	N^{03}	S^{95}	S^{96}	S^{00}	S^{01}	S^{03}	F^{95}	F^{96}	F^{00}	F^{01}	F^{03}
N^{95}	0.194	-0.152	-0.039	0.007	0.494	-0.064	-0.073	-0.058	-0.003	0.267	0.048	0.139	-0.054	0.194
N^{96}	1.000	0.130	-0.119	0.201	0.160	0.334	0.136	-0.102	0.104	0.199	0.368	0.109	0.205	0.052
N^{00}		1.000	-0.139	0.196	0.067	0.029	0.545	-0.100	0.213	0.051	0.049	0.123	-0.088	0.061
N^{01}			1.000	-0.363	-0.223	-0.295	-0.214	0.974	-0.300	-0.274	-0.293	-0.228	0.201	-0.205
N^{03}				1.000	0.192	0.284	0.282	-0.324	0.765	0.293	0.301	0.356	0.086	0.263
S^{95}					1.000	0.239	0.035	-0.221	0.088	0.244	0.093	0.094	0.075	0.208
S^{96}						1.000	0.154	-0.261	0.359	0.148	0.333	0.220	0.114	0.277
S^{00}							1.000	-0.167	0.345	0.140	0.201	0.259	-0.160	0.147
S^{01}								1.000	-0.262	-0.223	-0.258	-0.294	0.205	-0.303
S^{03}									1.000	0.257	0.232	0.314	0.033	0.220
F^{95}										1.000	0.556	0.298	-0.114	0.161
F^{96}											1.000	0.182	0.024	0.059
F^{00}												1.000	-0.144	0.902
F^{01}													1.000	-0.086

[95] – 1995; [96] – 1996; [00] – 2000; [01] – 2001; [03] –2003; marked correlation is valid for p < 0.005

The method of main components (Blackith and Reyment, 1971; Kachigan, 1986 and Suzuki et al, 1994) was used for data processing and determination of interrelations of element concentrations accumulated in the foliage of studied tree species (Table 14). 82.0 %

of total variability was explained by means of 7 factors. All weights of components in PC1 (first main component) to PC7 (last main component) are comparable for the years 1995–2003.

Individual components PC1 up to PC7 have different importance. PC1 accounts for 27.2% of relative variability and has the highest negative values for N and S in 2001 and positive values for N and S in 2003. PC2 accounts for 38.8 % of relative variability and has the highest negative values for N in 1995 and positive values for N and S in 2000. PC 3 accounts/explains 49.7% of relative variability and has the highest negative value for N in 1996 and for F in 2001 and positive value for F in 2003. PC4 (59.6% relative variability) has the highest positive value for N and S in 2001 and for F in 2000. PC 5 (67.9% of relative variability) has the highest negative value for N and S in 2001. PC 6 (75.2% of relative variability) has negative value for F in 1995 and 1996 and the highest positive value for S in 1996. PC 7 (82.0% of relative variability) has the highest positive value for N and S in 2003 and the highest negative value for S in 1996.

Table 14: Varimax PCA analysis of all samples of the foliage for the years 1995–2003

Component	PC 1	PC 2	PC 3	PC 4	PC 5	PC 6	PC 7
Dispersion	4.078	1.747	1.634	1.475	1.247	1.102	1.009
SD	2.020	1.322	1.278	1.214	1.117	1.050	1.005
Relative variability	27.189	11.648	10.894	9.833	8.315	7.345	6.729
Relative variability in %	27.2	38.8	49.7	59.6	67.9	75.2	82.0
N^{95}	0.095	*-0547*	0.103	0.062	-0.345	0.193	0.185
N^{96}	0.180	-0.183	*-0.416*	0.051	-0.118	-0.005	-0.450
N^{00}	0.149	*0.421*	-0.067	0.090	*-0.461*	0.270	-0.186
N^{01}	-0.343	-0.049	-0.162	*0.512*	-0.145	-0.133	0.076
N^{03}	0.345	0.140	-0.178	0.128	0.172	0.105	*0.452*
S^{95}	0.187	-0.411	-0.020	-0.020	-0.207	*0.512*	0.061
S^{96}	0.263	-0.045	-0.236	0.041	*0.320*	0.058	*-0.342*
S^{00}	0.229	*0.397*	-0.048	0.109	*-0.413*	0.086	-0.119
S^{01}	-0.336	-0.019	-0.234	*0.472*	-0.183	-0.133	0.116
S^{03}	0.320	0.219	-0.168	0.156	0.167	0.095	*0.485*
F^{95}	0.270	-0.220	-0.105	-0.079	-0.281	*-0.448*	0.250
F^{96}	0.266	-0.098	-0.329	-0.155	-0.095	*-0.502*	-0.072
F^{00}	0.317	-0.033	0.350	*0.424*	0.073	-0.206	-0.133
F^{01}	-0.054	-0.136	*-0.454*	0.228	0.330	0.254	-0.069
F^{03}	0.281	-0.118	*0.404*	0.429	0.155	-0.043	-0.209

^{95} – 1995; ^{96} – 1996; ^{00} – 2000; ^{01} – 2001; ^{03} – 2003

Fluorine is a non-metallic, negatively univalent element, one of the most reactive elements. It naturally occurs in compounds, mainly fluorite, cryolite and apatite. It is also naturally found in fluoro-acids and *nucleocidine*. It is indispensable for animals, but is not essential for bacteria, algae, fungi and higher plants. The element accumulates in *Acacia georginae, Dichapetalum* ssp., *Gastrolobium grandiflorum, Porifere Dysidea crawshayi*, bones and teeth. Its increased amount indicates the presence of emission, which comes from aluminium production, or other production technologies, as glass production, etc. Fluorine is also a part of emission arising from the combustion of fossil fuels. Mammals need it to strengthen their teeth. Excessive fluorine, however, gives rise to tooth fluorosis of cattle and game - e.g. tooth fluorosis of deer in the Žiar nad Hronom area. Its deficiency causes chlorosis or yellowing of young leaves, anaemia, haemolysis and growth reduction. Fluorine has a structural function in apatite, has antibiotic effects and correlates with heart disease. Concentration above 5 mg.kg^{-1}, especially in the form of F$^-$ and HF, is toxic for plants, and the dose of 2 g a day is lethal for human beings.

Bowen (1979) puts a limit value F for soil 200 mg.kg^{-1} and for plants at 0.02–24 mg.kg^{-1} . Total fluorine concentration in the world plant biomass is estimated by Markert (1992) at 3.682. 10^6 t. MAŇKOVSKÁ (1980) gives a limit value for spruce needles 8.7 mg.kg^{-1} F and Markert (1993) for pine tree 2.0 mg.kg^{-1} F. Hornvedt (1996) found linear dependence between fluorine concentration in the air and the leaves of *Sorbus aucuparia*. The values of fluorine ranged from 16 to 53 mg.kg^{-1} in the surroundings of 5 Norwegian aluminium plants, whereas he determined 4 mg.kg^{-1} as a limit value. INNES (1995) found in 2 years old needles of *P. abies* the values within 2.8-27.5 mg.kg^{-1} and in *P. sylvestris* within 3-11.5 mg.kg^{-1}. The concentration lower than 2 mg.kg^{-1} should be considered as a limit value (MAŇKOVSKÁ, 1996). Arithmetic mean of total fluorine concentration in leaves of all woody plants mentioned in the tion in leaves of individual species are as follows (in mg.kg^{-1}): *F. sylvatica* 5.8±2.6 (median 5.9), *Q. robur* 4.7±2.1 (median-4.9), *P. abies* 6.3±4.2 (median 6.2), *P. sylvestris* 7.8±14.9 (median 6.3) and *A. alba* 8.3±5.1 (median 8.0). The atlas of the maps of all woody plants (Maňkovská, 1996) shows, that fluorine concentration exceeds 5 mg.kg^{-1} in two-thirds of Slovak territory and are clearly associated with industrial plants. Total fluorine concentration above 10 mg.kg^{-1} has been determined in leaves of *P. abies, P. sylvestris and A. alba* in the Žiar valley and Central Spiš (Maňkovská, 1996).

Concentration of fluorine in Žiar valley was reduced in comparison with the years 2003/1995 in all studied groups of tree species. In the year 2003 the concentration of fluorine (in mg.kg^{-1}) in coniferous tree species varied in the range 6.6 ± 15.5 (1y) resp. 12.2 ± 21.6 (2y); broadleaved tree species 23.2 ± 56.6 and within 7.7 ± -4.2 in fruit tree species. The highest values of fluorine were found in the area very close to the aluminium plant (A pollution zone), Figure 2, Table 14. The differences between F concentration and pollution zones B, C and D were statistically insignificant. A marked drop of fluorine concentration was recorded for all studied tree species when compared the years 2003 and 1995.

Sulphur and nitrogen are structural elements. Increased concentration of both elements in plants is caused by polluted air. Sulphur is an important element in biogeochemistry of forest ecosystems on the basis of its role as essential plant nutrition. With damage to forest ecosystem it is necessary to consider three main reasons: damage to roots from humus complex, damage to foliage and redistribution of sulphur into older organs (older leaves, wood, etc.) (Rennenberger, 1994). Sulphur is an important nutrient limiting the growth of plants (INNES, 1995). Sulphur is a non-metallic element, which naturally occurs in valences - 2, (+3), +4, (+5) and +6. The most widespread states are -2 (sulphides) and +6 (sulphates). Sulphur is essential element for all organisms and it forms proteins. Its ecologically toxic forms are SO_4^{2-} and HSO_4^-. The element accumulates in noxious plants Cruciferae, Alium ssp., in sulphur bacteria, vertebrate hair and feathers. Sulphur is a constituent of amino acids (cysteine and methionine), coenzymes, muco-polysaccharide acids and sulphuric-acid esters. Its deficiency very much resembles the deficiency of nitrogen as it gives rise to interrib chlorosis of young leaves and yellowing of leaves. Considerably high concentration of sulphur in soil (gypsum) is well known. The effect of anthropogenic SO_2 emission on latest damage to forest and soil acidification is well known as well. Total sulphur concentration in world plant biomass has been estimated by MARKERT (1992) at 5.523. 10^{10} t. According to Bowen (1979), plants contain 1000–9000 mg.kg^{-1} S. BUBLINEC (1990) and Clement (1985) say that a sufficient concentration in spruce is 1100–1800 mg.kg^{-1} S and in oak and beech 1000–2000 mg.kg^{-1}. INNES (1995) found 750– 1620 mg.kg^{-1} S in two-year-old needles of *P. abies* and 970–1950 mg.kg^{-1} in *P. sylvestris*. Higher values should be considered undesirable. Materna and Mejstřík (1987) say that sulphur concentration in spruce needles ranges within 800–1000 mg.kg^{-1}, what corresponds to our data (MAŇKOVSKÁ, 1988). In air-polluted areas, sulphur concentration in needles is considerably increasing up to 5000 mg.kg^{-1} in the dry matter of 1-year-old needles, what has already an unfavourable effect. Arithmetic mean of total sulphur concentration in the foliage of all tree species in the Geo-chemical atlas (Maňkovská, 1996) is 2163 +1056 mg.kg^{-1} (median 1910 mg.kg^{-1}). Average sulphur concentration in the foliage of individual tree species are as follows (in mg.kg^{-1}): *F. sylvatica* 2242 ± 923 (median 2090), *Q. robur* 2236 ± 1088 (median 2120), *P. abies* 1959 ± 851 (median 1750), *P. sylvestris* 1952 ± 1010 (median 1730) and *A. alba* 2203 ± 943 (median 1940). Exogenous sulphur was found on 0.4% of the surface of analysed foliage of forest tree species. The obtained data on total sulphur concentration in the foliage of forest tree species are surprisingly high in comparison with our data obtained in 1975 (MAŇKOVSKÁ, 1988). They confirm increasing impact of sulphur oxides throughout Slovakia's territory. The concentration of total sulphur higher than 1000 mg.kg^{-1} is present on more than 4/5 of the Slovakia's territory. This concentration is exceeded for all tree species in all industrial areas, military area Lešť and in 5 selected mountainous forests. Concentrations of *sulphur* (mg.kg^{-1}) in coniferous trees were within the range 1091 ± 308 (1 y), 1003 ± 229 (2 y) resp., in broadleaved trees within 2570 ± 1109 and fruit trees 1758 ± 481 (Table 15). They confirm a marked impact of sulphur oxides in the whole Žiar valley. For all studied tree species a marked drop of sulphur was recorded in comparison of the years 2003/1995.

Atmospheric air is composed of about 4/5 volume proportions of elementary nitrogen. Inorganic compounds of nitrogen occur in nature in higher concentration only rarely with except for $NaNO_3$. Nitrogen is indispensable for living organisms, as it is one of elements forming proteins. Nitrogen is structural element and occurs in many organic compounds. Nitrogen is essential for bacteria, algae, fungi, higher plants as well as animals. It is a basic component of protoplasm and enzymes with a majority of metabolic functions. Its deficiency causes dwarfed growth or dwarfish growth, spindly growth of plant, scleromorphosis, yellowing of older foliage. Simple compounds of nitrogen today represent an extensive eco-toxicological problem, e.g. problem of sodium nitrites for animals, NO_2–emission, N_2O as greenhouse gas in the atmosphere. It is ecologically toxic in the form NO_3^- a NH_4^-. Total concentration of nitrogen in plant biomass all over the world is estimated by MARKERT (1992) at 4.602 .10^{10} t. BOWEN (1979) and MARKERT (1992) give for the soils the values 2000 mg.kg^{-1} and for plants 12 000 up to 38 000 mg.kg^{-1}. BERGMAN (1986) considers 13500–17000 mg kg^{-1} sufficient for spruce what is in accordance with the data by BUBLINEC (1990). Though INGESTAD (1962) and TAMM (1977) state, that 17000–25000 mg.kg^{-1} is indispensable for spruce optimal growth. For beech foliage BUBLINEC (1990) considers the values 19000–26000 mg kg^{-1} for oak foliage 18000–30000 mg kg^{-1}. INNES

(1995) found out in 2 y needles of *P. abies* the values 11010–16400 mg.kg^{-1} and in *P. sylvestris* 12500–23200 mg.kg^{-1}. Arithmetical mean of total concentration of nitrogen in the foliage of all tree species according to Atlas is 18165 ± 6432 mg.kg^{-1} (median 15900 mg.kg^{-1}). Average concentration of nitrogen in the foliage of respective tree species (MAŇKOVSKÁ, 1996) represents in mg.kg^{-1}: *F. sylvatica* 19750 ± 6755 (median – 17800), *Q. robur* 20923 ± 6170 (median – 21180), *P. abies* 16640 ± 5220 (median – 15300), *P. sylvestris* 16630 ± 5431 (median – 15600) and *A. alba* 17920 ± 5470 (median – 16900). In the atlas map of all tree species (MAŇKOVSKÁ, 1996) higher concentration of total nitrogen higher than 20000 mg.kg^{-1} is obvious in south and eastern Slovakia. These concentrations are exceeded in the foliage of *F. sylvatica* in the military area Lešť, in Central Spiš and industrial agglomeration Košice; *Q. robur* in Košice agglomeration and in Central Spiš and *P. abies* in Central Spiš.

Concentration of *nitrogen* (in mg.kg^{-1}) in coniferous tree species in Žiar valley varied within the range 13335 ± 2548 (1 year old) resp.12485 ± 2156 (2 years old); in broadleaved tree species within 28216 ± 7088 and fruit trees 24963 ± 5031 (Table 8).

Coefficient of molar ratio S/N in the foliage of coniferous trees ranged from 0.082 ± 0.121(1y) resp. 0.080 ± 0.176 (2y); resp; in broadleaved trees within 0.091 ± 0.156, and fruit trees within 0.070 ± 0.096. S/N ratio is a sensitive indicator of sulphur accumulation in the foliage of forest trees subjected to atmospheric pollution. Molar ratio of protein sulphur and protein nitrogen ranges from 0.05 to 0.15 (STEFAN et al., 1997) and it is relatively constant for all tree species.

S/N ratio is optimally balanced (Table 15) in more than 90% of coniferous and fruit tree species when compared with the limit range in 2003. In the years 1995–2001 it is redundant. In broadleaved tree species it is redundant and our results showed that capability of sulphur to increase exceeded in all cases the need of plants regarding protein synthesis.

Table 15: Coefficient of molar ratio S/N

Years	Coniferous tree species 1year old		Coniferous tree species-2 years old		Broadleaved tree species		Fruit tree species	
	x	SD	x	SD	x	SD	x	SD
1995	0.119	0.123			0.096	0.214	0.087	0.102
1996	0.169	0.199			0.142	0.253	0.149	0.178
1997	0.164	0.144			0.136	0.257	0.126	0.143
2000	0.123	0.107	0.119	0.096	0.131	0.235	0.146	0.173
2001	0.113	0.116	0.111	0.126	0.113	0.132	0.122	0.103
2003	0.085	0.016	0.071	0.008	0.092	0.025	0.068	0.010

CONCLUSION

1. Air pollution was reduced due to the introduction of a new technology of aluminium production. Substances polluting forest stands accumulated in the soil during more than 40 years. It cannot be expected that after the introduction of more modern technology this problem shall be fully eliminated. Only long-term monitoring can show the response of plants to substantial reduction of fluorine concentration in the

air, particularly when the concentrations of other pollutants remain quite high in the soil.

2. Studied tree species in Žiar valley are more subjected to the impact of a complex of factors connected with polluted air and soil, which are even increased due to unfavourable effects of biotic and abiotic injurious agents. In comparison of the year 2003 with 1995 the concentration of F has dropped significantly. The concentration of sulphur was slightly lower as well. The concentration of nitrogen is balanced. By means of nutrition ratios S/N we evaluated the state of the nutrition for studied tree species. Nutrition ratio S/N shows in all cases exceeding of plant need for sulphur in all cases for broadleaved, fruit trees and shrubs. In coniferous tree species the ratio S/N is balanced.

3. Anthropogenic loading of all tree species in Žiar valley, expressed by means of the coefficient of loading by air pollutants was as follows:

   – In 1995 the level of fluorine was exceeded 71 times, of arsenic 3.2 times, sulphur 2.2 times. Total loading of tree species by air pollutants in Žiar valley expressed by means of K_z coefficient represented 29.5 times higher loading;
   – In 1996 the level of fluorine was exceeded 42.5 times, arsenic 4.8 times, sulphur 3.2 times. Total loading of tree species by air pollutants in Žiar valley expressed by K_z coefficient represented 22.9 times higher loading;
   – In 1997 the level of fluorine was exceeded 35 times, of arsenic 10 times and sulphur 3.8 times. Total loading of all tree species by air pollutants in Žiar valley expressed by the coefficient K_z represented 19.4 times higher loading;
   – In 2000 the level of fluorine was exceeded 12.7 times, and of sulphur 3.1 times. Total loading of all tree species by air pollutants in Žiar valley expressed by K_z coefficient represented 7.9 times higher loading
   – In 2001 the level of fluorine was exceeded 9.5 times, of sulphur 2.3 times. Total loading of all tree species by air pollutants in Žiar valley expressed by K_z coefficient represented 5.9 times higher loading.
   – In 2003 the level of fluorine was exceeded 8.0 times, of sulphur 1.8 times. Total loading of all tree species by air pollutants in Žiar valley expressed by K_z coefficient represented 4.9 times higher loading.

4. Anthropogenic loading of all tree species in Žiar valley (pollution zone A, B, C) being expressed by means of the coefficient of loading by fluorine emissions (%) represented a significant decrease to 14.2% compared to the year 1995. We found also a significant decrease being given by the means of the coefficient of loading by sulphur emissions to 64.3% in comparison with 1995.

Years	1995	1996	1997	2000	2001	2003
Kz-F in %	100	75.2	61.9	22.5	16.8	14.2
Kz-S in %	100	114.3	135.7	110.7	82.1	64.3
Kz total in %	100	77.6	65.8	26.8	20.0	16.6

- Total loading by air pollutants of all tree species being given by means of the coefficient Kz represents 4.9 times higher loading, what is in comparison with 1995 only 16.6%.

5. The work summarizes basic information on the state of pollution of ground layer of the atmosphere not only by heavy metals but also by actinides (Th, U) and the elements of precious earths to the extent that has not been carried out up to now in Žiar valley. We used the method of bryomonitoring for this purpose. In comparison with the values from the cleanest locality in Europe (Central Norway) only 5 elements (Br, Cl, I, In, Mn) complied with the norm; 10 elements (Ba, Ca, Cs, Cu, K, Mg, Na, Rb, Se, Zn) represented slight loading (1–3 times higher increase) and 6 elements (Co, Fe, Hg, Ni, U, V) moderate loading (3–5 times higher increase). 16 elements (Ag, Al, As, Cd, Cr, Hf, La, Mo, Pb, Sb, Sc, Sr, Ta, Tb, Th, Yb) represented higher than 5 times increase.

6. The teeth of roe deer hunted in Lehôtka pod Brehy (A zone of endangerment) had the highest concentration of F (550–4308 mg. kg^{-1}). There is statistically significant difference between F concentration from the mentioned locality and localities Lutila and Bartošova Lehôtka (B zone of endangerment) and control locality Podlavice. F concentration dropped in A zone of endangerment by 35.7% for the recent 30 years.

7. On the basis of the analysis of diameter increment of beech in air-polluted area Žiar nad Hronom in the transect SSE in stands Forestry Management Unit Jalná and Forestry Management Unit Antol (Opatovce to Počúvadlo) we could draw conclusions that emissions from Žiar source affected more significantly the increment of forest stands only to the year 1990.

ACKNOWLEDGEMENTS

Please allow us to thank the company SLOVALCO Žiar nad Hronom, namely the director Ing. Milan Veselý for his active interest and for providing the funds. A special acknowledgement comes also to Ing. Roman Kohút for his open ten years collaboration. Dr. Richard Horndtvedt from the Forest Research Institute, Äs, Norway for his recommendations; Prof. Eiliv Steinnes from the University Trondheim for professional tests of the accuracy of the analyses.

REFERENCES

Aamlid, V., Venn, K., 1993: Methods of monitoring the effects of air pollution on forest and vegetation of eastern Finnmark, Norway. *Norw. J. Agric. Sci., 7,* p. 71–87.

Abrahamsen, G., 1980: Leaching of Plant Nutrients. In Drabløs, D., Tollan, A. (eds), *Ecological impact of acid precipitation*, Proc. Int. Conf. SNSF Proj. Norway, 196 pp.

Adriano, D.C., Doner, H.E., 1982: Bromine, Chlorine, and Fluorine. In Page, A.L., Miller, R.H., Keeney, D.R. (eds), *Methods of Soil Analysis. Part 2 - Chemical and microbiological Properties, American Society of Agronomy,* Madison, p. 449–483.

Altieri, A., del Caldo, L., Manes, F., 1994: Morphology of epicuticular waxes in *Pinus pinea* needles in relation to seasonal and pollution-climate. *Eur. J. For. Path., 24:* 79–91.

Arnesen, A.K.M., Abrahamsen, G., Sandvik, G., Krogstad, T., 1995: Aluminium smelters and fluoride pollution of soil and soil solution in Norway. *Sci. Total Environ., 163:* 39–53.

Arnesen, A.K.M. , 1997: Availability of fluoride to plants grown in contaminated soils. *Plant and Soil, 191*: 13–25.

Arnesen, A.K.M., Krogstad, T., 1998: Sorption and desorption of fluoride in soil polluted from the aluminium smelter at Ardal in Western Norway., *Water, Air Soil Poll., 103:* 357–373.

Ashmore, M., 1995: Critical levels for forestry in Europe., In H. Raitio, T. Kilponen (eds) *Critical Loads and Critical Limit Values,* Finnish Forest Research Institute, Research Papers 513, p. 27–35.

Ayodele, J.T., Ahmed, A., 2001: Monitoring air pollution in Kano municipality by chemical analysis of Scots Pine (*Pinus sylvestris* L.) needles for sulphur content. *The Environmentalist, 21: 145–151.*

Ayrasi, M., Pavlov, V., Reimann, C., 1997: Comparison of sulfur and heavy metal contents and their regional distribution in humus and moss samples from the vicinity of Nikel and Zapolarnij, Kola Penninsula, Russia. *Water, Air, Soil Poll., 98*: 361–380.

Baker, E.A., 1982: Chemistry and morphology of plant epicuticular waxes. In Cutler, D.F., , Alvin, K.L., Price, C.E. (eds), *The plant cuticle.* Academic Press, p. 139–165.

Barrow, N.J., Ellis, A.S., 1986: Testing a mechanistic model. III. The effects of pH on fluoride retention by a soil. *J. Soil Sci., 37:* 287–293.

Batič, F., Kalan, P., Kraigher, H., Šircelj, H., Simončič, P., Vidergar- Gorjup, N., Turk, B., 1999: *Water, Air, Soil Poll., 116:* 377–382.

Battisti, A., Tiberi, R., 1999: Effetti del inquinamento e dei cambiamenti climatici sulle popolazioni di insetti forestali. *Linea ecologica, 2:* 33–35.

Bellaloui, A. et al., 1999: Laboratory investigation of the control of acide mine drainage using alkaline papermillwaste. *Water, Air, Soil Poll., 111:* 57–73.

Bengt, A., Olsson, B.A., Lundkvist, H., Staaf, H., 2000: Nutrient status in needles of Norway spruce and Scots pine following harvesting of logging residues. *Plant and Soil, 223:* 161–173.

Berg, T., Røyset, O., Steinnes, E., Vadset, M., 1995: Atmospheric trace element deposition: Principal component analysis of ICP-MS data from moss samples. *Environ. Pollut., 88,* p. 67–77.

Berg, T., Røyset, O., Steinnes, E., 1995: Trace elements in atmospheric precipitation at Norwegian background stations (1989–1990) measured by ICP-MS. *Atmos. Environ,. 28,* p. 3519–3536.

Berg, T., Steinnes, E., 1997: Use of mosses (Hylocomium splendens and Pleurozium schreberi) as biomonitors of heavy metal deposition: From relative to absolute values. *Environ. Pollut., 98,* p. 61–71.

Bergman, W., 1986: Farbatlas Ernährungsstörungen bei Kulturpflanzen. *Fischer, Jena,* 124 pp.

Betrand,-F.R., 1998: The affects of fluoride on ecology. *Water-Sewage-&-Effluent (South Africa), 18* (4) p. 38.

Blackith , R.E., Reyment, R.A. 1971: *Multivariate morphometrics*. Academic Press, London, New York, p. 14–26, 146–189, 201–211.

Blagojevic, S., Jakovljevic, M., Radulovic, M., 2002: Content of fluorine in soils in the vinicity of aluminium plant in Podgorica [Montenegro, Yugoslavia]. *J. –Agric. Sci. (Yugoslavia), 47* (1) p. 1–8.

Bosman, B., Remacle, J., Carnol, M., 2001: Element removal in harvested tree biomass: scenarios for critical loads in Wallonia, South Belgium. *Water, Air, Soil Poll., Focus 1,* p. 153–167.

Bower, C.A., Hatcher, J.T., 1967: Adsorption of fluoride by soils and minerals. *Soil Sci., 103,* p. 51–154.

Braen, S.N., Weinstein. L.H., 1985: Uptake of fluoride and aluminium by plants grown in contaminated soil. *Water, Air, Soil Poll., 24,* p. 215–225.

Brännlund, R., Chung, Y. et al., 1998: Emissions trading and profitability: The Swedish Pulp and Paper Industry. *Environmental and Resource Economics, 12,* p. 345–356.

Brewer, R.F., 1966: Fluorine. In Chapman, H.D. (ed.), Diagnostic Criteria for Plants and Soils. Univ. *California Press, California, p.* 80-196..

Helrich, K., 1990: *Official Methods of Analysis.* Vol. 1. Association of Official Analytical Chemists, Inc., Virginia.

Hlawiczka, S., Dyduch, B., Fudala, J., 2003: Long-term changes of particulate emission in the industrial region of upper Silesia (Poland) and their effect on the acidity of rainwater. *Water, Air, Soil Poll., 142,* p. 151–163.

Horner, J.M., Bell, J.N.B., 1995: Effects of fluoride and acidity on early plant growth. Agric. Econ. Environ., 52, p. 205–211.

Horntved, T.R., 1995: Fluoride uptake in conifers related to emissions from aluminium smelters in Norway. *Science of the Total Environment, 163,* p.35–37.

Horntvedt, R. , Oyen,B. H., 1994: *Effekter av fluorider p°a skog ved norske aluminiumverk. Norsk aluminiumindustri og milj/o* (in Norwegian), Part 6, 27 pp. Alumuniumindustriens Milj/osekretariat, Oslo, Norway.

Hötzl, H., Rosner, G., Winkler, R., 1991: Correlation of [7]Be concentrations in surface air and precipitation with the solar cycle. *Naturwissenschaften, 78, p.* 215–217.

Hovdmand, M.F., Bille-Jansen, J., 1997: Atmospheric input to Danish spruce forests and effects on soil acidification and forest growth based on 12 years measurement. Water, Air, Soil Poll., 116, p. 75–88.

Hunter, I.R.,1994: *Results from the Interlaboratory sample exchange.* IUFRO, Working Group S1.02-08 Foliar Analysis. Natural Resources Institute, Kent, 18 pp..

Hutchinson, T.C., Bozic, L. , Munoz-Vega, G., 1986: Responses of five species of conifer seedlings to aluminium stress. *Water Air Soil Poll,. 31,* p. 283–294.

ICP, 1994: Manual on methods and criteria for harmonized sampling, assessment, monitoring and analysis of the effects of air pollution on forest. 3rd edition, Programme Coordinating Centre West, BHF, Hamburg.

Innes, J. L., 1995: Influence of air pollution on the foliar nutrition of conifers in Great Britain. Environ. *Pollut. 88, p.* 183–192.

Ištoňa, J., 1995: Methods of forest management and modeling growth processes in the conditions of air pollution" and a partial task "Logging and area forest arrangement under changed ecological conditions" in the forests affected by air pollutants in the surroundings of Žiar nad Hronom. Zborník referátov vedeckých prác z medzinárodnej konferencie LVÚ Zvolen.

Jianyun Ruan, Ming H. Wong, 2000: Accumulation of fluoride and aluminium related to different varietes of tea plant. *Scand. J. Forest Res., 8, p.* 498–509.

Kachigan, S. K., 1986: *Statistical Analysis. An interdisciplinary introduction to unvariate & multivariate methods.* Radius Press, New York, 377, 99 pp.

Kachigan, S.K., 1986: *Statistical Analysis. An interdisciplinary introduction to unvariate & multivariate methods.* Radius Press, New York, 377, 99 pp.

Karaban', R.T. , Rudneva, N.A., 1988 : Accumulation of metals caused by technogenic factors in soils and arboreal vegetation (in Russian). *Proceedings of the Institute of Applied Geophysics, 72,* p. 65–74.

Karaoz, M.O., 2003: Air pollution effects on forest trees in Balikeshir, Turkey. *Water, Air, Soil Poll., Focus 3,* p. 269–279.

Kaupenjohan, M., Zech, W., Hantschel, R., Horn, R., Schneider, B.U., 1989: Mineral nutrition of forest trees. A regional survey. In Schultze, E.D., Lange, O.L., Oren, R. (eds), *Forest decline and air pollution.* Ecological studies 77, Springer Verlag , Berlin, p. 182–294.

Kniebugl, J.: *Zhodnotenie stavu kvality ovzdušia v okrese Žiar nad Hronom* (Evaluation of the state of air quality in the district of Žiar nad Hronom). OÚ ŽP Žiar nad Hronom, apríl 1993, p. 1–8.

Koivisto, L., Myllyvirta, T., Sutinen, S., 1992: Microscopic Structure and S-content of Pine Needles in Industrial and Rural Areas in Southern Finland. In Sashwati, R., K"arenlampi, L., Hänninen, O. (eds), 7th International Bioindicators Symposium and Workshop on Environmental Health, Kuopio September 28–October 3, 1992, Abstract Book, Kuopio University Publications C. Natural and Environmental Sciences, 7, 33 pp.

Koptsik, G.N., Koptsik, S.V., Aamlid, D., 2001: Pine needle chemistry near a large point SO_2 source in northern Fennoscandia. *Water, Air, Soil Poll., 130,* p. 929–934.

Krause, C.R., Cannon, W.N., 1991: Epistomatal wax injury to Red spruce needles (Picea rubens Sarg.) grown in elevated levels of ozone and acidified rain. *Scanning Microsc., 5/4,* p. 1173–1180.

Lindberg, S. E., 1992: Atmospheric Deposition and Canopy Interactions of Sulfur., In D.W. Johnson, S. E. Lindberg (eds), *Atmospheric Deposition and Forest Nutrient Cycling,* SpringerVerlag, New York, p. 74–90.

Lofgren, S., Bringmark, L., Aastrup, M., Hultberg, H., Kindbom, K., Kvarnas, H., 2001: Sulphur balances and dynamics in three forested catchmetns in Sweden. Water, Air, Soil Poll., 130, p. 631–636.

Lomander, A., Johansson, M.B.,2001: Changes in concentrations of Cd, Zn,Mn, Cu and Pb in spruce *(Picea abies)* needle litter during decomposition. *Water, Air, Soil Poll., 132,* p. 165–184.

Lovett, G.M., 1992: Atmospheric Deposition and Canopy Interactions of Nitrogen. In D.W. Johnson, S. E. Lindberg (eds), *Atmospheric Deposition and Forest Nutrient Cycling,* Springer Verlag, New York, p. 152–166.

Lovett, G.M., Weathers, K.C., Arthur, M.A., Schultz, J.C., 2004: Nitrogen cycling in a northern hardwood forest: Do species matter? *Biogeochemistry, 67,* p. 289–308.

Madhoolika Agrawal, Jyoti Singh, 2000: Impact of coal power plant emission on the foliar elemental concentrations in plants in a low rainfall tropical region. *Environmental Monitoring and Assessment, 60,* p. 261–282.

Manes, F., 1999: Effetti della auinamento atmosferico su specie forestali in area mediterranea. *Linea Ecologica, 2,* p. 44–50.

Maňkovská, B., 1992: Chemical composition of solid particles on vegetative surface in Slovak forests. *Ekológia (ČSFR), 11,* 2, p. 205–214.

Maňkovská, B., 1995: Mapping of forest environment load by selected elements through the leaf analyses. *Ekológia (Bratislava), 14,* 2, p. 205–213.

Maňkovská, B., 1996: *Geochemický atlas Slovenska – Lesná biomasa* (Geochemical atlas of Slovakia – Forest biomass). Geologická služba Bratislava, ISBN 80-85314-51-7, 87 pp.

Maňkovská, B., 1996b: *Slovak Aluminium Industry and Local Environment.* Report 1995, LVÚ Zvolen, 64 pp.

Maňkovská, B., 1997: A variation in sulphur and nitrogen foliar concentration of deciduous and conifers vegetation in Slovakia. *Water, Air, Soil Poll., 96,* p. 329–345.

Maňkovská, B., 1997: Deposition of heavy metals in Slovakia – Assessment on the basic of moss and humus analyses. *Ekológia (Bratislava), 16,* 4, p. 433–442.

Maňkovská, B., 1997: *Slovak Aluminium Industry and Local Environment.* Report 1996, Lvú Zvolen, 72 pp.

Maňkovská, B., 1998: *Slovak Aluminium Industry and Local Environment.* Report 1997, Lvú Zvolen, 72 pp.

Maňkovská, B., Steinnes, E., 1995: Effects of pollutants from an aluminium reduction plant. *Science of the Total Environment, 163, p.* 11–23.

Manninen, S., Huttunen, S., Paavo Peräamäaki, P., 1977: Needle S fractions and S to N ratios as indices of SO_2 deposition. *Water, Air, Soil Poll., 95,* p. 277–298.

Markert, B., 1991: Multi-element analysis in plant material. In G. ESSER, OVERDIECK, D.(eds), *Modern Ecology: Basic and Applied Aspects,* Chapter 13, Elsevier, Amsterdam.

Markert, B., 1993. Interelement correlations detectable in plant samples based on data from reference materials and highly accurate research samples. *Fresenius J. Anal. Chem., 345,* p. 318–322.

Markert, B., HERPIN, U., Maňkovská, B., et al. 1996: A comparison of heavy metal deposition in selected Eastern European countries using the moss monitoring method, with special emphasis on the "Black Triangle". *Sci Total Environ., 193,* p. 85–100.

Maslov, Yu. I., 1978: Micros determination of sulphur in the plant material (in Russian). *Methods of biochemical analysis of plans,* LGU, Leningrad, p. 146–154.

Materna, J., Mejstøík, V., 1987: *ěělřčě Agriculture and forest management in polluted areas* (in Czech).. SZN, Praha, 152 pp.

Meisch, H.U., Kessler, M., Reinl, W., Wagner, A., 1986: Distribution of metals in annual rings of the beech (*Fagus sylvatica*) as an expression of environmental changes. *Experientia, 42,* p. 537–542.

Meriläinen, J.J., Hynynen, J., Palomäki, A., Veijola, H., Witick, A., Mäntykoski, K., Granberg, K., Lehtinen, K., 2001: Pulp and paper mill pollution and subsequent ecosystem recovery of a large boreal lake in Finland: a palaeolimnological analysis. *Journal of Paleolimnology, 26,* p. 11–35.

Mitschick, G., Fiedler, H.J.,1987: Zur Notwendigkeit von Reinigungschriften bei der Blattanalyse. Mengen -und Spurenelement. Arbeitstag. Agrowiss. und Chem. Ges. DDR, Jena 21.-22.12.1987, Leipzig, p. 44–51.

Muramoto, S., Nishizaki, H., Aoyama, I., 1991: Effects of fluorine emission on agricultural products surrounding an aluminum factory. *J.– –Environ. –Sci.–Health,Part –B, 26* (3), p. 351–356.

Mžp SR: Správa o stave životného prostredia Slovenskej republiky v roku 1994. SAŽPBanská Bystrica, 168 s.

Nabais, C., Freitas, H., Hagenmeyer, J., 2000: Dendroanalysis: A tool for biomonitoring environmental pollution? Biomonitoring of atmospheric pollution (with emphasis on trace elements) – BioMAP. International Atomic Energy Agency, TECDOc-1152, p. 130–135.

Neal, C., Smith, C..J., Walls, J., Billingham, P., Hill, S., Neal, M., 1990: Comments on the hydrochemical regulation of the halogen elements in rainfall, stemflow, throughfall and stream waters at an acidic forested area in Mid-Wales. *Sci.Total –Environ. (Netherlands), 91*(1), p. 1–11.

Nellemann, C., Thomsen, M.G., 2001: Long –term changes in forest growth: potential effects of nitrogen deposition and acidification. *Water, Air, Soil Poll., 128,* p. 197–205.

Nord, A.G., Tronner, A., Boyce, A.J., 2001: Atmospheric bronze and cooper corrosion as an environmental indicator. A Study Based on Chemical and Sulphur Isotope Data. *Water, Air, Soil Poll., 127*, p. 193–204.

Nyberg, L., Lundström, U., Söderberg, U., Danielsson, R., Van Hees, P., 2001: Does soil contamination acidification effect spruce needle chemical composition and tree growth? *Water, Air, Soil Poll., Focus 1,* p. 241–263.

Okda, N., Katayama, Y., Nobuchi, T., Ishimaru, Y., Aoki, A., 1990: Trace elements in the stems of trees IV. Radial distribution in mizumara (*Quercus mongolika* var. *grosseserata*), *Mokuzai Gakkaishi, 36,* p. 93–97.

Paoletti, E., LA Scala, S., Raddi, P., 1997: Leaf surface response to abiotic stress factors in a beech stand in central Italy. *Ekológia (Bratislava) , 16* (3), p. 281–293.

Percy, E., Cape, J.N. , Jagels, R., Simpson, C.J., (eds*), 1995: Air Pollutants and the Leaf Cuticle. NATO ASI Series,* Vol. G 36, Springer Verlag, Berlin- Heidelberg, p. 123–138.

Percy, K. et al., 1999: State of science and knowledge gaps with respect to air pollution impacts on forests: Reports from concurrent IUFRO 7.04.00 working party session. *Water, Air, Soil Poll., 116,* p. 433–448.

Phuc, H.V., Dam, N.T., 1998: Resistance ability of some multivoltine silkworm races against fluorine toxicant. Capacite de resistance de quelques races de vers a soie polyvoltins a un toxique fluore. *Sericologia (France). 38* (1), p. 151–154.

Phukan, S., Bhattacharyya, K.G,. 2003: Modification of soil quality near pulp and paper mill. *Water, Air, Soil Poll., 146,* p. 319–333.

Pradhan, G., Barik, K., 1999: Environment-friendly behaviour and competitiveness: A study of pulp and paper industry in India. Environ. *Resource Economics, 14,* p. 481–501.

Raddi, P., Moricca, S., Paoletti, E., 1994: Effects of acid rain and surfactants pollution on the foliar structure of trees species. In Percy, K.E., Cape, J.N., Jagels, R., Simpson, C.J. (eds) *Air Pollutants and The Leaf Cuticle.,* NATO ASI Series, Vol. G 36, Springer-Verlag, Berlin, Heidelberg, P. 205–216.

Rahn, K.A., 1976: The Chemical Composition of the Atmospheric Aerosol. Technical Report, Graduate School of Oceanography, University of Rhode Island, 265 pp.

Raitio, H., 1992: The Foliar Chemical Composition of Scots Pines in Finnish Lapland and the Kola Peninsula. in Tikkanen, E., Varmola, M., Katermaa, T. (eds), *Symposium on the State of the Environment and Environmental Monitoring in Northern Fennoscandia and the Kola Peninsula,* October 6–8, 1992, Rovaniemi, Finland. Arctic Centre Publications 4, p. 226–234.

Rennenberg, H., 1994: The fate of excess sulphur in higher plants. *Ann. Rev. Plant Physiol., 35,* p.121–153.

Rühling, A., Bargali, R., Maňkovská, B., et al., 1994: *Atmospheric Heavy Metal Deposition in Europe-estimation based on moss analysis.* NORD 9, Nordic Council of Ministers, Copenhagen, p. 53.

Rühling, A., Steinnes, E., 1998: *Atmospheric heavy metal deposition in Europe 1995–1996.* Nord 1998. Nordic Council of Ministers, Copenhagen.

Ruoho-Airola, T., Salmi, T., 2001: Episodicity of sulfate deposition in Finland. *Water, Air, Soil Poll. 130,* p. 529–534.

Saare, L., Talkop, R., Roots, O., 2001: Air pollution effects on terrestrial ecoszstems in Estonia. *Water, Air, Soil Poll. 130,* p. 1181–1186.

Samakovlis, E., 2003: The relationship between waste paper and other inputs in the Swedish paper industry. *Environ. Resource Economics 25,* p. 191–212.

Sanz, M.J., Calatayud, V., Calvo, E., 1995: Diferencias morfologicas en las ceras epiestomaticas de varias poblaciones de *Pinus sylvestris* L. de Castellòn y Teruel. Ecologia, 9, p. 201–211.

Schwarzl, B., Weiss P., 1997: Zusammenhänge zwischen Kenndaten zur Charakterisierung des Waldzustandes auf vier Dauerbeobachtungsflächen in Vorarlberg, Report 145, Umweltbundesamt Wien.

Senhou, A.,. Chouak, A., Cherkaoui, R., Moutia, Z., Lferde, M., Elyahyaoui, A., El Khoukhi, T., Bounakhla, M., Embarche, K., Gaudry, A., Ayrault, S., Moskura, M., 2002: Sensitivity of biomonitors and local variations of element concentrations in air pollution biomonitoring. *Journal of Radioanalytical and Nuclear Chemistry, 254,* 2 p. 343–349.

Sharma, G.K., 1993: Leaf epidermal and gross morphological adaptations in *Salix nigra* Marsh. (Salicaceae) in relation to environmental pollution. Journal of the Tennessee Academy of Science, 68 (3), p. 73–76.

Sinha, R.K., 1997: Fluorosis a case study from the Sambher Salt Lake region in Jaipur, Rajasthan, India. *The Environmentalist, 17,* p. 259–262.

Sikström, U., 2001: Effects of pre-harvest soil acidification, liming and N fertilization on the survival, growth and needle element concentrations of *Picea abies* L. Karst. seedlings. *Plant and Soil, 231, p.* 255–266.

Solberg, S., Kvindesland, S., Aamlid, D., Venn, K., 2002: Crown condition and needle chemistry of Norway spruce in relation to critical loads of acidity in south-east Norway. *Water, Air, Soil Poll., 140, p.* 157–171.

Stefan, K., Fürst, A., Hacker, R., Bartels, U., 1997: Forest Foliar Condition in Europe. Technical Report. EC and UN/ECE, Brussels, Geneva, p. 207.

Stefan, K. , 1995: International Cooperative Programme on Assessment and Monitoring of Air Pollution Effects on Forest. Report of 3rd Meeting of the Forest Foliar Experts Panel, Federal Forest Research Institute, Wien, November 6-8, p. 1–10.

Steinnes, E., 1980: Atmospheric deposition of heavy metals in Norway studied by analysis of moss samples using neutron activation analysis and atomic absorption spectrometry. *J. Radioana. Chem., 58*, p. 387–391.

Steinnes, E., 2000: Neutron activation techniques in environmental studies, *Journal of Radioanalytical and Nuclear Chemistry, 243,* 1, p.235–239.

Steinnes, E., Rambæk, J.P., Hanssen, J.E., 1992: Large scale multi-element survey of atmospheric deposition using naturally growing moss as biomonitor. *Chemosphere, 35,* p. 735–752.

Sutinen, S., Koivisto, L., Raitio, H., 1995: Neulasten hienorakenteen ja rikkipitoisuuden välinen yhteys. In Tikkanen, E. (ed.), *Kuolan saastep¨a¨ast ¨ot Lapin metsien rasitteena, Gummerus,* Jyväaskylla, 138 pp.

Suzuki, T.,Ohtaguchi, K., Koide, K., 1994: Correlation between flash points and chemical structures of organic compounds, using principal component analysis. *Int. Chem. Engin., 34,* 3, p. 393–402.

Tendel, J., Wolf, K., 1988: Distribution of nutrients and trace elements in annual rings of pine trees (*Pinus silvetris*) as an indicator of environmental changes, *Experientia, 44,* p. 975–980.

Tokareva, T., Schepaschenko, D., 2000: Selection of indices for the monitoring of spruce forests within impact zone of the metalurgical enterprice. *Water, Air, Soil Poll., 121,* p. 339–347.

Torseth, K., Aas, W., Soldberg,S., 2001: Trends in airborne sulphur and nitrogen compounds in Norway during 1985/1996 in relation to air mass origin, *Water, Air, Soil Poll., 130,* p. 1493–1498.

Trimbacher C., 1991: REM-Untersuchungen an Fichtennadeln besonders exponierter Standorte. *VDI-Berichte, 901,* p. 285–289.

Trimbacher C., 1996: Die Wachsqualität von Fichtennadeln am Schulterberg-Nordprofil. In Herman, F., Smidt, S. (eds), *Ökosystemare Studiem im Kalkalpin. Abschätzung der Gefährdung von Waldökosystemen,* FBVA-Berichte, 94, Dforstliche Bundesversuchsanstalt Vienna, Austria, p. 185–191.

Trimbacher, C., Weiss, P., 1999: Needle surface characteristics and element contents of Norway spruce in relation to the distance of emission sources. *Environ. Pollut., 105,* p. 111–119.

Trimbacher, C., Weiss, P., 2004: Norway spruce: A novel methods using surface characteristics and heavy metal concentrations of needles for a large/scale monitoring survey in Austria. *Water, Air, Soil Poll., 152,* p. 363–386.

Tuovinen, J.-P., Kangas, L., Nordlund, G., 1990: Model Calculations of Sulphur and Nitrogen Deposition. In Kauppi, P., Anttila, P., Kenttämies, K. (eds), *Acidification in Finland.* Springer-Verlag, Berlin, Heidelberg, p. 167–197.

Turunen M., Huttunen S., 1990: A review of the response of epicuticular wax of conifer needles to air pollution. *J. Environ. Qual., 19,* p. 35–45.

Tveite, B., Abrahamsen, G., Huse, M., 1994: Trees: Nutrition. In Abrahamsen, G., Stuanes, A.O., Tveite, B. (eds), Long-term Experiments with Acid Rain in Norwegian Forest Ecosystem. *Ecological Studies 104,* Springer-Verlag, New York, p. 140–179.

UNECE ICP Vegetation, 2003: Heavy metals in European mosses, 2000/2001 Survey, March 2003, 45 pp.

Vandersmissen, A., Blaude, M.N., Bloden, S., Ansay, M., 1993: Urinary fluor in cattle, an indicator of atmospheric pollution in Wallonia. Variations du fluor urinaire chez les bovins en Wallonie: un indicateur de pollution atmospherique. *Annales –de Medecine Veterinaire (Belgium), 137* (6) , p. 435–442.

Wahaab, R.A., 2002: Biological degradation of some organic compounds involved in the paper industry. *The Environmentalist, 22*, p.227–235.

Wayland, M., et al.. 1998: The effect of pulp and paper mill effluent on an insectivorous bird, the tree swallow. *Ecotoxicology, 7,* p. 237–251.

Weinstein, L.H., 1977: Fluoride and plant life. *Occupat. Environ. Medic., 19,* p. 49–78.

Wenzel, W.W., Blum, W.E.H., 1992: Fluorine speciation and mobility in F-contaminated soils. *Soil Science, 153* (5) p. 357–364.

Wenzel, W.W., Blum, W.E.H., 1992: Effects of fluorine deposition on the chemistry of acid luvisols. *Intern. J. Environ. Anal. Chem., 46* (1/3) p. 223–231.

Wulff, A., Karenlampi, L. 1993: 'The effect of the sulphur and fluoride by Pices abies needls near point origins. *Scand. J. Forest Res., 8,* p. 498–509.

Yumada, H., Hattori, T., 1977: Investigation of the relationship between aluminium and fluoride in plants. I. Relationship between aluminium and fluorine in tea leaves. Japanese Soil Science and Plant Nutrition, p. 253–261.

Zöttl, H.W., Hüttl, R.F., 1986: Nutrient supply and forest decline in Southwest-Germany. *Water, Air, Soil Poll., 31,* p. 449–462.

In: New Topics in Environmental Research
Editor: Daniel Rhodes, pp. 139-153

ISBN 1-60021-172-0
© 2006 Nova Science Publishers, Inc.

Chapter 6

USE OF MODERN STATISTICAL METHODS IN DEVELOPING ECOTOXICITY QSARS

Shijin Ren[1], and Hyunjoong Kim[2]*

[1]Johnson Diversey, Inc.
[2]Department of Applied Statistics, Yonsei University, Korea

ABSTRACT

In this study the use of seven modern statistical methods in developing ecotoxicity QSARs was investigated. The statistical methods used were general additive model (GAM), generalized unbiased interaction detection and estimation (GUIDE), least absolute shrinkage and selection operator version 2 (LASSO2), multivariate adaptive regression splines (MARS), neural networks (NN), projection pursuit regression (PPR), and recursive partitioning and regression trees (RPART). Traditional multiple linear regression (MLR) was also employed as a baseline method. A data set that contained the toxicity for 250 phenols acting by various mechanisms of toxic action and seven molecular descriptors was used for model development. Eight QSAR models were developed without regard to toxicity mechanism using the above-mentioned statistical methods. The resultant models were validated using the 10-fold cross validation method. For the data set under consideration, the model based on PPR was found to offer the highest modeling and predicting powers. The ability to identify toxicologically important parameters, transparency, and interpretability of the models based on the modern statistical methods and traditional MLR were discussed.

* Corresponding author. Address: Johnson Diversey, Inc. 8310 - 16th Street, Sturtevant, WI 53177, U.S.A. Phone: 1-262-631-4211; Fax: 1-262-631-4067; Email: shijin.ren@johnsondiversey.com

INTRODUCTION

Phenols are used in many industries such as coal conversion, metal casting, paper manufacturing, and resin production (Caza et al. 1999, Fang et al. 1996). A significant amount of phenols is discharged into the environment by different carriers (e.g., wastewater) and consequently the evaluation of the toxicity of phenols, especially their aquatic toxicity, is essential for environmental risk assessment purposes. Phenol toxicity data have been obtained using several bioassay systems involving sensor organisms of different trophic levels, e.g., protozoa (Cronin and Schultz, 2001), daphnids (Cronin et al., 2000), bacteria (Ren and Frymier, 2003), and tadpoles (Wang et al., 2001).

Following the acquisition of toxicity data has been the development of quantitative structure-activity relationships (QSARs) for phenols (Cronin et al., 2002). QSARs have been proven to be reliable tools for the hazard assessment of organic chemicals when little or no empirical data are available (Bradbury, 1995, Bearden and Schultz, 1997). QSARs aim at relating toxicity or other biological activity of chemical compounds to their molecular structures. To this end, three components are required: (1) a database with experimentally measured toxicity of a group of compounds, (2) descriptors characterizing the molecular structure and/or other properties, and (3) some methods to relate the previous two components. Currently, the most widely used methods to relate biological activity to molecular structures/properties are statistical methods.

Although occasionally, the literature shows the use of more complicated statistical methods in deriving QSARs, e.g., neural networks (Kövesdi et al., 1997, Kaiser, 2003, Schultz et al., 2003a) and recursive partition (Hawkins et al., 1997), most QSARs in toxicology are developed using regression analysis (Eriksson et al., 2003, Schultz et al., 2003b), especially multiple linear regression (MLR). However, as Cronin and Schultz (2003) pointed out, biology and the modeling of biology is a nonlinear phenomenon and always expecting a linear relationship in biological modeling is not realistic. Another issue in multiple linear regression is the assumption of normal distribution. Deviations from this distribution assumption are commonly encountered in real data sets but are frequently overlooked.

In a recent study by Cronin et al. (2002), the authors examined the use of multiple linear regression and partial least square (PLS) regression in developing QSARs for predicting the toxicity of phenols to *Tetrahymena pyriformis*. In addition to PLS, developments in the field of statistics have yielded a number of modern statistical approaches. Many of these newly developed statistical methods are nonlinear and/or nonparametric in nature, thus they are able to capture the nonlinearity exhibited in a data set and avoid the assumption of normal distribution. The aim of the present study was to extend the scope of the study of Cronin et al. (2002) to incorporate more statistical methods. To this end, the following statistical methods were under investigation in this study: general additive model (GAM), generalized unbiased interaction detection and estimation (GUIDE), multivariate adaptive regression splines (MARS), neural networks (NN), projection pursuit regression (PPR), recursive partitioning and regression trees (RPART), and least absolute shrinkage and selection operator version 2 (LASSO2). Detailed descriptions of the computing algorithms for the above methods are not the focus of this chapter and thus only brief introductions to them are provided in Table 1. However, key references are listed in Table 1 for the interested reader. One specific aim of this study was to investigate the improvement of the accuracy of phenol toxicity prediction using the modern statistical methods over the prediction accuracy of traditional multiple linear regression models.

Table 1. Modern statistical methods used in this chapter

Method	Brief description	Reference
General additive model (GAM)	GAM extends the notion of linear regression by allowing linear functions of the predictors to be replaced by smooth functions of the predictors. The model assumes that the smooth predictor function has an additive structure.	Hastie and Tibshirani (1990)
Generalized unbiased interaction detection and estimation (GUIDE)	GUIDE is a regression tree algorithm that can fit a multiple regression at each terminal node. The tree structure is chosen in such a way that the regression model is most significant for each node.	Loh (2002)
Multivariate adaptive regression splines (MARS)	MARS is an adaptive procedure for regression. It is a generalization of stepwise linear regression, but the regression is fitted using piecewise basis functions.	Friedman (1991)
Neural networks (NN)	NN can be viewed as a nonlinear statistical method. It consists of input, hidden, and output layers. The nonlinear model fitting is implemented in hidden layer with sigmoid function.	Müller (1990)
Projection pursuit regression (PPR)	PPR is an additive model using ridge function, which is estimated by some flexible smoothing method. It can be viewed as nonlinear regression using linear combination of variables.	Friedman and Stuetzle (1981)
Recursive partitioning and regression trees (RPART)	RPART is a piecewise constant regression tree method. CART (Brieman et al., 1984) provides its original algorithm. The tree structure is determined so that the variance of responses within each node is minimized.	Breiman et al. (1984)
Least absolute shrinkage and selection operator version 2 (LASSO2)	LASSO2 is similar to the ridge regression method. Rather than taking penalties on the square of the coefficient, it makes constraints on the absolute value of the coefficient.	Osborne et al. (2000)

METHODS

Data Set

The data set reported in the study of Cronin et al. (2002) was used in this study. This data set contained the toxicity data for 250 phenols evaluated with the *Tetrahymena pyriformis* testing system (Schultz, 1997), *which* were expressed as the negative logarithm of the 50% growth inhibition concentrations ($\log(IGC_{50})^{-1}$). The phenols in this data set were characterized by a variety of chemical structures and exhibited toxicity via several mechanisms. The values of a total of seven molecular descriptors were reported in the study of Cronin et al. (2002). These descriptors included the logarithm of the ionization-corrected octanol/water partition coefficient ($\log D$), the lowest unoccupied molecular orbital (LUMO) energy, molecular weight (MW), the negatively charged molecular surface area (*Pneg*), the sum of absolute charges on nitrogen and oxygen atoms in a molecule (ABSQon), the largest positive charge on a hydrogen atom (MaxHp), and the electrotopological state index for the hydroxy group (SsOH).

Model Development

As mentioned in *Introduction*, a specific aim of this study was to compare the prediction accuracies of the modern statistical models and that of multiple linear regression. For this reason, GAM, GUIDE, MARS, NN, PPR, RPART, and LASSO2 models as well as a MLR model were developed using the above-mentioned data set. All 250 phenols and seven molecular descriptors were used in model development and no observations or descriptors were removed (see *Discussion*). The squared correlation (R^2) between observed and fitted phenol toxicity and mean squared error (MSE) were recorded and used as indicators of model fitting. The statistical software R version 1.4.1 (The R Foundation, Vienna, Austria), which can be downloaded from the internet at http://www.r-project.org, was used for all model development and validation except for the GUIDE model. The software Guide version 1.05, which is downloadable from the internet at http://www.stat.wisc.edu/~loh/guide.html, was used to develop the GUIDE model. The key R codes and Guide inputs are provided in *Appendix*.

Model Validation

In the study of Cronin et al. (2002), model development and validation was performed using a data-splitting approach, i.e., the entire data set was split into a training and a validation subset and the training subset (containing 200 phenols) was used for model development and the validation subset (containing 50 phenols) was used for model validation. While this approach (i.e., data-splitting) is frequently taken, there might be some peculiar pattern contained in the training and/or validation data sets. As the same authors pointed out, model validation is highly dependent on the selection of the test or validation set. Due to the comparative nature of the present study, 10-fold cross validation (CV) was performed to ensure fair comparisons between the statistical models. Previous studies have shown that 10-fold CV is a reliable way to assess model validity (Hastie et al., 2001). As such, the whole data set containing all 250 phenols was divided into 10 disjoint subsets. Within each subset the approximate proportion of phenols acting by each of the mechanisms (except for pro-redox cyclers because of their very small number) was similar to that in the original data set. Selection of phenols within each mechanism category to be included in a subset was random. Data in every and each of the ten subsets were used to validation a model built on data in the other nine subsets. Note that in this way, each observation in the original data set was used in the validation set and training set once and nine times, respectively. The predicted mean squared error was calculated for each CV sample and denoted $PMSE_i$. At the end of the 10-fold CV process, the squared correlation (R^2_{cv}) between observed and CV predicted toxicity to all 250 phenols was examined. Additionally, the overall predicted mean squared error ($PMSE_{cv}$) was calculated at the end of the 10-fold CV process and used as a measure of model prediction capacity. The validation procedure described above was conducted for all models including the MLR model developed in this study after the 10 subsets for cross validation were created.

Model Predictive Capacity Comparison

In addition to using $PMSE_{cv}$ to compare the predictive capacity of each model developed, a rigorous statistical test was conducted. To enable a statistical test, the $PMSE_i$ values were used instead of $PMSE_{cv}$. The purpose of the test was to examine whether there was statistical difference among the eight statistical models in terms of model prediction accuracy while taking into account the variations caused by the selection of data used in a validation subset. To this end, a model was fit where $PMSE_i$ was the response and statistical method and CV sample were the factors, or mathematically,

$$PMSE_i = a + b \text{ Method} + c \text{ CV Sample} \qquad (1)$$

where a is a constant and b and c are vectors containing constants. Note that "Method" was a fixed factor and "CV sample" was a random factor. The difference between a fixed factor and a random factor and its impact on the resulting statistical model can be found in, e.g., Montgomery (2001). The effect of statistical models on $PMSE_i$ was studied by inspecting the statistical significance of the factor "method" in the model. For the purpose of convenience, this part of the study was conducted using the statistical software JMP 5.0 (SAS Institute, Cary, North Carolina). The method of expected means squares (EMS) instead of the method of restricted maximum likelihood (REML) was used in JMP model fitting.

RESULTS

Model Development

The results of model fitting for the eight statistical models are shown in Table 2. The R^2 values for model fitting ranged from 0.60 for LASSO2 to 0.87 for PPR. Correspondingly, the MSE calculated in the model fitting stage ranged from 0.31 for LASSO2 and 0.09 for PPR. All modern statistical methods provided a better fit of the phenol data than MLR except LASSO2. Many of the statistical methods under consideration, including the best model in this study (see later results), do not provide explicit forms of the model developed and therefore no mathematical expression describing any model was provided in this study.

Model Validation

The R^2_{cv} and $PMSE_{cv}$ values calculated at the end of the 10-fold CV process are also shown in Table 2. The R^2_{cv} values ranged from 0.54 for RPART to 0.68 for PPR, and the $PMSE_{cv}$ values ranged from 0.32 for RPART and LASSO2 to 0.23 for PPR. Using R^2_{cv} and $PMSE_{cv}$ as rough measures of model predictive capacity, results in this study indicated that, among the modern statistical methods, RPART and LASSO2 (and probably MARS) did not provide a higher predictive capacity than MLR for the phenol data set. The $PMSE_i$ values calculated during the 10-fold CV process are listed in Table 3. The average $PMSE_i$ values were qualitatively in agreement with the $PMSE_{cv}$ values. The standard errors of $PMSE_i$ suggested that NN and PPR gave the most consistent results for the CV data sets and thus were more robust than other methods.

Table 2. Summary of model fitting and 10-fold cross validation (total number of observation in model = 250)

	R^2	MSE	R^2_{cv}	$PMSE_{cv}$
GAM	0.73	0.18	0.63	0.26
GUIDE	0.65	0.24	0.61	0.26
MARS	0.70	0.21	0.59	0.29
NN	0.73	0.18	0.64	0.25
PPR	0.87	0.09	0.68	0.23
RPART	0.75	0.17	0.54	0.32
LASSO2	0.60	0.31	0.57	0.32
MLR	0.63	0.25	0.59	0.28

Model Predictive Capacity Comparison

A model as described previously in *Methods* was fit to test whether there were statistically significant differences between the predicting power of the eight models. Results of the tests with respect to random effects are shown in Table 4. "CV sample" was shown to be a significant factor ($p < 0.0001$), which was expected due to the inevitable variations caused by CV samples. More importantly, the p value for "method" was 0.0221, indicating that there was significant difference among the statistical models in terms of prediction power. A portion of the parameter estimates is shown in Table 5 (the parameter estimates for the intercept and CV samples were ignored). Note that there was no parameter estimate for MLR because in this model MLR was used as the "baseline" model and the parameter estimates in Table 5 represented change in $PMSE_i$ as "Method" changed from MLR to another statistical model. Examining the p values in Table 5 revealed that three models (LASSO2, PPR, and RPART) were significantly different from MLR in terms of predictive capacity. Considering the sign of the parameter estimate in Table 5, it can be seen that only PPR offered a statistically higher predicting power than MLR. This is consistent with the observations in Table 2. Figures 1 and 2 show the model fitting and CV predictions using the PPR model. Note that the PPR model did not provide satisfactory fit for two hydroquinones indicated in Figure 1. Given their small number (two out of 250) and based on the visual observation that they only moderately deviated from the fitted model, their impact on the resulting model was judged small and therefore they were not removed from model fitting (also see later discussion on treatment of outliers). In the study of Cronin et al. (2002), the authors also found that the toxicity of many compounds capable of being metabolized to quinones could not be adequately fitted by QSARs developed in their study.

Table 3. PMSE$_i$, their average, and associated standard error (SE) values of 10-fold cross validation (number of observation in training set = 225, number of observation in validation set = 25)

	CV 1	CV 2	CV 3	CV 4	CV 5	CV 6	CV 7	CV 8	CV 9	CV 10	Average	SE
GAM	0.35	0.56	0.21	0.32	0.42	0.15	0.12	0.15	0.17	0.11	0.26	0.15
GUIDE	0.40	0.52	0.18	0.16	0.39	0.28	0.18	0.22	0.19	0.10	0.26	0.13
MARS	0.57	0.63	0.28	0.19	0.37	0.21	0.15	0.17	0.21	0.12	0.29	0.18
NN	0.41	0.32	0.20	0.19	0.39	0.28	0.19	0.22	0.18	0.15	0.25	0.09
PPR	0.25	0.32	0.33	0.17	0.32	0.19	0.23	0.15	0.19	0.12	0.23	0.08
RPART	0.41	0.59	0.29	0.26	0.34	0.25	0.19	0.33	0.37	0.13	0.32	0.13
LASSO2	0.41	0.52	0.22	0.28	0.46	0.25	0.34	0.35	0.27	0.12	0.32	0.12
MLR	0.46	0.51	0.22	0.18	0.36	0.32	0.20	0.23	0.19	0.12	0.28	0.13

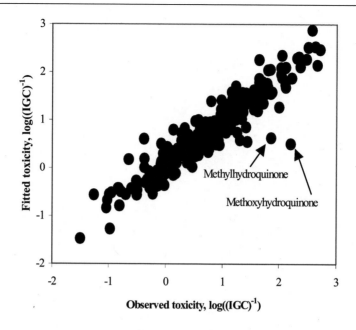

Figure 1. Observed versus fitted toxicity using the PPR model.

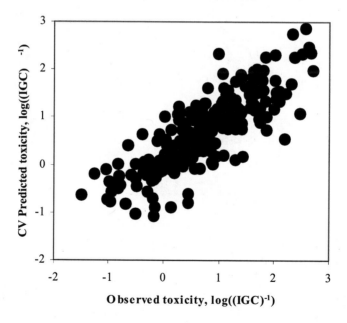

Figure 2. Observed versus 10-fold cross validation predicted toxicity using the PPR model.

Table 4. Tests with respect to random effects

Source	Sum of squares	Mean sum of squares numerator	Degrees of freedom numerator	F Ratio	Pr > F
Method	0.074	0.011	7	2.56	0.0221
CV Sample	0.94	0.10	9	25.30	< 0.0001

Table 5. Selected parameter estimates (parameter estimates for the intercept and CV samples were omitted)

Parameter	Estimate	Standard error	t Ratio	$Pr > |t|$
GAM	-0.020	0.019	-1.07	0.29
GUIDE	-0.013	0.019	-0.67	0.51
LASSO2	0.046	0.019	2.43	0.018
MARS	0.013	0.019	0.70	0.49
NN	-0.023	0.019	-1.23	0.22
PPR	-0.048	0.019	-2.53	0.014
RPART	0.040	0.019	2.13	0.038

DISCUSSION

The pitfalls in developing QSARs and desired characteristics of QSARs have been discussed thoroughly (Cronin and Schultz, 2003, Schultz and Cronin, 2003). One of the desirable features of QSARs is a high reliability of the toxicological data. As the authors pointed out, such data should ideally be "measured by a single protocol, even in the same laboratory and by the same workers." (Schultz and Cronin, 2003). Data obtained in this way are regarded more reliable than data compiled in the literature that come from various sources. The phenol toxicity to *T. pyriformis* data involved in the study of Cronin et al. (2002) were collected in the Biological Activity Testing and Modeling Laboratory (BATML) at the University of Tennessee and are a set of highly reliable data that conforms to the above-mentioned features. The high quality of the *T. pyriformis* data had been demonstrated by researchers outside of BATML (e.g., Mekapati and Hansch, 2002). Consequently, the *T. pyriformis* data is suitable for QSAR analysis and was therefore chosen in the present study.

The molecular descriptors used to develop QSAR model in the present study were taken directly from the study of Cronin et al. (2002) and no additional descriptors were calculated. In the study of Cronin et al. (2002), the authors calculated 108 descriptors and performed MLR with stepwise variable selection. The seven molecular descriptors used in the study of Cronin et al. (2002) were the results of the stepwise variable selection procedure. The authors also concluded that these descriptors were important for describing toxicity and that there was no redundancy among them. Therefore, these seven descriptors provided a suitable basis for the present study in which comparative assessment of statistical methods were made. Note that several of the modern statistical methods do not incorporate explicitly variable selection procedures. However, the computing algorithms ensure that those variables that are relatively less significant make less contribution to the resulting model. Although for methods such as MLR variable selection can be explicitly performed, this was not done in the present study (see *Methods*) because of the known non-redundancy among the descriptors. Additional descriptors other than the seven that were used were not considered in this study due to the potential problem of having spurious, unstable, or invalid models as explained by Cronin and Schultz (2003). As mentioned previously, the multiple regression approach with variable selection is frequently taken in developing QSARs. One of the advantages of this approach is the ability to identify potentially toxicologically important parameters by inspecting the statistical significant of the parameters in the regression model. By comparison, the modern statistical methods are less capable in this sense. A comparison of the seven modern methods and MLR with respect to the ability to identify important parameters is shown in Table 6.

Table 6. Comparison of statistical methods for ecotoxicity QSARs

	Ability to identify important parameters	Model transparency	Model interpretability
GAM	Low	Low	Low
GUIDE	Low-medium	Medium	Medium
MARS	Low	Low	Low
NN	Low	Low	Low
PPR	Low	Low	Low
RPART	Low-medium	Medium	Medium
LASSO2	Low	Low	Low
MLR	High	High	High

As mentioned in *Methods*, no outliers were removed in developing the statistical models. The removal of outliers from QSAR models has been a contentious issue for at least the past two decades (Cronin and Schultz, 2003). Outliers can be caused by experimental error. Some researchers have also pointed out that there may not be particular reasons that outliers occur (Tang et al., 1992). However, it is more generally agreed that, in the absence of unduly experimental error, outliers in a QSAR model suggest that they act by mechanisms of toxic action that are different from that of the majority of the compounds used to develop the QSAR. Inspecting outliers in QSAR model has provided a basis for many mechanism-related studies (e.g., Cronin et al., 2000). It has been realized that the most successful and toxicologically meaningful QSAR models are developed by separating compounds by their mechanisms of toxic action (Cronin and Dearden, 1995, Schultz et al., 1998). However, despite efforts to determine toxicity mechanism especially for phenols (e.g., Ren 2002a, 2002b), correctly identifying the mechanism of toxic action of a compound can often be difficult due to the complicated interaction between chemical compounds and living organisms. In a recent study, it was demonstrated that incorrect mechanism identification may introduce extra errors in addition to the intrinsic prediction errors of mechanism-based QSAR models (Ren, 2003). Therefore, the ability to predict toxicity without relying on information regarding toxicity mechanism is advantageous (Schultz and Cronin, 1999).

From a statistical modeling point of view, the existence of outliers suggests the inadequacy of a model in describing the data. Instead of removing outliers from an existing model, an alternative approach, which was taken in this study, is to find (a) better model(s) to account for the outlying behavior of certain observations. In the study of Cronin et al. (2002), it was found that different observations needed to be removed for different models. This was not considered appropriate in the present study because the present study aimed at comparing different statistical modeling approaches. Removing different observations from different models would impair the foundation of the comparisons made since at least theoretically all models would provide the same or similar fit and/or prediction accuracy if all the outlying observations were eliminated.

The QSAR models developed in this study aimed at relating toxicity to molecular descriptors without regard to mechanism of toxic action and for this reason no outliers were removed. Since phenols acting by several mechanisms are involved in the same models, the use of these models in mechanistic studies is compromised. On the other hand, these models convey the most information contained in the data set and can be used the predict phenol toxicity without discriminating toxicity mechanisms. In this regard, traditional MLR did not satisfactorily explain the variation in the phenol toxicity data set (see Table 2). Of note is the best model chosen in this study, i.e., the PPR model. This model resulted in an R^2 value of 0.87. In the study of Cronin et al. (2002), the R^2 values of the models developed ranged from 0.54 to 0.83, the latter of which was based on 180-185 observations after removing outliers. Clearly, the PPR model is superior because a higher R^2 value was achieved without removing any outlier. Direct comparison between the predictive capacity of the PPR model and the models in Cronin et al. (2002) is not appropriate because of the difference in data splitting and model validation. However, results of this study shown in Table 2 strongly suggest that the PPR model also had a higher predicting power compared to the seven-parameter multiple regression model.

The statistical criteria to evaluate the quality of QSAR models have been proposed by several researchers (e.g., Eriksson et al., 2003, Tropsha et al., 2003). The R^2_{cv} value is used as a criterion for model predictive capacity. An R^2_{cv} value of higher than 0.5 is generally considered good (Eriksson et al. 2003), and the associated QSAR model is considered predictive (Tropsha et al., 2003). A second criterion is that the difference between R^2 and R^2_{cv} should not exceed 0.3 (Eriksson et al., 2003, Walker et al., 2003). The PPR model had R^2 and R^2_{cv} values of 0.87 and 0.68 (Table 2), respectively, with a difference of 0.19. Therefore, the PPR model conformed to the above criteria. An additional consideration is that the prediction errors of a QSAR model should ideally be close to the experimental data being modeled, but should not be smaller than the errors of the experimental data. Otherwise the model may suffer from over-fitting. Cronin and Schultz (2001) pointed out that an error of 0.1 to 0.2 log units can be expected on even the most precise assay considering the intrinsic variability of biological measurement systems. Walker et al. (2003) stated that a general guide is that the errors of in vivo data are in the region of 0.3 log units. The $PMSE_{cv}$ value for the PPR model shown in Table 2 indicates that this model was not over-fitted.

It is understood that the better performance of the modern statistical methods including PPR is achieved at the sacrifice of model simplicity and transparency. A direct result of lack of model transparency is lack of interpretability. Several of the modern statistical models cannot be explicitly expressed and thus cannot be interpreted. The GUIDE and RPART models, which are regression tree approaches, can be expressed in the form of tree structure. While this enables model interpretation, model complexity increases as the tree structure becomes complex and the interpretation of a regression tree is not always easy. A comparison of the eight statistical models in terms of model transparency and interpretability is shown in Table 6. The importance of model transparency when developing QSARs has been fully discussed in the studies of Cronin and Schultz (2003) and Schultz and Cronin (2003). There is no question that simpler models such as MLR models offer great model transparency and interpretability. However, in the above-mentioned studies, it was also pointed out that the function of an ecotoxicological QSAR is to predict toxicity accurately. Eriksson et al. (2003) also pointed out that the need for interpretation of QSAR models depends on application and may not always be necessary. Therefore, in certain cases, prediction accuracy may have a higher priority than interpretability for QSAR models. The results of the present study indicate that when model transparency is not the primary concern, modern statistical methods can be employed to improve model fitting and prediction. Finally, it needs to be pointed out that, although the PPR model was identified as the best model for predicting phenol toxicity to *T. pyriformis* in this study, this model selection was dependent on the particular data set involved. Should a data set involving other endpoints or other testing organism be used, the best model might be different.

CONCLUSIONS

The use of seven modern statistical models, i.e., GAM, GUIDE, LASSO2, MARS, NN, PPR, and RPART, in addition to MLR, in developing QSARs for phenol toxicity to *T. pyriformis* was studied. QSAR models without regard to mechanism of toxic action were developed based on these statistical methods using a data set containing toxicity for 250 phenols and seven molecular descriptors. No outliers were removed in model development. The models were validated using 10-fold cross validation. For the particular data set, the highest modeling and predicting powers were offered by the PPR model among all eight models. In addition to model prediction, the eight models were compared in terms of their ability to identify toxicologically important parameter, model transparency, and model interpretability.

APPENDIX

Key R Codes

```
GAM:    obj<- gam(Toxicity~s(logD)+s(LUMO)+ s(MW)+s(Pneg)+s(ABSQon)
                +s(MW)+s(Pneg)+s(ABSQon)+s(MaxHp)+s(SsOH),data=x,family=gaussian())
MARS:   obj <- mars(x,y)
NN:     obj <- nnet(x,y,size=3,decay=1e-3,linout=T,skip=T,maxit=1000)
PPR:    obj <- ppr(x,y,nterms=7)
RPART:  obj <- rpart(y~logD+LUMO+MW+Pneg+ABSQon+MaxHp+SsOH,data=x)
LASSO2: obj  <-  l1ce(Toxicity~logD+LUMO+MW+Pneg+ABSQon+MaxHp+SsOH,
                data=x)
MLR:    obj <- lm(y~logD+LUMO+MW+ABSQon+MaxHp+SsOH, data=x)
```

Key Guide Inputs at Prompt

Guide: Advanced options, least squares, multiple linear, slower method, prune by cross-validation, 10-fold cross-validation.

ACKNOWLEDGEMENTS

The first author is grateful to Helen M. Delgado for her motivation and encouragements. The work of the second author was supported by the Basic Research Program of the Korea Science & Engineering Foundation (Grant No. R01-2005-000-11057-0).

REFERENCES

Bearden AP, Schultz TW. 1997. Structure-activity relationships for *Pimephales* and *Tetrahymena*: a mechanism of action approach. *Environ. Toxicol. Chem.* 16, 1311-1317.

Bradbury SP. 1995. Quantitative structure-activity relationships and ecological risk assessment: an overview of predictive aquatic toxicology research. *Toxcol. Lett.* 79, 229-237.

Breiman L, Friedman JH, Olshen JA, Stone CJ. 1984. *Classification and Regression Trees.* Wadsworth International Group, Belmont, CA, USA.

Caza N, Bewtra JK, Biswas N, Taylor KE. 1999. Removal of phenolic compounds from synthetic wastewater using soybean proxidase. *Water* Res. 33, 3012-3018.

Cronin MTD, Dearden JC. 1995. Review: QSAR in toxicology. 1. Prediction of aquatic toxicity. *Quant. Struct.-Act. Relat.* 14, 1-7.

Cronin MTD, Zhao YH, Yu RL. 2000. pH-Dependence and QSAR analysis of the toxicity of phenols and anilines to *Daphnia magna. Environ. Toxicol.* 15, 140-148.

Cronin MTD, Schultz TW. 2001. Development of quantitative structure-activity relationships for the toxicity of aromatic compounds to *Tetrahymena pyriformis*: comparative assessment of the methodologies. *Chem. Res. Toxicol. 14,* 1284-1295.

Cronin MTD, Aptula AO, Duffy JC, Netzeva TI, Rowe PH, Valkova IV, Schultz TW. 2002. Comparative assessment of methods to develop QSARs for the prediction of the toxicity of phenols to *Tetrahymena pyriformis. Chemosphere 49,* 1201-1221.

Cronin MTD, Schultz TW. 2003. Pitfalls in QSAR. *J. Mol. Struct. (Theochem) 622,* 39-51.

Eriksson L, Jaworska J, Worth AP, Cronin MTD, McDowell RM, Gramatica P. 2003. Methods for reliability and uncertainty assessment and for applicability evaluation of classification- and regression-based QSARs. *Environ. Health Perspect. 111,* 1361-1375.

Fang HHP, Chen T, Li YY, Chui HK. 1996. Degradation of phenol in wastewater in an upflow anaerobic sludge blanket reactor. *Water* Res. 30, 1353-1360.

Friedman JH. 1991. Multivariate additive regression splines. *Anls Stat. 19,* 1-141.

Friedman JH, Stuetzle W. 1981. Projection pursuit regression. *J. Am. Stat. Asso. 76,* 817-823.

Hastie TJ, Tibshirani RJ. 1990. *Generalized Additive Models.* Chapman and Hall, New York, NY, USA.

Hastie T, Tibshirani R, Friedman J. 2001 *The Elements of Statistical Learning.* Springer, New York, USA.

Hawkins DM, Rusinko A, Young SS. 1997. Analysis of a large structure-activity data set using recursive partitioning. *Quant. Struct.-Act. Relat. 16,* 296-302.

Kaiser KLE. 2003. The use of neural networks in QSARs for acute aquatic toxicological endpoints. *J. Mol. Struct. (Theochem) 622,* 85-96.

Kövesdi I, Dominguez-Rodriguez MF, Ôrfi L, Náray-Szabó G, Varró A, Papp JG, Mátyus P. 1997. Application of neural networks in structure-activity relationships. *Med. Res. Rev. 19*, 249-269.

Loh WY. 2002. Regression trees with unbiased variable selection and interaction detection. *Statistica sinica 12*, 361-386.

Mekapati SB, Hansch C. 2002. On the parametrization of the toxicity of organic chemicals to *Tetrahymena pyriformis*. The problem of establishing a uniform activity. *J. Chem. Inf. Comput. Sci. 42*, 956-961.

Montgomery DC. 2001. *Design and Analysis of Experiments*. 5th Edition. John Wiley and Sons, Inc., New York, NY, USA.

Müller B. 1990. *Neural Networks*: *An Introduction*. Springer-Verlag, New York, NY, USA.

Osborne MR, Presnell B, Turlach BA. 2000. On the LASSO and its dual. *J. Comput. Graphical Stat. 9*, 319-337.

Ren S. 2002a. Determining the mechanism of toxic action of phenols to *Tetrahymena pyriformis*. *Environ. Toxicol. 17*, 119-127.

Ren S. 2002b. Use of molecular descriptors in separating phenols by three mechanisms of toxic action. *Quant. Struct.-Act. Relat. 21*, 486-492.

Ren S. 2003. Ecotoxicity prediction using mechanism- and non-mechanism-based QSARs: a preliminary study. *Chemosphere 53*, 1053-1065.

Ren S, Frymier PD. 2003. Toxicity estimation of phenolic compounds by bioluminescent bacterium. *J. Environ. Eng. 129*, 328-335..

Schultz TW. 1997. TETRATOX: Tetrahymena population growth impairment endpoint – a surrogate for fish lethality. *Toxicol. Meth. 7*, 289-309.

Schultz TW, Sinks GD, Bearden AP. 1998. QSAR in aquatic toxicology: a mechanism of action approach comparing toxic potency to *Pimephales promelas*, *Tetrahymena pyriformis*, and *Vibrio fischeri*. In Devillers J (ed.), *Comparative QSAR*. Taylor & Francis, New York, NY, USA. pp51-109.

Schultz TW, Cronin MTD. 1999. Response-surface analyses for toxicity to *Tetrahymena pyriformis*: reactive carbonyl-containing aliphatic chemicals. *J. Chem. Inf. Comput. Sci. 39*, 304-309.

Schultz TW, Cronin MTD. 2003. Essential and desirable characteristics of ecotoxicity quantitative structure-activity relationships. *Environ. Toxicol. Chem. 22*, 599-607.

Schultz TW, Cronin MTD, Netzeva TI. 2003a. The present status of QSAR in toxicology. *J. Mol. Struct. (Theochem) 622*, 23-38.

Schultz TW, Cronin MTD, Walker JD, Aptula AO. 2003b. Quantitative structure-activity relationships (QSARs) in toxicology: a historical perspective. *J. Mol. Struc. (Theochem) 622*, 1-22.

Tang NH, Blum DJW, Nirmalakhandan N, Speece RE. 1992. QSAR parameters for toxicity of organic chemicals to *Nitrobacter*. *J. Environ. Eng. 118*, 17-37.

Tropsha A, Gramatica P, Gombar VK. 2003. The importance of being earnest: validation is the absolute essential for successful application and interpretation of QSPR models. *QSAR Comb. Sci. 22*, 69-77.

Wang X, Dong Y, Wang L, Han S. 2001. Acute toxicity of substituted phenols to *Rana japonica* tadpoles and mechanism-based quantitative structure-activity relationship (QSAR) study. *Chemosphere 44*, 447-455.

Walker JD, Dearden JC, Schultz TW, Jaworska J, Comber MHI. 2003. QSARs for new practitioners. In: Walker JD (ed.), QSARs for Pollution Prevention, Toxicity Screening, Risk Assessment, and Web Applications. SETAC Press, Pensocola, FL, USA. pp3-18.

In: New Topics in Environmental Research
Editor: Daniel Rhodes, pp. 155-221

ISBN 1-60021-172-0

Chapter 7

AN IONISING RADIATION EXPOSURE ASSESSMENT SYSTEM FOR THE ARCTIC ENVIRONMENT: THE EPIC FRAMEWORK

Justin Brown[1] and Mark Dowdall[2]

[1] Norwegian Radiation Protection Authority, Østerås, Norway
[2] Norwegian Radiation protection Authority, Polar Environmental Centre, Tromsø, Norway

ABSTRACT

Within the field of radiological protection it has historically been presumed that measures to ensure the protection of man from the effects of ionising radiation have also served to effect the protection of the environment. Recent times have seen this premise questioned on the basis of its inconsistency with environmental protection standards for other contaminants, the fact that it conflicts with the recommendations of some international advisory bodies and that it is, in some cases, demonstrably not true. Such questions have generated the need for a defensible and transparent system for ensuring the protection of the environment from ionising radiation. The Arctic environment is especially vulnerable to radioactive contamination for a number of reasons including the large number of potential and actual sources of contamination either within the Arctic itself or in locations where discharges may be transported to the Arctic and the specificities of Arctic ecosystems that impose enhanced vulnerabilities on the components of these ecosystems to radioactive contamination. For these reasons, the development of specific strategies and systems to ensure the protection of Arctic ecosystems from radioactive contamination are a matter of some concern.

The aim of the EPIC (Environmental Protection from Ionising Contaminants in the Arctic) framework was to develop a methodology for the protection of natural populations of organisms in Arctic ecosystems from radiation via the derivation of dose limits for different Arctic biota. The system was developed by collating information relating to the environmental transfer and fate of selected radionuclides through aquatic and terrestrial ecosystems in the Arctic, identification of reference Arctic biota that can be used to evaluate potential dose rates to biota in different terrestrial, freshwater and marine environments and modelling the uptake of a suite of radionuclides to the selected reference Arctic biota. This work then allowed for the development of a reference set of dose models for Arctic biota and the compilation of data on dose-effects relationships and assessments of potential radiological consequences for reference Arctic biota with the integration of assessments of the environmental impact from radioactive contamination with those for other contaminants.

This article serves to describe the EPIC framework and its development, the regulatory environment within which the framework was designed to function and presents a case study demonstrating the operation of the framework. Future development and issues of concern are also presented.

GLOSSARY

The following terms and definitions have been adopted or modified from ICRU report 65 (2001) and USDoE (2002).

Absorbed dose: Quantity of energy imparted by *ionising radiation* to unit mass of matter such as tissue. Unit *gray*, symbol Gy. 1 Gy = 1 joule per kilogram.

Actinide: A group of 14 elements with atomic number from 90 (thorium) to 103 (lawrencium) inclusive. All are radioactive.

Activity: Attribute specifying an amount of a *radionuclide*. Describes the rate at which transformations occur. Unit *Becquerel*, symbol Bq. 1 Bq = 1 transformation per second.

Aggregated transfer factor (T_{ag}): The aggregated transfer factor/coefficient, T_{ag}, is the mass activity density, A_m (Bq kg^{-1}) in a specified object per unit areal activity density, A_a (Bq m^{-2}) in the soil. A_a in this case refers to the depth-integrated activity per unit area in soil underlying the specified object.

Allometric: The allometric approach is based on the observation that many metabolic parameters, including basal metabolic rates, ingestion rates, biological half times etc., are related (as power functions) to the masses of organisms.

Alpha particle: Is a helium-4 nucleus, consisting of two protons and two neutrons, given off by the decay of many heavy elements, including uranium and plutonium.

Assessment endpoint: The biological effect inferred from the measurements or predictions and which the assessment framework is designed to study.

Assessment framework: Identification and demarcation of the assessment boundaries. In EPIC, the framework contains the process from problem formulation through to characterisation of the effects of radiation on individuals. The overall assessment system describes the tools, methods and information flow used to carry out the impact assessment.

Benthic: Pertaining to, or with the characteristics of, the benthos; also, the bottom region of a lake or sea.

Bioaccumulation: The process whereby an organism accumulates chemicals in living tissues to concentrations higher than those existing in the surrounding media (e.g., soil, water, food).

Bioaccumulation factor (BAF): The ratio of the concentration of a chemical in the tissue of an organism to its concentration in the surrounding media, in a situation where both the organism and its food are exposed and the ratio does not change substantially over time.

Bioconcentration : The net accumulation of a chemical by an aquatic organism as a result of uptake directly from the ambient water, through gill membranes or other external body surfaces.

Bioconcentration factor (BCF): The ratio of the concentration of a chemical in the tissue of an aquatic organism to its concentration in water, in situations where the organism is exposed through the water only and the ratio does not change substantially over time.

Biokinetic model: A mathematical model which incorporates metabolic rate equations and is dynamic (time-dependent).

Biological diversity (Biodiversity): The number and abundance of species found within a common environment. This includes the variety of genes, species, ecosystems, and the ecological processes that connect everything in a common environment.

Biological half-life: The time required for a biological system (e.g. animal) to eliminate, by natural processes, half the amount of a substance that has been absorbed into that system.

Biomagnification: The increase in concentration of a chemical in the tissue of organisms along a series of predator-prey associations, primarily through the mechanism of dietary accumulation.

Biomagnification factor (BMF): The ratio (unitless) of the concentration of a chemical in a predator organism at a particular trophic level to the concentration of the chemical in the tissue of its prey organism at the next lowest trophic level for a given ecosystem and chemical exposure.

Biosphere: The portion of Earth and its atmosphere that can support life.

Biota: The animal and plant life of a given region.

Bioturbation: Perturbation or disturbance of sediments or soils by one or more biological mechanisms.

Chronic: Refers to an extended continuous exposure to a stressor or the effects resulting from such an exposure.

Concentration factor (CF): In this report, the term has been applied specifically for aquatic ecosystems and is defined as the ratio of the concentration of the radionuclide in the organism or tissue (normally fresh weight) to that in water (normally filtered), assuming the system is under equilibrium.

Concentration ratio (CR): In this report, the term has been applied specifically for terrestrial ecosystems and is defined as the activity density of *reference organism* relative to that of soil (ICRU, 2001).

Cytogenetic: Observed effects in chromosomes that can be correlated with adverse hereditary or genetic effects.

Cytogenetic damage: Damage to chromosomes that can be detected on the microscopic level.

Decay: The process of spontaneous transformation of a radionuclide. The decrease in the activity of a radioactive substance.

Dose: Normally relates to the term *absorbed dose* as specified above.

Dose conversion factor (DCF): Represents the instantaneous dose rate per unit activity concentration of the radionuclide in an organism or in the environment. Synonym: DCC, Dose Conversion Coefficient.

Dose rate: Dose (normally *absorbed dose*) received over a specified unit of time.

Dose-effect: The relationship between dose (or dose-rate) and the gradation of the effect in an exposed individual or population, that is a biological change measured on a graded scale of severity.

Dose-response: A correlation between a quantified exposure (dose) and the proportion of an exposed population that demonstrates a specific effect (response).

Dynamic model: A mathematical model which incorporates time as an independent variable.

Ecosystem: The interacting system of a biological community and its non-living surroundings.

Ecological risk assessment: The process that evaluates the likelihood that adverse ecological effects may occur or are occurring as a result of exposure to one or more stressors.

Ecosystem: The interacting system of a biological community and its non-living surroundings.

Effect: A biological change caused by an exposure.

End-point: The final stage of a process, especially the point at which an effect is observed. A radiological or other measure of protection or safety that is the calculated result of an analysis or assessment.

Equivalent dose: The quantity obtained by multiplying the *absorbed dose* by a weighting factor (*radiation weighting factor*) to allow for the different effectiveness of the various ionising radiations in causing harm to tissue. Unit sievert, symbol Sv.

Exposure: The co-occurrence or contact between the endpoint organism and the stressor (e.g., radiation or radionuclide)

Exposure assessment: The process of measuring or estimating the intensity, frequency, and duration of exposures to an agent currently present in the environment or of estimating hypothetical exposures that might arise from the release of new chemicals into the environment.

Fecundity: The number of viable offspring produced by an organism; mature seeds produced, eggs laid, or live offspring delivered, excluding fertilized embryos that have failed to develop.

Fertility: In sexually reproducing plants and animals it is the number of fertilized eggs produced in a given time.

Food chain: A linear series of species linked by specific *trophic* or feeding relationships, e.g. plant-herbivore-carnivore.

Hazard: A condition or physical situation with a potential for an undesirable consequence, such as harm to heath or environment.

KERMA: Kinetic Energy Released in Material. It is a non-stochastic quantity relevant only for fields of indirectly ionising radiations (photons or neutrons) or for any ionising radiation source distributed within the absorbing medium. It represents the initial kinetic energy of the primary ionising particles produced by the interaction of the incident radiation per unit mass of interacting medium. In the SI system KERMA is measured in units of joules per kilogram or grays.

Linear energy transfer (LET): A measure of how, as a function of distance, energy is transferred from radiation to the exposed matter. Radiation with high LET is normally assumed to comprise of protons, neutrons and alpha particles (or other particles of similar or greater mass). Radiation with low LET is assumed to comprise of photons (including X-rays and gamma rays), electrons and positrons.

Measurement endpoint: Measured or predicted value that an assessment produces

Monte Carlo method/simulation: Of or relating to a problem-solving technique that uses random samples and other statistical methods for finding solutions to mathematical or physical problems.

Morbidity: A loss of functional capacities generally manifested as reduced 'fitness', which may render organisms less competitive and more susceptible to other stressors, thus reducing the life span.

Mortality: Death; the death rate; ratio of number of deaths to a given population.

Natural radionuclide: Radionuclides that occur naturally in significant quantities on Earth.

Occupancy factor: Refers to the fraction of the time that an organism expends in a specified habitat.

Octanol-water partition coefficient (K_{ow}): The K_{ow} is defined as the ratio of a chemical's concentration in the octanol phase to its concentration in the aqueous phase of a two-phase octanol-water system.

Phytoplankton: Passive or weakly motile suspended plant life; the plant subgroup of *plankton*.

Poikilotherm: An organism, such as a fish or reptile, having a body temperature that varies with the temperature of its surroundings; an ectotherm.

Pollution: The presence of matter or energy [e.g., smoke, gas, hazardous or noxious substances, light, heat, litter or a combination thereof] in sufficient quantities and of such characteristics and duration as to produce, or likely to produce, undesired environmental effects.

POPs: Persistent Organic Pollutants (POPs) are chemical substances that persist in the environment, bioaccumulate through the food web, and pose a risk of causing adverse effects to biota and the environment.

Radiation weighting factor: Its value represent the *relative biological effectiveness* of the different radiation types, relative to X- or gamma-rays, in producing endpoints of ecological significance.

Radiological protection: The science and practice of limiting the harm to environment from radiations.

Radionuclide: An unstable nuclide that undergoes spontaneous transformation, emitting *ionising radiation*.

Reference organisms: A series of entities that provide a basis for the estimation of radiation dose rate to a range of organisms which are typical, or representative, of a contaminated environment. These estimates, in turn, would provide a basis for assessing the likelihood and degree of radiation effects.

Relative biological effectiveness (RBE): For a given type of radiation, RBE is defined as:

$$RBE = \frac{\text{Dose of the reference radiation needed to produce the same effect}}{\text{Dose of the given radiation needed to produce a given biological effect}}$$

Response: The proportion or absolute size of an exposed population that demonstrates a specific effect. May also refer to the nature of the effect.

Risk: A measure of the probability that damage to life, health, property, and/or the environment will occur as a result of a given hazard. A technical estimation of risk is usually based on the expected value of the conditional probability of the event occurring times the consequence or magnitude of the event given that it has occurred.

Risk Assessment: A qualitative or quantitative evaluation of the risk posed to human health and/or the environment by the actual or potential presence and/or use of pollutants. It includes problem formulation, exposure and dose-response assessment and risk characterisation

Risk Characterisation: The synthesis of information obtained during risk assessment for use in management decisions. This should include an estimation of the probability (or incidence) and magnitude (or severity) of the adverse health or ecological effects likely to occur in a population or environmental compartment, together with identification of uncertainties.

Semi-natural ecosystem: Extensively (as opposed to intensively) used land.

Transfer factor (TF): Is defined as the ratio of the activity density (Bq/kg or Bq/l) of a radionuclide in the receptor compartment to that in the donor compartment. In this report the term transfer factor is used as a generic term that includes CRs, CFs and activity concentration relative to annual deposited activity.

Trophic level: Functional classification of organisms in an ecosystem according to feeding relationships from first level autotrophs through succeeding levels of herbivores and carnivores.

Zooplankton: Sub-group of plankton in aquatic ecosystems and which are animals.

INTRODUCTION

Sources and Potential Sources of Radioactive Contaminants to the Arctic Environment

There are several varied actual and potential sources of radioactive contamination to the European Arctic a number of which are of importance to both the terrestrial and marine environments of the region. These include the earlier atmospheric testing of nuclear weapons, discharges from the nuclear reprocessing plants of Western Europe (Aarkrog et al., 1987), the Chernobyl Accident of 1986, radioactive discharges to the Techa, Ob and Yenisey River systems (Academy of Science, 1991), dumped nuclear materials at Novaya Zemlya and in the Kara Sea, sunken nuclear submarines, civilian and military nuclear facilities on the Kola Peninsula, the use of Radionuclide Thermoelectric Generators (RTGs) in the Arctic region and various accidents involving nuclear materials. In addition to these, the production of technologically enhanced naturally occurring radioactive material (TENORM) as a by-product of extractive industries conducted or to be conducted in the Arctic should be considered as an additional source.

Global fallout from the atmospheric testing of nuclear weapons is one of the primary sources of radioactive contamination in the Arctic region. Of the 543 atmospheric weapons tests that have been carried out globally, 91 of these were conducted within the Arctic region by the Former Soviet Union (FSU) at the Novaya Zemlya test sites with a total yield of 239.6 Mt (UNSCEAR, 2000a). Aarkrog (1994) estimated fallout levels in the Arctic region of 20 PBq of ^{90}Sr and 30 PBq of ^{137}Cs from 87 of these tests alone. In the 70 to 80°N latitude band, UNSCEAR (2000a) determined average integrated deposition densities as a consequence of atmospheric testing of 0.68 kBq/m^2 of ^{90}Sr and 1.09 kBq/m^2 ^{137}Cs, the latter being in agreement with the lower end of an estimated ^{137}Cs cumulative deposition range of 1 to 5 kBq/m^2 as determined by AMAP (1997). The levels of atmospheric radioactive contamination reaching the Arctic region fell significantly in the years after the signing of the Limited Test Ban Treaty of 1963 (Barrie et al., 1992), with a resultant but somewhat slower reduction in levels in terrestrial matrices. During the early 1960's, underwater nuclear testing at the Chernaya Bay test site on the south western coast of Novaya Zemlya resulted in contamination of the bay's benthic environment with elevated levels of plutonium and cesium isotopes, as well as other radioactive isotopes. However, the mobility of many radionuclides in sediments is low and at present may only cause insignificant exposure for people. The exposure of biota to radioactive contaminants at these sites is unknown. Currently the inventory of plutonium isotopes in Chernaya Bay is similar to other sites exhibiting serious plutonium contamination, such as the most contaminated areas of Bylot Sound (location of a B-52 bomber accident) and the Irish Sea in the vicinity of the Sellafield reprocessing plant. Underground detonations were conducted during the period 1963 to 1989 at Novaya Zemlya and at Amchitka Island, Alaska. While fission products have been identified in air after underground nuclear detonations, (Bjurman et al., 1990), such detonations are assumed to have no significant impacts on the levels of radioactive contaminants in the marine environment. The predominant signature of radioactive fallout from atmospheric nuclear weapons testing in the Arctic environment of today is primarily via the long lived isotopes of plutonium (^{238}Pu, ^{239}Pu, ^{240}Pu) with contributions from ^{137}Cs and ^{90}Sr that have diminished since the time of deposition due to their relatively short half-lives. ^{241}Am, a daughter of ^{241}Pu, is also present due to radioactive ingrowth over the years since the initial deposition of its parent.

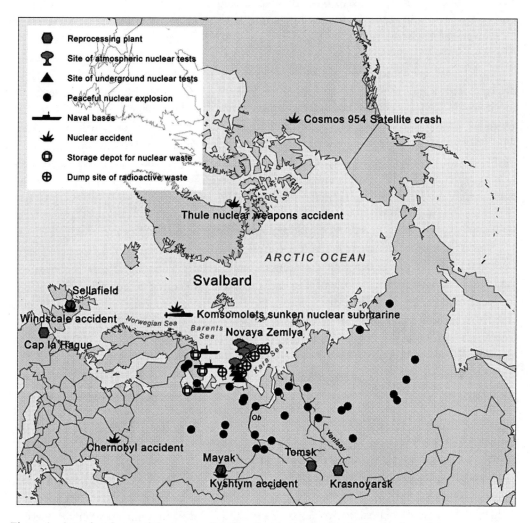

Figure 1. Actual and potential sources of radioactive contamination to the Arctic region.

A past and continuing source of anthropogenic radionuclides to the Arctic marine environment are European nuclear fuel reprocessing facilities at Sellafield in the United Kingdom, Dounreay in Scotland, and Cap la Hague in France. The highest discharges of radioactive material have occurred from the reprocessing facilities at Sellafield, UK. From the late sixties until the mid-eighties, releases of radiocaesium from the Sellafield facility were up to a factor of 100 higher than the releases from Dounreay and Cap la Hague, peaking in the mid seventies at around 5 PBq/a. Due to a stronger regulatory environment and plant improvements that have been implemented at the site since this time, releases of several of the primary radionuclides of concern, including ^{137}Cs and the actinides plutonium ($^{239+240}$Pu) and americium (^{241}Am) have declined appreciably over subsequent years. In 1994 the Enhanced Actinide Removal Plant (EARP) and the Thermal Oxide Reprocessing Plant (THORP) began operations at the Sellafield site. While the operation of these plants resulted in reduced discharges of some radionuclides such as $^{239+240}$Pu and ^{241}Am, plant operations increased the discharges of others, especially technetium (^{99}Tc) but also, to a much lesser extent, ^{60}Co and ^{90}Sr. Throughout the 1980's and early 1990's (1981 to 1993), ^{99}Tc was discharged from the Sellafield site at a rate of 1.9 to 6.6 TBq/a following an earlier release peak of 180 TBq/a during 1978. Commencement of EARP operation saw a step increase in discharges to a level close to the authorised limit (200 TBq/a) of 72 to 190 TBq/a during the period 1994 to 1996. A reduction in ^{99}Tc discharges has occurred during recent years to levels that are lower than the current revised authorised limit of 90 TBq/a. The reprocessing facility at Cap la Hague has been in operation since 1965 and although the total discharges of radioactive materials are much lower than for the Sellafield site, releases of ^{99}Tc during the period 1981 to 1990 exceeded those from Sellafield. Cs-137 discharges from the la Hague site peaked in 1971 at 240 TBq/a, but have been appreciably lower than for Sellafield over the duration of its operations as is the case for all discharges from Dounreay. The major discharges from Dounreay occurred in the 1960's and early 1970's, with lower peaks in 1968 and 1973 due to plant cleaning and decontamination procedures. The cumulative activity discharged from Dounreay up to 1986 was in the region of 10 PBq with ^{95}Zr/^{95}Nb, ^{144}Ce and ^{106}Ru representing 55 %, 17 % and 10 % of this activity respectively (CEC, 1990).

The most serious accident involving nuclear reactor operations to date occurred at the Chernobyl nuclear power plant in the Ukraine in April of 1986. Significant amounts of a variety of radionuclides were released to the atmosphere resulting in contamination of both the local environment and large areas across the Scandinavian countries of Finland, Sweden and Norway and over much of Western Europe. It is estimated that as a result of the Chernobyl accident approximately 131 PBq of radiocaesium (^{134}Cs and ^{137}Cs), 8 PBq of ^{90}Sr and 0.1 PBq of plutonium isotopes were released to the environment (AMAP, 1997). In addition to direct fallout from the atmosphere, the Arctic marine environment may also be contaminated by transport of contamination from the North Sea and the Baltic Sea, the catchments of both receiving considerably more radionuclides from Chernobyl than Arctic regions. Calculations based on ^{134}Cs/^{137}Cs ratios in the Kara Sea, in 1992, suggested that some 30 % of the ^{137}Cs contamination in the surface waters of the Kara Sea was derived from the Chernobyl accident at that time (Strand et al., 1993).

Several major nuclear facilities of various types are situated in and discharge to the drainage basins of the large Russian river systems, the Ob and the Yenisey. Discharges or accidental releases of radioactive materials from these facilities combined with surface run-off of radioactive fallout from atmospheric nuclear weapons testing may enter the river drainage systems and be transported downstream to the Kara Sea and subsequently into the wider Arctic region. The Mayak facilities, built in 1948 to produce ^{239}Pu weapons-grade material, discharged large quantities of radioactive waste into the nearby Techa River between 1949 to 1956. Current releases from the Mayak site are considerably reduced, since the last of the reactors producing weapons-grade plutonium was shut down in 1990. In addition to intentional discharges, the area around the Mayak site (~20000 km^2) was contaminated by the Kyshtym accident in 1957 when a storage tank containing highly radioactive material exploded. Between 1951 and 1963, a system of dams along the upper parts of the Techa was constructed in an attempt to retain most of the radioactive material, creating several artificial lakes along the river course (Borghuis et al., 2002). Failure of the dam system would result in a large scale discharge of radionuclides into the already contaminated Asanov Swamp and into the Techa and Ob river systems (JNREG, 2004). Other large-scale releases would occur if the Asanov swamp were to dry out after which spring floods could wash remobilised radionuclides into the river systems. Lake Karachay, which received Mayak discharges from 1951 onwards, has no outlet but caused contamination of the surrounding region during a dry period in 1967, when lake sediments were exposed and transported by winds. The lake bottom is now covered with blocks of concrete to prevent further resuspension, but radioactive material might leach from the sediments into groundwater and eventually into the Techa/Ob river system.

The Siberian Chemical Combine at Seversk near Tomsk is one of the largest nuclear weapons production facilities in the world. Since 1956, the plant has released contaminated cooling water into the river Tom, which ultimately drains into the Ob. The plant came to international attention in April 1993, when a chemical reaction caused an explosion in a tank containing fission products and uranium nitrate solution, contaminating an area of about 90 km^2. A recent report from the Russian Federation Security Council has stated that large amounts of radioactive wastes were stored within the industrial zone, some of which are retained in reservoirs, leading to fears over contamination of groundwater. The Krasnoyarsk Mining and Chemical Combine, recently renamed Zheleznogorsk, reprocesses spent nuclear fuel for the production of plutonium. Prior to 1992, contaminated cooling water from two reactors at the site was routinely discharged into the Yenisey River. At present liquid waste is stored in reservoirs or injected into deep holding wells, which may contaminate groundwater migrating into the Yenisey (Linnik et al., 2005).

It is difficult to estimate the impact on the Arctic region from these sources because the transport routes and the magnitude of transport are not sufficiently documented and because the data regarding discharges and radioactive inventory in the open literature contains inconsistencies. Observations conducted by Roshydromet (Vakulovsky et al., 1993) indicate that about 1 PBq of ^{90}Sr and 0.1 PBq of ^{137}Cs were transported by the Ob and Yenisey rivers during 1961 to 1989. In addition, approximately 200 TBq of ^{137}Cs have been transported to the Barents Sea by the rivers Pechora, Onega and Severnaya Dvina (Vakulovsky et al., 1993).

Between 1959 and 1991, the Former Soviet Union (FSU) dumped high, intermediate, and low level radioactive waste in the Arctic Seas including six nuclear submarine reactors and a shielding assembly from an icebreaker reactor that contained spent nuclear fuel. The solid waste and the nuclear reactors were dumped in the Kara Sea and in the fjords of Novaya Zemlya at depths of between 12 and 135 m and in the Novaya Zemlya trough at a depth of 300 m. The liquid low-level waste was dumped into the open Barents and Kara Seas. At the time of dumping experts estimated that the spent nuclear fuel constituted a total activity of 8.5 x 10^{16} Bq. Between 1992 to 1994, a joint Norwegian-Russian expert group has used sonar techniques and a remotely operated vehicle in an attempt to find and examine the waste materials. The exploratory cruises also took samples of water, sediments, and biota from the relevant areas. The results of these investigations indicate that there is no significant contamination in the Kara Sea in general. In fact, the levels of radionuclides in the water of the Kara Sea are lower than in many other marine areas such as the Irish, Baltic, and North Seas. However, higher levels of radioactivity in the immediate vicinity of the waste show that there is local contamination at the dumpsites whilst the major risks are over the long term after the containment systems around the dumped materials corrode and degrade.

In 1989, the Soviet nuclear submarine Komsomolets caught fire and sank to the southeast of Bjørnøya. The submarine contained a nuclear reactor with a radionuclide inventory including 2.7 PBq of ^{90}Sr and 3.0 PBq of ^{137}Cs and two nuclear warheads containing approximately 16 TBq of ^{239}Pu. Underwater monitoring at the site has shown elevated levels of ^{137}Cs and also indicated ^{134}Cs near the reactor section indicating that some leakage of radionuclides has occurred (Kolstad, 1995). However, conservative modelling of the possible releases of ^{137}Cs indicates that radionuclide concentrations in seawater and fish caused by past, present and probable future releases from the Komsomolets submarine are, or are likely to be, at least a factor of 100 lower than current concentrations in these media.

In 2000, the Kursk, a Russian Oscar II class attack submarine containing two 190 MW pressurized water reactors and 22 Granit cruise missiles sank in international waters in the Barents Sea. No indication of leakage from the submarine was observed from any dose rate readings or any of the measurements on environmental samples taken close to the Kursk immediately after the sinking, during subsequent operations at the site or during its final raising (Amundsen et al., 2001). The fact that no elevated radioactivity levels were observed indicates that the reactors had been shut down, as stated by the Russian authorities, and that the reactor compartment was not flooded with contaminated water. The section of the Kursk containing the two reactors and the cruise missiles was raised in 2001. On the 30th August 2003, the K-159, a decommissioned Russian November class attack submarine sank 5 km north west of the Kildin Islands in Russian territorial waters to a depth of 240 m while being towed on pontoons to the Polyarny shipyard for decommissioning,. The submarine contained two 70 MW pressurised water reactors which were shut down in 1989 but no nuclear missiles. The cores of the reactors have an estimated 800 kg of spent nuclear fuel with an inventory of between 2 and 4 PBq.

On the Kola Peninsula the Russian Northern Fleet and the civilian nuclear icebreaker fleet have their main bases. Approximately 100 nuclear vessels operate from these bases containing, in total, about 200 nuclear reactors. Aside from operational vessels about 80 decommissioned nuclear submarines awaiting dismantling are stationed at the military bases. Most of these submarines still contain their nuclear reactors and fuel. Plans exist to decommission 125 submarines during the next several years. However, many challenges exist in performing the dismantling work, minimising the risks of accidents and radiation doses to workers. Disposing of the nuclear materials poses a further challenge as storage facilities for spent nuclear fuel in the Kola Peninsula are already filled to capacity. The operations involved in the decommissioning of these submarines and related activities pose some risk to the Arctic environment should an accident or discharge of radioactivity occur. The Kola Nuclear Power Plant (NPP) represents a potential major source of radioactive contamination to the Arctic due to its high inventory and lack of containment. The Kola NPP has 4 pressurized water reactors that have been in operation since the early 1970's and 80's with an estimated total fission product inventory of approximately 10^{19} Bq (Stokke, 1997; JRNEG, 2002). According to Larsen et al. (1999) a worst case accident scenario involving a significant loss of cooling could result in the release of 26.7 PBq of ^{134}Cs and ^{137}Cs and 1.7 PBq of ^{90}Sr.

The remoteness of the Arctic and the difficulty of civil and military operations in the environment have led to nuclear materials being introduced as power sources for a variety of installations. Radionuclide Thermoelectric Generators (RTGs) are often used as power supplies, utilising radioactive decay, of typically ^{90}Sr, as a heat source. RTGs are located throughout Alaska and the Eurasian arctic region and are generally considered to pose little risk of contamination, although some RTGs have been reported as lost or stolen. Hypothetical dose-rates arsing from unshielded sources could be extremely high resulting in acute radiation sickness or lethal doses to vertebrate animals within several days although the area of extremely elevated exposures would be limited to a radius of 10s of metres from the RTG (Hosseini & Brown, 2005).

Vulnerability of the Arctic Environment to Radioactive Contamination

The prevalent perception of the Arctic as a pristine wilderness and the vulnerability of its ecosystems have contributed to an increase in the amount of interest and attention focused on the region. Much of this attention has been in relation to pollutant levels in the Arctic and its ecosystems, with radioactive contaminants being one of the most often discussed suite of pollutants. A number of factors have influenced the current focus on radioactivity within the Arctic regions, as evidenced by the radiological components of both the International Arctic Environmental Protection Strategy (IAEPS) and the Arctic Monitoring and Assessment Programme (AMAP, 1997). These include the relatively large number of sources of both actual and potential nuclear contamination that exist in the Arctic as introduced in the previous sections, the particular vulnerability of Arctic ecosystems to nuclear contamination (Wright et al., 1997) and the relative lack of knowledge with respect to both the occurrence and behaviour of radioactive contaminants in Arctic ecosystems and the possible effects of even low levels of radioactivity on High Arctic biota.

Although historically, the emphasis of radiological protection has been directed towards health impacts on humans, the need for developing a system for assessment of radiological impacts to both flora and fauna has come to the fore in recent times. This shift in emphasis has largely been due to the realisation that the previous philosophy of environmental radioprotection, encapsulated in the phrase *"if man is protected, then the environment is protected"*, is not sufficient to ensure the protection of biota from the effects of radiation (Pentreath, 1999). Related to this change in focus is the concept that the assessment of the impacts of anthropogenic radioactive contaminants on the environment in general, and the Arctic in particular, can only be conducted with reference to the intrinsic natural dose commitment upon which any further anthropogenic doses are subsequently superimposed. Fundamental to both of these concepts is a need for an improvement in the amount and the quality of information relating to the current level of radionuclides in High Arctic environmental components and a focussing of attention towards site-specific processes influencing the behaviour and occurrence of radionuclides in constituent matrices therein. Of added importance in the consideration of the impact of radioactivity on the Arctic environment is the acute sensitivity of public perception to levels of radioactive contamination. Given the productivity of the Arctic marine environment and the importance of that productivity to a number of industries, it is imperative to ensure public confidence with respect to levels of radioactive contamination in the Arctic.

In discussing the behaviour of radioactive contaminants in the Arctic environment and the possible effects of such contaminants on components of Arctic ecosystems, it is worth considering the specificities of Arctic radioecology and how and why these aspects necessitate Arctic specific protection systems. Marine long-range transport of radioactive contaminants from European reprocessing plants and coastal waters contaminated by

Chernobyl fallout is principally mediated through oceanic circulation in the North Atlantic and Arctic Seas. The general circulation pattern (with respect to European reprocessing facilities) describes Atlantic water flowing through the Irish Sea and English Channel, via the North Sea to become incorporated with Baltic Sea outflow through the Skagerrak and forming the north flowing Norwegian Coastal Current. As the Norwegian Coastal Current continues northwards, it progressively mixes with Atlantic water coming from the Norwegian Atlantic Current, until the Norwegian Atlantic Current splits at the western boundary of the Barents Sea into the North Cape Current and the West Spitsbergen Current that flows north along the western coastline of Svalbard. Transit times of radionuclides from Sellafield to the Arctic region, specifically the Barents Sea, via this route have been estimated to be of the order of 3 to 6 years (Kautsky, 1987; Dahlgaard, 1995; Brown et al., 2002a) Models of the dispersion of radionuclides from the European reprocessing plants to the Arctic have shown good overall agreement with experimental data (e.g. Nies et al., 1999; Iosjpe et al., 2002; Karcher et al., 2004) and in addition, have highlighted mesoscale variability in surface concentrations of radionuclides, which may have important implications for future monitoring strategies. It has been suggested that incorporation of radionuclides as well as other pollutants, into the ice cover in the Arctic Seas, may result in significant transportation of contaminants from one area to another. Contamination of ice with radionuclides occurs from in situ seawater contamination, atmospheric deposition onto existing sea ice cover and through the incorporation of contaminated suspended material from terrestrial run-off and contaminated bottom sediments in seasonally formed coastal ice. The formation of seasonal coastal sea ice occurs along long swathes of the European Arctic coastline and of particular interest, in the Kara Sea, in the shallow coastal areas of the Ob and Yenisey estuaries and the coastal areas off Novaya Zemlya (e.g. Vinje and Kvambekk, 1991; Dethleff et al., 1998; Landa et al., 1998). Kara Sea ice has been shown to travel north round the tip of Novaya Zemlya, into the Barents Sea and southwest towards Svalbard (e.g. Vinje and Kvambekk, 1991; Nurnberg et al., 1994; Landa et al., 1998). Levels of ^{137}Cs and $^{239+240}$Pu of sediments entrained in sea ice from across the Arctic Basin have been reported to be in the range of 0.2 to 78 Bq/kg and 0.02 to 1.8 Bq/kg respectively (e.g. Meese et al., 1997; Landa et al., 1998). During the spring and summer, contaminated sediments may be deposited during ice melting, which can occur in the ice-melting zone along the polar front in the Svalbard area (Loeng, 1991). Furthermore, high levels of primary production associated with the polar fronts may lead to increased fluxes of certain radionuclides to marine sediments through active scavenging of nuclides from the water column during the production period (Føyn and Sværen, 1997). Radionuclides present in the marine environment may then be available for biological uptake by marine biota and possible subsequent transfer through marine and marine/terrestrial food webs. Indeed, some marine biota such as crustaceans, molluscs and marine algae exhibit very high uptake rates of certain anthropogenic and natural radionuclides (e.g. Pentreath et al., 1982; Aarkrog et al., 1997; Brown et al., 1999) that may have important consequences for Arctic ecosystems in the event of significant levels of ambient contamination.

There is much evidence to suggest that the in situ physical conditions of the Arctic region may hypothetically alter radionuclide transfer to biota (Sazykina, 1995, 1998), at least in the case of poikilotherms. Indeed, the slower digestion and metabolism of cold water animals resulting in slower efflux rates than in warm water species has been cited as a possible reason that differences may be observed in biological uptake within Arctic marine environments

(Fisher et al., 1999). The modifying influence of Arctic climatic conditions upon the expression of radiation induced effects has been considered in some detail by Sazkyina et al. (2003). The development of radiation effects in poikilothermic Arctic organisms is expected to occur more slowly because of low environmental temperatures. However, low temperatures, extreme seasonal variations in incoming solar radiation and lack of nutrients are physical and chemical environmental stressors of Arctic organisms which limit biodiversity. These also make Arctic ecosystems potentially more vulnerable to contaminants than organisms in other European climatic regions (AMAP, 1997).

In the terrestrial environment, the principal factors that govern the transport and biotic uptake of radionuclides (persistence, solubility, nutrient competition and location/trophic level of biota within ecosystems) are all affected to varying degrees by Arctic-specific processes. In the marine environment, the same can be said of the controls and the mechanisms by which radionuclides are transported to and within the Arctic area. Effects of climate on both the moisture content and organic input into Arctic soils largely determine the retention, mobilisation and behaviour of radionuclides within this matrix. In many Arctic regions, ^{137}Cs depth penetration within the soil column is minimal, despite the main deposition outside of Chernobyl affected areas occurring primarily in the 1950 and 60's. Typically, ^{137}Cs is detected predominantly within the upper soil layers (0 to 5 cm), in association with organic material rather than the underlying mineral horizons (e.g. Taylor et al., 1988; Baskaran et al., 1991; Stranberg, 1997). Arctic freeze-thaw cycles can have physical and chemical effects on the vertical distribution of radionuclides in these soils. These effects on soil chemistry exert some control over the movement and solubility of radionuclides between and within soils and the overlying snowpack. Such movement can promote a surge of contaminants in runoff associated with the initial spring meltwater (Johannessen and Henriksen, 1978). Soil horizons can undergo severe distortion due to high pressures generated by the freezing of soil that result in frost heave (see for example, Nakano, 1990) or by the slipping of saturated layers (solifluction). The unique environment of the Arctic has produced many adaptations in the ecosystems that are found there, which can increase the vulnerability of the organisms involved and the environment in general to radioactive contamination. This is perhaps most evident in a consideration of Arctic terrestrial food chains, which tend to be extremely short. In this regard, the role of lichens and mosses, which are highly efficient in their uptake and retention of radioisotopes, in the transfer of radionuclides to herbivores has received a great deal of attention (e.g. Gaare and Staaland, 1994). An as yet unexplored transfer mechanism that may have significance for Arctic radioecology is the potential of seabirds, through faecal deposits, to transfer radionuclides from the marine to the terrestrial environment or to condition soils, via nutrient input, such that the affected soils have a greater capacity for the adsorption of radionuclides. It has been shown that seabird faeces are the principal source of heavy metal input to Arctic soils (Headley, 1996) and that transfer can occur of these metals to vegetation growing on faecal-affected soils (Godzik, 1991).

The role of Arctic vegetation species in the accumulation and retention of radionuclide contaminants is closely linked to the overall nutrient status of the Arctic terrestrial environment. The enhanced nutrient status of faecal-affected soils subsequently causes an increase in both the diversity and quantity of vegetation growing in these areas (Eurola and Hakala, 1977) and therefore provides enhanced grazing for the herbivores of the region. The consumption of such vegetation by herbivores and further trophic transfer may result in novel or increased exposure to radionuclide contaminants.

The Requirement for Environmental Protection

There are already numerous multi-lateral environmental agreements (MEA's) that constitute legal frameworks for the conservation aspects of environmental protection. Initially, these were designed to regulate the exploitation of wildlife and to maintain their economic utility. More recently, as attitudes and scientific understanding have developed, the focus has changed from the protection of endangered species, to conservation of both species and their habitats. A major shift in conservation agreements occurred at the1992 UNCED Earth Summit in Rio de Janeiro, with the introduction of the Convention on Biological Diversity (CBD). The summit sought to bring together issues of human use and management of land and sea, nature conservation and the requirement for sustainability (Larsson et al., 2002a) and several relevant documents emerged in which a number of general principles for environmental protection were laid down. An example can be found in The Rio Declaration (UNCED, 1992) which emphasises, in Principle 4, the issue of sustainable development, stating that *'in order to achieve sustainable development, environmental protection shall constitute an integral part of the development process and cannot be considered in isolation from it.'* The issue of sustainable development was the key subject of the successor to the Rio Earth Summit: the UNCED World Summit on Sustainable Development held in Johannesburg, August-September 2002.

The trend in environmental protection MEA's has been reflected in international agreements relating to the management of radioactivity in a specific manner. Examples include the protection of the marine environment (OSPAR, 1998) and conventions on waste safety (e.g. the Joint Convention on the Safety of Spent Fuel Management and on the Safety of Radioactive Waste Management (UN, 1996)). The second principle of the IAEA Safety Fundamentals for the Management of Radioactive Waste (IAEA, 1995) states that, *'Radioactive waste shall be managed in such a way as to provide an acceptable level of protection of the environment'*. From these and other considerations, five basic principles, which reflect a world view or overlapping consensus, have been identified by the International Atomic Energy Agency (IAEA, 2002) as being relevant to the issue of environmental protection, including from ionising radiation. These are:

1. *Conservation and preservation.* The recognition that certain species are threatened or endangered (e.g. IUCN, 2000) and thus require protection from human activities. This applies not only to the conservation of wild species themselves but extend to their habitat.
2. *Sustainability.* This includes the right to economic development; the integration of development with environment protection, the sustainable use of natural resources and equity for future generations.
3. *Maintenance of biodiversity.* Although agreement on the exact meaning of the word biodiversity has not been achieved, the term is generally accepted to cover the diversity of habitats, the diversity of species and the genetic variability within species.

4. *Environmental justice*. This addresses issues of liability, compensation and distribution. The principle accounts for the fact that inequity can and does arise from the distribution of environmental benefits and harms and attempts to redress this imbalance by redistributing benefits or compensating from harm caused.
5. *Human dignity*. This principle concerns a respect for human-dignity, rights and self-determination.

Translation of these vague "political" aspirations into a legal framework and quantitative assessment system is not entirely straight-forward. Although a certain amount of consensus on the principles has emerged from various meetings and conferences in recent years (e.g., Strand and Oughton, 2002; Oughton and Strand, 2003), there can be different interpretations and applications of the principles themselves. For example, one implication that might be derived from the principle of conservation, as normally applied, but not restricted, to endangered species, is the requirement to protect selected flora and fauna at the individual level. Indeed, in the UK for instance, many species, including common as well as threatened or endangered ones, are protected at the individual level against deliberate harm being inflicted on them (Pentreath, 1999). This is in contrast to the basic axiom of other assessment systems (e.g. USDoE, 2002) where the "population", with all the concomitant difficulties in characterising such a group, is the entity of concern. The principle of biodiversity also implies the protection of individual organism's not just populations, in some cases. The loss of even one member from an endangered species might lead to a significant loss from the gene pool. Trans-generational equity (sustainability principle) might be addressed by ensuring that the end-points selected in the assessment system are appropriate for demonstrating the viability of organisms and their habitat in the foreseeable future. It follows that any assessment framework should therefore be compatible with such considerations allowing assessments to be made for individual organisms where necessary but being flexible enough to allow assessment of impacts at higher levels of the biological hierarchy (e.g. populations, communities etc.).

Other matters relating to sustainability, environmental justice and human dignity are broader issues that will need to be addressed at an overarching management level (Robinson, 2002). These include assessment of economic, social and ethical issues, including decisions about the role of stakeholders and the acceptability of risk distribution over time and space (Oughton 2001, 2003). It is not possible to envisage how such principles might be directly addressed within an assessment system other than to say that the application of such principles may help to define the limits of our system. Issues of conflict could arise from an evaluation of human requirements vis-à-vis pure environmental protection considerations. For example, it may be possible to demonstrate "scientifically" that a particular species is not suffering any observable biological harm from current or prospective contamination levels, but broader issues impacting upon the ideal of protection, such as the exploitation of the organism by indigenous peoples (which could be linked to the principle of human dignity), can only be addressed using value judgements.

Finally, MEAs can be termed "soft laws" in the sense that they are not strictly enforceable. Their enforcement is instead via national legislation that draws up the regulatory measures necessary to meet the objectives of the MEAs and these in turn usually result in "hard" law (Larsson et al., 2002a). A system allowing quantitative impact assessments to be conducted should enable the assessor to robustly and transparently demonstrate that national legislation is being enforced (or being violated as the case may be).

The Arctic Legal Regime

The Arctic region consists of territories of various nations (Iceland, Canada, USA, Norway, Sweden, Russia, Finland and Denmark), and as such has no overall and binding legal regime. As for elsewhere, the framework for environmental protection of the Arctic is constituted by the national laws of individual countries. However, global treaties and norms to a larger and larger extent influence the national laws – something that is undoubtedly linked to the special status of the Arctic environment as discussed previously. In particular, treaties related to the marine environment have influenced the domestic laws of these countries and much of the focus of environmental protection of the Arctic has therefore been marine conservation.

The Arctic legal system consists of a collection of diverse agreements and the guiding body is the Arctic Council. The Arctic council emerged from the Arctic Environmental Protection Strategy (AEPS), which was adopted by the eight Arctic countries in 1991. The AEPS was one of two agreements on the protection of the Arctic environment produced in 1991: the other being the Declaration on Protection of the Environment. Five years later in 1996, the Foreign Ministers of the Arctic states agreed in the Ottawa Declaration to form the Arctic Council to be a *"high-level forum intended to provide a means for promoting co-operation among Arctic states... on common Arctic issues, in particular issues of sustainable development and environmental protection in the Arctic"*.

The objectives of the AEPS were:

1. to protect the Arctic ecosystems, including humans,
2. to provide for the protection, enhancement and restoration of environmental quality and the sustainable utilization of natural resources including their use by local populations and indigenous peoples in the Arctic,
3. to recognize and to the extent possible, seek to accommodate the traditional and cultural needs, values and practices of the indigenous peoples, as determined by themselves, related to the protection of the environment,
4. to review regularly the state of the Arctic environment, and
5. to identify, reduce, and as a final goal, eliminate pollution.

The AEPS proposed six priority areas for action: persistent organic contaminants, oil pollution, heavy metals, noise, radioactivity, and acidification. The Arctic Council is assessing the environmental impact of these six pollutants through different working groups such as Arctic Monitoring and Assessment Programme (AMAP), Conservation of Arctic Flora and Fauna (CAFF), Protection of the Arctic Marine Environment (PAME), and Emergency Preparedness and Response (EPPR) Programme.

Several existing global agreements apply to the Arctic. For the marine environment, these are the 1973 International Convention for the Prevention of Pollution from Ships (MARPOL), the 1972 Convention on the Prevention of Marine Pollution by dumping of waste and other matter (London Convention) and the Law of the Sea Convention. The major international treaty on trans-boundary air pollution is the 1979 Convention on Long-Range Trans-boundary Air Pollution (LRTAP). Other significant global treaties to protect the atmosphere include the ozone regime, consisting of the 1985 Vienna Convention for the Protection of the Ozone Layer and the 1987 Montreal Protocol on Substances that Deplete the Ozone Layer; the climate change treaty, including the 1992 United Nations Framework Convention on Climate Change and its 1997 Kyoto Protocol, and the new POPS treaty, 2000.

Biodiversity is covered on a global scale by the 1992 Convention on Biological Diversity. Protection of marine mammals and fish on a global scale is considered by the 1946 International Convention for the Regulation of Whaling (ICRW), and the UN Convention on Straddling Stocks and Highly Migratory Stocks. Furthermore, polar bears are protected through the 1973 Agreement on the Conservation of Polar Bears and Their Habitats. In addition, the Arctic states have concluded a number of agreements bilaterally and regionally to conserve selected species.

All Arctic states are parties to the Ramsar Convention on Wetlands of International Importance especially as Waterfowl Habitat; the World Heritage Convention (with the exception of Iceland), the Biodiversity Convention (with the exception of the USA). Norway and Sweden are parties to the Convention on the Conservation of Migratory Species or Wild Animals (the Bonn Convention).

The 1989 Basel Convention on the Control of Trans-boundary Movements of Hazardous Wastes and their Disposal has as a guiding principle that hazardous wastes should be treated as close to where they are produced as possible. In the Arctic area, this convention has relevance in connection with imports of wastes for economic gains.

In the area of radioactive pollution, a number of treaties are of importance to the Arctic such as the 1986 Convention on Early Notification of a Nuclear Accident, the 1994 Convention on Nuclear Safety, and the 1997 Joint Convention on the Safety of Spent Fuel Management and on the Safety of Radioactive Waste Management.

Specific environmental issues such as control of environmental impacts of mining and biodiversity protection are areas for which the Arctic legal regime is incomplete. Furthermore, despite indigenous rights and land claims, the indigenous peoples of the Arctic have not been fully integrated into the legal regime. The regime also suffers from being unenforceable, lacking specific commitments, targets and timetables for action, and under-funding.

THE EPIC ASSESSMENT FRAMEWORK

The aim of the EPIC (Environmental Protection from Ionising Contaminants in the Arctic) project was to develop a methodology or framework for the protection of natural populations of organisms in Arctic marine and terrestrial ecosystems from radiation, achieved via the derivation of dose limits for different Arctic biota. The project therefore aimed to (i) collate information relating to the environmental transfer and fate of selected radionuclides through aquatic and terrestrial ecosystems in the Arctic; (ii) identify reference Arctic biota that can be used to evaluate potential dose rates to biota in different terrestrial, freshwater and marine environments; (iii) model the uptake of a suite of radionuclides to reference Arctic biota; (iv) develop a reference set of dose models for reference Arctic biota; (v) compile data on dose-effects relationships and assessments of potential radiological consequences for reference Arctic biota; (vi) and integrate assessments of the environmental impact from radioactive contamination with those for other contaminants. The EPIC project was funded under the European Community's 5th Framework, Copernicus II Programme and started in the winter of 2000. The project had a 36 month duration and involved the collaboration of the Norwegian Radiation Protection Authority (Coordination) with The Centre for Ecology and Hydrology, UK, The Institute for Radiation Hygiene, Russia and SPA TYPHOON, Russia.

Basic Elements of an "Exposure Assessment" System for Environmental Protection

The exposure assessment component of the protection framework introduced in this document refers to the process of measuring or estimating the intensity, frequency, and duration of exposures to radionuclides currently present in the Arctic environment or of estimating hypothetical exposures that might arise from future releases. A system based on this approach would allow the considerable volume of available data pertaining to radioactive contamination of and, radiation effects on, the Arctic environment to be organised in a systematic manner. Basic, and therefore essential, components of this system include a reference set of organisms that could act as representative of the larger ecosystem, a set of quantities and units allowing consistent comparison of the effects from different radiation types, a set of dose models to allow calculation of absorbed dose and tabulated dose-effects relationships to allow interpretation of the doses received. Within this system a transparent, defendable impact assessment could be performed.

The common definition of "reference organism" is: "*a series of entities that provides a basis for the estimation of the radiation dose rate to a range of organisms that are typical, or representative, of a contaminated environment. These estimates, in turn, would provide a basis for assessing the likelihood and degree of radiation effects*". (Larsson et al., 2002b). The basic unit for expressing exposure information to flora and fauna is the absorbed dose (or dose rate) in units of Gy (or Gy per unit time). The practical application of the system of dosimetry based around the absorbed dose forces consideration of the empirical observation that the same absorbed dose of differing radiations can produce differing degrees of effect in the same biological endpoint. That is, the radiations can differ in their qualitative effect. For example, there is a very substantial body of experimental evidence to indicate that the absorbed dose of high linear energy transfer (LET) radiation (α-particles) required to produce a given biological effect is less than that of low LET radiation (β-particles and γ-rays) - the relative biological effectiveness (RBE) phenomenon. For human radiological protection practice, this phenomenon is taken into account by applying dimensionless radiation weighting factors (w_r) to the absorbed doses from the different radiations, and summing, to give a quantity called the equivalent dose. It should be emphasized, however, that values of w_r defined for the purpose of human radiation protection cannot be applied without reservation to other organisms and biological endpoints.

The whole system has been built around the objective to assess doses and effects for individual organisms. This is a pragmatic approach, based on the observation that the great preponderance of exposure data relate to effects on individual organisms, and is also compatible with the underlying principles of conservation and biodiversity, where the focus is often placed on the protection of individual organisms. Furthermore, there is no evidence to suggest that radiation effects can be expressed at high levels of biological organisation such as populations without first being observable at the individual level (Larsson et al., 2002a). A feature of EPIC has been the categorisation of effects data under "umbrella" end-points. This has followed the guidance presented by Pentreath, (1999) and others (e.g. IUR, 2002) to consider mortality, morbidity, reproductive success and scoreable cytogenetic damage. The biological endpoint "reproductive success" is of particular interest because this tends to be the most radiosensitive endpoint that ultimately influences the viability of a defined population and relates the assessment to the underlying principle of sustainability.

Scope of the Assessment

The geographical extent of the work behind the development of the EPIC system is presented in Figure 2 and has been described in more detail in Beresford et al. (2003). The assessment methodology, as presented, is limited in terms of the radionuclides considered for reasons of practicability. An initial list of 13 radionuclides (radioisotopes of caesium, strontium, iodine, technetium, plutonium, americium, carbon, hydrogen, uranium, radium, thorium and polonium) is broadly representative of (i) routine release scenarios from power plants and reprocessing facilities, (ii) accidental releases and (iii) naturally-occurring or technologically-enhanced naturally-occurring (TENORM) radionuclides. The selected radionuclides cover a broad range in relation to environmental mobility and biological uptake and hence the system should be flexible enough to allow other radionuclides to be assessed with the provision of appropriate parameters. For aquatic systems, radioisotopes of P, Mn, Co and Zn were also considered for biological transfer as they are routinely released into the waters of the study area. With respect to the derivation of "background" exposures arising from naturally-occurring radionuclides in soils, water and sediment, dose conversion factors were derived for members of ^{238}U and ^{232}Th decay chains (see Golikov & Brown, 2003).With respect to the analyses of the transfer of radionuclides from the point of release/input to the resultant activity concentration observed within reference flora and fauna, a decision was made to focus mainly on the biological uptake. This was made with a view to the generic applicability of the system, assuming that reference media concentrations would be predictable or measurable. This removed the requirement for a consideration of environmental (physical) transport models.

Three broad Arctic ecosystem categories were selected for further consideration, namely: terrestrial, freshwater and marine. The starting point for the assessment has been selected to be a unit concentration in the organisms' habitat, e.g., unit activity concentration per litre of water in the case of the aquatic environment and a unit activity concentration per kg of soil or unit deposition per m^2 in terrestrial environments. In the absence of monitoring data, it is assumed that the assessor will have access to appropriate models to allow activity concentrations in abiotic compartments of the environment to be calculated.

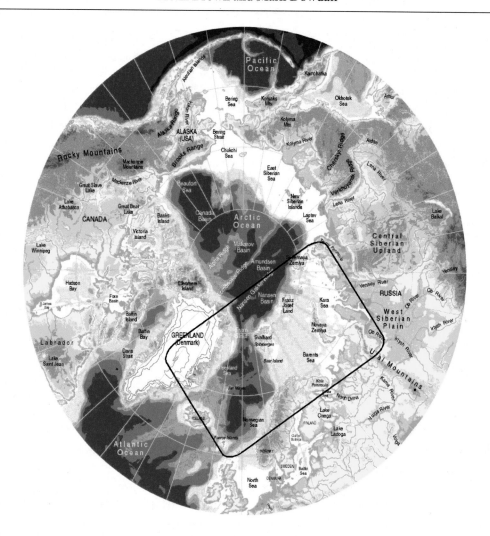

Figure 2. The Arctic region studued within the EPIC framework (from AMAP, 1997 and Beresford et al., 2003).

Stages in the Assessment

The stages in the EPIC assessment are depicted in Figure 3. The initial stage of the assessment requires the selection of appropriate reference biota and suitable representative organisms (normally defined at the species level) with concomitant collation of life history data sheets. Following this step, the exposure assessment is conducted using the basic methodology outlined in this chapter. Methods for deriving the transfer and fate of radionuclides in Arctic ecosystems are necessary during this procedure as are methods for deriving (weighted or unweighted) dose-rates. Once exposures for reference biota have been derived, they need to be interpreted in terms of biological effects. The assessment approach presented here has been compared, where appropriate, to the approaches taken for non-radioactive contaminants.

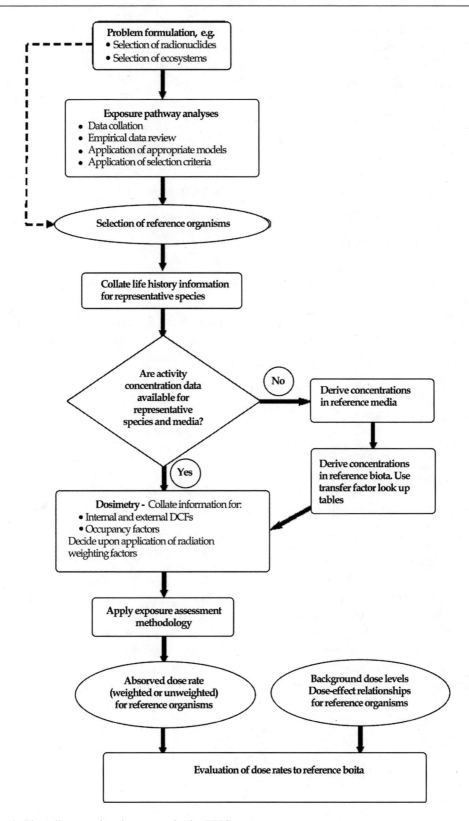

Figure 3. Flow diagram showing stages in the EPIC exposure assessment

Exposure Assessment

The whole-body absorbed dose-rate is used as a measure of the reference organism exposure to ionising radiation, expressed in units of Gy per year, and is the sum of internal and external absorbed dose rates:

$$\dot{D}^j_{total} = \dot{D}^j_{int} + \dot{D}^j_{ext}$$ [1]

where,

$\dot{D}^j_{total}$ is the total absorbed dose rate received by organism j (Gy a^{-1}),

$\dot{D}^j_{int}$ is the internal absorbed dose rate received by organism j (Gy a^{-1}),

$\dot{D}^j_{ext}$ is the external absorbed dose rate received by organism j (Gy a^{-1}).

It may be appropriate to introduce radiation weighting factors to take account of the differing biological effectiveness of different types of ionising radiation. For this reason, the radiation emission types for each radionuclide have been split into the categories of α, β and γ. Introduction of weighting factors leads to the weighted absorbed dose:

$$\dot{D}^j_{total,weighted} = \dot{D}^j_{int,weighted} + \dot{D}^j_{ext,weighted}$$
$$\dot{D}^j_{int,weighted} = w_\beta \dot{D}^j_{int,\beta} + \dot{D}^j_{int,\gamma} + w_\alpha \dot{D}^j_{int,\alpha}$$ [2]
$$\dot{D}^j_{ext,weighted} = w_\beta \dot{D}^j_{ext,\beta} + \dot{D}^j_{ext,\gamma} + w_\alpha \dot{D}^j_{ext,\alpha}$$

where,

w_β and w_α are the radiation weighting factors for beta radiation, and alpha radiation, respectively,

β, γ, and α denote the contributions to absorbed dose rate from beta particles, gamma ray photons, and alpha particles, respectively.

Contributions from low energy beta particles and alpha particles to external radiation will usually be negligible, but may need to be considered for organisms whose dimensions are of the same order as the range of these radiation types in tissue - typically, in the sub-millimetre range. For simplicity of explanation, the following paragraphs describe the methods for calculation of (unweighted) absorbed dose rates to organisms. Extension of the method to calculate weighted absorbed dose rates is described in subsequent paragraphs.

The external dose rate, averaged over different habitats, can be determined by the following equation:

$$\dot{D}^j_{ext} = \sum_z v_z \sum_i C^{ref}_{zi} * DCF^j_{ext,zi}$$ [3]

where,

C_{zi}^{ref} is the average concentration of the radionuclide i in the reference media of a given habitat z (Bq kg^{-1} (soil or sediment) or Bq m^{-3} (water)),

$DCF^{j}_{ext,zi}$ is the dose conversion factor for external exposure defined as the ratio between the average concentration of the radionuclide i in the reference media corresponding to the habitat z and the dose rate to the organism j (Gy a^{-1} per Bq kg^{-1} or Bq m^{-3})

v_z is the occupancy factor, i.e. fraction of the time that the organism j expends in habitat z.

The derivation of external unweighted DCFs for reference terrestrial biota are discussed later in this article and presented in numerical form in Golikov and Brown (2003).

The internal dose rate (for biota in both aquatic and terrestrial environments) can be derived from the activity concentration in the selected reference organism using the following equation:

$$\dot{D}^{j}_{int} = \sum_i C^{j}_i * DCF^{j}_{int,i}$$ [4]

where,

C^{j}_i is the average concentration of the radionuclide i in the reference organism j (Bq kg^{-1} fresh weight),

$DCF^{j}_{int,i}$ is the radionuclide-specific dose conversion factor (DCF) for internal exposure defined as the ratio between the average concentration of the radionuclide i in the organism j and the dose rate to the organism (Gy a^{-1} per Bq kg^{-1} fresh weight).

The derivation of internal unweighted DCFs for reference terrestrial biota are discussed in the relevant section of this article and presented in numerical form in Golikov and Brown (2003). If no data are available on the activity concentrations in reference organisms, methodologies are available to allow these values to be estimated and this is discussed in more detail in subsequent sections.

Golikov and Brown (2002) discussed the issue of appropriate radiation weighting factors and noted that the final choice of radiation weighting factor for alpha particles will depend on the selection of reference organism, end-point and dose (or dose-rate) range. It was considered appropriate that calculations of absorbed dose should be split into low LET and high LET components in order to facilitate the incorporation of a radiation weighting factor once consensus has been achieved. A provisional recommendation concerning the application of an α-radiation weighting factor in the range of 5-20 was made. Furthermore, a weighting factor of 3 was recommended for application to low energy β. In view of the way in which DCFs have been presented in Golikov and Brown (2003), i.e. into components of α, β and γ radiation, it has not been possible to apply a weighting factor for low β in most cases. However, ^{3}H is known to emit a large component of low beta radiation and earlier studies (e.g. Straume and Carsten, 1993) have shown that a radiation weighting factor in excess of unity might be appropriate for this particular radionuclide.

The weighted internal DCFs for a given radionuclide and reference organism become:

$$\left[DCF^{j}_{\text{int},i,low\beta}\right]_{w} = DCF^{j}_{\text{int},i,\beta} * w_{\beta} \qquad\qquad [5]$$

$$\left[DCF^{j}_{\text{int},i,\alpha}\right]_{w} = DCF^{j}_{\text{int},i,\alpha} * w_{\alpha} \qquad\qquad [6]$$

$$\left[DCF^{j}_{\text{int},i,Total}\right]_{w} = \left[DCF^{j}_{\text{int},i,\beta}\right]_{w} + \left[DCF^{j}_{\text{int},i,\alpha}\right]_{w} + DCF^{j}_{\text{int},i,\gamma} \qquad [7]$$

where,

$\left[DCF^{j}_{\text{int},i,\beta}\right]_{w}$; $\left[DCF^{j}_{\text{int},i,\alpha}\right]_{w}$ and $\left[DCF^{j}_{\text{int},i,Total}\right]_{w}$ are "weighted" DCFs for low β, α and all radiation types respectively, being specific to radionuclide i and reference organism j, w_{β}; w_{α} are radiation weighting factors, $DCF^{j}_{\text{int},i,\gamma}$ is the DCF for γ radiation for radionuclide i and reference organism j.

It should be noted that these weighted DCFs have not been included in the tables presented in Golikov and Brown (2003). By way of example a w_{α} of 10 has been applied to alpha radiation components. In the exceptional case of tritium, ^{3}H, a weighting factor of 3 has been applied. For all other β, and γ, the radiation weighting factor has been set to unity.

Selection of Data

In some cases, it will be necessary to predefine the evaluation area, i.e. site boundary or area of elevated contamination, and then collate data from within these boundaries. The subsequent method of "averaging" data or selecting which data are appropriate for the assessment is currently a point for contention and will depend upon the purpose of the assessment. For example, in the context of an assessment to demonstrate compliance in line with the IAEA criterion of protecting a population of organisms, the maximally exposed individual is chosen as the point of reference (IAEA, 1992): the dose rate to this individual must not exceed the defined dose limit. In such a case, it may be necessary to characterise the distribution of values from an empirical data set (e.g. field sampled values of activity concentrations, CFs etc.) and then derive a model generated population from which an appropriate percentile can be selected (see Wilson and Hinton, 2002). Such an approach might be limited by assumptions required about the form of the distribution and the fact that the distribution of absorbed dose rates to individual organisms will not necessarily be the same as the distribution of results for environmental contamination based on samples taken within a particular area - because mobile organisms will receive absorbed dose rates which reflect a spatial average over their home range. Alternatively, the average absorbed dose rates to a relatively small subset of the population (in line with the critical group approach for humans) would be more tractable, and would be equally valid as an approach to protecting population of wild organisms.

In both cases, choices will have to be made about what fraction of population is appropriate for assessment: in the first, the size of the percentile, in the second the size of the chosen subset. However, here, flexibility should be seen as an advantage since what is appropriate will in turn be dependent on other factors such as the size of population, number of offspring, etc. A direct consideration of the uncertainties involved in the exposure assessment have not been addressed within the EPIC assessment framework, although it is acknowledged that there are many sources and that such considerations are recognised as being important. Specifically, however, it is recommended that both the range, expected values (e.g. transfer factors, activity concentrations in reference media and biota etc.) and where possible concomitant statistics (including arithmetic mean, standard deviation, number of observations etc.) be tabulated. Such data may have utility not only in compliance situations (where maximum values may be required) but also within sensitivity and uncertainty analyses.

Exposure Estimates: Interpretation

There are currently no dose limits in place that can be applied when evaluating whether biota within Arctic environments are being protected from exposure to ionising radiation. In order to assess the potential consequences of exposures to radiation on non-human biota, arguably, two points of reference may be used. These are (a) natural background dose rates and (b) dose rates known to have specific biological effects on individual organisms. This dual approach is in accordance with that discussed by Pentreath (2002). With respect to natural background dose rates information on expected levels in Arctic and/or related environments are discussed in Sazykina et al. (2003) and reconsidered from the perspective of dose standards in a later section of this article. With respect to the second point of reference, dose-effects relationships for reference (or related) Arctic biota have also been considered in great detail in EPIC Deliverable Report 5 (Sazykina et al., 2003). An overview of this work in the context of the EPIC assessment framework is provided in this article. Furthermore, possible implications for the development of dose limits for the Arctic, based on these findings, are discussed in the relevant section.

The information provided in these sections should allow the significance of derived dose-rates to be evaluated, albeit in a preliminary way, in terms of their implications for environmental impact. At this stage, and within the remit of the work presented here, it would be premature to derive concrete dose limits, although it is hoped that the results could provide relevant guidance and input to decision making processes.

Reference Organisms - Selection

The EPIC framework approach requires the selection of reference organisms during the initial stages of the assessment, a subject that has been addressed previously by Beresford et al. (2001). For freshwater, marine and terrestrial environments, selection criteria have been applied in order to select a reference organism suite although this constitutes only a subset of numerous other criteria that could be applied (see for example Pentreath and Woodhead, 2001). The criteria applied in Beresford et al. (2001) were:

1. *Ecological niche.* This was simply applied as a requirement to have at least one representative from each trophic level.
2. *Intrinsic radiosensitivity.* In this case comparison was made between the acute lethal doses expressed by various organism groups.
3. *Radioecological sensitivity.* i.e. identification of which organisms are likely to be most exposed either through an expression of relatively high radionuclide bioaccumulation or relatively high activity concentrations in their habitat.

4. *Distribution.* Preference was given to those organisms that were year-round residents in the Arctic.
5. *Amenability to research and monitoring.* This criterion involved an assessment of whether data sets documenting activity concentrations in various groups of organism were available from monitoring studies and whether future research might be conducted upon the various groups (e.g. exposure experiments etc.).

The lists of selected reference organism lists are used as a basis for deriving appropriate environmental transfer data information and selecting suitable target geometries/phantoms for dosimetric modelling. With respect to these points, it is apparent that the identification of actual species (or in some cases families or classes of organisms) representing each of the broadly defined groups would be helpful in some instances. This is true in the case of deriving food-chain model parameters where detailed information is often required, beyond a generic consideration, with respect to organism characteristics. It is also true in the case of geometry construction where quantitative information on size, shape and density are required and can be derived, simply and transparently, from a consideration of real flora and fauna. Examples of suitable representative species or selected reference organisms chosen for the EPIC framework, giving preference to species ubiquitous throughout the European Arctic and the availability of appropriate data are presented in Tables 1 - 3.

Life history data have been collated for most representative species in Arctic marine and terrestrial ecosystems. Recommended CR/CF values are provided within the EPIC framework for both terrestrial and marine systems although in the case of the former ecosystem, data availability limited this exercise to only a few radionuclides for many of the reference biota considered.

Table 1. Reference organisms and representative families/species for terrestrial Arctic ecosystems.

Reference organism	Representative species	Availability of information		
		Life history	CR	DCF
Soil micro-organism	Not applicable	No		No
Lichens & Bryophyte	Cladonia spp.	Yes	*	No
Gymnosperm	Juniperus spp., Larix dahurica, Picea obovata	Yes	*	Yes (plant roots)
Monocotyledon	Carex spp., Luzula spp., Festuca spp.	Yes	*	Yes (plant roots)
Dicotyledon	Vaccinium spp.	Yes	*	Yes (plant roots)
Soil invertebrate	Collembola & mites	Yes	*	Yes
Herbivorous mammal	'Lemmings and voles' (Dicrostonyx spp., Myopus spp., Lemmus spp., Microtus spp., Clethrionomys spp. & Eothenomys spp.)	Yes	*	Yes
			*	
	Reindeer (Rangifer tarandus)	Yes		Yes
Carnivorous mammal	'Foxes' (Vulpes vulpes & Alopex lagopus)	Yes	*	Yes
Herbivorous bird	Lagopus spp.	Yes	*	Yes
Egg from ground-nesting bird	Lagopus spp.	Yes		Yes

* CRs not available for all radionuclides

Table 2. Reference organisms and representative families/species for Arctic freshwater ecosystems.

Reference organism	Representative species	Availability of information		
		Life history	CF	DCF
Benthic bacteria	Not applicable	No	No	No
Aquatic plants	'Freshwater monocotyledons' (e.g. Carex spp.)	No	No	No
Phytoplankton	Not applicable	No	No	No
Zooplankton	Rotifera	No	No	No
Insect larvae	Chironomid spp.	No	No	No
Pelagic planktotrophic fish	Coregonus peled (northern whitefish), Coregonus laveretus (cisco) & Coregonus albula (shallow-water cisco)	No	*	No
Pelagic carnivorous fish	Esox lucius (pike)	No	*	No
Benthic fish	Coregonus lavaretus (cisco) & Salvelinus alpinus (Arctic char)	No	*	No
Carnivorous mammal	Mustela lutrecla (mink)	No	No	No
Fish egg	Not applicable	No	No	No

* Some information available in Beresford et al (2003)

Table 3. Reference organisms and representative families/species for Arctic marine ecosystems

Reference organism	Representative species	Availability of information		
		Life History	CF	DCF
Benthic bacteria	Not applicable	No	No	No
Phytoplankton	Not applicable	Yes	Yes	No
Macroalgae	Fucus spp.	Yes	Yes	No
Pelagic crustacean	Pandalus borealis	Yes	Yes	Yes
Benthic mollusc	Mytilus edulis	Yes	Yes	Yes
Polychaetes	Arenicola marina Lumbrineris spp.	Yes	Yes	No
Pelagic planktotrophic fish	Boreogadus saida (polar cod) Mallotus villosus (capelin) Clupea harengus (herring)	Yes	Yes	Yes
Benthic crustacean	Cancer pagurus	*	Yes	Yes
Pelagic carnivorous fish	Gadus morhua (cod)	Yes	Yes	Yes
Benthic fish	Pleuronectes spp. (e.g. Pleuronectes platessa, plaice)	Yes	Yes	Yes
Sea bird	Larus spp.	Yes	Yes	Yes
Carnivorous mammal	'Seals' (Erignathus barbatus, Phoca hispida, Phoca groenlandica)	Yes	Yes	Yes
Fish egg	Not applicable	No	No	No

* Life history data available for European Lobster (*Homarus gammarus*)

In the Arctic terrestrial ecosystem, DCFs for plant roots were derived for *Vaccinium* spp. and these may be applied for Gymnosperms and Monocotyledons. As shown in Tables 1 to 3 DCFs are not available for all reference organisms. No DCFs for freshwater were derived. Phantoms that correspond in dimensional terms may be suitably adopted from the marine list. For example, the DCF for cod may suitably be used as a proxy for pike. For the case of micro-organisms/bacteria in both Arctic terrestrial and aquatic environments, it has been shown by Pröhl et al. (2003) that the absorbed dose will be dominated to a large extent by the external component of the dose. If dose rates to these organisms require calculation, simple assumptions can be made. For example it can be assumed that the organism resides in an infinite absorbing medium and that all radiation energies are absorbed by the organism. DCFs for phytoplankton, macroalgae and polycheates were not been derived. In view of the radioresistance of marine flora and the lack of data on polychaetes (uptake and dose-effect information), it was considered unlikely that these organism types would feature strongly in any environmental impact assessment.

It is not the intention of the framework to be overly-prescriptive with respect to reference organisms. The lists of both reference organisms and representative organisms could be adopted by those wishing to conduct an impact assessment in the Arctic but when specific information concerning a particular release of radioactivity is available it may be appropriate to conduct a new exposure pathways analysis. This may, of course, result in the selection of modified lists although the information presented for dose conversion factors and transfer factors may not be compatible with these organisms. In such a case, transfer information would need to be re-collated and new modelling work (e.g. dosimetric models for the derivation of DCFs) conducted.

The EPIC framework requires that basic ecological information be collated for each of the selected flora and fauna. The specific organism attributes that should be considered relate directly to the subsequent assessment of exposure. For example, information should be provided on habitat and, where applicable, the fractional occupancy of various organisms in their habitats. This information is important for the weighting of external dose-rates in order to account for the behaviour of the organism (see relevant section). Guidance on the types of ecological information required for reference fauna is displayed in Table 4. It should be noted that some of the information specified in Table 4 is redundant for the purpose of conducting the impact assessment as described. Essentially, only information on the dimensions and habitat of a particular organism are required to allow informed application of appropriate DCFs with occupancy factors being required to subsequently use these. Organism mass, life expectancy and feeding habits have been used in some cases to provide appropriate values for allometric relationships, which have subsequently been implemented within the dynamic radioecological models as described. The additional information, e.g. home range, special life-cycle data etc. may be useful in the application of a more detailed ecological risk assessment (e.g. Sample et al., 1997) or in the parameterisation of models simulating how populations might respond to radiation induced changes in individual attributes (e.g. Woodhead, 2003).

Table 4. Ecological information required for Arctic reference fauna.

Information	Assessment	Comments
(i) Latin and common English name of the selected species.	Simple[1]	
(ii) Biota dimensions (mass, dimensions)	Simple[1]	Dimension – represent as ellipsoid and defined length, width depth. Required for geometry configuration
(iii) Habitat – configuration and occupancy factors	Simple[1]	Required for target source configuration – external dose assessment. - Marine – e.g. pelagic, benthic; - Terrestrial – e.g. at soil surface, in soil (depth and orientation) Occupancy factors – fraction of time spent in different habitats – required for average dose-rate calculation
(iv) Habitat (dynamic)	Advanced[2]	Examples: - The animal spends parts of its life cycle in different habitats (e.g. meroplanktonic larvae) - The animal hibernates (where and when?) Information required in the calculation of integrated doses
(v) Distribution – Home range.	Advanced[2]	Information required in the calculation of integrated doses
(vi) Average life expectancy	Advanced[2]	Information required in the calculation of integrated doses
(vii) Feeding habits	Advanced[2]	e.g. main prey species Information required for input to ecological models
(viii) Additional information on lifecycle	Advanced[2]	e.g. viviparous fish, periods spent in freshwater Information required in the calculation of integrated doses; sensitive periods in life-cycle

[1]Simple assessment – basic information required for the calculation of dose-rates.

[2]Advanced assessment – possibly beyond the scope of initial EPIC aspirations. However, such information may prove useful in the parameterisation of food-chain and exposure models.

DERIVING ACTIVITY CONCENTRATIONS IN REFERENCE ORGANISMS

Several approaches have been explored in the process of deriving concentrations in the bodies of reference flora and fauna. These are addressed in detail in Beresford et al. (2003) – an overview of how recommended values were derived is provided here.

Empirically-derived Transfer Factor Approach

This approach assumes that information is available on activity concentrations in a predefined reference material, i.e. filtered water in aquatic environments (Bq l⁻¹) or surface soil in terrestrial environments (Bq kg⁻¹).

Overview of Approach

When the concentrations in the reference organisms are not available, these can be calculated by multiplying the concentrations in the reference media with the appropriate Concentration Ratios (CR) or Concentration Factors (CFs).

For the terrestrial ecosystems the CRs are defined as:

$$CR_{b,i} \text{ (dimensionless)} = C_{b,i}/C_{soil,I} \qquad [8]$$

where,

$CR_{b,i}$ = Concentration ratio for reference organism b and radionuclide i;
$C_{b,i}$ = Activity concentration of radionuclide i in whole body of reference biota (Bq kg⁻¹, fresh weight);
C_{soil} = Activity concentration of radionuclide i in surface soil (Bq kg⁻¹ d.w.)

For the aquatic ecosystems the transfer factor, commonly known as Concentration Factor (CF), are defined as:

$$CF_{b,i} \text{ (dimensionless or l kg}^{-1}\text{)} = C_{b,i}/C_{aq} \qquad [9]$$

where

$CF_{b,i}$ = Concentration Factor for reference organism b and radionuclide i;
C_b = Activity concentration of radionuclide i in whole body of reference biota (Bq kg⁻¹, fresh weight); C_{aq} = Activity concentration of radionuclide i in aqueous phase (Bq l⁻¹ or Bq kg⁻¹) - normally filtered water.

CRs in Arctic Terrestrial Environments

The database of the transfer of the EPIC radionuclides from soil to reference organisms was generated predominantly from literature review of published data (western and Russian-language publications) and data provided by Russian partners in EPIC. More than 300 publications (refereed literature, books, institute reports and conference proceedings) were reviewed. The species selected as representative of Arctic reference organisms were especially targeted within the literature review. The review was not restricted to studies conducted within the European Arctic because of the paucity of data specific to this area. Much data was rejected from the review as the level of detail within the original publications was insufficient to enable their use with any degree of confidence. The review also provides statistical information (mean, maximum, minimum) for each radionuclide and reference organism category.

For animals whole-body fresh weight activity concentrations were used. Where activity concentrations for organs were reported, this required assumptions to be made concerning the distributions of radionuclides within the body of the animal. For plants all values were converted to dry matter values (in some cases literature values were reported as fresh or ashed weights).

Both CRs and aggregated transfer factors (Tag; Bq kg^{-1} in organisms: Bq m^{-2} in soil) were reported in Beresford et al. (2003). However for the purposes of consistency and ease of use within the assessment framework, values appear only as CRs, Tags having been converted by authors assuming a soil bulk density of 0.78 g DM cm^{-3} for Arctic soils (Batjes 1995) and a sampling depth of 10 cm.

An overview of the empirical transfer factor data coverage is presented in Table 5. It is apparent that very little transfer factor data was available for radionuclides other than radiocaesium and radiostrontium. Data was available for many of the reference organisms for natural radionuclides; these data were dominated by studies from within the EPIC area. No Arctic specific data for the transfer of actinide elements from soil–biota were found during this review. Even for these well-studied radionuclides, very little information is available on transfer to selected representative organism groups, e.g. for lemmings and voles (*Microtus spp./Lemmus spp.*).

Table 5. Coverage of empirical transfer factors for Arctic terrestrial reference organisms (values given in columns show number of data (T$_{ag}$ or CR) found for each radionuclide).

Reference organism	Representatives pecies	Cs	Sr	I	Tc	Pu	Am	C	H	U	Ra	Th	Po
Lichens+bryophytes	Cladonia spp.	388	356	-	-	-	-	-	-	1	6	6	5
Gymnosperms		22	13	-	-	-	-	-	-	11	4	2	-
Dicotyledons	Vaccinium spp.	457	63	-	-	-	-	-	-	10	7	6	4
Monocotyledons		435	321	-	-	-	-	-	-	-	1	-	2
Herbivorous mammal	Microtus spp. /Lemmus spp.	4	-	-	-	-	-	-	-	2	17	2	-
Herbivorous mammal	Rangifer tarrandus	845	365	-	-	-	-	-	-	-	16	6	42
Carnivorous mammal		12	8	-	-	-	-	-	-	1	17	2	3
Herbivorous bird		56	51[a]	-	-	-	-	-	-	4	31	4	-

[a] Lagopus spp. only

Consequently there is only sufficient data to provide recommended transfer parameters for application in the exposure assessment for some of the radionuclide – reference organism combinations. The approach suggested by Higley et al. (2003) was implemented, in combination with suitable soil-plant transfer values for dietary components, to determine soil-biota transfer values for Arctic reference organisms by Beresford et al. (2003). Where comparison was possible, predicted values generally compared well to the available measurements for some radionuclides (e.g. Cs and U) but not for others (e.g. Pu, Am and Th). The initial model was simplistic and did not include soil ingestion which could result in underestimated values for those radionuclides with low plant uptakes. Beresford et al. (2004) revised these estimates assuming a soil ingestion rate of 10 % dry matter intake for herbivores

(USDoE 2002) and 6 % for fox (Sample and Suter 1994). For Cs and Pu isotopes, gastrointestinal absorption factors for soil associated radionuclides were taken from Beresford et al., (2000), Am absorption was taken to be the same as Pu, and all other radionuclides were assumed to have the same bioavailability as herbage associated radionuclides, Beresford et al. (2000) having suggested this as a valid assumption for Sr and I. Daily dry matter ingestion rates were predicted using the allometric relationships of Nagy (2001) for carnivorous mammals (fox), rodents (vole) and galliformes (*Lagopus* spp.); intakes of grass and lichen by reindeer were taken from Golikov (2001). Voles were assumed to eat grass, *Lagopus* spp. to eat Vaccinium spp., and fox to consume the soft tissues of voles. Estimates were made for animals of average age for each species. Predicted transfer values for Cs, U and Sr were generally comparable with the range of observed data, although predicted values for Ra were high compared with observed data. The inclusion of soil ingestion improved comparisons with the observed data for Pu, Am and Th.

For ^{14}C a specific activity approach was used to derive transfer parameter (Galeriu et al., 2003; Beresford et al 2003). For ^{3}H an approach was developed (including limited Arctic specific parameters) enabling (unlike other biota assessment frameworks) organically bound and body water ^{3}H concentrations to be derived (Galeriu et al., 2003; Beresford et al., 2003). For both ^{14}C and ^{3}H CR values represent the ratio of activity concentration in biota to that in air (Bq m^{-3}).

CFs in Arctic Freshwater Environments

CF data for Arctic freshwater environments are limited to few species and few radionuclides. Mean values ± standard deviation pertaining to CFs for ^{137}Cs (water -muscle) and ^{90}Sr (water - bone) have been provided for 4 species of fish from Arctic Russian lakes. For all other radionuclides and organism types, other methodologies must be applied in the derivation of transfer information as discussed below in the following section.

CFs in Arctic Marine Environments

Site-specific radionuclide CF values for Arctic marine biota were collated within the EPIC framework for European Arctic sea areas including the Norwegian, Barents, White, Kara, and Greenland Seas. CF values were calculated for Arctic fish, birds, sea mammals, zoobenthos, and macroalgae for the following radionuclides ^{90}Sr, ^{137}Cs, ^{239}Pu, ^{240}Pu, and ^{99}Tc based upon a number of literature reviews. Collated data were for the period 1961-1999, and a summary is provided in Table 6. For some radionuclide-organism combinations, data for neighbouring sea regions (i.e. the North Sea and North Atlantic) were also used because of the scarcity of Arctic-specific data. For all other radionuclide-biota combinations very few data were available.

Where there are no Arctic specific transfer data, generic information for the world's oceans (IAEA, 1985 and IAEA 2004) would have to be used in an assessment of this type although it is recognised that such data tend to be biased towards edible marine organisms and the edible parts of these organisms.

**Table 6. Summarised information on the number of data
compiled from Arctic marine biota from Beresford et al., (2003).**

Reference organism group	Caesium-137	Strontium-90	Plutonium-239,240	Technecium-99	Total
Fish	630	37	23	1	691
Bird	55	-	6	-	61
Mammal	175	17	15	-	207
Crustacea	41	7	8	8	64
Mollusc	31	-	10	5	46
Macroalgae	116	14	46	18	194
Invertebrate*	33	3	10	-	46
Total	1081	78	118	32	1309

*Includes data for species such as *Strongylocentrothus* spp., foraminefera and polychaetes.

By comparing region specific data sets with recommended generic values for CFs (IAEA, 1985 and IAEA, 2004), the hypothesis that transfer to Arctic biota differs from that observed in temperate areas was tested for ^{90}Sr, ^{137}Cs, ^{239,240}Pu and ^{99}Tc. Despite the general paucity of data and large uncertainties regarding radionuclide CFs to reference biota, the use of Arctic-specific CFs for Sr, in the case of crustaceans and fish, and Pu, in the case of molluscs, is preferable because differences with generic CFs were apparent (Brown et al., 2004). The review of Beresford *et al.* (2003) provides mean CF values that may be applied in an exposure assessment. These values have been used in conjunction with other data derived from other literature sources and modelling methodologies in order to produce the look-up tables, providing recommended radionuclide-specific CFs for reference organism groups within the EPIC framework.

Management of Information Gaps

Several approaches may be adopted in cases where no transfer factors are available (see Copplestone *et al.*, 2001). These include:

1. A transfer value (fresh weight activity concentration in organism: fresh weight activity concentration in soil) of 1 is recommended as being generally conservative for terrestrial environments. There will be exceptions where this assumption is not conservative (e.g. for radiocaesium) but in these cases data will generally be available for some organism groups for these radionuclides on which an expert judgement can be based.
2. For aquatic systems, the highest available concentration factor for a specified radionuclide considering all reference organism types can be adopted as a conservative estimate in cases where no data exist for the specific organism of interest
3. Consider if transfer can be justifiably ignored. For some organisms exposed to beta/gamma emitters the total dose is likely to be dominated by external radiation (e.g. a worm inhabiting soil contaminated by gamma-emitters).

4. For some radionuclides transfer values for radionuclides with a similar biogeochemical behaviour could be employed. For instance, transfer values for Pu could be used to estimate Am activity concentrations.

Limitations in the Application of Equilibrium Transfer Factors

The application of concentration ratios provides a simply implemented methodology to estimating radionuclide concentrations in biota. Similar approaches have been suggested by most other developers of assessment frameworks (e.g. USDoE 2002; Copplestone et al., 2001). However it is acknowledged within EPIC that the CR/CF approach is open to criticism for a number of reasons:

1. it provides no information concerning the types of processes/mechanisms in operation during biological uptake, (although the amalgamation of these processes into one parameter can conversely be considered to be an advantage),
2. the relationship between the radionuclide concentration in an abiotic compartment (e.g. soil, water) and within (the organs or whole body of) a high trophic-level organism, deriving most of its contaminant load from ingested food, may not be a simple, linear one,
3. the assumption that the system is under equilibrium, a requirement for CRs/CFs to be truly applicable, is often invalid,

In numerous cases, application of CR/CF recommended values would not provide robust prognoses for activity concentrations in biological compartments. Therefore the numerous limitations associated with CFs renders the application of dynamic models desirable.

Dose Models for Arctic Environments

The EPIC framework has used reference organisms as the basis for further dosimteric modelling. The selection of appropriate reference phantoms has been addressed in a previous section of this article. The actual dimensions of the organisms have been based, in most cases, on the adult form of representative organisms and were specified in Golikov and Brown (2003). For the derivation of DCFs, ellipsoids have been used to represent the various geometric forms of representative plants and animals.

Due to the complexity of the processes involved and the enormous variability of organisms and their natural habitats, it was not possible to derive external dose conversion factors (DCFs) for all possible exposure conditions. Therefore, typical exposure situations appropriate to and based around the geometries for reference organisms were selected for detailed consideration. These are:

1. For the DCFs pertaining to species living *in the soil*, two source descriptions were assumed: (a) a uniformly contaminated volume source for natural radionuclides

and (b) a planar isotropic source, located at the depth 0.5 g·cm^{-2} in the soil[1], for artificial radionuclides.

2. For the DCFs pertaining to species living *on the ground*, two source descriptions were assumed: (a) a semi - infinite volume source for natural radionuclides and (b) a planar isotropic source located at a depth of 0.5 g·cm^{-2} in the soil for artificial radionuclides.

3. For the DCFs pertaining to aquatic species at the sediment/water interface, two source descriptions were assumed: (a) a volume source with a depth of 5 cm for artificial radionuclides[2] and (b) a semi - infinite volume source for natural radionuclides.

Numerous models already exist for the purpose of deriving absorbed doses to individual organisms including the analyses and solution of dose distribution functions, conservative approaches (whereby all radiations emitted by radionuclides within the organism are absorbed) and Monte Carlo methodologies, (e.g. IAEA, 1979, Copplestone *et al.*, 2001; USDoE, 2002, Pröhl *et al.*, 2003). Dose conversion coefficients have been derived for generic biota (Amiro, 1997) and specific reference plants and animals (Pröhl *et al.*, 2003). A review of some of these approaches is to be found in Golikov & Brown (2002).

Methodology for Deriving Absorbed Doses

The deployed method for deriving absorbed doses is based on an approximation defining the dose distribution of radiation within an organism's body. This distribution can be defined using two functions:

1. Dose attenuation function describing the dose at any point along the path length for radiation travelling through matter. This can be solved using exact numerical methods.

2. Chord distribution function describing numerous possible path lengths within the body. This can be calculated using a Monte Carlo methodology for each specific geometry.

External doses to organisms from radionuclides present in soil or in the water column were calculated using a variant of the simple formula for a uniformly contaminated isotropic infinite absorbing medium: This equation approximates the dose rate to an organism immersed in an infinite contaminated medium but neglects density differences between the organism and the medium. Furthermore, it allows for self shielding by the organism itself, and averages the dose rate throughout the volume of the organism. This approach has been used to calculate the external dose from β- and γ-radiation for organisms buried in soil or free swimming in the water column; the relevant concentrations being those in the soil or water media as appropriate.

---

[1] This represents a (thin) surface layer contamination selected to represent a period shortly after a deposition episode.

[2] A depth of 5 cm was arbitrarily selected to represent common artificial radionuclide profiles – bioturbation and post depositional migration of radionuclides often lead to the rapid development of a finite layer of contamination.

The estimation of external exposures at the interface of environments with different densities is more complex than cases pertaining to infinite, uniformly-contaminated environments. A two-step method has been used within EPIC. In the first step, the kerma in a specified location (above the soil/air interface, in soil at the given depth) is derived. In the second step, the ratio of the dose in an organism and the kerma is calculated for the different organisms and radionuclides.

A model, entitled DOSE3D was developed which could be used to calculate internal and external doses (dose-rates) for user-defined geometries, the computer program being composed of two component parts:

1. Geometry module – this part of the program allowed the user to create a geometry and subsequently manipulate and view this object. The module dealt with a variety of shapes including ellipsoids, spheres, cylinders, conical cylinders and egg-shaped (i.e. irregular ellipsoid) objects. A 3-dimensional solid array was generated from the original mesh. A Monte Carlo algorithm was subsequently employed in order to calculate chord/segment distributions.
2. Dose module – This part of the program used chords data output from the geometry module, in the form of histograms, to derive absorbed fractions or dose rates. Absorbed fractions could be calculated for α, β and γ radiation types. The user selected the energy (monoenergetic α and γ or maximum and average for β) and scaling factors allowed calculations to be performed for a phantom of larger size but the same shape.

The program is currently available in 2 forms, one which can be used to carry out calculations for (1) simple situations whereby activity concentrations are uniformly and homogeneously distributed within the organisms and/or its environment and (2) more complex situations whereby differential activity concentrations between organs can be defined and absorbed fractions and dose rates calculated for the sets of organs involved.

Using this model it was possible to derive absorbed fractions and dose rates for a large suite of radionuclides for any user-defined geometry and target source configuration.

DCFs

In addition to the original list of 13 radionuclides originally selected within EPIC, radionuclide specific DCFs were also been derived for ^{238}U and ^{232}Th decay series for the purpose of allowing background dose rates to be calculated. All radionuclides with half-lives greater than 1 day were treated separately and were presented with their own DCF. All progeny with half-lives less than 1 day were included within the DCF value of the parent. In cases where decay chains branch (e.g. ^{212}Bi and ^{234}Th), the DCF value was weighted according to the yield of daughters. Further details concerning the models developed within the project and the derivation of DCFs in EPIC can be found in Golikov and Brown (2003). Weighted DCFs have been derived using provisional weighting factors of 3 for ^{3}H (all other β-emitters have been assigned a radiation weighting factor of 1) and 10 for alpha radiation. For an overview of these DCF values see Tables 7 and 8. The application of a dose-rate within radiological assessments has a distinct advantage in the sense that it allows radiation exposures arising from numerous radionuclides and sources, i.e. internal and external, to be integrated within a single, unified measurement. A disadvantage with the application of absorbed dose(rate) relates to the observation that exposures to different radiation types cause varying degrees of biological damage (as discussed previously) and thus a biological weighting factor needs to be applied to the various categories of radiations emitted by selected radionuclides to account for this. The methodology to circumvent this disadvantage is not difficult to implement, however, the fact that the relative biological effectiveness of different radiation types is dose-rate, species and end-point dependent means that consensus on appropriate radiation weighting factors is not easily attained.

Table 7. Arctic aquatic reference organisms - exposure pathways considered.

Reference organism	DFCs derived
Pelagic planktotrophic fish	Internal
	External (from water column)
Pelagic carnivorous fish	Internal
	External (from water column)
Benthic crustacean	Internal
	External (from water column)
	External (from water bottom sediment)
Benthic fish	Internal
	External (from water column)
	External (from water bottom sediment)
Bivalve mollusc	Internal
	External (from water column)
	External (from water bottom sediment)
Sea bird	Internal
	External (at air/water interface)
	External (on soil/air interface from source in soil)
Pelagic crustacean	Internal
	External (from water column)
Carnivorous mammal	Internal
	External (from water column)
	External (on soil/air interface from source in soil)

DOSE EFFECT RELATIONSHIPS

The approach taken within EPIC with regards to analyses of dose-effects relationships was to collate and organise data around the reference organism categories as defined earlier in this article and to focus on dose-rates and biological endpoints that are of relevance from the perspective of Arctic environmental protection. For this purpose, the compilation of data focused on the effects of chronic radiation exposure at dose rates well below those that are known to cause mortality of organisms. And, from the wide variety of radiation effects reported in the open literature, emphasis was placed upon those which are important for the survival and reproduction of organisms *in the wild*. Furthermore, information was arranged in a form that would facilitate the development of appropriate Arctic dose limits, providing a scientific basis for the regulations in the radiation protection of the environment. To this end, a preliminary scale of the severity of radiation effects at different levels of chronic exposure to aid decision making was considered useful.

Table 8. Arctic terrestrial reference organisms - exposure pathways considered.

Reference organism	DCFs derived
Soil invertebrate	Internal
(Collembola)	External (on the soil/air interface)
Soil invertebrate (mite)	Internal
	External (on the soil/air interface)
	External (100 cm underground)
Herbivorous mammal	Internal
(lemming)	External (on the soil/air interface)
	External (100 cm underground)
Herbivorous mammal (vole)	Internal
	External (on the soil/air interface)
	External (50 cm underground)
Herbivorous mammal	Internal
(reindeer)	External (on the soil/air interface)
Herbivorous bird	Internal
	External (on the soil/air interface)
Bird egg	Internal
	External (on the soil/air interface)
Carnivorous mammal	Internal
	External (on the soil/air interface)
	External (100 cm underground)
Plant roots	Internal
	External (at the depth 0-30 cm)

Data concerning dose-effects relationships on radiation effects in reference (or related) Arctic biota available from Russian and other former Soviet Union sources was collated. The compiled data were concentrated on the effects in radiosensitive species in Arctic terrestrial and aquatic ecosystems, such as mammals, fish, and sensitive groups of plants (e.g. pines) less attention being given to radioresistant species. In line with approaches taken elsewhere (e.g. Woodhead and Zinger, 2003) data was organised under "umbrella" end-point categories, namely:

1. Morbidity (worsening of physiological characteristics of organisms; effects on immune system, blood system, nervous system, etc.);
2. Reproduction (negative changes in fertility and fecundity, resulting in reduced reproductive success);
3. Mortality (shortening of lifetime as a result of combined effects on different organs and tissues of the organism);
4. Cytogenetic effects;
5. Ecological effects (changes in biodiversity, ecological successions, predator-prey relationships);

6. Stimulation effects;
7. Adaptation effects.

Background Dose-rates

One reference point for assessing the significance of a particular level of radiation exposure may be defined by the natural background radiation. In the Arctic, as everywhere on the Earth, terrestrial and aquatic organisms are exposed to natural sources of ionising radiation, including cosmic rays, radionuclides produced by cosmic ray interactions in the atmosphere, and radiations from naturally-occurring radionuclides, which are ubiquitously distributed in all living and non-living components of the biosphere (Whicker & Schultz, 1982).

The typical dose rates of natural background exposure for different types of organisms in the Arctic are discussed in Sazykina et al. (2003). These dose rates have been derived using data on the activity concentrations of natural radionuclides in Arctic aquatic ecosystems for several reference organism groups and representative species. The doses were estimated by the methods described in earlier studies (IAEA, 1976, 1979; Kryshev and Sazykina, 1995; Kryshev et al., 2001, 2002), taking into account the geometrical characteristics of organisms and ionising radiation sources. Typical annual doses to terrestrial vertebrate under generic conditions were been taken from Whicker and Shultz (1982).

Preliminary Relationships "Dose Rate – Effects" for Chronic Low-LET radiation

The EPIC database "Radiation effects on biota" provided the extensive sets of data from Russian/FSU publications, which can substantially enlarge the knowledge of radiobiological effects in northern wildlife (Sazykina et al., 2003). These data were found sufficient to develop the preliminary dose-effects relationships for northern biota in the terrestrial and aquatic environment although it may additionally be necessary, in the context of management, to develop specific scales documenting the likely effects of radiation exposure for selected reference organisms. An example is provided in Table 9. Further information, for other reference organism groups, can be found in Sazykina et al. (2003).

Effects of Chronic High-LET Radiation on Wild Organisms

In order to revisit the issue of relative biological effectiveness and the application of appropriate radiation weighting factors, data pertaining to biota exposure to high LET, i.e. α-radiation, were treated separately. The effects of high-LET radiation on wildlife, represented in the EPIC database, related mainly to the areas of enhanced natural radioactivity (U, Th) in the Komi Region of Russia. The EPIC database also included the results of some experiments with exposure of aquatic organisms to solutions of ^{238}U or ^{232}Th.

Table 9. Dose-effects relationships for developing roe of cold-water fish; chronic exposure from radionuclides in aquatic media during the whole period of fish egg development (Sazykina et al., 2003).

Exposure	Effects
Chronic 5×10^{-8} Gy d^{-1}	Slight stimulation of salmon's egg development
Chronic $< 10^{-4}$ Gy d^{-1}	Effects are insignificant
Chronic $(1-2) \times 10^{-4}$ Gy d^{-1}	First effects appeared: some cytogenetic changes in blood of fore-larvae
Chronic $(1-5) \times 10^{-3}$ Gy d^{-1}	Decrease in survival of eggs, appearance of dead and abnormal embryos, in some cases damaged were 30-50% of eggs
Chronic 3×10^{-2} Gy d^{-1}	Considerable decrease in survival of roe, mortality about 50%
Chronic 0.13-0.33 Gy d^{-1}	Practically total death of roe

The comparison of dose-effects and concentration effects relationships for these radionuclides lead to the conclusion that the high chemical toxicity of ^{238}U and ^{232}Th dominates over radiotoxicity. Alpha-emitting radionuclides, characterized by low specific activity and high chemical toxicity, were therefore not suitable for the purpose of evaluating the radiation weighting factors for high-LET radiation. Further refinement of radiation weighting factors beyond the considerations afforded this topic previously was not possible following the EPIC dose-effects review.

Radiation Effects in Arctic Organisms

One of the hypotheses explored within EPIC, which has clear relevance to the derivation of Arctic specific dose limits, is that Arctic flora and fauna manifest effects quite differently, following exposure to radiation, compared to similar organisms under temperate conditions. Testing of this hypothesis was difficult because there are very few radiobiological studies that have relevance for the Arctic. Nonetheless some limited data are available.

For example, fish have been observed to survive for much longer time periods following high dose (i.e. approx 20 Gy) acute exposures at low temperatures, commensurate with those observed in Arctic environments, compared with higher temperatures, commensurate with those observed in temperate environments (Keiling et al., 1958). On the other hand, other experimental studies have shown the repair of radiation damage in cells and tissues is not effective at very low temperatures (see references in Sazykina et al., 2003).

From a further consideration of general radiobiological laws and peculiarities of metabolic processes in Arctic organisms, several further inferences may be derived. Anticipated impacts of ionising radiation, characteristic to Arctic conditions might include:

1. Lesions in cooled animals (e.g. poikilothermic or hibernating animals) and plants might be expected to be latent. However, if the organisms become warm, lesions are rapidly revealed.
2. Because the development of embryos and young poikilothermic organisms in the Arctic occurs slowly at low temperatures, Arctic organisms may receive much higher doses under conditions of chronic exposure, for a specified dose-rate, during the

radiosensitive stages of ontogenesis when compared with similar species in the temperate climate.

3. Low biodiversity of the Arctic ecosystems provides a more limited potential for compensatory replacement of damaged species by others.

4. Long-distance migrations of many animals in the Arctic may result in mitigated exposure regimes because the animal will spend less time in contact with a localised hot-spot of contamination.

Combining Effects Assessments for Radioactive and Non-radioactive Substances

Biological effects of hazardous substances, such as radionuclides, POPs and heavy metals, can be measured at different levels of biological organisation, from the molecular to the ecosystem level. Biomarkers[3] measurable at a molecular level respond early, but are not readily interpreted in terms of possible effects at higher levels of biological organisation (e.g. individual or populations). In contrast, biomarkers with clear ecological relevance, such as population declines or reduced reproductive rates, respond too late to have diagnostic or preventive value.

At the molecular or cellular level of organisation, effects of various substances may be crudely separated into genotoxic (i.e. act mainly by damaging DNA) and non-genotoxic substance categories. The former group includes chemically active species, or substances that can be activated, bind to or modify DNA directly, or indirectly *via* radicals. The non-genotoxic substances range from non-specific irritants and cytotoxins to natural hormones, growth factors, and their analogues (UNSCEAR, 2000). Most of the POPs referred to in AMAP (2002) are non-mutagenic (a common underlying mechanism seems to be disruption of the hormone system).

Even though the primary molecular and cellular effects of various POPs, heavy metals and radionuclides are often very diverse, comparison of toxicity may be performed using suitable (umbrella) end-points. The umbrella end-points used in EPIC have been described previously. A similar, but more detailed approach is being developed for POPs using, in addition to mortality and reproduction effects, biological markers based on subtle, low dose effects (e.g. on liver enzymes). Carcinogenic effects are also considered – stating whether a POP is mutagenic or functions as a tumour promoter. In the Arctic, the major concern of POPs is long-term chronic exposures as organisms are exposed to low levels over their entire lifetime. In this context, the major effects of concern are those that may affect reproduction and survival at the individual and population level. An overview of toxic properties of important POPs is given in AMAP (2002).

End-points such as mortality and effects on reproduction are also important in connection with heavy metal studies - most experiments considered in AMAP, focus on "clinical signs and symptoms of lethal and sub-lethal toxicity" (AMAP, 1998). An overview of reported effects threshold levels in tissues of main animal groups are given in AMAP (1997).

---

[3] Almost any biological change, from molecular to ecological, can serve as a biomarker; however, the term most often refers to changes at sub-cellular level.

In a "real" contamination situation, biota will be exposed to complex mixtures of various types of hazardous substances (and other environmental stressors). It is thus important to consider the possibility of combined effects[4] of toxicants in Arctic areas. Studies of interactions have indicated that, at least at high exposures, the action of one agent can be influenced by simultaneous exposures to other agents. The combined effects may be greater or smaller than the sum of the effects from separate exposures to the individual agents (UNSCEAR 2000a).

Even though interactions between non-radioactive contaminants and radionuclides/radiation exposure have not been extensively studied for non-human biota, two separate, but connected, general influences may be distinguished: (1) effects of co-exposure to non-radioactive contaminants on accumulation kinetics and internal tissue distribution of radionuclides; and (2) possible modifying influence of co-contaminants on the biological effects induced by the exposure to ionising radiation (Woodhead & Zinger, 2003).

A well balanced conclusion on the combined actions of two agents can only be given if the dose-effect relationship of both agents separately and of the combined exposure are known and can be analysed using a model in which the interactions can be consistently and quantitatively defined. The majority of studies on combined effect, including those with radiation, do not meet these conditions (UNSCEAR 2000b).

EXAMPLES OF THE ASSESSMENT PROCESS

In order to facilitate the application of the exposure assessment methodology described in the preceding sections of this document, an application in the marine environment is provided.

Marine Environment

Introduction

A "worst case" release scenario at the Kola NPP as described by Larsen *et al.* (1999) was considered for this example. A summary of the scenario and activities of ^{137}Cs, ^{134}Cs, and ^{90}Sr released to the atmosphere is presented below:

Source:	VVER-440/230	
Accident scenario:	Large Loss of Cooling accident	
Release scenario:	Fission product release	45 min
	Reactor vessel melt-through	250 min
	End of scenario	1800 min
Nuclides:	^{137}Cs	14.0 PBq
	^{134}Cs	18.7 PBq
	^{90}Sr	1.7 PBq

---

[4] Combined effects can be defined as: "The joint effects of two or more agents on the level of molecules, cells, organs, and organisms in the production of a biological effect" (UNSCEAR 2000b)

It was assumed that the released radioactivity was deposited in the Barents Sea (*i.e.* box 27 in Figure 4). The NRPA marine box model was employed to simulate sea water and sediment activity concentrations in the first 20 years after this hypothetical accident. The box model is an improved version of the compartmental model (Nielsen *et al.*, 1997). The model is based on the modified approach for box modelling (Iosjpe *et al.*, 2002), which includes dispersion of radionuclides during time (non-instantaneous mixing in oceanic space). This approach was created in order to provide a better and more realistic/physical approach comparing to traditional box modelling. The NRPA model water boxes structure was developed with regards to improved description of Polar, Atlantic and Deep waters in the Arctic Ocean and the Northern Seas (Karcher and Harms, 2000). The model ice module is available for the description of radionuclide exchanges between water and ice phases, between the suspended sediment in the water column, bottom sediment and the ice sediment, the exchanges of radionuclides between the ice boxes.

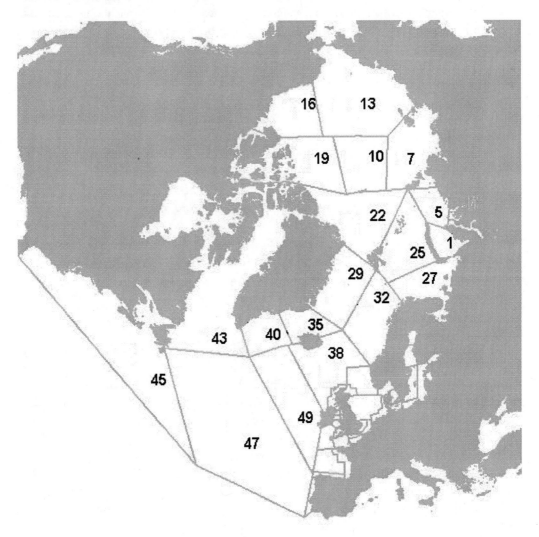

Figure 4. The structure of the surface boxes in the NRPA marine box model

Exposure Assessment Methodology

The list of reference organism, as specified in Table 3 was adopted for further analyses. Simulations were subsequently run for the following reference organisms (representative species in parentheses): Carnivorous pelagic fish (Atlantic cod); benthic fish (plaice); bivalve mollusc (blue mussel); sea bird (herring gull); and carnivorous mammal (harp seal).

The activity concentrations of ^{137}Cs, ^{134}Cs, and ^{90}Sr associated with the reference organisms were calculated by applying appropriate CF's to radionuclide activity concentrations in (filtered) sea water derived using the marine box-model for the specified release scenario. As an example, calculated activity concentrations of ^{137}Cs in reference organisms for the specified scenario are displayed in Figure 5.

Simplifying assumptions were made with respect to occupancy factors, v: for benthic biota (bivalve mollusc and benthic fish) it was assumed that the organisms are continually present at the sediment-water interface at all times. For pelagic fish and sea mammals it was assumed that the organisms are totally immersed in water at all times. For sea birds it was (somewhat arbitrarily) assumed that gulls spend 1/3 of their time on the water surface; 1/3 of their time in the inter-tidal zone; and the rest of their time in non-contaminated areas (e.g. in the air). Internal and external dose conversion factors (DCFs) were extracted from the relevant Tables in Golikov & Brown (2003). In order to calculate external doses to sea birds in the inter-tidal zone, it was assumed that the external DCFs for soil also apply here. Sediment activity concentrations (Bq kg^{-1} DW) – predicted using the marine box model – were consequently converted to kBq m^{-2} (assuming a density 0.78 g cm^{-3}, and a soil depth of 10 cm).

The exposure assessment methodology presented previously was used to calculate doses to the selected reference organisms: external exposure (Eqn. 3); internal exposure (Eqn. 4) and total exposure (Eqn.1), using activity concentrations, occupancy factors and internal and external DCFs. Distribution between external and internal exposure are visualised in Figure 6 using external dose rate fractions (i.e. external dose rate divided by total dose rate). Total dose rates from ^{137}Cs, ^{134}Cs, and ^{90}Sr are displayed in Figure 7. From life-history data sheets it was evident that all of the representative species considered may live for 20 years or more. Consequently, integrated doses were calculated for the whole simulation period (20 years). These integrated doses are presented in Table 10.

Results

As displayed in Figure 5, activity concentrations of ^{137}Cs in sea water decrease rather rapidly, from 46, 6.8, and 1.3 Bq m^{-3} for years 1, 5, and 10, respectively. In contrast, sediment concentrations of ^{137}Cs seem to be rather stable for the whole simulation period, reaching a maximum about 6-7 years after the accident. Sea birds exhibit the highest activity concentrations within the reference organism group. This is due to relatively large CF values for gulls.

Excluding the first year, external doses (mainly from sediments) dominate predicted total doses to benthic organisms (i.e. bivalve molluscs and benthic fish). Internal doses, which vary as a function of bioaccumulation as defined by CFs account for virtually the entire total dose rate to pelagic organisms (i.e. pelagic fish and sea mammals). Sea birds exhibit dose-rates that combine characteristics, i.e. internal exposure dominates in the first 10 years, whereas external dose contributions increase to about ¾ of the total dose after 20 years. The concentration dynamics of radionuclides in the water column and sediment determine the dynamics of dose rates for all marine organisms. As shown in Figure 7, sea birds receive the highest predicted doses for the first 10 years after the hypothetical accident, whereas benthic organisms become the most exposed group for periods in excess of 10 years. Pelagic organisms receive total dose rates of comparable size to benthic organisms during the first years, but since doses to these organisms are only dependent on water concentrations, dose rates decrease quite rapidly (cf. Figure 5). In contrast, total doses to benthic organisms level off due to external exposure from sediments (cf. Figure 6). In general, doses calculated for this example were low compared to natural background levels for marine reference organisms. Table 10 indicates that sea birds receive the highest total dose (20 years), benthic organisms lie in-between and pelagic organisms receive the lowest doses from a hypothetical "worst case" accident at Kola NPP. The large CF for radiocaesium (notably based on limited information and therefore uncertain) for sea birds seems to be of most importance for the relatively high predicted dose for this reference organism.

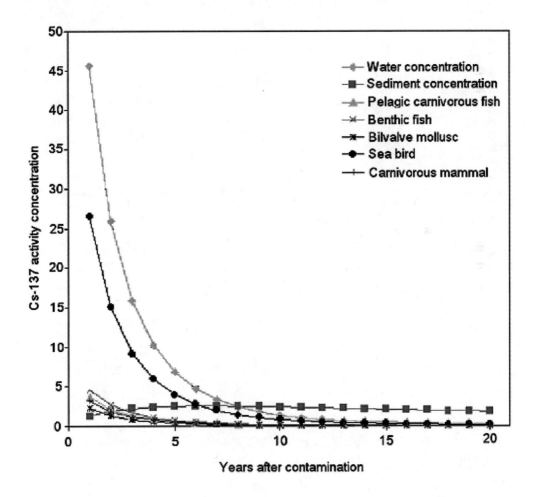

Figure 5. Predicted ^{137}Cs activity concentrations in water (Bq m^{-3}), sediments (Bq kg^{-1} DW) and reference organisms (Bq kg^{-1} FW) from the Barents Sea.

Table 10. Total doses (^{137}Cs, ^{134}Cs, and ^{90}Sr) to reference Arctic marine organisms for the whole simulation period (20 years).

Reference organism	Representative species	Integrated total dose (20 y) Gy
Pelagic carnivorous fish	Cod	$2.8 \cdot 10^{-5}$
Benthic fish	Plaice	$8.0 \cdot 10^{-5}$
Bivalve mollusc	Blue mussel	$6.2 \cdot 10^{-5}$
Sea bird	Herring gull	$2.3 \cdot 10^{-4}$
Carnivorous mammal	Harp seal	$5.0 \cdot 10^{-5}$

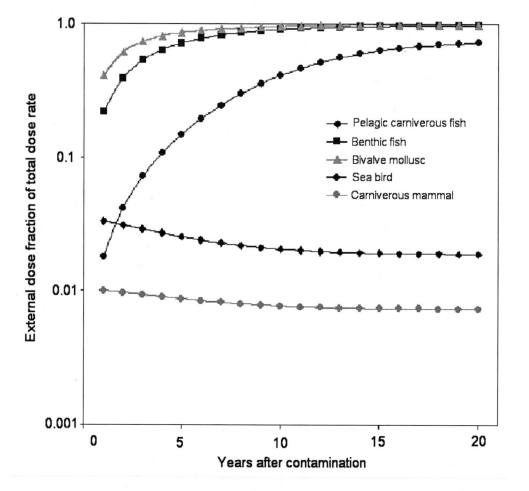

Figure 6. External dose fractions of total dose rate (^{137}Cs, ^{134}Cs, and ^{90}Sr) to reference organisms from the Barents Sea.

CRITERIA AND STANDARDS FOR ARCTIC BIOTA

The dose-effects relationships for low-LET radiation derived from the EPIC framework, in conjunction with recommendations and results from other international programmes/projects are a valuable input to the development of internationally agreed safety guidance for protection of wildlife from ionising radiation. Any assessment guidance should utlimately include standards and criteria. According to risk management terminology, these have been distinguished by the following definitions: standards are normally regulatory or legal limits, either dose limits or environmental concentrations, and criteria refer to guides or factors that may be used to aid management decisions such as levels of exposure above which adverse environmental effects may occur (these are normally not legally binding).

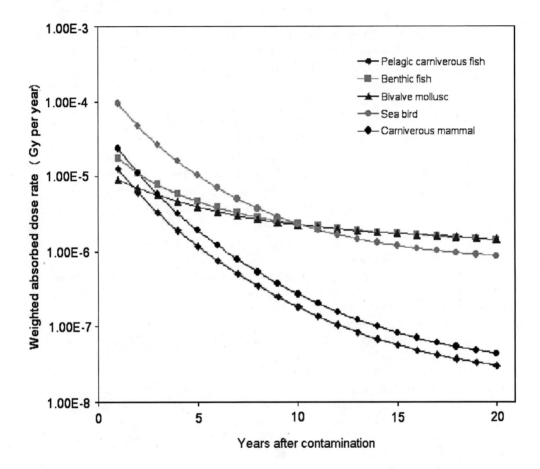

Figure 7. Predicted weighted dose rates (^{137}Cs, ^{134}Cs, and ^{90}Sr) to reference organisms from the Barents Sea (Gy a^{-1}).

The Derivation of Dose Limits

As stated earlier, no international agreed regulations exist for protecting natural flora and fauna from the detrimental effects of ionising radiation. A main concern for environmental regulations is the establishment of radiation safety standards for biota. Such standards would apply to normal operating activities of industries dealing with technogenic/natural radionuclides, which are associated with a chronic exposure of flora and fauna at comparatively low dose rates (with accumulated doses well below those likely to lead to increased mortality) (IAEA, 1976).

International Developments

There have been several review publications on radiobiological effects in wild nature (IAEA, 1976, 1992; Blaylock and Trabalka, 1978; NCRP, 1991; Polikarpov, 1998; Turner, 1975; Woodhead, 1984; UNSCEAR, 1996). In most cases, the intention of the authors was to focus attention on the effects of chronic low-dose exposures, but these data were very limited. As a result, the existing reviews refer largely to studies of radiation effects from acute exposure at high doses; hence these data are not directly relevant to environmental concerns. A major problem in the evaluation of the severity of environmental effects and subsequent derivation of standards for non-human organism's exposure has been the lack of available data on effects at low-level chronic radiation in international publications.

In the 1990s, international reviews of radiation effects on flora and fauna were published by the IAEA (1992) and UNSCEAR (1996). Based on summaries of available radiobiological literature, including some data from Russian sources, these documents provide the following set of preliminary conclusions on the thresholds of observable radiation effects for terrestrial and aquatic biota:

IAEA Report (1992, Summary):

"Chronic dose rates of 1 mGy d^1 to even the more radiosensitive species in terrestrial ecosystems are unlikely to cause measurable detrimental effects in populations and that up to this level adequate protection would therefore be provided".

"In the aquatic environment it would appear that limiting chronic dose rates to 10 mGy d^1 or less to the maximally exposed individuals in a population would provide adequate protection for the population";

UNSCEAR Report (1996, Para. 264):

"For the most sensitive animal species, mammals, there is little indication that dose rates of 10 mGy d^1 to the most exposed individual would seriously affect mortality in the population. For dose rates up to an order of magnitude less (1-2.4 mGy d^1), the same statement could be made with respect to reproductive effects.

For aquatic organisms, the general conclusion was that maximum dose rates of 0.4 mGy h^{-1} (≈10 mGy d^1) to a small proportion of the individuals in aquatic populations and, therefore, lower average dose rates to the whole population would not have any detrimental effects at the population level."

Furthermore, it was stated that for *"the most sensitive plant species, the effects of chronic radiation were noted at dose-rates 1-3 mGy h^{-1}. It was suggested that chronic dose-rates less than 0.4 mGy h^{-1} (≈10 mGy d^1) would have only slight effects in sensitive plants but would be unlikely to produce significant deleterious effects in the wider range of plants present in natural plant communities."*

The conclusions of the IAEA and UNSCEAR reports specified the ranges of chronic dose rates, which are of concern in the environmental protection of flora and fauna. None of these dose rate levels were intended as recommendations for radiation protection criteria, although they clearly could have implications for the development of such criteria and standards.

Dose limits have been applied in other situations as exemplified by the approach advocated by the USDoE (2002). The limits used by the USDoE have been established earlier based on the findings of numerous reviews considering the effects of ionising radiation on flora and fauna (e.g. NCRP, 1991; IAEA, 1992) and relate to the protection of populations of wild organisms. A dose limit of 10 mGy d^{-1} is applied to aquatic animals and terrestrial plants and a dose limit of 1 mGy d^{-1} applied to terrestrial animals.

Although these basic recommendations, and in the latter case dose-limits, exist, their applicability directly within the context of the EPIC framework is limited for two reasons:

1. For reasons discussed in the introductory section, there are reasons to believe that Arctic climatic conditions influence the expression of radiation induced effects and, furthermore, that Arctic ecosystems are potentially more vulnerable to contaminants than organisms in other European climatic regions. The dose limits derived for temperate environments may, therefore, be unsuitable for direct application to the Arctic.

2. The dose limits considered above relate to the protection of populations of wild flora and fauna. In contrast, the approach taken in the EPIC framework focuses on environmentally-relevant endpoints at the individual organism level, hence all data collation and subsequent analyses is made at the individual level.

With respect to environmental protection, it is important to derive dose-effects relationships for a large range of exposures, providing a scale of severity of radiation effects on natural biota following the increase in irradiation levels. Such information will further facilitate the derivation of appropriate dose-standards and has therefore been a key theme for the EPIC framework.

From the information compiled within EPIC, a preliminary scale which maps observed biological effects onto ranges of absorbed dose has been constructed (Table 11). Dose-effect relationships have been thus tabulated for the generic groups: Arctic terrestrial animals, Arctic terrestrial plants and Arctic aquatic animals. The table also includes the "background" dose-rate range observed under natural conditions.

A general conclusion can be drawn, that the threshold for deterministic radiation effects in wildlife lies somewhere in the range 0.5-1 mGy d^{-1} for chronic low-LET radiation. This is in broad agreement with the conclusions made by UNSCEAR (1996). Having said this, the extrapolation of biological effects observed at one level of biological organisation to a higher level is no simple matter. Although minor effects on morbidity in sensitive vertebrate animals are observed at the dose range specified above, populations of highly productive vertebrate organisms (mice, some ubiquitous fish species) are viable at dose rates in the order 10 mGy d^{-1}. The establishment of dose limits may therefore depend not only on the types of organism that require protection but on the level of protection, e.g. protection of viable populations versus protection of individuals from a particular radiosensitive species.

The generalised conclusions, within EPIC, regarding the threshold dose-rates at which various effects are observed are consistent with earlier studies. From the available information it is, therefore, not possible to justify any Arctic specific dose-standards at the present time. Assumptions of Arctic vulnerability might provide justification for applying an additional safety factor to any derived dose limits, e.g., that standards be set at say a factor of ten lower than those derived for other for ecosystems. Having said this, the data set upon which such a conclusion is drawn is limited in scope (see below) and the hypothesis relating to whether there is a unique expression of radiation-induced biological damage under Arctic conditions remains to be properly tested.

Table 9. Scale mapping absorbed dose-rates onto effect (Sazykina *et al.*, 2003).

Absorbed dose rate (Gy d^{-1})	Effect
10^{-6} -10^{-5}	Natural radiation background for Arctic/northern organisms
10^{-4} to 5×10^{-4}	Minor cytogenetic effects. Stimulation of the most sensitive species
5×10^{-4} to 1×10^{-3}	Threshold for minor effects on morbidity in sensitive vertebrate animals.
2×10^{-3} to 5×10^{-3}	Threshold for effects on reproductive organs of vertebrate animals, decrease of embryo's survival.
5×10^{-3} to 10^{-2}	Threshold for life shortening of vertebrate animals. Threshold for effects in invertebrate animals. Threshold for effects on growth of coniferous plants.
10^{-2} to 10^{-1}	Life shortening of vertebrate animals; chronic radiation sickness. Considerable damage to coniferous trees.
10^{-1} to 1	Acute radiation sickness of vertebrate animals. Death of coniferous plants. Considerable damage to eggs and larva of invertebrate animals.
> 1	Acute radiation sickness of vertebrate animals; lethal dose received within several days. Increased mortality of eggs and larva of invertebrate animals. Death of coniferous plants, damage to deciduous plants.

Table 12. Summary of natural background dose rates for marine reference organisms, derived from EPIC Deliverable Report 5 (Sazykina et al., 2003).

Ecosystem	Organism	Dose-rate (µGy d^{-1})
Marine	Phytoplankton[a]	0.5 - 2.1
	Zooplankton[a]	0.6 - 4.1
	Crustaceans[a]	2.7 - 14
	Molluscs[a]	2.7 - 13
	Macrophytes[a]	1.7 - 12
	(Benthic) Fish[a]	1.3 - 10
	Waterfowl[a]	0.5 – 1.6
Freshwater	Fish	1.4 – 2.2
Terrestrial	Generic vertebrate[b]	Circa 3.2

[a] Derived for the Kara Sea – it is assumed that phytoplankton, zooplankton and waterfowl receive all external irradiation from the water column whereas crustaceans, molluscs, macrophytes and benthic fish receive all external irradiation from sediment;

[b] Generic terrestrial vertebrate in a temperate environment (from Whicker & Shultz, 1982).

Furthermore, the problem of evaluating the appropriate weighting factors for high-LET radiation in the context of wildlife protection is still unsolved. It was evident from the analyses of available data (Sazykina *et al.*, 2003) that heavy alpha-emitting radionuclides with very low specific activity and chemical toxicity can not be used for the purpose of w_r estimations, because the bulk of observed effects on biota are associated with chemical toxicity of these elements. The safety regulations for these radionuclides (e.g. ^{238}U, ^{232}Th) are more appropriate to establish for each radionuclide separately. As discussed previously, background dose rates have been derived for Arctic and/or related ecosystems albeit at a simple level. This information is summarised in Table 12.

It should be noted that background dose-rates for Arctic terrestrial flora and fauna are particularly poorly defined and information for freshwater environments is limited to only a few reference organism types. Used in conjunction, information for reference organisms, relating to doses at which various effects are observed and background dose rates might be used to inform management decisions. Such an approach would be in line with the "derived consideration levels" discussed by Pentreath (2002).

Concentration Standards

Another way to organise the implementation of standards is through the setting of concentration standards. Such methods have been applied both in the US and Russia and are briefly introduced below.

Biota Concentration Guides (BCG) – US Approach

A prominent example is the US DoE's graded approach for evaluating radiation doses to aquatic and terrestrial biota (USDoE, 2002). This assessment methodology is in essence a compliance tool whereby doses to aquatic flora and fauna can be evaluated against specified limits on radiation doses to these biota. Having defined the dose rate limits, as described previously, biota concentration guides (essentially limiting radionuclide concentrations in sediments and water) for specified radionuclides are derived by dividing this limit by external and internal dose rates per unit concentration in sediment or water. In other words, at the BCG concentration, dose rates to biota will attain the dose limit. An example of the BCG is shown in Eqn. 10.

$$ BCG_{s,i,ra} = \frac{365 DL_{ra}}{C_{ra}\left[\left(LP_{s,i,ra} DCF_{\text{int},i}\right)+\left(DCF_{iext,i}\right)\right]} \tag{10} $$

where,

$BCG_{s,i,ra}$ = Biota concentration Guide, i.e. concentration of radionuclide "*i*" in sediment (Bq kg^{-1}), based on screening level assumptions that numerically equates to the Dose Rate DL_{ra} to riparian animal,

DL_{ra} = Recommended dose limit for riparian animals (1 mGy d^{-1}),

C_{ra} = Correction factor for area or riparian animal residence time,

$LP_{s,i,ra}$ = Lumped parameter (dimensionless) – ratio of the activity concentration in riparian animal to sediment concentration of radionuclide "*i*".

The methodology uses a sum of fractions rule, whereby activity concentrations measured in sediment and water are divided by corresponding BCGs for all radionuclides considered.

The sum of fractions should be < 1 for compliance to be demonstrated. The graded approach, advocated by the DoE, involves a data assembly phase wherein sources, receptor and routes of exposures are considered and environmental activity concentration data collated. Following this, a general screening phase can be employed using default parameters and maximum activity concentrations. Failing this, successively more detailed levels of analyses are employed including site-specific screening (site representative parameters and condition utilised), site specific analyses (using site appropriate kinetic allometric modelling tools) and finally a site specific biota dose assessment (employing an eco-risk framework).

Control Concentrations (CC) - Russian Approach

There are no official criteria for radiation protection of flora and fauna in Russia. However, the issue has been under consideration since the 1970s, mainly in the context of the establishing the control concentrations of radionuclides in marine areas ensuring the safety of the human population, as well as marine fauna and flora. In earlier work (Shekhanova, 1983), attempts were made to establish control levels (working limits) of the radionuclide content in sea water, with consideration for hygienic and radioecological criteria of limiting the exposure of humans and marine biota. These problems were also discussed in several publications (Sazykina, 1996; Sazykina and Kryshev 1999; Kryshev and Sazykina, 1998). In recent years, a methodology was developed for radionuclide permissible levels in sea water, based on the current requirements for ensuring the radiation safety of the population and the environment (Sazykina and Kryshev, 1999).

It was proposed that the maximum permissible concentrations (control levels) of radionuclides in seawater should be estimated in order to ensure radiation safety of both humans and marine biota, using both hygienic and radioecological criteria. Control levels of concentrations were calculated for each radionuclide separately; as several radionuclides are present in sea water, the permissible levels are calculated using standard rules for mixed contaminants. From hygienic (human protection) criteria, the control concentrations of radionuclides in sea water were calculated under the following conditions: radiation dose to the population from consumption of marine foodstuffs should not exceed 10 % of the permissible dose limit (1 mSv a^{-1}); dose is assessed for a critical population group with considerable consumption of marine foodstuffs. These hygienic criteria satisfy Russian and international standards for ensuring the radiation safety of the human population (IAEA, 1996).

From radioecological criteria, the control concentrations of radionuclides in sea water ensuring the radiation safety of marine flora and fauna were calculated using the following guidelines:

1. radiation dose to sea animals should not exceed 100 mGy a^{-1};
2. radiation dose to sea plants should not exceed 1000 mGy a^{-1}.

These doses correspond to about 1 % of LD$_{50}$ (at which 50 % of the organisms die after single exposure). Under conditions of chronic exposure, doses exceeding 10 mGy d^{-1} to aquatic fauna can be ecologically significant. Dose assessments were made for critical groups of marine biota characterized by the highest exposure level at a given content of radionuclides in sea water. Using the radioecological criteria, the control concentrations were determined with the following relationship:

$$X_k = PC_{ik} / (F_{ik} B_{ik} + F_{dk} B_{dk}), \text{ [11]}$$

where,

X_k is the control concentration of the radionuclide k in sea water; PC_{ik} is the ecological dose limit for the ith group of marine organisms from exposure to the radionuclide k, Gy a^{-1},

F_{ik} is the concentration factor of the radionuclide k in the ith group of marine organisms,

B_{ik} is the dose factor for the ith group of marine organisms on internal exposure to the radionuclide k, Gy a^{-1}/Bq kg^{-1}; F_{dk} is the concentration factor of the radionuclide k in bottom sediments; B_{dk} is the dose factor for the ith group of marine organisms on external exposure to the radionuclide k from bottom sediments, Gy a^{-1}/Bq kg^{-1}.

The control concentrations of radionuclides in sea water calculated from radioecological criteria are presented in Table 13. Fish and molluscs are the critical groups of marine organisms for most radionuclides.

Table 13. The control concentrations (CC) of radionuclides in sea water calculated from the radioecological criteria, Bq l^{-1} ((Sazykina & Kryshev, 1999) relevant to the seas of the Russian North).

Radionuclide	CC	Critical group	Radionuclide	CC	Critical group
^{3}H	1700000	Mammals	^{99}Tc	1000	Mollusks
^{51}Cr	6000	Fish	^{106}Ru	30	Mollusks
^{54}Mn	8	Fish	^{129}I	1100	Algae
^{59}Fe	4	Fish	^{131}I	400	Algae
^{60}Co	2	Fish	^{134}Cs	13	Fish
^{59}Ni	850	Fish	^{137}Cs	30	Fish
^{63}Ni	1100	Fish	^{144}Ce	6	Fish
^{65}Zn	11	Fish	^{147}Pm	200	Fish
^{89}Sr	120	Fish	^{152}Eu	7	Fish
^{90}Sr	60	Fish	^{154}Eu	5	Fish
^{95}Zr	3	Fish	^{239,240}Pu	6	Mollusks
^{95}Nb	8	Fish	^{241}Am	1	Mollusks

The control concentrations (CC) for each radionuclide, calculated from hygienic and radioecological criteria, are compared, and the lower of the two values is selected; this value is considered as the maximal permissible level of radionuclide in seawater ensuring the protection of both humans and marine biota. The hygienic criteria was found to provide more rigid restrictions than radioecological ones for most radionuclides; the radionuclides ^{241}Am, ^{239}Pu, ^{240}Pu, ^{60}Co, and ^{65}Zn, which are characterized by high values of accumulation in individual marine foodstuffs, have the lowest CC; for tritium CC in sea water are higher than the specific activities established for fresh water (this is associated with the fact that tritium does not accumulate in marine foodstuffs and sea water is not used for drinking). At present, the existing concentrations of radionuclides (^{90}Sr, ^{137}Cs, ^{239}Pu, ^{240}Pu and some others) in sea water of the Arctic Seas are 10^3-10^4 times lower than CC.

Limitations with the Concentration Standards Approach

Concentration standards combine information on dose effects and environmental transfer and uptake. For the same assumed dose effect relationship in an organism the derived concentration standard will be lower in ecosystems having high transfer and bioaccumulation. Thus if limits were based on concentration standards rather than dose standards, then there would be clear grounds for having Arctic specific criteria, since there is a reasonable amount of evidence that transfer and uptake parameters under Arctic environments are different, for some radionuclides, compared to those observed under temperate conditions.

From a methodological point of view, the "permissible concentration" approach, which was developed in Russia for the marine environment, could be extended for terrestrial and freshwater ecosystems. However, there are some practical difficulties in estimating the reference radionuclide transfer parameters for terrestrial/freshwater ecosystems. In the seawaters of standard salinity, the chemical composition of seawater is maintained at a constant level, therefore, in equilibrium, the concentration factors for radionuclides accumulation in biota are the same within the whole marine area. In contrast, in freshwater ecosystems, each lake/river has unique composition of waters and sediments, which modify the site-specific radionuclide-transfer parameters. Average values of concentration factors and transfer parameters estimated for lake/river ecosystems of a large region have very high uncertainty. In the terrestrial ecosystems, soils of different types also demonstrate a large range of uncertainties in the values of radionuclide transfer parameters. Therefore, the databases of transfer parameters for terrestrial ecosystems cannot be averaged in the same manner as for marine environment; and it may be more appropriate to use site-specific data.

With these points in mind, a "concentration standard" approach has not been advocated within the framework of EPIC. It is felt that the uncertainty associated with such values would be too large to be sensibly applied. The process of establishing dose limits is still incomplete and although much progress has been made with respect to the derivation of appropriate transfer factors for Arctic reference organisms, further refinement is still clearly required.

COMPATIBILITY OF THE EPIC EXPOSURE ASSESSMENT FRAMEWORK WITH OTHER ENVIRONMENTAL IMPACT ASSESSMENT METHODOLOGIES

Comparison with Other Assessment Frameworks

Other assessment systems have been considered at some length elsewhere (Larsson *et al.*, 2002a) and there is no justifiable reason to repeat this exercise here. However, some general observations from Larsson *et al.* (2002a) are appropriate for consideration in this report. Assessment methodologies often include three major phases:

1. Entry characterisation – describe sources so that factors relevant to the assessment including physico-chemical form, magnitude of discharge, temporal variation in input etc. are provided.

2. Exposure analyses/assessment – predict the exposure of the substance to the assessment endpoint. This might be a concentration in a specific organ or for radiation, absorbed dose-rate to whole body.

3. Effects analyses/assessment – analyse concentration or dose-effects relationships in order to identify concentrations/doses at which harmful effects are observable for selected endpoints.

The EPIC assessment framework is compatible with such an approach but has not involved a detailed analysis of "entry characteristics". The assessment methodology is designed to be generically applicable and within the constraints of the framework it is not possible to explore whether this general approach can accommodate all possible input and ensuing radiation exposure scenarios. It is recognised, for example, that the suite of radionuclides discharged for any given scenario might not be a subset of the limited set considered within EPIC. It is also recognised that the physico-chemical form may lead to quite different environmental behaviour of radionuclides compared to the generic case. Under such situations the assessor would be advised to conduct a site-specific analysis.

Several differences between assessment systems (20 pathway based systems were analysed of which 11 considered impacts/risks of non-radioactive hazardous substances) have been identified by Larsson *et al.,* (2002a). These differences and the way in which the EPIC system can be classified in accordance with the various approaches adopted are listed below:

1. *Aim of the assessment.* These vary and include compliance with regulatory standard (e.g. USDoE, 2002), impact assessment for authorised releases (Copplestone *et al.,* 2001), assessment of hazards associated with chemical releases (e.g. Environment Canada, 1997) and a tool to develop environmental standards. The aim of the EPIC system includes aspects of many of these other aims. The system is initially being developed to allow realistic environmental impact assessment to be conducted in Arctic environment following releases of radioactivity. However, it is envisaged that the EPIC methodology may be used to inform the derivation of recommended standard/limits for the Arctic. With such standards in place the methodology could be used in a compliance situation (although it is recognised that such an outcome would involve sanction by Arctic countries at a national level).

2. *Degree of specificity.* This arises at the problem formulation stage and often depends on the aim of the assessment. The difference is most pronounced when comparing screening-level assessments using generic, and often conservative data/model parameters with site-specific assessments using more "realistic" information. The EPIC system has been developed to lie somewhere between these extremes, using regional-specific, 'best estimate' data-sets/models as oppose to conservative estimates. The general methodology should, however, be applicable to both screening and site specific assessments.

3. *Assessments vary with respect to the number of 'levels' employed in the system.* An example of a multi-tiered approach is provided by USDoE compliance methodology (USDoE, 2002). EPIC is essentially a single-tiered approach essentially for reasons pertaining to its envisaged application (see point (i)). Multi-tiered approaches are clearly suitable for application in compliance situations to remove the requirement for detailed, labour-intensive analyses, unless absolutely necessary. The EPIC system

has a degree of complexity built in, allowing realistic impact assessment for the Arctic to be conducted. However, the system could be modified to a compliance tool if such a need arises.

4. *The point in the assessment at which risk characterisation is conducted,* i.e. comparison between a standard/limit and measured/predicted quantity differs. As considered earlier in the article risk characterisation is only addressed within the EPIC system, by evaluating dose-rates to reference organism in relation to documented dose-rate response relationships to inform management decisions. Standard/limits are not employed by the system although it is envisaged that such limits may be recommended for the Arctic in the future based on part on EPIC project data sets.

5. *The choice of endpoint varies between systems.* This encapsulates differences in the type of ecosystem to be assessed, the type of effect and species to be studied, the level of biological hierarchy to be studied and/or protected. Systems vary with respect to guidance given on the selection of measurement endpoints (e.g. the concentration of a contaminant or measurable effect in a selected organism) and assessment endpoints (the effect that is inferred from the measurement endpoint which the assessment is designed to study/protect). Some frameworks include a predefined choice of endpoint others leave the choice to the assessor. The choice of measurement endpoint within EPIC is the activity concentration and derived dose rate for reference organisms. The use of critical organisms (used in site specific assessments) and reference organisms (generic studies) are used in some systems. The selection of reference organisms within EPIC has been predefined and the criteria employed in the selection are compatible with other systems. For EPIC the choice of assessment endpoints covers the umbrella biological effects categories mortality, morbidity, reproductive success and cytogenetic damage – a choice that should cover most envisaged application requirements for the system. The level of biological hierarchy to be protected is often taken to be the population – probably based on the observation that humans are prepared to accept, in many cases, the limited culling of numerous species for human use. Some systems (e.g. Environment Canada, 1997) also consider the protection for individuals under some circumstances.

6. *Difference in the extrapolation between measurements and assessment endpoints.* Many systems adopt an approach whereby a wide range of 'reference' organisms is selected in order to represent all species within an ecosystem. It is assumed that the test organisms, from which dose-response data were derived, do not need to be present in the environment. However, the range of reference organisms studied should have some relationship with these test animals allowing extrapolations to be made. In contrast, other systems select organisms in line with specific assessment goals. For example, sensitive organisms may be chosen based on their known sensitivity to a toxin and the effects estimated for these organisms are extrapolated to higher levels of biological hierarchy. The EPIC system takes elements of some of these varying approaches, a broad suite of reference organisms has been selected but the selection of each group was informed by a number of important generic considerations.

7. *Effects data analyses.* Based mainly on observations from non-radioactive substances, Larsson *et al.* (2002a) report that differences are evident in which effects

are deemed relevant and the statistical significance and/or acceptability of tests. Various statistical methods are also applied to effects data in order to establish a 'safe' level below which no adverse effects are observed in the endpoint of concern. Since the EPIC system is not being primarily developed to derive standards, this type of effects data analysis falls beyond the remit of the project.

Compatibility with MARINA II Methodology for Assessing Doses and Radiation Impacts on Marine Biota

The recent MARINA II Update project, together with the assessment of radiation exposure to human population, considered a specific task of assessing the dose rates to, and estimating the possible radiobiological effects on, representative non-human organisms, inhabiting the marine waters of the North-East Atlantic within the OSPAR area (EC, 2002).

An assessment methodology was identified for the estimation of doses and radiation impact on marine biota, based on the current 'state-of-art' in the dosimetry of non-human organisms, and available information of the effects of chronic radiation exposure on aquatic organisms. The methodology includes the following components: identification of biological endpoints of concern; selection of region-specific organisms for assessment; adaptation of dosimetric models for dose calculations; radiological assessment for marine biota (EC, 2002). This is in line with the EPIC approach.

Biological Endpoints of Concern

Four umbrella endpoints were adopted to be inclusive of all relevant effects of radiation at the level of individual organisms: morbidity, reproduction, cytogenetic effects, and mortality – compatible with those considered within EPIC. Following the conclusions of comprehensive reviews on radiation effects in non-human organisms (NCRP, 1991; IAEA, 1992; UNSCEAR, 1996), dose rates of chronic exposure within the range 1-10 mGy d^{-1} (10^{-3}-10^{-2} Gy d^{-1}) have been considered as the levels at which minor radiation effects on the morbidity, fertility and fecundity of individual aquatic animals begin to become apparent first in laboratory studies, and, at higher exposure, in natural populations.

To evaluate the possible harm to biota, the dose rates to organisms inhabiting the industry-impacted marine areas were compared with the available information on the effects of chronic radiation exposure in aquatic organisms.

Selection of Reference Organisms

It was practically impossible to perform radioecological assessment for every species from the thousands inhabiting the waters of the North-East Atlantic. This problem was mitigated by selecting a limited set of representative marine organisms, including molluscs (mussel and winkle/limpet), large crustaceans (crab and lobster), and fish (cod and plaice). The contamination of these region-specific species is studied within radioecological monitoring/research programmes and databases on the concentrations of radionuclides are available for these organisms. In the radiological assessment, the use of region-specific organisms throughout the whole OSPAR region provided an advantageous possibility to compare on a unified basis the doses/effects to biota in different local sites of the North-Atlantic. These approaches are in line with those recommended within EPIC.

Dosimetry of Marine Organisms

In the MARINA II Update study, dose rates to representative marine organisms have been calculated using the existing dosimetric approaches; adaptations were made to take into account the sizes and habits of the region-specific organisms. Dose conversion factors were calculated for recommended representative organisms and different radionuclides. To account the differences in the relative biological efficiency (RBE) of α-, β-, and γ- emitters, as a conservative assumption, a radiation weighting factor (w_r) of 20 has been selected for α-emitting radionuclides, and factor of 1 for other radionuclides. The dosimetric approaches are similar to those developed within EPIC with the exception of the selection of radiation weighting factors: by way of example, a w_α of 10 has been selected for the alpha component of radiation and a w_β of 3 has been applied to ^{3}H.

Compatibility with Developments Made Internationally: ICRP, IUR, IAEA

The International Union of Radioecology (IUR), considers that there is already sufficient information to start introducing an overall framework for the systematic protection of the environment from ionising radiation, drawing upon specialist reviews and interpretations of the large amount of radiobiological and radioecological information that has been gathered over the last fifty years (IUR, 2002). The basic elements of the system advocated by the IUR have been discussed at some length elsewhere (Pentreath, 1999; Strand et al, 2000; Strand & Larsson, 2001) but are essentially the same as that being developed within EPIC and FASSET. However, the organisation has also highlighted the need to plug some gaps in our knowledge and to improve upon existing databases. The IUR point to the fact that an increased interest in environmental protection has highlighted a number of knowledge gaps in the scientific data on sources and effects of radiation in non-human species, making the following observations:

1. Although the transfer of radionuclides is quite well known within some food-chains, there are very little data on the behaviour of radionuclides in non-temperate zones and on uptake to species that do not form part of the human food chain.
2. There is a need to develop both transfer models (flux, dynamic, ecosystem, etc.) and genotoxicological biomonitoring techniques that are capable of allowing impact assessments at a variety of species, population and ecosystem levels and that could also deal with other environmental stressors.
3. Mathematical models should be developed and applied to relate the effects of radiation on individuals (particularly with regard to early mortality, reproductive success, and cytogenetic damage) to potential impacts at the population level.
4. Knowledge of the doses and effects of background radiation is lacking, as are dose-effect relationships, including information on RBE for a variety of species, doses and

dose rates. Interaction of radionuclides with other stressors, including possible synergistic effects, is only just starting to be investigated.

These observations are pertinent to the discussions relating to the EPIC framework and emphasise the fact that although basic tools may be available for assessing impacts of ionising radiation on the environment, large areas of data paucity and knowledge gaps are prevalent.

The International Commission on Radiological Protection (ICRP), have revised their previous stance encapsulated by the paraphrase "*if man is protected from ionising radiation, the environment is also adequately protected*" (ICRP, 1991) to a position wherein a Committee (ICRP Committee 5) has been established to address environmental protection issues and plans are being made to incorporate their findings into the revised basic recommendations of the Commission (which are concerned with all aspects of radiological protection). An ICRP Task group completed a report on the protection of non-human species from ionising radiation, in 2002 (ICRP, 2002) and Committee 5 are currently (early 2006) in the process of producing a report on the concept and use of reference animals and plants for the prupose of environmental protection. The elements of the ICRP approach are consistent with those proposed by the EPIC projects having been based, to a large extent on the same ideas (see Pentreath, 1999). However, a number of ideas have been developed further in order to address how the system to protect man may be combined with the system to protect the environment under a common front (Strand and Holm, 2002). In the process of revising their basic recommendations of human radiological protection, the ICRP is exploring the possibility of moving away from dose-effects assessment based purely on human dose effects data and the hypothesis of a no threshold linear response relationship (with the implication that any small increment in radiation exposure carries with it a small incremental increase in risk) to a more embracing and understandable approach based on bands of concern with explicit reference to background dose rates (Pentreath, 2002). This would be consistent with the proposed dose assessment approach for flora and fauna, i.e. *Derived consideration levels*, where data could be presented as scales of dose-effects levels to facilitate different management options. Essentially, consideration levels for flora and fauna could be compiled from 2 sets of information namely (i) logarithmic bands of dose rates relative to natural dose rates and (ii) dose rates that are known to have an effect on selected biological endpoints including reproductive success, mortality, morbidity and scoreable cytogenetic parameters. Pentreath (2002) envisages that in adopting such an approach for any given situation involving environmental contamination by radionuclides, management decisions would be facilitated by information on two bands of concern. The first would relate to members of the public and be based on Reference Man and secondary data sets, the other would relate to the environment and be based on consideration levels based on primary and secondary reference organisms. After its initial work on compiling information in the 70's and up to the early 90's (see for example IAEA, 1976, IAEA, 1992), the IAEA has also taken up renewed interest in environmental protection, including an evaluation of the ethical and legal issues. Two reports have been published (IAEA, 1999, 2002) and the agency has organized a number of specialist meetings that have been successful in establishing a consensus on both the need for a system of protection and some fundamental ethical principles of environmental protection. The IAEA is in the process of developing a safety standard that will provide the basis for the assessment of radioactive materials on the environment, or living components of it and for the technical components of environmental management decisions (Robinson, 2002). The assessment component of the IAEA work programme is heavily influenced by the system being developed under FASSET and EPIC and is likely to adopt many of the methodologies developed within these projects.

CONCLUSION

General Conclusions

Within the frame of the EPIC project the following major steps were made in the direction of the development of a practical methodology for radiological assessment of the Arctic/northern wildlife:

1. A set of region-representative species have been selected which are characteristic for the marine, freshwater and terrestrial areas of the European Arctic. The selected species satisfy all/most of the selection criteria, they form large populations, and their natural areas of geographical distribution cover the whole or the greater part of the marine areas of the European Arctic. The contamination of the selected species is studied within radioecological monitoring/research programmes, so the databases on the radionuclide concentrations are available for most of the selected organisms.
2. Site-specific radioecological information have been collated concerning the assessment of concentration factors (CFs) of radionuclides in Arctic biota.
3. Models and computer codes were developed in order to calculate internal and external doses to non-human organisms; dose-conversion factors have been calculated for a set of reference Arctic organisms and a number of radionuclides.

The EPIC database compiled forms a large collection of information relating to radiation effects on Arctic biota covering a very wide range of radiation dose rates to wild flora and fauna: from below 10^{-5} Gy d^{-1} up to more than 1 Gy d^{-1}. A great variety of radiation effects are registered in the EPIC database encompassing effects from stimulation at low doses up to death from acute radiation syndrome at high doses. Based on information compiled in the EPIC database, the preliminary dose-effects relationships were derived for terrestrial and aquatic animals of northern climatic zone, also for terrestrial plants. The dose-effects relationships provide a preliminary scale of severity of radiation effects at increasing levels of chronic radiation exposure. Furthermore, information on background dose-rates were derived for selected reference organisms in terrestrial, freshwater and marine environments. Together, these data sets could inform decision making processes and provide input towards the development of Arctic dose standards.

Needs for Further Development of Assessment Methodology

Despite the availability of large data sets, it should be noted that large information gaps exist. With regard to the transfer of radionuclides in the environment, it was not been possible to derive transfer information for all radionuclide-reference organism combinations. This is especially true in the cases of freshwater and terrestrial environments where data paucity is often great. Even basic information relating to activity concentrations of natural radionuclides in Arctic environments are limited in coverage and thus render the derivation of background dose rates highly uncertain. The existing information concerning the effects of chronic exposure on Arctic wildlife does not cover all groups of sensitive species; for instance, there is a lack of data on large and long-lived Arctic animals, such as seals, polar bears, foxes, which probably are the most radiosensitive animals in Arctic ecosystems. There is also a deficiency of special experimental studies of those peculiarities in metabolism and biochemical composition of Arctic organisms, which may modify the response of Arctic organisms to ionising radiation compared with organisms from warmer climatic zones.

Effects of some natural alpha-emitting radionuclides (U, Th) on wildlife demonstrate the complex simultaneous action of chemical toxicity and high-LET radiation. In the consideration of these radionuclides a problem arises in developing a unified methodology for combined assessment for chemical toxicity and radiation on biota. The problem of evaluating the appropriate weighting factors for high-LET radiation in the context of wildlife protection is still unsolved. It became evident, however, that heavy alpha-emitting radionuclides with very low specific activity and high chemical toxicity can not be used for the purpose of w_r estimations, because the bulk of observed effects on biota is associated with chemical toxicity of these elements. The safety regulations for these radionuclides (e.g. ^{238}U, ^{232}Th) are more appropriate to establish for each radionuclide separately.

There is a requirement to collate further information on natural radionuclides in Arctic environments through field studies. Furthermore there is a requirement to refine and test existing dynamic models simulating the behaviour and fate of radionuclides in Arctic ecosystems. Empirical data are also required in defining transfer factors for numerous radionuclides and reference organism types.

The EPIC database provides a large collection of data related to radiation effects on wildlife under the conditions of chronic exposure. At present, the radiation impacts in the datasets are given mostly as they appeared in the source publications, i.e. activity concentrations in biota and environment, and/or author's dose estimates. A detailed dose assessment, using modern models for dose-to-biota calculations, is required to provide reliable estimations of dose rates for the EPIC datasets, and make dose reconstructions in cases there only "radionuclide concentration-effects" data were available from source publications.

There is a lack of experimental data on radiation effects in typical Arctic organisms, bespoke experimentation being required to determine if extreme Arctic conditions influence the response of biota to ionising radiation exposure.

REFERENCES

Aarkrog, A. Radioactivity in Polar Regions - Main Sources. *J. Environ. Radioactivity. 1994, 25,* 21-35.

Aarkrog, A.; Boelskifte, S.; Duniec, S.; Hallstadius, L.; Holm, E.; Smith, J.N. Estuar. Coast. *Mar. Sci. 1987, 24,* 637-647.

Aarkrog, A.; Baxter, M.S.; Bettencourt, A.O.; Bojanowski, R.; Bologa, A.; Charmasson, S.; Cunha, I.; Delfanti, R.; Duran, E.; Holm, E.; Jeffree, R.; Livingston, H.D.; Mahapanyawong, S.; Nies, H.; Osvath, I.; Li, P.Y.; Povinec, P.P.; Sanchez, A.; Smith, J.N.; Swift, D. *J. Environ. Radioactivity. 1997, 34,* 69-90.

Academy of Science. J. Radiobiol. 1991, 31, 436-452.

AMAP. (Arctic Monitoring and Assessment Programme). Arctic Pollution Issues: A State of the Arctic Environment Report; AMAP: Oslo, Norway, 1997, 87 pp

AMAP. (Arctic Monitoring and Assessment Programme). Arctic Pollution, 2002. AMAP: Oslo, Norway, 2002; pp 111 + xii

Amundsen, I.; Lind, B.; Reistad, O.; Gussgaard, K.; Iospje, M.; Sickel, M. The Kursk Accident; StålevernRapport 2001:5; Norwegian Radiation Protection Authority: Østerås, Oslo, 2001; pp 1-36.

Amiro, B.D. *J. Environ. Radioactivity. 1997, 35,* 37-51.

Barrie, L.A.; Gregor, D.; Hargrave, B.; Lake, R.; Muir, D.; Shearer, R.; Tracey, B.; Bidleman, T.F. *Sci. Tot. Environ. 1992, 122,* 1-74.

Baskaran, M.; Kelley, J.J.; Naidu, A.S.; Holleman, *D.F. Arctic. 1991, 44,* 346-350.

Batjes, N.H. *A Homogenized Soil Data File for Global Environmental Research: a Subset of FAO, ISRIC, and NRCS profiles* (version 1.0), Working paper 95/10; International Soil Reference and Information Centre (ISRIC): Wageningen, The Netherlands, 1995, 43 pp.

Beresford, N.A.; Mayes, R.W.; Cooke, A.I.; Barnett, C.L.; Howard, B.J.; Lamb, C.S.; Naylor, G.P.L. *Environ. Sci. Technol. 2000, 34,* 4455-4462.

Beresford, N.A.; Wright, S.M.; Sazykina, T. Reference Arctic organisms; Deliverable Report 1 for EPIC, EC Inco-Copernicus project ICA2-CT-2000-10032; Centre for Ecology and Hydrology: Grange-over-Sands, United Kingdom, 2001; 43 pp

Beresford, N.A.; Wright, S.M.; Brown, J.E.; Sazykina, T. *Review of approaches for the estimation of radionuclide transfer to reference Arctic biota*; Deliverable Report 3 for EPIC. EC Inco-Copernicus project ICA2-CT-2000-10032. Centre for Ecology and Hydrology: Grange-over-Sands, UK. 2003; 40 pp

Beresford, N.A.; Broadley, M.R.; Howard, B.J.; Barnett, C.L.; White, P.J. *J. Radiol. Protect. 2004, 24,* A89-A104.

Bjurman, B.; Degeer, L.E.; Vintersved, I.; Rudjord, A.L.; Ugletveit, F., Aaltonen, H.; Sinkko, K.; Rantavaara, A.; Nielsen, S.P.; Aarkrog, A.; Kolb, W. *J. Environ. Radioactivity. 1990, 11,* 1-14.

Blaylock, B.G.; Trabalka, J.R. *Adv. Radiat. Biol. 1978, 7,* 103-152.

Borghuis, A.M.; Steenhuisen, F.; Brown, J.E.; Sickel M. *Sci. Tot Env. 2002, 291,* 155-165.

Brown, J.E.; Kolstad, A.K.; Brungot, A.L.; Lind, B.; Rudjord, A.L.; Strand, P.; Føyn L. 1999, *Mar. Poll. Bull. 2002a, 38,* 560-571.

Brown, J.E.; Iospje, M.; Kolstad, K.E.; Lind, B.; Rudjord, A.L.; Strand P. *J. Environ. Radioactivity. 2002, 60,* 49-60.

Brown, J.; Børretzen, P.; Dowdall, M.; Sazykina, T.; Kryshev, I. *Arctic, 2004, 57,* 279-289.

CEC. The Radiological Exposure of the Population of the European Community from Radioactivity in North European Marine Waters - Project 'Marina'; Radiation Protection Report 47; Directorate of Nuclear Safety, Impact of Industry on the Environment and Waste Management; Directorate General Environment, Consumer Protection and Nuclear Safety, EUR 12483 EN, 1990. 571 pp.

Copplestone, D.; Bielby, S.; Jones, S.R.; Patton, D.; Daniel, P.; Gize, I. *Impact Assessment of Ionising Radiation on Wildlife*; R&D Publication 128; Environment Agency: Bristol, United Kingdom, 2001; 222 pp

Dahlgaard, H.; Chen, Q.; Herrmann, J.; Nies, H.; Ibbett, R.D.; Kershaw, P.J. *J. Mar. Sys. 1995, 6,* 571-578.

Dethleff D.; Loewe P.; Kleine E. *Cold Reg. Sci. Technol. 1998, 27*(3), 225-243.

EC (European Commission). 2002. MARINA II. Update of the MARINA Project on the Radiological Exposure of the European Community from Radioactivity in North European Marine Waters. European Commission Annex F. In: MARINA II. Update of the MARINA Project on the Radiological Exposure of the European Community from Radioactivity in North European Marine Waters http://europa.eu.int/comm/environment/ radprot.

Environment Canada. Environmental assessments of the Priority Substances under the Canadian Environmental Protection Act. Guidance Manual, Version 1.0; Chemical Evaluation Division, Ecosystem: Quebec, Canada, 1997: pp 199.

Eurola, S.; Hakala, U.K. *Aquilo Series Botanical.* 1977, 15, 1-18.

Fisher, N.S.; Fowler, S.W.; Boisson, F.; Carroll, J.; Rissanen, K.; Salbu, B.; Sazykina, T. G.; Sjoeblom, K. L. *Environ. Sci. Technol. 1999, 33,* 1979-1982.

Føyn, L.; Sværen, I. ICES J. Mar. Sci. 1997, 54(3), 333-340.

Gaare, E.; Staaland, H. In Nordic Radioecology: The Transfer of Radionuclides through Nordic Ecosystems to Man; Dahlgaard, H.; Ed.; *Elsevier: Amsterdam, The Netherlands,* 1994; pp 303-334.

Galeriu, D.; Beresford, N.A.; Melintescu, A.; Avila, R.; Crout, N.M.J. In International Conference on the Protection of the Environment from the Effects of Ionising Radiation; IAEA-CN-109; *International Atomic Energy Agency:* Vienna, Austria, 2003; pp 186-189.

Godzik, B. *Polar Research. 1991, 9*(2), 121-131.

Golikov V. Yu. Operational models for calculation of internal and external doses in the Arctic. Deliverable for the EC Inco-Copernicus project AVAIL (contract No. ERB IC 15-CT980201). Institute of Radiation Hygiene: St Petersburg, Russia, 2001, 77 pp

Golikov, V.; Brown, J.E. Report on Currently Available Internal and External Dose Models. Deliverable Report 2 for EPIC. EC Inco-Copernicus Project ICA2-CT-2000-10032; Norwegian Radiation Protection Authority, Østerås, Norway, 2002; pp 1-38.

Golikov, V.; Brown, J.E. Internal and External Dose Models. Deliverable Report 4 for EPIC. EC Inco-Copernicus project ICA2-CT-2000-10032. Norwegian Radiation Protection Authority: Østerås, Norway, 2002; pp. 1-52.

Headley, A.D. *Sci. Tot. Environ. 1996, 177,* 105-111.

Higley, K.A.; Domotor S.L.; Antonio E.J. *J. Environ. Radioactivity. 2003, 66,* 61-74.

Hosseini, A.; Brown, J.E. In Proceedings from the 2nd International Conference on Radioactivity in the Environment, 2-6 October 2005, Nice, France; Strand, P.; Børretzen, P.; Jølle, T.; Eds.; Norwegian Radiation Protection Authority: Østerås, Norway, 2005; pp 553-556.

IAEA (International Atomic Energy Agency). Effects of Ionising Radiation on Aquatic Organisms and Ecosystems; Technical Reports Series No. 172*; International Atomic Energy Agency*: Vienna, Austria, 1976. 131 pp

IAEA (International Atomic Energy Agency). Methodology for Assessing Impacts of Radioactivity on Aquatic Organisms; Technical Reports Series. No. 190; *International Atomic Energy Agency*: Vienna, Austria, 1979; pp 43-96.

IAEA (International Atomic Energy Agency). Sediment Kds and Concentration Factors for Radionuclides in the Marine Environment; Technical Report Series No. 247; *International Atomic Energy Agency*: Vienna, Austria, 1985; 73 pp

IAEA (International Atomic Energy Agency). Effects of Ionising Radiation on Plants and Animals at Levels Implied by Current Radiation Protection Standards; Technical Report Series No. 332; *International Atomic Energy Agency*: Vienna, Austria, 1992: 74 pp

IAEA (International Atomic Energy Agency). The Principles of Radioactive Waste Management; Safety Series No 111 F; *International Atomic Energy Agency*: Vienna, Austria, 1995: 24 pp

IAEA (International Atomic Energy Agency). International Basic Safety Standards for Protection Against Ionising Radiation and for the Safety of Radiation Sources; Safety Series N 115; *International Atomic Energy Agency*: Vienna, Austria, 1996; 353 pp

IAEA (International Atomic Energy Agency). Protection of the Environment From the Effects of Ionising Radiation; a Report for Discussion; IAEA-TECDOC-1901; *International Atomic Energy Agency:* Vienna, Austria, 1999; 53 pp

IAEA (International Atomic Energy Agency). Ethical Considerations in Protecting the Environment from the Effects of Ionising Radiation; a Report for Discussion; IAEA-TECDOC-1270; *International Atomic Energy Agency*: Vienna, Austria, 2002; 29 pp

IAEA (International Atomic Energy Agency). Sediment K_ds and Concentration Factors for Radionuclides in the Marine Environment; Technical Reports Series No. 422; *International Atomic Energy Agency*: Vienna, Austria, 2004: pp 1-95.

ICRP (International Commission on Radiological Protection). Recommendations of the International Commission on Radiological Protection; Publication 60 Annals of the ICRP 21; Pergamon Press: Oxford, United Kingdom, 1991; 201 pp

ICRP (International Commission on Radiological Protection) (2002). http://www. icrp.org/draft_nonhuman.htm

ICRU (International Commission on Radiation Units and Measurements). Quantities, Units and Terms in Radioecology; ICRU Report 65; Nuclear Technology Publishing: Ashford, United Kingdom, 2001; pp 1-44.

IUCN (International Union for Conservation of Nature and Natural Resources). IUCN Red List of Threatened Species; IUCN Publications Service Unit: Cambridge, United Kingdom, 2000; 61 pp

IUR (International Union of Radioecology), (2002). Protection of the environment: Current status and future work. IUR Report 3:2002. Østerås, Norway; 23 pp

Iosjpe, M.; Brown, J.; Strand, P. J. *Environ. Radioactivity. 2002, 60,* 91-103.

Johannessen, M.; Henriksen, A. *Water Resour. Res. 1978, 14,* 615-619.

JRNEG (Joint Russian-Norwegian Expert Group for Investigation of Radioactive Contamination in the Northern Areas). Long term Consequences of Potential Contamination in the Northern Areas: Northern Norway and Murmansk Oblast; Summary Report; StrålevernRapport 2002:5; Norwegian Radiation Protection Authority: Østerås, Norway, 2002; pp 1-120.

JNREG (Joint Russian-Norwegian Expert Group for Investigation of Radioactive Contamination in the Northern Areas). Impacts on Man and the Environment in Northern

Areas from Hypothetical Accidents at "Mayak" PA, Urals, Russia; Norwegian Radiation Protection Authority: Østerås, Norway, 2004; pp 1-104.

Karcher, M.J.; Harms, I.H. In Transport and Fate of Contaminants in the Northern Seas; Iosjpe M.; Ed.; Norwegian Radiation Protection Authority: Oslo, Norway, 2000, 80 pp

Karcher, M.J.; Gerland, S.; Harms, I.H.; Iosjpe, M.; Heldal, H.E.; Kershaw, P.J.; Sickel, M. *J. Environ. Radioactivity. 2004, 74,* 185-198.

Kautsky, H. *Deutsche Hydrographische Zeitschrift. 1987,* 40, 49-69.

Keiling, R.; Bloch, J.M.; Vilain, J.P. *Annales Radiol. 1958, 1,* 381.

Kolstad AK. Expeditions to Komsomolets in 1993 and 1994; NRPA report 1995:7. Norwegian Radiation Protection Authority: Østerås, Norway; 1995, 66 pp.

Kryshev, I.I.; Sazykina, T.G. *J.Environ. Radioactivity. 1995, 29,* 213-223.

Kryshev, I.I.; Sazykina, T.G. *Radiat. Protect. Dosim. 1998, 75,* 187-191.

Kryshev, A.I.; Sazykina, T.G.; Kryshev, I.I.; Strand, P.; Brown, J.E. *Environ. Modell. Softw. 2001, 16,* 697-709.

Kryshev, A.I.; Sazykina, T.G.; Strand, P.;Brown, J.E. In Proceedings of the 5th International Conference on Environmental Radioactivity in the Arctic and Antarctic, St.Petersburg, 16 – 20 June 2002; Norwegian Radiation Protection Authority, Østerås, Norway, 2002; pp 326 – 329.

Landa E.R.; Reimnitz E.; Beals D.M.; Pochkowski J.M.; Winn W.G.; Rigor I. *Arctic. 1998, 51,* 27-39.

Larsen, E.; Holo, E. N.; Saltbones, J.; Stokke, E. Kola consequence analyses - Evaluation of cases from a hypothetical accident at Kola Nuclear Power Plant; StrålevernRapport 1999:10; Norwegian Radiation Protection Authority: Østerås, Norway, 1999; pp 2-59.

Larsson, C-M.; Brewitz, E.; Jones, C. Formulating the FASSET assessment context; Deliverable 2: Part 1. Deliverable Report for the EC Project FASSET (Contract No. FIGE-CT-2000-00102); Swedish Radiation Protection Authority, Stockholm; 2002a, 77 pp.

Larsson, C-M.; Strand, P.; Brown, J.E. In Proceedings from the International Conference on Radioactivity in the Environment, Monaco, 1-5 September 2002; Børretzen, P.; Jølle, T.; Strand, P.; Ed.; Norwegian Radiation Protection Authority: Østerås, Norway, 2002b; pp 39-42.

Linnik V.G.; Brown J.E.; Dowdall M .; Potapov V.N.; Surkov V.V.; Korobova E. M.; Volosov A.G.; Vakulovsky, S.M.; Tertyshnik, E.G. *Sci. Tot. Environ. 2005, 339,* 233-251.

Loeng, H. *Polar Res. 1991, 10,* 5-18.

Meese, D.A.; Reimnitz, E.; Tucker, W.B.; Gow, A.J.; Bischof, J.; Darby, D. *Sci. Tot. Environ. 1997, 202,* 267-278.

Nagy, K.A. Nutrition Abstracts and Reviews. 2001, 71, 21-31.

Nakano, Y. *Cold Reg. Sci. Technol. 1990, 17,* 207-226.

NCRP (National Council on Radiation Protection and Measurements). *Effects of Ionising Radiation on Aquatic Organisms*; NCRP Report N 109; NCRP: Bethesda, MD, 1991; 115 pp

Nielsen, S.P.; Iosjpe, M.; Strand, P. *Sci. Tot. Environ. 1997, 202,* 135-146.

Nies, H.; Harms, I.H.; Karcher, M.J.; Dethleff, D.; Bahe, C. *Sci. Tot. Environ. 1999, 237,* 181-191.

Nurnberg, D.; Wollenburg, I.; Dethleff, D.; Eicken, H.; Kassens, H.; Letzig, T.; Reimnitz, E.; Thiede, *J. Mar. Geol. 1994, 119,* 185-214.

OSPAR Convention (1998): Convention for the Protection of the Marine Environment of the North-East Atlantic., Sintra Statement, Ministerial Meeting of the Ospar commission, Sintra 22-23 Jul. 1998. Summary Record OSPAR 98/14/1, annex 45.

Oughton, D.H. (2001). In: *Values in Decision Making On Risk* (VALDOR); Statens strålskyddsinstitut: Stockholm, Sweden, 2001; pp 1-4.

Oughton, D. H. *Journal of Environmental Radioactivity. 2003, 66,* 3-18.

Oughton, D.H.; Strand, P. In Protection of the Environment from Ionising Radiation. International Atomic Energy Agency: Vienna, Austria, 2003; pp 129-136.

Pentreath, R.J.; Jefferies, D.F.; Talbot, J.W.; Lovett, M.B.; Harvey, B.R. Transuranic Cycling Behaviour in the Marine Environment; IAEA-TECDOC-265; International Atomic Energy Agency: Vienna, Austria, 1982; pp 121-128.

Pentreath, R.J. *J. Radiol. Prot. 1999, 19,* 117-128.

Pentreath, R.J. *J. Radiol. Prot. 2002, 22,* 45-56.

Pentreath, R.J.; Woodhead, D.S. *Sci. Tot. Environ. 2001, 277,* 33-43.

Polikarpov, G.G. *Radiat. Protect. Dosim. 1998, 75,* 181-185.

Pröhl, G.; Brown, J.; Gomez-Ros, J.-M.; Jones, S.; Woodhead, D.; Vives, J.; Taranenko, V.; Thørring, H. Dosimetric models and data for assessing radiation exposure to biota; Deliverable 3 to the Project "FASSET" Framework for the assessment of Environmental Impact, contract No. FIGE-CT-2000-00102; Swedish Radiation Protection Authority: Stockholm, Sweden, 2003, 103 pp

Robinson, C. In Proceedings from the International Conference on Radioactivity in the Environment, Monaco, 1-5 September 2002; Børretzen, P.; Jølle, T.; Strand, P.; Eds.; *Norwegian Radiation Protection Authority*: Oslo, Norway, 2002; pp 29-30.

Sample, B.E.; Suter II, G.W. *Estimating exposure of terrestrial wildlife to contaminants Report ES/ER/TM-125*; Oak Ridge National Laboratory: Oak Ridge, TE; 1994, 49 pp

Sample, B.E.; Aplin, M.S.; Efoymson, R.A.; Suter II, G.W.; Welsh, C.J.E. *Methods and Tools for Estimation of the Exposure of Terrestrial Wildlife to Contaminants; Oak Ridge Report - ORNL/TM-13391*; Oak Ridge National Laboratory: Oak Ridge, TE, 1997; pp 1-113.

Sazykina, T.G. In Environmental Radioactivity in the Arctic; Strand, P.; Cooke, A.; Eds.; *Norwegian Radiation Protection Authority*: Østerås, Norway, 1995, pp 159-161.

Sazykina, T.G. In Proceedings of the International. Symposium on Ionising Radiation: Protection of the Natural Environment. Stockholm, 20-24 May, 1996, pp.153-159.

Sazykina, T.G. *Radiat. Protect. Dosim. 1998, 75,* 219-222.

Sazykina, T.G.; Kryshev, I.I. *Atom. Energy.* 1999a; 87/4; 302-307.

Sazykina, T.G.; Jaworska, A.; Brown, J.E. Dose-effects relationships for reference (or related) Arctic biota: Deliverable Report 5 for the EPIC project (Contract no. ICA2-CT-200-10032); Norwegian Radiation Protection Authority: Oslo, Norway; 2003; pp 1-119.

Shekhanova, I.A. *Radioecology of fish.* Publ.House "Light and Food Industry": Moscow, 1983, 208 pp.

Stokke, E. *Kola Nuclear Power Plant - Consequence Assessment for Hypothetical Severe Accidents. Source Term Assessment*; Report No. IFE/HR/F-97/1088; Institute for Energy Technology: Halden, Norway, 1997, 56 pp.

Strand, P.; Rudjord, A.L.; Salbu, B.; Christensen, G.; Foyn, L.: Lind, B.; Bjørnstad, H.; Bjerk, T. In Environmental Radioactivity in the Arctic and Antarctic - Proceedings of the

International Conference on Environmental Radioactivity in Arctic and Antarctic, Kirkenes, 1993; Strand, P.; Holm, E.; Eds.; *Norwegian Radiation Protection Authority*: Østerås, Norway, 1993, pp 31-34.

Strand, P.; Brown, J.E.; Larsson, C.M. Radiat. *Protect. Dosim. 2000, 92,* 169-175.

Strand, P.; Larsson, C.M. (2001). In Radioactive Pollutants. Impact on the Environment; Brechignac, F.; Howard, B.J.; Eds.; EDP Sciences: Les Ulis, France, 2001; pp131-145.

Strand, P.; Holm, L.E. In Proceeding from the International Conference on Radioactivity in the Environment, Monaco, 1-5 September 2002; Børretzen, P.; Jølle, T.; Strand, P.; Eds.; *Norwegian Radiation Protection Authority*: Østerås, Norway, 2002; pp 35-38.

Strand, P.; Oughton, D.H. In Proceedings from the International Conference on Radioactivity in the Environment , 1-5 september,2002 Monaco; Børretzen, P.; Jølle, T.; Strand, P.; Eds.; *Norwegian Radiation Protection Authority*: Østerås, Norway, 2002; pp. 31-34

Straume, T.; Carsten, A.L. *Health Phys.* 1993, 65, 657-672.

Strandberg, M. Arctic. 1997, 50, 216-223.

Taylor, H.W.; Svoboda, J.; Henry, G.H.R.; Wein, R.W. *Arctic. 1988, 41,* 293-296.

Turner, F.B. *Adv. Radiat. Biol. 1975, 5,* 83–145.

UN (United Nations). UN Waste Convention: Joint Convention on the Safety of Spent Fuel Management and on the Safety of Radioactive Waste Management, Annex 1; United Nations: NY, 1996; 86 pp.

UNCED (United Nations Conference on Environment and Development). Rio Declaration on Environment and Development; United Nations: NY, 1992.

UNSCEAR (United Nations Scientific Committee on the Effects of Atomic Radiation). Effects of Radiation on the Environment, Annex to Sources and Effects of Ionising Radiation (1996 Report to the General Assembly, with one Annex), UNSCEAR, UN, New York, 1996 108 pp.

UNSCEAR. (United Nations Scientific Committee on the Effects of Atomic Radiation). Sources and effects of ionizing radiation; Volume 1 Sources; United Nations: NY, 2000a; 654 pp.

UNSCEAR (United Nations Scientific Committee on the Effects of Atomic Radiation). UNSCEAR 2000 Report to the General Assembly, with scientific annexes. Volume II: EFFECTS. Combined effects of radiation and other agents Annex H; United Nations: NY, 2000b; 120 pp.

USDoE (U.S. Department of Energy). A graded approach for evaluating radiation doses to aquatic and terrestrial biota; Technical Standard DoE-STD-1153-2002.; U.S. Department of Energy: Washington D.C., 2002.

Vakulovsky S.; Nikitin, A.; Chumichev, V. In Environmental Radioactivity in the Arctic and Antarctic; Strand, P.; Holm, E.; Eds.; *Norwegian Radiation Protection Authority*: Østerås, Norway, 1993; pp 177-182.

Vinje T.; Kvambekk A.S. *Polar Res. 1991, 10,* 59-68.

Whicker, F.W.; Schultz, V. *Radioecology: Nuclear Energy and the Environment* ; CRC Press Inc.: Boca Raton, FA., 1982; Vol. 2, 212 pp.

Wilson, M.D. & Hinton, T.G. In Proceedings of the Third International Symposium on the Protection of the Environment from Ionizing Radiation (SPEIR 3), Darwin, Australia 22-26th July 2002; Dept. of Environment and Heritage: Canberra, Australia, 2002; pp 69-76.

Woodhead, D.S. In Marine Ecology; Kinne, O.; Ed.; John Wiley, London, United Kingdom, 1984: Vol. 5, pp 1111-1287.

Woodhead, D.S. *J. Environ. Radioactivity. 2003, 66,* 181-213.

Woodhead, D.; Zinger, I. Radiation effects on plants and animals. FASSET Deliverable Report 4. Contract No FIGE-CT-2000-00102; Norwegian Radiation Protection Authority: Østerås, Norway, 2003, 196 pp

Wright, S.M.; Strand, P.; Sickel, M.A.K.; Howard, B.J.; Howard, D.C.; Cooke, A.I. *Sci. Tot. Environ. 1997, 202,* 173-184.

INDEX

D

F

G